Louis Laloy (1874-1944) on Debussy, Ravel and Stravinsky

Louis Laloy (1874–1944) on Debussy, Ravel and Stravinsky

Translated, with an introduction and notes, by

Deborah Priest

Routledge
Taylor & Francis Group
LONDON AND NEW YORK

First published 1999 by Ashgate Publishing

Reissued 2018 by Routledge
2 Park Square, Milton Park, Abingdon, Oxon, OX14 4RN
711 Third Avenue, New York, NY 10017, USA

Routledge is an imprint of the Taylor & Francis Group, an informa business

A Library of Congress record exists under LC control number: 99031934

Phototypeset by N^2 productions

ISBN 13: 978-1-138-35126-4 (hbk)
ISBN 13: 978-1-138-35129-5 (pbk)
ISBN 13: 978-0-429-43540-9 (ebk)

Contents

Acknowledgements

The idea for this book arose after Fisher Library at the University of Sydney allowed me to keep a microfilmed copy of Laloy's *Claude Debussy* (1909), which meant that it was on hand whenever I had the idea of browsing through it. Since then, staff at other Australian university libraries and at the Australian National and Victorian State Libraries have gone out of their way to help me with research inquiries. At the Sydney Conservatorium of Music Library, Jackie Luke, Catherine Bryant and Claire McCoy have exercised patience and ingenuity in obtaining inter-library loans and checking details of copyright. I am also grateful for the assistance I received at the British Library, the Bibliothèque Nationale de France, the Bibliothèque-Musée de l'Opéra and the Paris Conservatoire.

As the work took shape I benefited more than they probably realize from discussions with Dr Nigel Butterley, Lewis Cornwell, Roy Howat, Elizabeth Powell and Richard Toop. Dr Françoise Grauby of the Department of French Studies at the University of Sydney and Prof. John Humbley of the Laboratoire de Linguistique Informatique, Université de Paris XIII gave their advice on linguistic matters. For specialist help with annotations I would like to thank Dr Alan James of the Classics Department at the University of Sydney, Prof. Thomas J. Mathiesen of Indiana University, Mr Yen Yung Yang, Mme Myriam Chimènes of the Centre de Documentation Claude Debussy and Mme Catherine Massip of the Département de la Musique, Bibliothèque Nationale de France. M. Vincent Laloy willingly provided documents from the family archive, and obligingly answered my many questions. M. Manuel Rosenthal was kind enough to write to me with his memories of Laloy.

I would like to acknowledge the contribution of research assistants Michael Black, Marie-Hélène Coudroy-Saghaï, Peter Hollo, Eurydice Jousse and Anna Maslowiec, and thank Brian Brennan, Craigie Macfie and my sister, Joanne Hardwick, for the encouragement which was so valuable and so warmly given at certain stages of the project. The research was funded by grants from the Sydney Conservatorium of Music, the University of Sydney and the Australian Research Council.

I would like to thank M. Vincent Laloy for permission to quote and to translate extracts from Laloy's books, and to reproduce photographs, letters and other material. Thanks are also due to Editions Musicales Durand for permission to quote passages from Debussy scores. Permission was requested from W. W. Norton & Co. to quote from the translation of Mallarmé's *L'Après-midi d'un faune* contained in W. W. Austin, ed., *Debussy. Prelude to 'The afternoon of a faun'* (1970). Permission was also requested from Cassell Publishing Ltd to translate an extract from Laloy's article on *Pelléas et Mélisande* contained in F. Aprahamian, ed., *Essays on music: an anthology from 'The listener'* (1967). All efforts have been made to identify and contact the copyright holders of the other articles by Laloy translated, in part or whole, in the present volume, but these efforts have been unsuccessful. The publisher will be pleased to hear from copyright holders and to make appropriate acknowledgements in any future editions of this book.

List of plates

Preface

My interest in Louis Laloy began some years ago when I discovered his *Claude Debussy* (Paris, 1909), the first French biography of the composer. I felt the book said things about Debussy which needed to be said and simply were not to be found in any of the current literature: I had in mind Laloy's analysis of Debussy's musical language, and also his highly perceptive exploration of the connections between Debussy's music and French literature of the period, not to mention that the final chapter contained one of the very few contemporary accounts of Debussy's requirements of performers.

Composers, performers and analysts to whom I showed the biography expressed interest and enthusiasm and I formed the idea of looking further into Laloy's writings. Beginning with his memoirs, *La Musique retrouvée, 1902–1927* (Paris, 1928) I embarked on a search for his other books, and for his reviews and articles. What I found showed me that Laloy was a new source of information on the life and æsthetic stance not only of Debussy, but of many French composers from the first four decades of this century, and also on the reception of their works. I have chosen Debussy, Ravel and Stravinsky as the focus of the present volume because of the quantity of Laloy's writings about them. There is more material about Debussy than about Ravel and Stravinsky, since Laloy knew Debussy more intimately, but his observations and opinions about the two later composers are nonetheless equally powerful and original. It is also interesting to read Laloy's articles about Dukas, Satie, *Les Six* and composers from earlier periods, which are equally insightful and written with his characteristic elegance and humour.

The search in itself was fascinating and challenging. No compilations of this material have been made previously, and indeed but for short extracts quoted in two books by Léon Vallas, in an article on Debussy's piano music by Guido M. Gatti written in 1921, and in Roger Nichols's *Debussy remembered* (Portland, Oregon, 1992) Laloy's writings on Debussy are very little known; his writings on Ravel and Stravinsky are even less so. Some of the newspapers and periodicals to which Laloy contributed are held in Australian libraries, but I needed to make two trips to Paris to search the remainder, to obtain others of his books, and also to examine archival material held at the Bibliothèque Nationale de France and the Conservatoire and Opéra libraries. In addition, the Laloy family archive provided a rich source of correspondence and other material.

Laloy's breadth of culture produces a wide range of references to history, literature, the visual arts and other disciplines. I have annotated any references which might not be clear to English readers, and also added brief details about lesser-known composers, current events and the like. In translating the extracts I have aimed for a style which has a flavour of the period, so I have opted for some older-style vocabulary and retained Laloy's occasional use of the first person plural to express his own views. I have given most composers' names as Laloy gives them, but spelled 'Mussorgsky' as it would have been spelled in English in Laloy's time. At times I have added the original French of a phrase in a note, if it sheds light. For ease of reading the number of commas has been greatly reduced, but I have not altered Laloy's occasional very long, unclear sentences: these and a small number of errors are signs that, like all music critics, he sometimes had to write quickly. Minor mistakes in names, titles of works and dates of composition have been corrected without comment; the few more significant errors, probably slips of memory, have been annotated. In texts of Laloy's period the word *musicien* can mean either *musician* or *composer*, and I have chosen between the two translations depending on the context.

Many writers of the period use ellipses for expressive reasons, as well as occasionally to indicate omissions: to avoid confusion, editorial ellipses are given as '[. . .]'. In English titles, I have adopted the recent practice of using very few capital letters, but in French I have followed a more conservative usage so as to give more of a flavour of the period. For ease of reading, I have used more capital letters than the French do for names of institutions, so: 'Ballets Russes' rather than 'Ballets russes', 'Ecole Normale Supérieure' rather than 'Ecole normale supérieure', and so on.

Only two of Laloy's books are currently in print: *Aristoxène de Tarente et la musique de l'antiquité* (1904, repr. Minkoff, Geneva, 1973) and *La Musique retrouvée, 1902–1927* (1928, repr. Desclee de Brouwer, Paris, 1974). With one exception, all the books by Laloy mentioned in the present volume are held in the Bibliothèque Nationale de France. *The future of music; coming changes outlined in regard to composer, conductor and orchestra* (London, [1910]), a translation of Laloy's article 'La Musique de l'avenir', was consulted at the British Library. Periodicals from which extracts have been translated are held in the Bibliothèque Nationale de France (BNF). Volume numbers have not been given for periodical articles dated earlier than 1918 because of the absence of volume numbering for certain key holdings at the BNF. Letters written to Laloy by Ravel and others are held in the Laloy family archive. Many of Debussy's letters to Laloy have been published in F. Lesure, ed., 'Correspondance de Claude Debussy et de Louis Laloy (1902–1914)', *La Revue de musicologie*, vol. 48, no. 125 (1962), pp. 3–40; some others appear in *La Musique retrouvée*. A number of the letters are contained in Lesure's *Claude Debussy. Correspondance 1884–1918* (Paris, 2nd ed. 1993) which has been translated as *Debussy letters* (London, 1987), ed. F. Lesure and R. Nichols.

Introduction

Louis Laloy and the Paris music scene

Louis Laloy - scholar, writer, musicologist and music critic - was a central figure in the musical scene in Paris in the early decades of the twentieth century. Sadly forgotten today, like other music critics of his time, by all but specialists, he deserves a place in the history of French music by virtue of his relationships with composers, and also because of his ability to stay abreast of new musical trends and to explain them lucidly and elegantly to his readers. In fact Laloy's explanations of new directions in music in his time remain fresh today, and he has insights to offer us about this music which are not to be found in more recent literature.

Laloy's acuity of perception and astonishing breadth of scholarship would make him a fascinating object of study in his own right, and the fact that he was on terms of friendship with most of the major French composers in the years from 1902 to World War II establishes him as a key source for the period. Outstanding among critics for his depth of musical knowledge and his almost always balanced reviews, Laloy was greatly admired and valued by his contemporaries. In a tribute written after Laloy's death, the organist Marcel Dupré praised 'his vast culture, his prodigious erudition, allied to a profound sensibility' and remarked that 'an entire generation owes a great deal to him.' The musicologist Michel Brenet described him as 'a writer who was able to be simultaneously a real artist and a true scholar [...]' Emile Vuillermoz thought that 'he had a paradoxical wealth of culture, and he was able to carry its crushing weight with the lightness and grace of a dilettante' and Romain Rolland 'admired and loved [his] original, rich and multiple personality, overflowing with the most diverse, the most solid, the most brilliant of talents; a scholar, artist, writer, musicologist and sinologue of the first rank [...]'[1]

Born in the Jura region, in eastern France, in 1874, Laloy moved to Paris with his family as a child. He was educated at the Lycée Henri IV, the Ecole Normale Supérieure and then the Sorbonne, where he was one of the first doctoral candidates in music history. He studied piano, violin and double bass, but his aim as an instrumentalist was to become familiar with scores rather than to be a concert performer. While preparing his doctorate, he also studied counterpoint and composition at the Schola Cantorum, an institution renowned for its interest in early music and for the lucid teaching of two of its founders, Vincent d'Indy and Charles Bordes.[2]

There followed a career of the greatest diversity and intellectual penetration. Laloy began to write articles and concert reviews in 1901, at first for *La Revue musicale* of which he was unofficially editor-in-chief,[3] then for *Le Mercure musical* which he co-founded with Jean Marnold.[4] From 1907 he contributed to *La Grande revue*, which he also edited, and he was co-founder of a short-lived periodical entitled *L'Année musicale* (1911–1913). He also wrote for a variety of other Parisian newspapers and periodicals: *La Chronique des arts et de la curiosité*, *Comœdia*, *Le Courrier musical*, *La Joie musicale*, *Excelsior*, *L'Ere nouvelle*, *Le Figaro*, *Le Gaulois*, *La Gazette des beaux-arts*, *Le Journal des débats*, *Le Mercure de France*, *La Nouvelle revue française*, *Le Pays*, *La Revue des deux mondes*, *La Revue de Paris* and *Le Temps*.[5] A small number of articles by Laloy appeared in periodicals in Russia, England, Italy and the USA. His output of music journalism covered, in addition to the standard repertoire, new music by Debussy, Fauré, Dukas, Ravel, Stravinsky, Satie and *Les Six*, and extended beyond concert reviews to include substantial articles on subjects as diverse as non-Western music, cabaret, music-hall, the second wave of Wagnerism in about 1909, and government policy as it affected music.[6]

In 1906–1907, Laloy lectured in music history at the Sorbonne, temporarily replacing Romain Rolland. He lectured there again in 1920, and also at the Conservatoire from 1936 until his retirement in 1941. More important than teaching in Laloy's career, however, was his involvement in the theatre. Laloy had met the influential director of the Théâtre des Arts, Jacques Rouché, while the latter was editor of *La Grande revue*. Rouché invited Laloy to work with him, at a time when he was bringing Parisian stage practice – scenery, lighting – up to date with developments introduced in Russia, Berlin and London by Stanislavsky, Gordon Craig and others.[7] The Théâtre des Arts staged several works in which Laloy collaborated: his translation of the thirteenth-century Chinese play *Le Chagrin dans le palais de Han* (*The trouble in the Han palace*) with incidental music by Gabriel Grovlez; *Les Dominos*, a ballet based on music by Couperin, and

Dolly, a ballet based on the suite by Fauré. When Rouché accepted the prestigious post of Director of the Opéra in 1914, Laloy went with him as Secretary-General, and he continued in that position until 1940.

It will already be evident that Laloy's musical interests were diverse. A list of his books on music indicates just how wide-ranging they were. The first was *Aristoxène de Tarente et la musique de l'antiquité* (1904, repr. Geneva, 1973) which had been his doctoral dissertation: it remains one of the most lucid studies in the field and, together with his *Lexique d'Aristoxène* (1904), was highly praised by his contemporary musicologists. *Rameau* (1908) coincided with the revival of interest in that composer's music at the Schola Cantorum and elsewhere. Laloy's *Claude Debussy* (1909, rev. 1944) was the first French biography of the composer. It was followed by *La Musique chinoise* (1912, repr. 1979), *La Danse à l'Opéra* (1927), and a detailed and much-admired book of memoirs, *La Musique retrouvée, 1902–1927* (1928, repr. 1974), then *Une heure de musique avec Beethoven* (1930) and *Comment écouter la musique* (1942).[8] The Laloy family papers reveal that he also signed publishers' contracts for, but did not finish, books on Mozart and Chopin, and that at the time of his death in 1944 he was working on a massive *Fastes de la musique française* (*Annals of French music*).

Laloy's intellectual curiosity and capacity were such, however, that he extended his studies way beyond music to include languages, mathematics and philosophy.[9] Proficient in French, English, German, Russian and Italian as well as Greek and Latin, Laloy published translations of various literary works and books about music. These included the Mimes of Herodas, lectures on Wagner by Guido Adler, and Oscar von Riesemann's *Mussorgsky* (Paris, [1940]); he also prepared singing translations of *Boris Godunov* and Mozart's *Idomeneo* (Act III). He studied mathematics to a level where he was able to understand the lectures Einstein gave in Paris in 1921. Overriding these interests, however, was his fascination with Chinese language and culture. He spoke fluent Mandarin, lectured on Chinese culture and metaphysics at the Institut des Hautes Etudes Chinoises, and translated Chinese literary works into French. In 1931 he was sent to China on a cultural mission for the French government. Laloy had many friends among the Chinese community in Paris, and adopted Chinese elements (including dress, and opium use) into his lifestyle to such an extent that he was known to friends and acquaintances as 'le Chinois'.[10]

Some of Laloy's contemporaries lamented that with such exceptional abilities he did not forge a high-level career in government or academia. However, he had no desire for power or influence, preferring to follow the dictates of his own curiosity; still, he was no dilettante, rather pursuing each line of inquiry to its end before passing on to another. As a writer, he had an elegant, flexible style with a sensitivity to rhythm and the melody of the French language which mark him out from most of his contemporary music critics. In this as in many other areas he had exceptional ability. He read widely in French literature as well as the literatures of other languages. His articles quote or refer to writers ranging from Pascal to Jean Cocteau, as well as Chinese and Greek philosophers, and it was to Laloy that Debussy turned for help in understanding certain words when he planned to set *Quant j'ai ouy le tabourin* by the fifteenth-century French poet Charles d'Orléans. At times it is possible to pick up in Laloy's writing a tone of Baudelaire or Mallarmé, or of the period corresponding to the music he is reviewing, and there are Proustian overtones in the title which he chose for his memoirs, *La Musique retrouvée* (*Music revisited*).

Laloy's friends among musicians included Debussy, Ravel, Stravinsky, Ricardo Viñes, Poulenc, Auric and the critics Romain Rolland and Jean Marnold. He was on terms of acquaintance with Diaghilev, M.-D. Calvocoressi, Manuel de Falla, Albert Roussel and Satie – though this last was a relationship of mutual antipathy – and on their visits to Paris he met Rimsky-Korsakov, Richard Strauss and Bartok. His wife, Susanik (Chouchik), was a noted pianist and teacher and his sister-in-law, Marguerite Babaïan, was a professional singer. Among his other friends were the writers André Breton, Colette, André Gide, Jacques Maritain and Jean Cocteau, and the sculptor Auguste Rodin.

Laloy's music criticism is marked not only by an ability to understand new compositions while other critics were still reacting to them with shock, horror and condemnation, but also by an attitude of progressiveness and receptivity to new developments in æsthetics and musical language. An article on 'La Musique de l'avenir' ('The music of the future'), published in *Le Mercure de France* in 1908, outlined his vision of developments in instrument-making and orchestration, including the invention of mechanical instruments and the use of electricity for the organ.[11] In a review of *Le Sacre du printemps* in 1914, Laloy showed his familiarity with the recently expounded philosophy of Italian Futurism and the musical instruments devised by Luigi Russolo, and he remained abreast of the changes in musical language and æsthetics which occurred in the 1920's. Laloy differs from most of his contemporary critics in discussing the theory of Debussy's new directions in harmony and in giving his readers a historical perspective on current musical trends, for example by discussing timbre and in particular Rameau's departure from standard eighteenth-century practice.

Laloy's æsthetic position was influenced by the philosopher Henri Bergson, who had taught him at the Lycée Henri IV, and to whose ideas he referred in *La Musique retrouvée* and elsewhere.[12] Bergson's philosophy, a reaction against positivism, emphasized intuition and 'spiritual energy', and rather than abstract time emphasized psychological time which he considered the foundation of the inmost nature of consciousness. The influence of Bergson's ideas is clearest in Laloy's early writings, particularly the article 'Claude Debussy. La simplicité en musique' (1904) and *Claude Debussy* (1909). Later, the influence of Chinese philsophy is more evident, for example in his reviews of Stravinsky's *Le Sacre du printemps* and *Le Rossignol*. At times Laloy's Roman Catholicism comes to the fore, in his descriptions of composers, and especially when he expresses his conviction that Gregorian chant is a fundamental part of the musical heritage of all French composers.[13]

Laloy stands out from his contemporary critics because of his ability to appreciate, understand and evaluate new works: this is particularly clear in the case of the most revolutionary works, including *Pelléas et Mélisande*, the *Histoires naturelles* and *Le Sacre du printemps*. His reviews maintain a tone of judicious balance and, despite his intimate connection with Debussy and the teaching posts he held at the Conservatoire and elsewhere, he remained an independent voice, free of what the French call *l'esprit de parti* during a period when schools and alliances were many and varied, constant only in their continual presence.[14] This is not to say that he was not outspoken: his reviews contain some memorably dismissive remarks, about certain minor composers and also about Elgar ('a good pupil, [. . .] a good public servant'; the *Enigma* variations and *The dream of Gerontius* have an 'administrative character') and Massenet (whose music has 'a perpetual smile' and an 'obsequious grace', and who in any case borrowed his formula from Gounod).

There are a certain number of errors in dates, facts and the titles of compositions in Laloy's writings, perhaps because he seems often to be writing from memory. Additionally, *La Musique retrouvée* needs to be read with the caution that it was written in 1928, and up to twenty-five years had elapsed since some of the events it describes. The same point should be made about the articles on Debussy published in the 1930s and 1940s. Some of the anecdotes which Laloy recounts, such as the description of Debussy's visits to Mallarmé's salon, might be thought to convey only a general impression or atmosphere, but others, particularly those which report things composers said, do ring true: examples are remarks by Rimsky-Korsakov and the story of Debussy's all-night conversations with Pierre Louÿs.

It is in Laloy's articles, books and lectures about Debussy that his ability and passion as a critic reach their highest point. The impression made by these writings is perhaps best expressed by Romain Rolland: 'No critic has, I believe, so subtly penetrated the art and genius of Debussy. Some of his analyses are a model of intelligent intuition. It seems that the critic's mind has identified with that of the composer.'[15] Although Laloy eulogized Debussy - describing him as 'of unalloyed nobility' and referring to his music as 'this earthly paradise' - he did so with such perceptiveness about the music's æsthetic aims and the means by which they were achieved that his enthusiasm is rarely an embarrassment. Most composers would count themselves highly fortunate to have such an apologist.[16] Laloy was certainly not the only critic to have insight into Debussy's aims and the technical expertise to analyse his music: articles by Paul Dukas, Lionel de la Laurencie, Jean Marnold and Emile Vuillermoz are also noteworthy and would bear study today.[17] However, Laloy applied himself to the task of elucidating Debussy's music in an ongoing, consistent and perhaps more imaginative way which no doubt had to do with the intuitive understanding and close friendship between the two men. Whether it was in reviews of performances, in longer, more in-depth articles, in books, or in what would now be called pre-concert talks at privately sponsored recitals, Laloy took on the role of explaining Debussy's music to a public which was sometimes puzzled and confused, at a time when the majority of other critics were also puzzled and confused - and every indication is that Debussy approved and was grateful for Laloy's public utterances.

Debussy and Laloy first met after Laloy wrote an article on the prelude to *Pelléas et Mélisande*. The article was not a review but an 'Exercice d'analyse' on the first four bars of the prelude, and it was published in *La Revue musicale* in November 1902.[18] Impressed, Debussy invited Laloy to visit him: this must have been before 4 December 1902, for a letter from Debussy to Laloy about a matter obviously already under discussion bears that date. Laloy describes the visit in *La Musique retrouvée*. It was the start of a friendship and musical collaboration which was to last until Debussy died.[19]

At first Laloy's role in Debussy's life was to further his interests: he arranged performances of his music at the salons of the Comtesse Greffuhle and the Princesse de Cystria, and helped to obtain the award of the Légion d'honneur for Debussy after the success of *Pelléas et Mélisande*. It seems to have been Laloy who encouraged Debussy to record some of his music with Mary Garden for the Compagnie Française du Gramophone in 1904. Gradually the friendship deepened, nurtured by conversation and, after Laloy's marriage in 1906, regular weekly evenings of dinner and bridge. Their mutual social circle, entertained more often than not at Debussy's home, included Stravinsky, Satie, Déodat de Séverac, André Caplet, Gabriele D'Annunzio, Désiré-Emile and Germaine Inghelbrecht, Franz and Louise Liebich, Pasteur Vallery-Radot, Walter Rummel and Ricardo Viñes. Debussy came to depend on Laloy's help in negotiations with concert organizers, performers and publishers, and in 1909 Laloy used his government connections to secure Debussy's nomination to the Conseil Supérieur of the Conservatoire. They worked together on several theatrical projects, and Laloy wrote the text for Debussy's last composition, the *Ode à la France*.[20]

The friendship between Debussy and Laloy was strong. In the words of the composer Gustave Samazeuilh, 'Claude Debussy, who chose his friends well, admitted him into the bosom of his family, and appreciated in him the most loyal and delicate of friends.' By 1908, Debussy was writing to Laloy that their friendship was 'of such a calibre that it seems to me to be almost invulnerable.' Not everything Debussy wrote to Laloy has survived, but eighty-two letters, notes and telegrams have been collected by François Lesure.[21] They reveal a considerable personal and domestic intimacy: Debussy writes about mutual acquaintances, the events of his daily life and the dealings he had with performers and publishers, and Laloy was one of the friends he approached for help in obtaining loans when he was in financial difficulties. Though the correspondence with Laloy does not have the degree of openness found in Debussy's letters to Robert Godet or Jacques Durand, it does indicate strong interest and affection, as for example on 13 September 1905: 'Write to me as soon as you can. I'm anxious to know what you're doing ... like a brother.' And later that year, on 4 November: 'When do you return? Be sure to let me know, for I must see you, I have so many things to tell you!'

The most severe test of the friendship occurred during the scandal following the attempted suicide of Debussy's first wife, Lilly, and his involvement with Emma Bardac. At a time when Debussy lost many of his friends, Laloy remained loyal, as did Robert Godet, Paul-Jean Toulet, Jacques Durand, Paul Dukas, Charles Koechlin, Ricardo Viñes and Satie. Laloy said that, after the crisis, he waited a few months as 'it seemed to me that he could not wish for anything but silence', then wrote to reassure Debussy of his friendship.[22] Debussy replied on 14 April 1905:

> My dear friend,
>
> I want to say first of all that you have never ceased to be so! And now your friendship has become even dearer to me through your simple ... but unusual – gesture in writing to me as you just have, with a sympathy and understanding which also mind their own business. And I've seen such desertions taking place all around me ...! enough to make me forever disgusted with everything called human. Nevertheless I'd been wanting to write to you for a long time (telepathy certainly isn't child's play), telling myself that you could not be like the others, and basing my faith on the memory of past conversations in which we enjoyed exchanging something more than mere words![23]

As a result of his closeness to Debussy, Laloy can give us insight into aspects of his inner life. For example, on 15 October 1907 Debussy, who was depressed and questioning his domestic situation, wrote to Laloy: '... there is no calm in my soul! Is it the fault of the feverish landscape that is this part of Paris? Am I definitely not made for the domestic life? So many questions which I don't feel strong enough to answer.' Laloy says that 'Debussy [...] from time to time had a sense of an account which destiny had to settle with him,' and mentions a letter in which he 'wondered whether he was not paying for some "forgotten error" in his life'. In another letter, Debussy gave a clue to his emotional state when he referred to *La Chute de la maison Usher* 'as if he sensed the same maleficent influence around him.'[24]

Laloy also tells numerous anecdotes about Debussy's everyday life. There is an entertaining account of a dinner with Gabriele D'Annunzio, around the time of *Le Martyre de saint Sébastien*, at which Debussy, whose tastes in food were notoriously plain, refused to try the more exotic Chinese dishes which had been prepared. There are descriptions of Debussy's habits, his study, his way of speaking, his interest in gossip, his piano playing, and even his singing:

> One day when I went to see Debussy and found him alone as usual, at the first words of welcome he went to the piano,

> impatient and perplexed like someone who has brought a surprise, but when the time comes to show it doubts whether it will be well received. The surprise was 'Le Faune' [from *Fêtes galantes* II], sung in his bass voice, almost whispering, while his soft hands, gliding over the keys, imitated the flute and tambourin.[25]

We know from accounts by Jacques Rouché and others that evenings at Laloy's home at Bellevue, just outside Paris near Meudon,[26] included the ritual of opium-smoking, and the question arises whether Debussy himself smoked opium. Laloy, whose use of opium was moderate, does not mention the subject, but the answer seems to be that Debussy did not: no accounts of his using it have ever come to light, and it is clear from remarks he made to the writer Paul-Jean Toulet that he was strongly opposed to it:

> If the condition of being friends did not forbid all painful discussions, I would have told you long ago how much I regretted your relationship with opium . . . an imagination as delicate as yours must expressly suffer for it. And here is life warning you, a little roughly (as it always does) that you have nothing to do with this sinister drug [. . .][27]

According to Debussy's stepdaughter Dolly Bardac, Debussy said that Laloy had an intellect the like of which he had never seen.[28] As François Lesure points out,[29] Laloy was the only university intellectual among Debussy's friends: given what we know about Debussy's abhorrence of academicism, this fact says something about the absence of dryness in Laloy's thinking, and also perhaps about his intuitive powers. Debussy described Laloy to Victor Segalen in 1907 as 'Bon critique. Solide.'[30] and on 15 July 1910 concluded a letter to his friend and publisher Jacques Durand in terms complimentary to both Durand and Laloy: 'I must leave you now and go to Bellevue to see Laloy, one of the men with whom – in your absence – one can exchange something other than tittle-tattle and scurrilous remarks!'[31] Although Debussy's opinions about others tended to vary depending on the person to whom he was writing, it is worth noting that Laloy is the only critic about whom he made such appreciative comments – his letters to Paul Dukas and Pierre Lalo are less fulsome, and the ambivalence of his attitude to the latter, the music critic of *Le Temps*, is well documented – and that they were never gainsaid in other contexts.

It is clear that conversations between Debussy and Laloy were much more protracted than their letters but, tantalizingly, there is little information about them. There must have been many, during the evenings following their weekly dinners together and at other times, and both men felt that their talks were an important part of their relationship. Debussy's reference to 'conversations in which we went somewhat beyond exchanging mere words' was quoted above; Laloy, always more given to analysis, described the way they talked to one another as follows:

> [I]t was not taste alone that linked me to Debussy. Although our existences were far removed from each other both by events, and by the feelings which arose from them, it was still easy for us to communicate not those feelings themselves, but their subsequent resonances, which were in harmony. Thus we exchanged not confidences but reflections, prolonged into silence, while each of us applied what had been said to his own case, whence came to mind another remark which brought us together once again.[32]

Over the course of years their talks must have ranged widely over music, literature, philosophy and the people they knew. Certainly the topics of discussion would have included French and other literatures, the music of Rameau, which was then being rediscovered in France, and popular genres they both enjoyed, such as cabaret and music-hall.[33] Debussy would have drawn benefit from Laloy's deeper knowledge of Chinese philosophy and also of non-Western music, in particular Chinese, Japanese and Cambodian.

Though Debussy had had some knowledge of Oriental culture since the 1890s, it seems clear that Laloy aroused his interest to new heights.[34] The *Estampes* (*Etchings*), the first of which is entitled 'Pagodes,' date from 1903, soon after the friendship between Laloy and Debussy began. Later Debussy dedicated 'Et la lune descend sur le temple qui fut' ('And the moon goes down over the temple which once was', *Images* II) to Laloy: Laloy confirms that the title is 'de style chinois.'[35] We know that Debussy had jade animals and pieces of Chinese pottery in his study; Laloy also owned Chinese *objets d'art*, which Debussy would have seen on visits to his home. In a letter to Laloy dated 2 August 1909, Debussy says that he 'began the day well by reading some Chinese poems translated by Laloy. They are very fine and we must talk about them again.' It is also interesting to note that references to Confucius and other Chinese philosophers in Debussy's reviews occur only from 1903 onwards; the same can be said for Classical Greek authors, and we may surmise that Laloy, with his Classical education, was an influence there too.

Laloy hoped to persuade Debussy to contribute to *Le Mercure musical*, the periodical which he co-founded in 1905, but Debussy never did so. Laloy was not alone in failing to persuade Debussy to write reviews: he turned down requests from Paul Flat for *La Revue bleue* in 1904, from René Doire for *Le Courrier musical* in 1910 and from André Gide for *La Nouvelle revue française* in 1913, and in any case virtually stopped writing music criticism between mid-1903 and 1912. In a letter to Laloy dated 2 May 1905, Debussy made the excuses he was to make so often:

> I dare not promise you something for your first issue, being brutalized with worries of all kinds to the point where, soon, I won't even have the strength to laugh about them - which I should - but reserve a spot for me under the heading 'Entretiens avec M. Croche' ['Conversations with Monsieur Croche']. He is a man with whom I spent a lot of time in the past, let's hope I meet him again?

On 10 March 1906, Debussy wrote with another refusal, and this time described the frustration he felt with music criticism in Paris:

> It's very kind of you to be so insistent on the subject of Monsieur Croche... but he's no longer very well in touch with the musical *mores* of his age. What's the point, in any case, of spelling out his opinions to people who don't listen! Music is currently split up into lots of little republics in which everyone is determined to shout louder than the man next door. The result is such horrible music, one begins to fear a taste for the 'other sort of music' may not long survive; and it's no consolation to see a sort of pretentious mediocrity gaining ground. It's not only irritating but positively harmful.
>
> You know, better than I do, the standard of writings about music. Today, if you don't know what to do or, especially, what to say, you improvise some art criticism!
>
> As for the artists themselves, they've taken to profound dreaming about æsthetic problems - the strange thing is, they generally talk more rubbish than the other lot... altogether not very stimulating!
>
> Don't you agree, we ought to adopt a more guarded attitude?

> We need to preserve a little of the 'mystery', which is eventually going to be rendered 'pervious' by all this gossip and tittle-tattle, with the artists joining in like so many aged actresses.
>
> Certainly there are things that need saying. But who to? Who for? For people who oscillate between Beethoven and Maurice Ravel! It's lucky really that no one of our generation is a genius: in my view that would be the hardest and most ridiculous position of all to be in. When are you coming to play bridge?[36]

On 25 December 1906 he again declined to give Laloy a contribution, pleading pressure of engagements, but interestingly, in the same letter he foreshadowed plans for a selection of articles.

> I am thinking for the future of a series of notes, opinions, etc. [. . .] left to me by poor Monsieur Croche who decided to die. – This most delicate of men thought that I couldn't decently continue 'conversations' in which the Void conducted a dialogue with Nothing-at-All![37] – So he leaves me the freedom: either to publish the papers, or to burn them. Together we'll see what's best done about it.

Debussy continued to discuss the idea with Laloy, but it did not come to fruition until the last years of his life. In February 1914, in preparation for a proposed edition by the publisher Dorbon, he wrote to Laloy asking him to spare him an hour to work on the proofs. This edition did not eventuate; the articles were eventually published in book form by Dorbon in 1921, as *Monsieur Croche*.

Debussy's name appeared on a list of contributors to *Le Mercure musical*, but he never did contribute. Laloy removed the announcement of the 'Entretiens avec Monsieur Croche' in July 1906 but only removed Debussy's name from the list of contributors in July 1907. A letter dated 13 September 1905 gives some idea as to the reasons why Debussy was reluctant to write for *Le Mercure musical*: it was a serious musicological review and, with the exception of Laloy, he was always ill at ease in the company of intellectuals.

> Really, apart from you, dear friend, the people at *Le Mercure musical* are sinister; above all, they are terribly well-informed, I really cannot see what poor Monsieur Croche would do among so many hardy specialists? I would like very much to tell you of his death in these terms:
>
> 'Monsieur Croche *anti-dilettante*, rightly disheartened by the

> musical mores of our times, passed away quietly amid general indifference. By request no flowers, and above all no music.'
>
> Don't hold it against me ... I would like you to succeed and I fear you are too delicate, too well brought up for the people at reviews.

Laloy and Debussy's first collaborative work was to be a ballet, *Masques et bergamasques*. As Laloy tells it, Diaghilev needed works for the Ballets Russes and in 1909 'had the idea of approaching Debussy, whom I went to see with him. It was agreed that I would draw up the scenario.'[38] The work was to be a *divertissement*, set in Venice, and lasting about fifty minutes. On 27 July 1909, Debussy wrote to tell Laloy that he had decided to write the scenario himself. The letter mentions another joint project, which was never begun, and also gives an insight into the quality of their communication:

> Why are you at Rahon par Chaussin [Laloy's country estate in the Jura] instead of 80, avenue du Bois-de-Boulogne? ... where it would be much easier for me to tell you of my decision, come what may, to write the scenario for the Russo-Venetian ballet.
>
> May all the gods whose job it is to guard friendships prevent you from thinking I've forgotten ... the other arrangement - which you remind me of so tactfully.
>
> I hope you'll be willing to extend your forgetfulness of past wrongs to continuing your moral support in the dealings I shall have to have one day with these people? As you so rightly say, 'they speak and think Russian' and you are the only one who can help me.
>
> I humbly admit that the impulse to take this decision so abruptly came from what I know to be the bad side of my character ... launching out enthusiastically, only to lose heart later. But I do treasure, in a secret corner of my heart, the idea of working with you on Æschylus' *Oresteia* ... in that we shall be completely our own masters, with all the time we need and not bothered either by Russia or the place de la Madeleine [i.e. Diaghilev or Debussy's publisher, Durand].
>
> I won't offer any further explanations, as you've got me used to your habit of understanding the things I don't say. It may not look like it, but it's much more cunning than Œdipus' game with the Sphinx.[39]

Another letter, written on 30 July 1909, explains and apologizes further. However, a rupture with Diaghilev led to the work's being abandoned before any music had been written, and Debussy wrote to Laloy on 2 August in terms which leave no doubt about the hostility he felt towards Diaghilev at that time:

> Kipling said that 'the Russian is a charming fellow until he tucks in his shirt . . .'
>
> Our mutual Russian imagines that the best way to act towards his fellow men is first of all to lie to them. This perhaps requires more talent than he possesses, and I confess that in friendship I don't play those games.
>
> Anyway, everything is as it should be between us, and that's certainly what matters, more than Diaghilev and his treacherous Cossack regiment.[40]

Their next collaboration was in 1913–1915. Laloy, who was to work as Secretary-General of the Opéra under the newly appointed Director, Jacques Rouché, tells the story:

> Debussy was one of the first composers whom Monsieur Rouché approached for a new work. Returning to Verlaine who had inspired such admirable songs from him in his youth, Debussy thought at first of a ballet on the *Fêtes galantes*, and I presented him with a scenario which introduced in turn the different pieces from that set.[41]

The work was to be an opera-ballet, a choice of genre which was connected with their shared interest in the music of Rameau. However, the project was eventually abandoned because of legal problems. The poet Charles Morice had previously adapted Verlaine's *Fêtes galantes* for the stage, and insisted on his right to impose his version.[42] Debussy did not want to work with Morice, whose libretto he described to Laloy in disparaging terms on 30 November 1913:

> It was enough, as you will demonstrate, to have taste and sensitivity – to banish above all the *tours de force* with which Moriceoblat[43] seems to pull out that poor Verlaine's lines like bad teeth! . . . It [Laloy's libretto] has the best pretexts for making real music, and I am very happy. (You wouldn't have an old coat that once belonged to J. Ph. Rameau?!)[44]

Seven pages of sketches survive; a libretto in Laloy's hand is in the possession of the Laloy family. (See Plate 8.)

Later they began a project of reworking *Le Martyre de saint*

Sébastien as an opera. Laloy says that after the original performance in 1911,

> Debussy remarked like all of us that the music was too short in comparison to the recited poem and was not well adapted to it, and formed the idea of revising his composition so that everything in it was sung. The text had to be abridged and revised. We were to carry out this work together. With his customary generosity, Gabriele D'Annunzio gave us full discretion.[45]

Laloy said he 'set to work too slowly' and had scarcely begun the revisions when war intervened,[46] but his memory must be in error here, for Debussy wrote to Jacques Durand on 1 November 1917: 'Laloy and I have been working on the operatic version of *Le Martyre de saint Sébastien*. It's an improvement; isn't it strange that in some 3,995 lines there should be so little substance? Just words, words ... I think we'll manage it all the same.'[47]

Their last collaborative effort was an *Ode à la France*, for soprano, chorus and orchestra. Begun in 1916, it is a patriotic work reflecting Debussy's attitude towards the war. Debussy was too ill to complete it. Laloy prepared a vocal score from sketches which were discovered some years after Debussy's death, and from his own rough copies. The work was orchestrated by Marius-François Gaillard with the consent of Laloy and Emma Debussy; it was published by Choudens in 1928 and performed in the same year. Laloy gives an account of the work's history in an article, 'La Dernière œuvre de Claude Debussy: l'*Ode à la France*', which is translated on pp. 231–235.

Laloy's *Claude Debussy*, the first French biography of the composer, was published in 1909, and Debussy seems to have been more than happy with it.[48] On 29 April 1909, before publication, he wrote to Laloy:

> I congratulate the company [the publisher Dorbon] for the pleasure it is going to give me to read you. You are the only one who knows what Claude Debussy is – without bass drum, or embroidery –
>
> And we know what we can both get out of it – especially me –[49]

On 27 July he approved the last chapter, which covers performance practice, and later that year, on 10 September, he acknowledged receiving a copy of the book in terms which tend to confirm its credentials as a true representation of his æsthetic and technique, and also demonstrate the value he placed on Laloy's friendship and comprehension:

> My dear friend,
>
> A long time ago already, you were pretty much the only person to understand *Pelléas*; you know how much joy that gave me, you also know that from that day a friendship began which neither things nor men have been able to disturb . . .
>
> Today I received the detailed, charming narrative you have been pleased to write on Claude Debussy. If I am not sure of being absolutely all you say I am, the emotion of being understood from so close up ('but unaffectedly,' as the other one says [i.e. Golaud, in Act III Scene 3 of *Pelléas et Mélisande*]) is absolute.
>
> There's something acute about it like a shining a bright light into the shadows of the mind; it's burglary with the burgled congratulating the burglar.[50]

We may safely assume that the biographical material derives from Debussy, and it seems likely that the comments about Debussy's compositions, together with the analysis of his style presented in the fifth chapter, are based on or at least consistent with ideas Debussy had expressed to Laloy in conversation. Laloy does not go into detail about individual works, but discusses Debussy's style at some length, also setting it against the background of Romanticism and the Russian school. The book includes an autograph score excerpt from *Rondes de printemps*, which was to be published the following year by Durand. *Claude Debussy* was admired at the time by the more scholarly critics, including Maurice Emmanuel and Emile Vuillermoz, and it remained influential until the 1940s. It was quoted in numerous articles and in other Debussy biographies such as Daniel Chennevière's *Claude Debussy et son œuvre* (Paris, 1913) which acknowledges that biographical details have been borrowed from Laloy, and Robert Jardillier's *Claude Debussy* (Dijon, 1922) which is written very much on the Laloy model.

In *Claude Debussy*, *La Musique retrouvée* and elsewhere, Laloy provides information about Debussy which is unavailable from other sources. (Only details not found in the translated extracts will be mentioned here.)

- Debussy's first *envoi de Rome*, *Almanzor*, is to be regarded as lost.[51]

- Laloy recounts the comment made by Debussy's composition teacher Ernest Guiraud when Debussy showed him music he had written for Théodore de Banville's play, *Diane au bois*: 'Well, this is all very interesting, but you must put it away for later. Or else you will never have the Prix de Rome.'[52]

- Louise Liebich's biography of Debussy quotes an interesting snippet of information from a letter which has not survived:

> 'It is not possible to publish the *Suite bergamasque*,' wrote Debussy one day to Monsieur Louis Laloy; 'I am still in need of twelve bars for the Sarabande.' And as none of his previous ideas had satisfied him, sooner than publish the piece with the slightest defect he preferred to wait patiently for the right inspiration.[53]

- Laloy tells us that after Maeterlinck's mistress, the singer Georgette Leblanc, was rejected for the role of Mélisande in the 1902 performances of *Pelléas et Mélisande*, 'Debussy received a directive visit from his illustrious collaborator, and remained so taken aback by it that later he said to me again, "I have trouble believing it happened."' Laloy considered Georgette Leblanc, whom he did not know in 1902 but met later, 'very intelligent and likable, but as unmusical as possible.'[54]

- Very interestingly, a letter from Debussy to Laloy casts doubt on the authenticity of some of Debussy's most frequently quoted aphorisms. Paul Landormy's interview with Debussy, published in *La Revue bleue* on 2 April 1904 under the heading 'L'Etat actuel de la musique française' ('The current state of French music'), is the source of well-known comments such as 'The musical genius of France is something like fantasy in sensibility' and 'Music must humbly seek to give pleasure.'[55] However, the day after the interview was published, Debussy disowned at least some of the quoted comments in a letter to Laloy:

> Have you read an article by Landormy in *La Revue bleue* in which he reports a conversation with C. Debussy? It's extraordinary how poorly this so-called musician hears . . .

Laloy provides valuable first-hand information about the reception of Debussy's works, particularly in the years before 1910 when the novelty of Debussy's musical language provoked strong reactions among audiences. At times Laloy describes these reactions and proffers explanations for them. He says that in the 1890s the public was astonished, taken aback, by the gentle, voluptuous atmosphere that was so new: at concerts it was common to hear comments that the harmony was insane, or that there were things that would make your hair stand on end. He goes into detail about the phenomenon known as Debussyism (*le Debussysme*) to which he devotes a chapter of *La Musique retrouvée* and a long article entitled 'Claude Debussy et le Debussysme' (1910). Defined by one of the Debussyists as 'an epic struggle between a few devotees of Debussy's music and the masses, which were resolutely hostile,'[56] Debussyism began with the *générale* - the public dress rehearsal - of *Pelléas et Mélisande* on 28 April 1902. The 'Debussyists' (*les debussystes*) were young, and not all were professional musicians: many were students and artists. Although the Debussyists included the composers Ravel, Louis Aubert, Raoul Bardac, André Caplet, Alfredo Casella, Maurice Delage, Gabriel Grovlez, Jean Huré, Charles Koechlin, Jean Roger-Ducasse and Florent Schmitt,[57] it was of course principally music critics who perpetuated Debussyism, and the most active were Laloy, Jean Marnold and Emile Vuillermoz.[58] The movement gave rise to a furore in the Paris press, with a great many articles written - many of them ill-informed or wide of the mark and some, such as Jean Lorrain's 'Les *Pelléastres*', greatly angering Debussy.[59]

Laloy says that the Debussyists wanted Debussy to write another *Pelléas*, and some were bitterly disappointed when in 1905 *La Mer* did not sound like the music associated with the sea in that opera. Debussy found it impossible to repeat himself: 'Convinced that a work is a special case, he refused to write a second *Pelléas*, which would have had the greatest chances of success.'[60] Debussyism continued to be discussed in the press until about 1910, by which time Debussy was established as the pre-eminent composer of his time. Even while it was raging, Laloy was able to put the phenomenon of Debussyism into historical perspective:

> Debussy had his Debussyists, as Wagner his Wagnerians, Rameau his *ramistes* or *ramoneurs*; and these devoted partisans were pursued with a ferocious hatred and the most heated sarcasm. It is an eternal spectacle. No improvement in anything

> has ever been wanted by the majority, but by a tiny handful of believers, who at first are accused of madness, or of all crimes. This handful increases all the time and, a few centuries having passed, the masses finish up deeming good what they once anathematized; but only so as to draw rules from it, which in turn will condemn without appeal any work suspected of inventiveness.[61]

Laloy's views of Debussy's historical position and musical development are found mainly in his *Claude Debussy*, though he returns to these themes in articles written later, particularly 'Claude Debussy et le Debussysme' (1910) and 'Le Théâtre de Claude Debussy' (1920). After Romanticism and the partial liberation achieved by Mussorgsky, he sees Debussy as 'the saviour, because he came at the appointed time, because he had contemplated the example of the sister arts, and above all because he had listened to the voices of nature.'[62] Laloy considers *Pelléas et Mélisande* such an important landmark in the history of music that he begins *La Musique retrouvée* from 1902, the year of the first performances, and calls the last chapter 'Vingt-cinq ans après' ('Twenty-five years later'). He admires the work for its depiction of everyday feelings - and he says the same of *La Damoiselle élue*, which he links to *Pelléas et Mélisande*. He calls *Pelléas* 'a masterpiece of emotion and simplicity', 'music without formulae, in which everything comes from the heart, music with no idle developments, modelled on the drama, or rather on life itself, of which the words of the drama were only a pale reflection.'[63] Its historical significance, Laloy maintained, was that it broke Wagner's long-standing domination over French music: '[Wagner's] uncontested reign only came to an end in 1902: *Pelléas et Mélisande* did not make us forgetful of *Parsifal*, of *Tristan und Isolde*, of the *Ring*, but it relegated them to the past.'[64]

In discussing Debussy's musical æsthetic, Laloy emphasizes two points: naturalness (*le naturel*) and connections or parallels with the other arts. There is much discussion in the early chapters of *Claude Debussy* of literature, and also of painting. Echoing Paul Dukas' well-known comment, Laloy considers that 'the most profitable lessons came to him not from composers, but from poets and painters.'[65] Debussy's affinity with nature is a recurring theme throughout Laloy's reviews and articles, and is associated with the notion of simplicity which Laloy also stresses. The theme of naturalness and simplicity is very much in keeping with the views Debussy puts forward in his own reviews and articles, including this well-known comment by his mouthpiece, Monsieur Croche:

> My favourite music is those few notes an Egyptian shepherd plays on his flute: he is part of the landscape around him, and he knows harmonies that aren't in our books. The 'musicians' hear only music written by practised hands, never the music of nature herself. To see the sun rise does one far more good than hearing the *Pastoral* symphony. What's the use of such incomprehensible art?[66]

There are also consistencies between Laloy's and Debussy's views: both speak of 'the mysteries of music', and of the need to maintain the French tradition of taste and elegance; also, there are anti-academic remarks in Laloy, though fewer than in Debussy. However, it is a matter of consistencies rather than similarities, for Laloy's style of argument is lengthier and more rigorous than Debussy's, and their writing styles are very different. Laloy is revealed as a thinker in his own right: he is by no means simply a mouthpiece for Debussy.

Measuring Debussy's music against some common labels for his readers' benefit, Laloy raises the question of whether Debussy is closer to Classicism or Romanticism, and decides in favour of the former:

> Between Classics and Romantics, if a choice must be made, [Debussy's music] will side with the former, but not as part of their school. It asks for order, on condition that instructions from a previous authority do not go with it, and it asks to remain the master, following the dictates of the mind.[67]

Laloy uses the terms Symbolism and Impressionism, although - like other critics of the period - not very often. One might speculate that Laloy was cautioned by Debussy's famous remark about 'what idiots call Impressionism', but in fact these terms and their definitions were much less of an issue at the time than they are in present-day writings about the period. Laloy does not define the terms, but comes closest to doing so in this passage from *Claude Debussy* (1909):

> Music is the Symbolist art par excellence, since it represents movements, forms and colours only by means of sounds, that is of sensations to which no conventional signification can be attached, and which, having no direct relation to objects, suggest all but show nothing. And it also has a particular aptitude for

> Impressionism: what was felt in a moment is less at risk of being altered by a transposition than by a reproduction, which incites control and aims to be faithful.[68]

Impressionism involves 'momentary nuances of feeling', 'unaltered freshness' of emotion and 'pictures – all vibrations in the air and effects of light'.[69] However, Laloy considers Debussy primarily a Symbolist by virtue of his intuitive sense of the correspondences between aspects of experience. Writing of *Ibéria*, he says that it 'is not a document; it is an "image", shaped first of all in his mind, and contemplated with an inward eye before being manifested outside. This is what we might have expected from an artist who has never abdicated before nature and, far less an Impressionist than a Symbolist, has only prized appearances for the emotion they reveal.'[70]

Laloy concluded that Debussy was 'the composer who, better than the poets themselves, fulfilled the wishes of Symbolism'[71] and suggested: 'It is possible that [...] *Pelléas et Mélisande* is the masterpiece of Symbolism, and the *Nocturnes* that of Impressionism.'[72]

Laloy passes on Debussy's opinions about other composers: he reports quite a number in *La Musique retrouvée*, including some derogatory comments about minor composers of the period, and a remark to the effect that anyone would think Schumann 'orchestrated in his cellar.' Laloy says that when Richard Strauss' *Salome* was performed in Paris in 1907,

> Debussy paid homage to a competence which was at times that of a conjuror, rather than of an artist, and did not delude himself either about the treacherous vulgarity of the ideas which had pretensions to be noble, like the music of the prophet Jochanaan, or a wicked taste for causing the listener pain. 'Sometimes he pulls the wool over their eyes, thinking they would never notice, or else he scratches them raw, he scratches them to the bone.'[73]

And Laloy gives us an insight into the important question of Mussorgsky's influence on Debussy:

> 'I went, like anyone else, to Bayreuth,' Debussy told me, 'and I wept my due at *Parsifal*. But when I came back I got to know *Boris Godunov*, which cured me.' However Mussorgsky could not be entirely to the taste of an artist who was so attentive to

> purety of style and the balance of proportions. 'It's never quite finished,' he used to say a little bitterly.[74]

Laloy's analysis of Debussy's musical language is perhaps the most valuable of his contributions to Debussy studies. The fifth chapter of *Claude Debussy* (1909) presents a summary of Debussy's style and technique in works up to and including *Rondes de printemps*: part of the chapter is translated on pp. 81–83. It is an impressive analysis which was far ahead of its time, and which remains unique. Laloy discusses the nature of Debussy's harmony, his orchestration and his flexible approach to modality in a way which perhaps leaves little more to be said about the essence of the composer's musical thinking.[75]

> The melody is under no compulsion, not even to emancipate itself from the major scale; often no notes are found which Mozart would not also have allowed. [...] It is, furthermore, improper to speak of scales, because a scale is a rule. Here the melody perpetually changes the order and nature of the intervals. This is music without scales [...]
>
> The orchestration resorts to doubling at the unison only if it is necessary for reinforcement or gradation; in every other place, it prefers unblended colours; through their proximity they set each other off, react and come into play. [...]
>
> The harmony is the image of the melody; like the melody, it is very regular on occasion, and even particularly fond of the root-position triad. But it also likes many other chords, which until then had been counted among the dissonances and which it recognizes as consonant: it imposes no enforced consequence on them, no resolution; it relishes in each of them a special charm, which is enough.

Some of the points made in this chapter recur in Laloy's later reviews, including 'Claude Debussy et le Debussysme' (1910) where he also radically redefines consonance and dissonance, making the far-sighted statement that 'we are reaching a period in which every chord, whatever its composition may be and even if it cannot be reduced to harmonics, can count as a consonance.'[76] Elsewhere Laloy also discusses Debussy's concision and unity of style, the simplicity of his melodic ideas, the adherence between thought and expression, and his rhythm, 'which is no longer that of beats and bars[, but] that of lines and contours [...]'[77]

Laloy's writings are also a good source of information about Debussy performance practice. The last chapter of *Claude Debussy* is devoted to the subject, and gives specific advice to pianists, other instrumentalists, singers and conductors: it is translated on pp. 107–109. In some of his reviews, Laloy's comments about the performances he has heard give valuable hints for interpreting particular works: for example, in 'Sirènes', the third of the *Nocturnes*, the female chorus should produce 'a dispersed murmur, coming from no one knows where', and he says that a constant tempo is necessary in order to achieve fluency in the *Prélude à l'Après-midi d'un faune*.[78] Laloy's credentials as an authority on Debussy performance practice are excellent: not only did his wife study piano with the composer, but Laloy attended performances and rehearsals with him, and Debussy gave specific approval of the last chapter of *Claude Debussy*. Furthermore, most of Laloy's recommendations are consistent with those of others who have written on the subject, including the singer Jane Bathori and the pianists Marguerite Long and René Dumesnil, and with Debussy's own stated views (for example that the fifth finger of the virtuoso is 'a pest').

On a number of occasions, Laloy also describes Debussy's own playing, and reinforces descriptions by Alfredo Casella and others of Debussy's 'soft hands' and the sound he produced from the piano. After a concert in 1914 in which Debussy accompanied the violinist Arthur Hartmann, Laloy wrote:

> The power of the magic will be understood by all who have once heard this supernatural piano in which sounds are born of the impact of the hammers, with no brushing against the strings, then rise up into transparent air, which combines but does not blend them, and evaporate in iridescent mists. Monsieur Debussy tames the keyboard with a spell which is beyond the reach of any of our virtuosi.[79]

At the end of his life, Laloy recalled 'that supple, living touch, with the hands always on the keys, palpating and feeling out the sound, which was needed for his music as for that of Couperin, Rameau, Schumann, Chopin, the authors he loved.'[80] In the 1930s, Laloy expressed his great admiration for Gieseking's performances of Debussy, in a passage which also recalled the intimacy which had allowed Laloy to become an authentic exponent of Debussy's music:

> Monsieur Walter Gieseking is the only pianist today whose touch reminds me of Debussy. Closing my eyes, I could believe I was again in that study, at the end of the avenue du Bois-de-

> Boulogne, on one of the evenings when my illustrious friend was in the mood to sit down at the piano. All that was missing was the too-frequent puffing of the Ceinture railway, and from time to time an angry exclamation under his breath when a note escaped him, for he had not practised for a long time. These are accidents which do not happen to a Gieseking. But in interpretation, there can be no mistake about the resemblance. Those who have heard Debussy know what this encomium is worth.[81]

Laloy knew Ravel less well than he did Debussy. They would have known each other in 1902, at the time of the first performances of *Pelléas et Mélisande*, as they both went to most of them: Ravel was there with other members of the ardent group of artistic supporters known as the *Apaches*. However, Laloy was not one of the *Apaches*, and he and Ravel never became close friends despite having numerous friends and acquaintances in common, among them Cocteau, Diaghilev, Roussel, Auric, Manuel Rosenthal, Maurice Delage, M.-D. Calvocoressi and Ricardo Viñes.[82] Ravel attended dinners and musical evenings at Laloy's home, and Laloy's summing-up of their relationship was: 'I was always on friendly, but not intimate, terms with Ravel.' Ravel's own ventures into music journalism do not seem to have brought him into contact with Laloy, but the two men would have had dealings during the years when Laloy was working with Jacques Rouché: *Ma mère l'Oye* was staged at the Théâtre des Arts, and *Daphnis et Chloë*, *L'Heure espagnole* and *Khovanchina* – an adaptation of Mussorgsky's incomplete opera by Ravel and Stravinsky – were performed at the Opéra. Two surviving letters from Ravel to Laloy, from 1906 and 1922, discuss performances in which Laloy had an organizing role, and are written in cordial terms.[83, 84] Ravel dedicated a song, *Tripatos* (1909) to Laloy's sister-in-law, the singer Marguerite Babaïan, and he is known to have spoken approvingly of Laloy's ballet based on Fauré's *Dolly* suite. As in the case of Debussy, Ravel's acquaintance with Laloy raises the question of whether Ravel used opium. It seems clear that he did not: he told Manuel Rosenthal, 'No, I find it unnecessary, I don't know what it can provide. I've often been offered it, by the Delages, among others, but I don't feel the need of it.'[85]

Laloy was what the French call *un inconditionnel* – an unconditional admirer – of Ravel. His writings on Ravel begin with a review of *Shéhérazade* in 1904, and continue beyond the composer's death; they include a substantial article on Ravel's works for music theatre. Some sources state that towards the end of his life Laloy was working on a book on Ravel. There is, however, no trace of such a book among the Laloy family papers: it is possible that the manuscript was destroyed along with other documents during World War II.

In the two scandals which occurred in the early part of Ravel's career, Laloy wrote articles in support of him. The first of the scandals, the controversy surrounding Ravel's exclusion after the preliminary round of the Prix de Rome competition in 1905, is discussed in an article from *Le Mercure musical*: see pp. 239–240. The second scandal, usually known as the *affaire Ravel*, followed the first performance of the *Histoires naturelles* at the Société Nationale in 1907. This *affaire* was sparked by a review by Pierre Lalo in *Le Temps*, where he claimed that the work reminded him of Debussy. Lalo's reviews provoked widespread and vehement reviews in the Paris press. Laloy, along with Jean Marnold, Georges Jean-Aubry and M.-D. Calvocoressi, strongly supported Ravel and it is interesting to read Laloy's reviews of the work in this context: see pp. 247–252.

Laloy's writings on Ravel attempt to explain aspects of his æsthetic and technique to the musical public. A passage from *Comment écouter la musique* analyses his compositional technique in a general way:

> After Debussy, Ravel (1875–1937), who was very attentive to his example, nonetheless remained faithful to the lessons of Fauré. The melody, barely altering a leading note, remains closely tied to the major scale; the ingenious chords are joined without seeming to be by legitimate junctions. There is something secret about this music. Whence its bewitching charm, and the sharply pointed emotion which catches us unawares and pierces the heart.[86]

In some of his reviews and articles Laloy discusses the change which occurred in Ravel's style during the 1920s, when the Sonata for violin and cello, the Sonata for violin and piano, *L'Enfant et les sortilèges* and the *Chansons madécasses* showed a tendency towards directness and concision: '[N]ot content to reduce a thought to its simplest expression, he goes further, into ellipsis and allusion, and rather than pronouncing all the notes of a chord succeeds in suggesting them through the movement of the melodious lines.'[87] Laloy's observations are confirmed by a remark which Ravel made in his 'Esquisse autobiographique' ('Autobiographical sketch') about the Sonata for violin and cello: 'I think this sonata marks a turning-point in the evolution of my career. Sparseness is pushed to extremes. Renunciation of harmonic charm; an increasingly marked reaction in favour of melody.'[88]

Despite his overall enthusiasm for Ravel's music, Laloy did not admire the works for piano:

> As for the piano pieces (*Pavane*, *Jeux d'eau*, *Miroirs*), they are of prodigious technique and rare colour; but [...] everything does not flow from one source: and at times one senses a slight overload of ornamentation. That is why I have never been able to raise myself to the heights of enthusiasm with regard to these works that some of our friends reached in a single bound; even the magic of Ricardo Viñes was not always enough to hold me under the spell and ward off the hint of arbitrariness which arises from time to time.[89]

An exception was *Gaspard de la nuit*, which Laloy considered confident and stylish. Many of Laloy's reviews have praise for Ricardo Viñes, who gave the first performance of so many works by Debussy and Ravel. Considering him to be 'not a virtuoso, but a magician of a pianist',[90] Laloy paid tribute to his abilities as follows: 'Monsieur Ricardo Viñes has a marvellous sense of harmony, and he also has fingers of fire [...] I do not hesitate to place [him] in the first rank not only as a pianist but as an artist of our time.'[91]

Laloy's principal contribution to Ravel criticism was his perceptive analysis of Ravel's musical personality. When the *Histoires naturelles* were first performed in 1907, Laloy was one of the few critics to admire the work, and indeed he felt that it was the most self-revealing of Ravel's compositions. Laloy saw Ravel as primarily a humorous composer, writing that 'a man like this is not completely himself when he not secretly poking fun.' He found wit in Ravel's piano playing, and admired the musical jokes and 'mocking smile' in *L'Heure espagnole*, where he also noted the tenderness which Ravel's music reveals towards children, toys and animals. Considering 'the seriousness of human feelings' to be outside Ravel's domain, Laloy said that he preferred his humorous music to 'the slight hint of sentimental affectation which mars, for my taste, the *Pavane* or "La Vallée des cloches".' Laloy identified the humorous element in Ravel most impressively in the above-mentioned articles on the *Histoires naturelles*, creating a striking and memorable image:

> Maurice Ravel's thought is naturally circumspect, penetrating, and inclined to make fun of whatever moves him. A mocking

> hobgoblin lives in his mind, singing and playing bells, for Ravel discovers in the blink of an eye the unexpected comedy and as it were the secret grin inside all things. And this light ironic touch, far from lessening the emotion, on the contrary quickens it and makes it more poignant; nothing is closer to tears than this smile [. . .]

Later, in *La Musique retrouvée*, he commented:

> As for my advice to listen to the 'mocking hobgoblin', perhaps it was not so bad, since after the *Histoires naturelles* Maurice Ravel wrote *L'Heure espagnole*, on the comedy by Monsieur Franc-Nohain, and quite recently, with Madame Colette, *L'Enfant et les sortilèges*.[92]

Laloy's appreciation of Ravel, as both man and artist, is summed up in a moving tribute written on the occasion of Ravel's death:

> French music has just been plunged into mourning by the death of Maurice Ravel, one of the most ingenious and exquisitely sensitive of composers, whose works will remain as a unique monument to what can be produced by taste and knowledge when both are carried to the last point of refinement. His solitary life, dedicated to his art, did not prevent him from relishing the pleasures of society, where his charming mind was greatly appreciated. He was a very true friend, a man of honour, a pure and noble artist.[93]

Letters from Debussy to Laloy early in 1907, after publication of Laloy's first review of the *Histoires naturelles*, reveal something of Debussy's opinion of Ravel. On 22 February, Debussy wrote:

> I have received the second issue of the *S.I.M.*. . . and am astonished to read that a man of your taste deliberately sacrifices such a pure, instinctive masterpiece as [Mussorgsky's] *The nursery* to the intentional Americanism of M. Ravel's *Histoires naturelles*. Despite Ravel's undeniable skill, these songs can only be 'displaced' music. So leave such things to the valet Calvocoressi![94]

Debussy returned to the subject on 8 March, and it is clear that Laloy must have defended his views:

> As for Ravel, I recognize the marks of your usual ingenuity ... Even if I don't feel he's quite found 'his way,' he'll be able to thank you for pointing one out to him ...
>
> But, between ourselves, do you really believe in 'humorous' music? For a start, it doesn't exist on its own; there always has to be a pretext, either words or a situation ... Two chords with their feet in the air, or in any other curious position, will never be intrinsically humorous and could only become so in an empirical manner.
>
> I agree with you Ravel is extraordinarily gifted, but what annoys me is the attitude he adopts of being a 'conjurer', or rather a Fakir casting spells and making flowers burst out of chairs ... The trouble is, a conjuring trick always has to have a build-up and after you've seen it once you're no longer astonished.
>
> For the moment I'm happy if people find it entertaining. Given the way people torment and annoy music, she might be glad to hear the excuse that her only function is to bring a smile to the lips![95]

These letters – and the second review, which was published soon after – make it clear that Laloy was no mere acolyte of Debussy, but held firmly to opinions formed on the basis of his own judgement.

Another aspect of Ravel's musical personality – the question of whether his music is unemotional and artificial – is also discussed by Laloy, and in a way that is consistent with Ravel's own comments on the subject. Laloy is referring to audiences and some critics when he writes:

> Because Ravel had a horror of bombast and because he was able to discover affinities between notes or sounds that but for him would escape us, he was accused of dryness and artifice. That was a great mistake.[96]

The question of artificiality is complex, as is suggested by a well-known comment by the critic M.-D. Calvocoressi, who knew the composer very well: 'One might say, indeed, that artificiality is natural to Monsieur Ravel.'[97] However, as regards dryness, some light is shed by a remark Ravel made about his own personality, to the effect that 'the Basques feel very deeply but rarely show it, and then only to very few.'[98] And the well-known lines by Tristan Klingsor, the poet of *Shéhérazade*, also refute any suggestion that Ravel was dry or unemotional:

> Et le cœur ironique et tendre qui bat sous
> Le gilet de velours de Maurice Ravel [. . .]
>
> And the tender, ironic heart which beats beneath
> The velvet waistcoat of Maurice Ravel [. . .]

Debate raged in the first decade of the century as to whether Ravel was to be regarded as merely an imitator of Debussy, or whether he had a recognisable style of his own. Pierre Lalo accused Ravel of plagiary in *Jeux d'eau* even though, as Ravel himself pointed out, at the time the piece appeared the only major piano work by Debussy was the suite *Pour le piano*, which could not possibly have served as a model. Even though he was a student of Fauré, most critics called Ravel a Debussyist, and Ravel did fit the description in so far as he attended all the early performances of *Pelléas*. However, he had an individual style, and in 1904 Laloy was one of the first to recognize it:

> Undoubtedly these two are minds from the same family, but the analogy should not be exaggerated, nor should the disdainful epithet of imitator be flung at Monsieur Ravel: his music is not an imitative music; it has a personal accent and, in particular, shows evidence of a taste for pictorial detail which is not encountered in Monsieur Debussy. It cannot be disputed that the influence of the latter is obvious, but the greatest geniuses began by having masters and models, and one could choose worse.[99]

In 1907 it was clear that Laloy saw Ravel as an individual when he wrote, 'I am aware [. . .] of what he can do for our music', and in 1908, several years in advance of most critics including M.-D. Calvocoressi, he described Ravel as 'a personality which can be loved or hated, but whose independence and interest can not fail to be recognized.' Interestingly, a few years later Laloy also analysed the differences between Ravel and Florent Schmitt, concluding that Ravel is more refined and takes care of the smallest detail, whereas Schmitt is 'a thinker, more preoccupied with order and sequence.'[100]

The relationship between Ravel and Debussy has been much discussed, and is perhaps more complex than most writers suggest. Besides the controversy over the issue of imitation in the mind of the musical public, there was also the specific difficulty over the question of plagiary between certain compositions. Laloy mentions this problem in his description of the relationship:

> He knew and very sincerely admired Debussy. I did all I could to prevent a misunderstanding between them, but too many hare-brained busybodies seemed to take pleasure in making it inevitable, for example sacrificing Debussy's quartet to Ravel's, or else raising absurd questions of priority between the 'Habanera' and the second of the *Estampes*. The two composers then stopped seeing each other; as their esteem was mutual they both – as I can vouch – regretted the rupture.[101]

Laloy's description is certainly consistent with Ravel's remark in 1912 that 'It's probably better for us, after all, to be on frigid terms for illogical reasons.' Indeed one might speculate that the rift between Debussy and Ravel was one reason why Laloy and Ravel did not become closer.

It is not clear when Laloy and Stravinsky met, but we know that Debussy and Stravinsky were both invited to Laloy's home soon after the first performance of *L'Oiseau de feu* in June 1910, which had been their first meeting. Such invitations evidently continued: in 1912 Stravinsky and Debussy performed part of the piano-duet version of *Le Sacre du printemps* on Laloy's Pleyel piano, and a note from Laloy to Stravinsky written in November 1916 invites him to dinner with Debussy, with the comment, 'Debussy feels that you are avoiding him.' Stravinsky and Laloy would have had professional as well as social encounters: *Les Abeilles*, *Le Chant du rossignol*, *Pulcinella*, *Mavra*, *Le Baiser de la fée* and *Perséphone* were all performed at the Opéra during Laloy's time there. Laloy mentions that in 1922, soon after it was finished, Stravinsky played *Les Noces* to him on the piano, and he also tells of a mutual Chinese friend who painted a portrait of Stravinsky in the 1920s. It seems reasonable to speculate that they would have discussed mutual friends and acquaintances, particularly Diaghilev, and also current æsthetic issues. The topic of player-pianos would have interested them both: Stravinsky wrote compositions and arrangements for the Pleyela and Aeolian during the period when he knew Laloy, and Laloy, always interested in new musical developments, discusses these instruments in *La Musique retrouvée*.

Laloy gives glimpses into Stravinsky's musical life, and even some affectionate descriptions of his physical appearance. After Stravinsky's reading of *Le Sacre* with Debussy, Laloy wrote of 'a slender young man, with a kind, curious face. Sitting at the piano, he is transported by passion, his hands run dizzily across the keyboard, unleashing unknown sounds; he rises, staggers, but he smiles, happy with his composition [. . .]' Elsewhere Laloy refers to 'the strange, striking formulae which he spits out so cuttingly',[102] and a short announcement of the return of the Ballets Russes to Paris in 1920, published in *Excelsior*, paints a picture of Stravinsky, 'this small, pale-faced man', bounding from a car to hurry to a rehearsal of *Petrouchka*, 'staring into space, unaware of anyone'.[103]

Although the friendship was not as intimate as that between Laloy and Debussy, it was closer than the relationship between Laloy and Ravel, and their professional relationship was also closer. A comment Stravinsky made to Laloy about *Le Rossignol* indicates a warmth between the two men: '*Le Rossignol* is a present I've given you. It's a flask of marc-brandy I've slipped into your pocket.'[104] It seems clear that Stravinsky had respect for Laloy's abilities: he mentions him in correspondence as one of two people in the Paris music scene who knew Russian, and a letter of condolence which Stravinsky sent to Laloy's wife after his death praises him as 'the most representative of French music critics.'

We might speculate that Debussy discussed the different phases of the friendship between him and Stravinsky with Laloy, and also his opinions of Stravinsky's music. However, Laloy mentions these things only briefly, glossing over the well-documented fluctuations in the friendship:

> *L'Oiseau de feu* was given by the Ballets Russes in 1910. The sparkling orchestral writing still draws heavily on Rimsky-Korsakov, though with intense moments, as in the poignant lullaby towards the end of the work, which points to a different type of sensibility. In 1911, we had *Petrouchka*, a marvel of liveliness and freshness. Debussy was immediately captivated by a music very different from his own in movement and density, but of no less pure quality. For him Stravinsky felt admiration that was never contradicted. Composers of genius both, they understood each other immediately and their prompt friendship was never disturbed.[105]

Laloy championed Stravinsky's music from 1912 onwards and, though he admired some works more than others, he was still an enthusiastic supporter in the 1930s. He reviewed performances of most of Stravinsky's major compositions from these years, and seems to have followed Stravinsky's artistic metamorphoses with characteristic penetration. While virtually every other Parisian music critic was expressing outrage at the radically new language of *Le Sacre du printemps*, Laloy wrote of 'a superhuman music, a revealing of the elemental powers', 'an intoxication, an ecstasy, an annihilation'. When other critics were thrown by Stravinsky's changes of stylistic direction in the 1920s, Laloy seems to have understood, writing that 'since [1914] I have continued to follow Stravinsky in all the developments of his thinking, and as with Debussy I have admitted that he was right each time he left the path he himself had traced out and went boldly in search of unknown truths.'[106] Laloy again voiced his support for Stravinsky's determination to forge his own path, in a review of *Perséphone* written in 1934, where he also gives an overview of Stravinsky's stylistic evolution up to that point:

> Monsieur Stravinsky attains in this work a simplicity which could be called Classical although it does not recall, or rather because it does not recall in any way, the procedures consecrated before his time by the practice of the masters in order to achieve that effect. He has been striving towards it for a long time, restraining at all costs the dazzling ardour which so seduced us in *L'Oiseau de feu*, *Petrouchka* and *Le Sacre du printemps*. We were able to admire unreservedly certain works in this second manner, like *Le Rossignol* and *Histoire du soldat*, in which the reform had not yet been carried to its furthest point and so left him his freedom of movement, and his richness of colour. But other works betrayed a voluntary abstention and from time to time donned borrowed forms. He continued, however, deaf to our cries of alarm, digging in stony ground, plunging into the night, and he did well, for he is now coming out of the tunnel into the light, into another land where his wishes are fulfilled.[107]

Laloy's favourite of Stravinsky's works was *Le Rossignol*, because of its Chinese elements:

> A masterpiece, as has been declared here right from the first. A pure masterpiece. Superhuman music, not, as with a certain fanatic of pride [i.e. Wagner], through renunciation, negation and defiance, but through the exaltation of gentleness, calm and love. Supernatural music, but without anything sham; a magic

> mirror in which matter becomes transparent, space luminous, and in which every perceptible appearance, while not vanishing, lets itself be penetrated right to the point where it joins the invisible, the ineffable, the non-existent.
>
> The revelation of *Le Rossignol* takes possession of our soul and renews it; only the revelations of *Parsifal*, *Boris Godunov*, *Pelléas et Mélisande* and *Saint Sébastien* are comparable.[108]

Although Laloy discusses the modality of *Le Rossignol* and comments on the orchestration of several works, his reviews of Stravinsky's compositions contain less technical analysis than his reviews of works by Debussy and Ravel. He writes more about aesthetics and about Stravinsky's evolution as a composer; in fact this is also the case with other critics of Laloy's generation, including Pierre Lalo, perhaps because they had not had formal training in the compositional techniques which Stravinsky was using.

Laloy devotes a considerable amount of discussion to Stravinsky's neoclassicism and the related issue of his anti-Romanticism. He complains about Stravinsky's 'intention to deprive himself' in some of his neoclassical works, while noting *Histoire du soldat*, *Renard*, *Mavra* and *Oedipus rex* among the exceptions. *Les Noces* provoked a particularly forthright response:

> Strictly reduced to melody and movement, austere as a church chant and as fervent, the work provoked an enthusiastic reception in which, despite my best efforts and to my great regret, I have never been able to join wholeheartedly. [. . .] But what repulses me [. . .], I confess to my shame, is the austere set purpose. In vain people tell me, and in vain I repeat to myself that a reaction against charm was necessary, that the fewer instruments an artist has at his disposition, the better he shows his muscular strength, that he is curious to test out his idea, as one tests a steel bar, by cutting it away to the critical point where it will break, and that it is quite right that the composer, in order to take a bigger leap, should rein himself in. These are reasons, and therefore poor reasons, if I keep them in my mind when I should simply be all eyes and ears. It is the case with *Les Noces*: I cannot forget, when I listen to it and watch it in the theatre, the precepts of the æsthetic it serves to verify, I have thoughts of hygiene, and I see the reins.[109]

Stravinsky's preference for the Apollonian over the Dionysian, his elevation of order and discipline over elements of an emotional character, and his concern with making objects, are echoed in a number of Laloy's remarks. Laloy commented that after the three big ballets and *Le Rossignol*, 'Stravinsky, through artistic scruples, solemnly renounced the attractions of Romanticism as if they were a diabolical temptation and, acting as his own executioner, imposed on himself the austerity of a Classical or neoclassical style, with much use of discipline and maceration [...]'[110] He thought that the Concerto for piano and wind orchestra imposed 'Classical discipline on the inborn passion of the author's mind,' and of *Perséphone* he wrote: 'This music is all in one block, and everything is set firm; there are no external details [...] No oscillation [of the melody] betrays a stirring of the heart: that would be Romanticism.'

Laloy stressed Stravinsky's position as the predominant French composer between the two World Wars, and in 1934, the year in which Stravinsky became a French citizen, he declared, 'Monsieur Stravinsky today belongs to France, which has made his reputation and where he lives, as much as in his country of origin.'[111] He also expressed admiration for Stravinsky's abilities as a conductor, writing in 1938:

> [F]amous throughout the world, he travelled a great deal, especially in America where several concert tours made a true conductor of him. Today we again find the impetuous ardour which was sometimes wasted in ineffectual gestures when he first stood before an orchestra, but it is enriched and rendered more supple by experience; it has taken on a precision and freedom which puts every note in its place, measures the volume of sound exactly, and imposes a sustained rhythm on the ensemble.[112]

Besides Ravel and Stravinsky, Laloy's circle after World War I included Henri Bergson, Colette, Jean Cocteau, André Gide, Jacques and Raïssa Maritain, Serge Lifar, Auric, Falla, Poulenc and Roussel. Indeed, far from being an exponent only of Debussy, Laloy championed the works of the younger generation of composers, particularly Poulenc and Auric. Laloy's friendship with these two composers dates from late 1923 and 1924 when he went to Monte Carlo for performances by the Ballets Russes, after which he reviewed Poulenc's *Les Biches* and Auric's *Les Fâcheux*.[113] The second of Poulenc's *Deux novelettes* (1927-1928) is dedicated to Laloy, but it was to Auric that Laloy was particularly close. 'The more we talk, the more we find to say', Laloy wrote in *La Musique retrouvée*, declaring that, of post-war composers, 'my favourite is Auric, because in him mind and talent are equal.' The libretto of Auric's opéra-comique *Sous le masque* (1927) is by Laloy, as is the scenario of his ballet *Les Enchantements d'Alcine* (1928), and Auric dedicated his *Petite suite* for piano to Laloy's wife Chouchik. Auric's loyalty continued well beyond the critic's death: he became President of the Société des Amis de Louis Laloy, and in 1974 contributed a preface to the reprinted edition of *La Musique retrouvée*, in which he wrote of 'the happy and unforgettable chance to know Louis Laloy (and, I believe, to know him well).'

Laloy was a staunch supporter of *Les Six* as a whole, and summarized his impressions of the group as follows:

> Of all its blooms, I prefer Auric's *Les Fâcheux*, and Darius Milhaud's second symphony, although at the same time I am not insensitive to the freshness of Poulenc, the seriousness of Honegger, the vivacity of Durey, the elegance of Germaine Tailleferre.[114]

Recognising that the influence of Debussy on *Les Six* was 'deadly' (*funeste*), he took the view that the young composers were lucky to have met Satie, who provided what Auric called a lesson in simplicity.[115] Laloy's relationship with Satie himself, however, was troubled: in fact the two men loathed each other. Satie, who was generally quick to take offence, felt a strong antipathy towards many music critics, including Jean Marnold and Henri Gauthier-Villars (Willy), but his loathing reached a peak where Laloy was concerned, and his writings are scattered with ironic and derogatory comments about him. Satie also held a grudge against Laloy for introducing Poulenc and Auric to opium, and the friendship of those two composers with Laloy seriously damaged their relationship with Satie. Laloy expressed his own view strongly in 1930: 'Erik Satie, who was [the mentor of *Les Six*], detested me, and made no secret of it. His character was odious to me, and I told him so to his face.'[116] As for Satie's music, Laloy liked the *Gymnopédies* and some of the *Préludes flasques*, but his favourite work was *Jack-in-the-box* (1899, staged as a ballet in 1926) because in that work 'He is no longer frowning, or pulling faces at himself. He yields himself up, without mental reservation, to the ingenuousness of his heart which a morose destiny almost always forced him to hide as if he were ashamed of it.'[117] In *La Musique retrouvée*, Laloy expounded the unusual idea that Satie was gifted with the same genius as Debussy, but that his different character and personality meant that it produced very different results: see pp. 104–105.

The crowning point of Laloy's involvement with the younger generation of composers was his collaboration with Albert Roussel on an opera-ballet, *Padmâvatî*. (See Plate 12.) First performed in 1923 at the Opéra, where Laloy continued to work as Secretary-General, the work drew on his and Roussel's mutual interest in the Orient and enjoyed considerable and continued success. Laloy also worked with Georges Migot to produce a 'symphonie lyrique et chorégraphique' entitled *Hagoromo* (1920–1921). Though Laloy was by this time in late middle age, his attitude to music and the other arts remained progressive and he was active in fostering the careers of the younger generation of composers. He brought to this later period the same perceptiveness and the same penetration of intellect that he had exercised over the music of Debussy. In evaluating his place in the French musical scene in the 1920s it would be hard to go beyond a tribute written by Jacques Maritain: 'Louis Laloy is certainly the most erudite and the most judicious of music critics [. . .] he has a remarkably young, open and penetrating mind.'

Notes

1 For further evaluations of Laloy's character and work by his contemporaries, see 'Hommage à Louis Laloy (1874–1944)', *L'Information musicale*, vol. 4, no. 151 (31 March 1944), pp. 245–247.

2 Some counterpoint exercises and compositions (mostly simple songs and piano pieces) by Laloy survive from this period. Together with folk-song settings and other pieces written in the 1940s, they are contained in the Laloy family archive. Laloy described d'Indy's course at the Schola Cantorum in *La Musique retrouvée*, pp. 68–92 and also in 'Promenades et visites musicales. - III. Une nouvelle école de musique: Le cours de M. Vincent d'Indy', *La Revue musicale* (November 1901), pp. 393–398.

3 This periodical was founded in 1901 under the title *La Revue d'histoire et de critique musicales*, and from no. 10 (1902) was known as *La Revue musicale*. It continued until 1912, and is not to be confused with the periodical of the same title founded by Henri Prunières in 1920, which continues today.

4 This periodical went through numerous changes of name before it ceased publication in 1914. The main versions of its title were: in 1905 *Le Mercure musical*; in 1907 *Le Mercure musical et bulletin français de la S.I.M.* [*Société Internationale de Musique*]; from 1908–1909 *Bulletin français de la S.I.M.*; in 1910–1911 *S.I.M. Revue musicale mensuelle*; in 1912–1913 *Revue musicale S.I.M.*, and in 1914 *La Revue musicale, S.I.M. et Courrier musical.*

Full details are given in Sadie (1980), vol. 14, p. 464 and Thoumin (1957), p. 48.

[5] Two of these, *L'Ere nouvelle* and *Le Gaulois*, have not been investigated for the present study.

[6] Laloy's journalistic output also includes articles on politics and military matters. The newspaper *Excelsior* published a large number of these in the years immediately before and after World War I, many under the pseudonym 'Jean Villars'.

[7] See L. Laloy, 'L'Opéra', in Rohozinski (1925), vol. 1, ch. 1, p. 97. Laloy discusses Rouché's innovations in general terms in *La Musique retrouvée*, p. 200ff.

[8] The place of publication is Paris unless otherwise stated.

[9] Laloy is perhaps the only music critic ever to have called for Latin and Greek to be taught at the Paris Conservatoire: see 'Les Etudes classiques au Conservatoire', *Le Courrier musical*, vol. 24, no. 3 (July 1922), p. 219.

[10] Laloy's translations and writings about China include *Légendes des immortels; d'après les auteurs chinois* (Paris, 1922); *Contes magiques, d'après l'ancien texte chinois de P'ou Soung-lin* (Paris, c.1925); *Poésies chinoises* (Paris, 1944); 'La Musique et les philosophes chinois', *La Revue musicale*, vol. 6, no. 4 (1 February 1925), pp. 132–139; 'Opium, fumée d'opium et morphine', *La Grande revue* (25 June and 10 July 1911), pp. 786–800, 116–128; 'La Convention d'opium', *La Grande revue* (25 July 1912), pp. 385–388, and, with H. Jou-Kia, 'Histoire de la révolution chinoise', *La Grande revue* (25 May 1912), pp. 225–243. Laloy described his experiences in China in *Miroir de la chine: présages, images, mirages* (Paris, 1933); this book has been translated into English by C. A. Phillips as *Mirror of China* (New York, 1936).

[11] *Le Mercure de France* (1 December 1908), pp. 419–434. Extracts are reproduced in *La Musique retrouvée*, pp. 179–184. The article was translated into English by Louise Liebich and published as a short monograph under the title *The future of music; coming changes outlined in regard to composer, conductor and orchestra* (London, [1910]).

[12] See, for example, *La Musique retrouvée*, pp. 28–29 and 'M. Henri Bergson et la musique', *Comœdia* (9 February 1914), p. 3. A letter from Bergson to Laloy dated 30 June 1928 is reproduced in Plate 9.

[13] Laloy expounds this idea in 'Le Chant grégorien et la musique française', *Le Mercure musical* (15 January 1907), pp. 75–80. In *La Musique retrouvée*, p. 63ff., he gives an account of chant performances he heard during visits to the Benedictine abbey at Solesmes in 1901 and 1903.

[14] See Laloy's article on 'Les Partis musicaux en France', *La Grande revue* (25 December 1907), pp. 790–799. For an overview of music criticism in France before World War I, see Goubault (1984).

[15] Rolland (1914), p. 203n.

[16] Only once, in a review of *La Mer*, does Laloy come close to voicing adverse criticism of Debussy's music: see pp. 194–195.

[17] See, for example, *Les Ecrits de Paul Dukas sur la musique* (Paris, 1948); L. de la Laurencie, 'Notes sur l'art de Claude Debussy', *Le Courrier*

musical (1 and 15 March 1904), pp. 141–149, 181–185 and *Le Goût musical en France* (Paris, 1905); Jean Marnold's articles on the *Nocturnes* in *Le Courrier musical* (1 and 15 March, 1 May, 15 December 1902), pp. 68–71, 81–84, 128–133, 293–295, and Emile Vuillermoz, 'Claude Debussy', a lecture transcript published in *Le Ménéstrel*, vol. 82, nos 24 and 25 (11 and 18 June 1920), pp. 241–243, 249–251.

18 *La Revue musicale* (November 1902), pp. 471–473. Later Laloy revised the article and included it in *La Musique retrouvée* under the title 'Sur deux accords' ('On two chords'). The latter version is translated in the present volume: see pp. 163–165.

19 The extract from *La Musique retrouvée* is translated on pp. 47–50.

20 Debussy evidently took an interest in Laloy's own ventures. For example, on 30 November 1911 he wrote to Paul-Jean Toulet, using a characteristic style of humour: 'Excuse us for tomorrow evening, dear Toulet, we have to help our friend Laloy endure "the trouble in the Ham [sic] palace"' [*Le Chagrin dans le palais de Han*, which was being performed at the Théâtre des Arts].

21 F. Lesure, 'Correspondance de Claude Debussy et de Louis Laloy (1902–1914)', *La Revue de musicologie*, vol. 48, no. 125 (1962), pp. 3–40. Some of the letters also appear in *La Musique retrouvée*.

22 *La Musique retrouvée*, p. 143

23 Mon cher ami,

> Je veux avant tout vous dire que vous n'avez jamais cessé de l'être! Et voilà que cette amitié me devient encore plus chère par le geste simple ... mais si rare – que vous venez de faire en m'écrivant comme vous venez de le faire avec une sympathie clairvoyante qui s'interdit de piétiner dans votre vie sans précaution. Puis, j'ai vu de telles désertions se faisant autour de moi ... ! à être écœuré à jamais de tout ce qui porte le nom d'homme. Pourtant (la télépathie n'est certainement pas un jeu d'enfants) j'avais depuis longtemps le désir de vous écrire, me disant que vous ne pouviez pas être comme les autres, appuyant ma certitude sur le souvenir d'anciennes conversations où nous aimions échanger un peu plus que des mots!

Interestingly, in conversation with Edward Lockspeiser in 1935, Laloy reported Debussy's words to him about marrying Emma, who was wealthy: 'You know what that makes me look like.' ('Vous savez de quoi ça me donne l'air.')

24 *La Musique retrouvée*, pp. 229–230

25 *Claude Debussy* (rev. ed. 1944), p. 90

26 The address was 17 bis, rue des Capucins.

27 Letter of 28 August 1903. In another letter, dated 15 March 1911, Debussy begged Toulet to 'pay a little more attention to the barbaric and whimsical way you treat your wretched body.' Tosi (1929), pp. 21 and 62

28 Madame G. de Tinan (Dolly Bardac), foreword to Charette (1990), p. xiv. Madame de Tinan, who lived in the Debussy household after 1904, also lists Laloy first among Debussy's most loyal friends, ahead of Paul-Jean Toulet and André Caplet. Part of the reason for this description may be that,

according to a story known within the Laloy family, Laloy acted as a go-between in an amorous relationship between Debussy and his stepdaughter. It seems Laloy kept their letters at home, hidden in a desk with a secret drawer. (The whereabouts of these letters is no longer known.)

29 Lesure (1994), p. 251

30 Joly-Segalen and Schaeffner (1961), p. 74. The remark is in Segalen's notes of a conversation on 8 October 1907, in which Debussy also commented on two other music critics: 'Lalo: just the gift of the gab. Feels nothing. Marnold: woolly writing.'

31 'Je vous quitte pour aller à Bellevue voir Laloy, un des hommes avec lesquels - vous n'étant pas là - on peut échanger autre chose que des potins ou des rosseries!'

32 See p. 49.

33 In *La Musique retrouvée*, p. 198, Laloy confirmed Debussy's interest: 'I had long loved [circus and music-hall burlesque. In 1904] I spoke admiringly with Debussy, who commended me, of Bostock the lion-tamer and his American orchestra, led by a cornet virtuoso, which was a precursor of jazz.' Bostock is mentioned in a letter from Debussy to Laloy on 21 April 1904.

34 For discussion of the other Orientalists Debussy knew, see Howat (1994), pp. 45–46.

35 *La Musique retrouvée*, p. 177. Also see p. 208.

36 Lesure and Nichols (1987), pp. 167–168

37 'où le Néant dialoguait avec le vague Rien-du-Tout!'

38 *La Musique retrouvée*, p. 194

39 Lesure and Nichols (1987), p. 209. Words in square brackets have been added by the present writer.

40 In *La Musique retrouvée*, p. 197, Laloy says that *Masques et bergamasques* was taken up again in about 1911, though this time he did not become involved, and that the result of the negotiations was the ballet *Jeux* in 1913. We can only assume that, as at some other times, Laloy is writing from memory, and in this case is mistaken.

41 *La Musique retrouvée*, p. 210

42 Charles Morice's title was *Crimen amoris*. See Lesure (1986), pp. 17–23.

43 'Moriceoblat' is an characteristic play on words, perhaps with *blatte*, a cockroach or slater, or more probably with *oblat*, an oblate or lay brother. Charles Morice (1861–1919), who was an idealist and mystic, published a book in 1913 explaining his reasons for remaining in the Roman Catholic faith.

44 'Il suffisait, ainsi que vous le démontrez, d'avoir du goût et de la sensibilité - bannir surtout les tours de force avec lesquels Moriceoblat semble arracher les vers de ce pauvre Verlaine, comme de mauvaises dents! . . . Il y a là les meilleurs prétextes à faire de la vraie musique, et je suis bien content. (Vous n'auriez pas un vieil habit ayant appartenu à J. P. Rameau?!)'

45 See pp. 118–119.

46 *La Musique retrouvée*, p. 212

[47] Lesure and Nichols (1987), p. 334

[48] Two books on Debussy, written in English, had appeared the previous year: W. H. Daly, *Debussy* (Edinburgh, 1908) and Louise Liebich, *Claude-Achille Debussy* (London, 1908, repr. 1925).

[49] 'Je félicite la compagnie du plaisir qu'elle va me donner de vous lire. Vous êtes le seul qui sachiez ce qu'est Claude Debussy – sans grosse caisse, ni broderies – Et nous savons ce que nous pouvons en tirer l'un et l'autre – surtout moi –'

[50] See Plate 3.

> Il y a déjà longtemps vous avez été à peu près le seul à comprendre *Pelléas*; vous savez toute la joie que j'en ressentis, vous savez aussi que de ce jour commençait une amitié que ni les choses, ni les hommes n'ont pu troubler.
>
> Aujourd'hui je reçois l'histoire minutieuse et charmante qu'il vous a plu d'écrire sur Claude Debussy. Si je ne suis pas sûr d'être absolument tout ce que vous dites, l'émotion d'être compris d'aussi près («sans affectation d'ailleurs», comme dit l'autre) est absolue.
>
> Cela a quelque chose d'aigu comme une vive lumière projetée dans l'ombre de la pensée; c'est du cambriolage où le cambriolé félicite le cambrioleur.

This appreciative letter is in contrast with a letter Debussy later wrote to René Lenormand, the author of an *Etude sur l'harmonie moderne* (Paris, 1913). Lenormand's book takes the approach of itemizing elements of harmonic vocabulary. It quotes extensively from Debussy's compositions, and on 25 July 1912 Debussy took Lenormand to task: 'You are sometimes ruthless in divorcing your quotations from their context.' The letter's conclusion leaves little doubt about Debussy's opinion: 'But enough! Too bad about the dead, and the wounded who will be put out of their misery. That's how it always is with wars. And may I congratulate you exceedingly on a task which demanded manifold abilities.' Lesure and Nichols (1987), p. 260

[51] *Claude Debussy* (1909), p. 17. The work is more often referred to nowadays as *Zuleima*. An *envoi de Rome* was a composition which a winner of the Prix de Rome sent back from Rome to the Académie des Beaux-Arts, the section of the Institut de France charged with administering the Prix de Rome competition.

[52] *Claude Debussy* (1909), p. 14

[53] L. Liebich (1908), p. 11

[54] *La Musique retrouvée*, p. 99

[55] Debussy (1987), pp. 272–273

[56] Vallery-Radot (1938), p. 391

[57] Also see *La Musique retrouvée*, p. 129ff.

[58] In 1905 the critic Camille Mauclair ironically identified an illness called 'Debussyitis' (*la 'Debussyte'*): 'a rather strange illness' which 'seems to have seriously harmed many young musicians in the past three years, but [. . .] has raged among music critics above all, to the point where several have gone raving mad.' 'La "Debussyte"', *Le Courrier musical* (15 September 1905), p. 501

[59] Jean Lorrain published this article first in *Le Journal* on 22 January 1904, and later as part of a book, *Pelléastres* (Paris, 1910). For reactions to *Pelléas* in the Paris press, see p. 59, and also Goubault (1984), p. 375ff.

[60] *Claude Debussy* (rev. ed. 1944), p. 109. Also see p. 120.

[61] *Claude Debussy* (1909), pp. 31–32

[62] See p. 81.

[63] See p. 66.

[64] *La Grande revue* (10 February 1913), p. 624. Laloy went further than Debussy in his criticism of Wagner: he disliked the artifice of elaborating melodic patterns and cadences from German folk music in *Götterdämmerung*, and he complained often about what he called 'the cement of his orchestration.' In a phrase almost as memorable as Debussy's about Wagner being a sunset taken for a sunrise, Laloy wrote, 'Wagner did not invent anything, he only misused everything.' ('Wagner n'a rien inventé, il n'a fait qu'abuser de tout.') Quoted by 'J. E.' (Jules Ecorcheville?) in *S.I.M. Revue musicale* (15 March 1910), p. 207n.

[65] See p. 54.

[66] Lesure and Langham Smith (1977), p. 48

[67] *Claude Debussy* (rev. ed. 1944), p. 82

[68] *Claude Debussy* (1909), pp. 78–79

[69] See pp. 70 and 196.

[70] See p. 216.

[71] See p. 215.

[72] *Claude Debussy* (1909), p. 79

[73] 'Tantôt il donne des vessies pour des lanternes, pensant qu'ils n'y verront rien, ou bien il gratte jusqu'au sang, il gratte dans le sang.' *La Musique retrouvée*, p. 171

[74] '«J'ai été, comme un autre, à Bayreuth, me disait Debussy, et j'ai pleuré mon dû à *Parsifal*. Mais à mon retour j'ai connu *Boris Godounov*, qui m'a guéri.» Pourtant Moussorgski ne pouvait plaire entièrement à un artiste aussi attentif à la pureté du style et l'équilibre des proportions. «Ce n'est jamais fait», disait-il avec un peu de dépit.' *La Musique retrouvée*, p. 132

[75] The revised edition (1944) covers Debussy's later works; however, the chapter on Debussy's musical language is substantially the same in both editions.

[76] See p. 91.

[77] *Claude Debussy* (1909), p. 81

[78] *Le Courrier musical*, vol. 225, no. 8 (15 April 1923), p. 149

[79] *Comœdia* (9 February 1914), p. 2

[80] *Claude Debussy* (rev. ed. 1944), p. 2

[81] *La Revue des deux mondes*, vol. 103, no. 18 (15 November 1933), p. 469

[82] The composer Manuel Rosenthal recalls meeting Laloy in company with Ravel and Maurice Delage. His impression was that Delage was closer to Laloy than to Ravel because Delage also knew the Far East, and used to spend evenings and nights smoking opium with Laloy. (Private communication)

83 The second of these letters is reproduced in Plate 10.

84 Ravel was one of the founding members of the Société Musicale Indépendante (S.M.I.), formed in 1910 by a group of composers aiming to establish a more progressive society than the Société Nationale. A letter from Laloy to Bartok dated 31 March 1910 seems to suggest that Laloy was also involved, but no other details have come to light.

85 'Non, je trouve ça inutile. Je ne vois pas ce que ça peut apporter. On m'en a proposé souvent, les Delage, entre autres, mais je n'en éprouve pas le besoin.' Marnat (1995), p. 132

86 *Comment écouter la musique*, p. 63

87 See p. 266.

88 'Je crois que cette sonate marque un tournant dans l'évolution de ma carrière. Le dépouillement y est poussé à l'extrême. Renoncement au charme harmonique; réaction de plus en plus marquée dans le sens de la mélodie.' Ravel (1938), p. 214 (22)

89 See p. 250.

90 *Le Mercure musical* (15 February 1906), p. 165

91 *Le Mercure musical* (15 May 1905), p. 39

92 See p. 252.

93 *La Revue des deux mondes*, vol. 108, no. 43 (1 February 1938), p. 707

94 'Je reçois le n° 2 de la *S.I.M*.... et m'étonne d'y lire qu'un homme de votre goût sacrifie délibéremment le pur et instinctif chef-d'œuvre qu'est *Chambre d'enfants* à l'américanisme voulu des *Histoires naturelles* de M. Ravel. Malgré l'indéniable habileté de celui-ci, elles ne peuvent être que de la musique «déplacée». Laissez donc cela au valet de chambre Calvocoressi!'

95 Lesure and Nichols (1987), pp. 177–178

96 See p. 264.

97 Calvocoressi (1913), p. 785

98 Myers (1960), p. 111

99 Review of *Shéhérazade*, *La Revue musicale* (1 June 1904), p. 291. See p. 246.

100 'Le Quintette de Florent Schmitt', *La Nouvelle revue française* (August 1909), p. 79

101 See p. 252.

102 See p. 60.

103 *Excelsior* (10 May 1920), p. 4

104 See p. 288.

105 *La Musique retrouvée*, p. 205

106 See p. 287.

107 See p. 306.

108 See p. 284.

109 See pp. 293–294.

110 *La Revue des deux mondes*, vol. 106, no. 31 (15 January 1936), p. 455

111 *La Revue des deux mondes*, vol. 104, no. 21 (1 June 1934), p. 696

112 *La Revue des deux mondes*, vol. 108, no. 43 (1 January 1938), p. 227

113 'A Monte-Carlo. Festivals français', *Le Courrier musical*, vol. 26, no. 3 (1 February 1924), p. 76

114 'Le "Groupe des six"', *Le Courrier musical*, vol. 32, no. 1 (1 January 1930), p. 5

115 *La Musique retrouvée*, pp. 272–273

116 'Le "Groupe des six"', *Le Courrier musical*, vol. 32, no. 1 (1 January 1930), p. 5. For Auric's impression of the relationship, see Orledge and Nichols (1995), p. 116. According to Laloy, the animosity began in 1913, when Satie took offence at an article Laloy wrote about him, in particular one word at the end: *falot*. Laloy says he intended to make pun on two meanings of the word: a person who is comical or droll, and a hand-lantern. Satie took it in a third, newer acceptation, which Laloy says he had not thought of: someone who is insignificant to the point of being comical. The article is reproduced in *La Musique retrouvée*, pp. 256–258.

117 *La Musique retrouvée*, pp. 274

On Debussy

Laloy's friendship with Debussy

Laloy first met Debussy in late 1902, after his article on the prelude to *Pelléas et Mélisande* was published in *La Revue musicale.* Writing twenty-five years later, he describes the meeting and also recounts some anecdotes from Debussy's earlier life.

Notes begin on p. 50.

La Musique retrouvée, pp. 119–124[1]

This article attracted Claude Debussy's attention and, not content with thanking me, he expressed a desire to meet me and asked me to go and see him. This was the beginning of a friendship which every year grew more intimate and secure, as he later put it better than I:

> 10 September 1909
>
> My dear friend,
>
> A long time ago already, you were pretty much the only person to understand *Pelléas*; you know how much joy that gave me, you also know that from that day a friendship began which neither things nor men have been able to disturb . . .[2]

Not without some apprehension, I climbed for the first time a rather dark staircase, at number 58 rue Cardinet, where he lived in a small flat on the fifth floor. I am shy, in the sense that I feel embarrassed before a new face like an explorer in an unknown land; I carefully test out the lie of the land with a fear of committing *faux pas* which often produces precisely that result, until the contact points are brought together and the current of sympathy can flow. What is more, when one likes a work, it is always an adventure to meet its author. In every case, there is a resemblance between the two. On this point I agree entirely with Romain Rolland. But it can happen that the resemblance is well hidden, and the thoughts an author puts into what he creates are those he does not use at all in his everyday life, which may be filled with dross. Or else, knowing what is expected of him, he wears a mask and puts on a face to suit the circumstances, reeking of lies. Then one can only make out a little of his true nature through chinks and by benefiting from a slip. Such were my fears, but I was soon reassured.[3]

His study was to the right of the dining room; the table in front of the window, a rosewood upright piano at the back. A little later the house of Pleyel, which was always generous to artists, offered him a fine mahagony instrument which he joyfully showed and played to me. The visitor's armchair was to his left and almost directly opposite his own. That is where he invited me to sit and, bowing his head slightly to evade my protests, began by congratulating me. I felt at ease straight away, firstly because of his sinuous face which reminded me of the Far East, calm out of courtesy, and above all because I sensed that he was being careful, just as I was, not to offend the stranger, and not to assert anything unless he was sure the other would understand.

He spoke in a low, clear voice, using short sentences, and in a burst, without ever searching for words, he would suddenly lay down a marvellous image.[4] He had a poet's mind. I do not know whether, as certain old friends of his have thought necessary to assert, he was completely ignorant about literature when he was at the Conservatoire. But it is certain that, better than anyone else, he had since made up for lost time. It was no accident that, from the time he returned from Rome, he was the only one among his friends to seek out the elite of writers, and consult for example Henri de Régnier, who has since told me the story, about the text of his *Proses lyriques*, when Catulle Mendès was there, quite ready to undertake the task; he also frequented Stéphane Mallarmé's coterie which was closed to the uninitiated, and to which I do not believe any other musician ever gained entry. That is where he had seen Whistler take hold of a drawing by Odilon Redon, and ask which way up it should go, and seen Verlaine take a seat by the fire, fill his pipe and demand a large absinthe. Another day he had met Pierre Louÿs, that exquisite conversationalist, and stayed talking to him until first light when the two friends waited for a café in the Bois de Boulogne to open, to sit over their cups of chocolate for another few hours.

All he had brought back from a trip to Russia were some very pleasant memories of the gypsies and their improvisations.[5] But an old musician named de Brayer had given him a score of *Boris Godunov*, before the revision by Rimsky-Korsakov, in the original edition, which was then almost unprocurable. He had been unwise enough some years earlier to lend this copy to an artist who never returned it, and could only speak to me about it from memory, with deep feeling.[6]

At the Conservatoire, he had retained good memories of Guiraud, his composition teacher, but had only stayed briefly in César Franck's organ class. When he was improvizing, the old master kept saying to him, over and over, 'Modulate! Modulate!' So much so that one day, to the horror of the class, he replied, 'Why do you want me to modulate when I'm fine in this key?' This was his sincerity of emotion protesting against a figure of musical rhetoric which is but an artifice if it is not necessitated by some inflection of the mind.

His piano teacher, Marmontel, had disgusted him slightly with Beethoven by putting words to a melody in the finale of the *Pathétique* sonata, which was the examination piece that year, in order to increase its expressiveness: 'O pauvre mère, douleur amère' ['Oh, poor mother, bitter sorrow']. It was only in the following year that he won second prize, with a Fantasy by Chopin.[7] He liked Chopin very much and it was he who made me understand the poetry in a repertoire which too many virtuosi only treat as an exercise in technical difficulties. But, in order for the beauty of the sounds to be revealed, it needs a lightness in the delineation which is not within the scope of ordinary pianists. Although he had not practised for a long time, Debussy still had a delicate touch and supple fingers which seemed to mould the sound that was overtaken by the rapidity of his soft, agile hands, and to spread it out smoothly in fluid, transparent layers.[8]

He responded deeply to the passion of Schumann and all its restless tenderness, exalted nobility and unfulfilled wishes, with the regret however that Schumann had put the ideas best suited to the orchestra into his works for piano, and that the instrumentation of his symphonies was dull and heavy. 'You'd think,' he said, 'that he orchestrated in his cellar.'

Soon, at his request, I acquired the habit of going to see him almost every week, on Saturday afternoons. It would be just the two of us. On only one occasion Jean Marnold, whom I did not yet know, took part in the conversation, but did not disturb its unanimity: we were discussing François Couperin, whom all three of us loved for the wealth of his imagination.

But it was not taste alone that linked me to Debussy. Although our existences were far removed from each other both by events, and by the feelings which arose from them, it was still easy for us to communicate not those feelings themselves, but their subsequent resonances, which were in harmony. Thus we exchanged not confidences but reflections, prolonged into silence, while each of us applied what had been said to his own case, whence came to mind another remark which brought us together once again.[9]

We also felt quite free, however, when we were in a different mood, to push serious thoughts to the back of our mind and reach a unanimous opinion on the events of the day, the silly ways of a person we knew, or our favourite tobacco. From time to time, he would come out with me to buy a cake for the evening's dessert. He was made for the opulent life and up to that point had floundered in poverty with no hope of escaping from it. It was obvious to me that he was suffering as a result, but he put on a brave face, and he even managed to say that he was perfectly happy. I strongly supported his views at that time and I think he was grateful to me.

Notes

1 This is Chapter XVII of *La Musique retrouvée*, 'L'Amitié de Claude Debussy' ('Claude Debussy's friendship').

2 The original French is quoted on p. 40 n. 50.

3 Laloy later recalled:

> Few friends crossed the threshold, and even fewer pupils. The message of his music, however, had won him the good feeling of some fervent spirits far and wide, but they kept their distance, instructed by the example of the music itself to respect the soul of others. He was not in the mood to gather a school around him and could give no other lessons than in taste, which were accessible to rare adepts.
>
> *Claude Debussy* (rev. ed. 1944), p. 86

This recollection was noted down many years after the event, but it is consistent with Debussy's own assertion that 'There is no Debussy school. I have no disciples. I am myself.'

4 Elsewhere Laloy writes of '... his bulging, sulky child's forehead, the lively expression in his eyes, which he would suddenly turn away, his broken voice [...]' *La Musique retrouvée*, p. 101. Some other contemporaries also described Debussy's way of speaking, including Alfredo Casella who wrote: 'Debussy's voice was unprepossessing, being hoarse (and this was aggravated by the abuse of tobacco), and he spoke in an abnormal, nervous, jumpy way.' Casella (1933), p. 1. Pasteur Vallery-Radot's analysis is more detailed:

> He spoke in a soft voice, without affectation, slowly, searching for the right word to make an image. From time to time he would stop in the middle of a sentence as a horse hesitates before an obstacle: he could not find the term which would be the raiment of his thought. He expressed himself as a visual person who knew how to look and he could always bring out the dominant feature. His sentences were often steeped in imprecision, in order to render the uncertainty of an idea or an impression, with a word bursting forth

suddenly, vibrantly. One was under the spell of his sensitivity, and at the same time one feared it, for he would become irritated at an unexpected noise, a light that was too garish, an ill-placed word.

Vallery-Radot (1938), pp. 398–399

5 In his biography of Debussy, Laloy writes about this episode, and the passage reads as if he were reporting a conversation between them. He says that while in Russia in the employ of Madame von Meck, Debussy 'became well acquainted [. . .] with the gypsies, who in the taverns in and around Moscow first gave him the example of music without rules. But he did not even think of writing down one of their melodies.' *Claude Debussy* (1909), p. 15

6 Compare *Claude Debussy* (1909), p. 22. According to Lesure (1994), *passim*, the story is that Jules de Brayer, the administrator of the Concerts Lamoureux, had discovered a vocal score of *Boris Godunov* at the home of Saint-Saëns, and had become a propagandist for the work. Lesure says that in 1889 Robert Godet lent Debussy the score with de Brayer's permission, and later returned it to him.

7 Laloy's memory seems to be in error here. While studying with Marmontel, Debussy won two second prizes for performing Chopin, with (part of?) the F minor concerto in 1874, and the first Ballade in 1875.

8 'Bien que ne travaillant plus depuis longtemps, Debussy avait gardé une délicatesse de toucher et une souplesse des doigts qui semblaient modeler le son gagné de vitesse par ses mains mollement agiles, et l'étendre sans choc en nappes fluides et transparentes.'

9 'Mais ce n'est pas le goût seul qui me liait à Debussy. Bien que nos deux existences fussent très éloignées l'une de l'autre et par les faits, et par les sentiments qui en étaient la conséquence, nous pouvions cependant aisément nous communiquer non ces sentiments eux-mêmes, mais leurs résonances ultérieures, qui étaient en harmonie. Ainsi nous échangions non pas des confidences, mais des réflexions, prolongées en silence, pendant que chacun en faisait l'application à son cas particulier, d'où lui venait à l'esprit une autre remarque où nous nous rencontrions encore.'

Early influences on Debussy

Claude Debussy (1909), pp. 48–52

Claude Debussy did not follow the teachings of Franck, and he was too sensitive to the bad taste of naive outpourings ever to be touched by them. He was won over by the grandeur of Wagner, but not for long: only *La Damoiselle élue* attests to some degree of admiration; there is none in *Printemps*, and Wagner is completely rejected in the compositions which follow. Moreover, only with *Parsifal*, that work of peace and renunciation, can a degree of kinship be found for him: it is the general tempo, a little slow and solemn; it is the character of the orchestra which, despite its delicacy, is eloquent here. But the melody has a clarity of outline which Wagner never attained, and almost always stands out in full light, above the murmuring harmonies; the vocal line has none of those great leaps and imperative accents proper to the German language and unwisely copied by so many of our composers; even when the vocal line takes up themes first stated by instruments, the simplicity of the themes allows it to remain natural; development is always stopped just at the point where it would become artificial; but Wagner, on principle, always goes beyond this point. Most importantly, he did not understand this heavenly candour: he had no part in the essential idea of the work, and only provided it with certain stylistic figures. This explains why, in due course, those slight imprints were obliterated without a trace.

The Russian composers certainly helped Debussy to detach himself from Wagner. After the mists surrounding the Grail and Valhalla, he loved their mosaic-like orchestra, and it was by inclination that he gave a piano-duet performance of Rimsky-Korsakov's *Capriccio espagnol* with René Chansarel on 20 January 1894, at a concert given by the Société Nationale. But, for his own part, these crude contrasts and savage rhythms were not what he was looking for. He wanted a type of painting in which all the tones connected with each other across space, even though they never blended; and the reason he could isolate the dreamlike flute line at the beginning of the *Prélude à l'Après-midi d'un faune* was to create an immediate effect around it of the burning light and the 'bushy sleeps' in the air where the nymphs' rosiness dissolves. As for the *Nocturnes*, the undulation of 'Nuages', which reminds some people of an accompaniment pattern in a Mussorgsky song, and the end of 'Fêtes' where a wreath of triplets is inflected with chromatic steps as in Balakirev's *Tamara*, are no more than coincidences: for nothing is further from Russian art and its primitive solidity than these tableaux where all that subsists of things is their envelope of changing light.[1]

The same holds for certain resemblances between *Pelléas et Mélisande* and *Boris Godunov*: for example, in one a solemn line rising and falling within the interval of a fourth depicts monastic calm, and in the other the turmoil of two minds which are already culpable; we must conclude what we already knew: that two composers are equally entitled to take the same notes in opposite acceptations. We might also think that Mussorgsky encouraged Debussy to find a truer vocal line. But each goes about it in his own way: the former knows no middle ground between the characteristic aria and exact transcription of spoken language. This middle ground is precisely what the latter is seeking; he wants a melody which is faithful to the accents of speech, but still musical in itself. Finally, *Boris Godunov* consists of separate episodes, with no connections established between them by the music, whereas a coherent thread is woven around *Pelléas*, clearly expressing the fatal progression of the emotions.

Much more than the Russian composers,[2] it was the folk musicians, especially the gypsies from around Moscow, who left Debussy a lasting memento. These gypsies are not counterfeit, like our own, and they do not brandish seductive bows: they sing, for the pleasure of hearing themselves. Their rhythms are lively, their melodies warm and sweet; they improvise them, as they do their accompaniments, by instinct alone: music is their life. To the young Frenchman who listened to them ecstatically, they were a lesson in imagination.[3] They advised him boldly to follow all the impulses of his mind; they guaranteed that, even when his impulses went against the rules, the results would be harmonious. They delivered him from the discipline that weighed so heavily on his spirit, they showed him a natural charm, a bravura which came from the heart, and introduced him to the meaning of those supple capriccios which the Russians borrowed from them also, but only for ornamentation and the pleasure of Orientalism. Had it not been for them, it is possible that the *Prélude à l'Après-midi d'un faune* would not have had the same tenderness of expression. And the String quartet, where the music, obedient to every emotion, bubbles forth like a gentle spring, could be dedicated to them.

It is obvious in any case that the procedures are quite different, since it is a matter of establishing and putting in place effects which improvisers discover find by happy inspiration. Thus, just as Wagner and Mussorgsky resemble Debussy through certain turns of style, not in their quality of mind, the gypsies certainly gave him the model and perhaps even the idea of a certain character, not the means to reproduce it. The most profitable lessons came to him not from musicians, but from poets and painters.

Notes

[1] '[. . .] car rien n'est plus éloigné de l'art russe, et de sa solidité primitive, que ces tableaux où il ne subsiste, des choses, que leur enveloppe de changeantes clartés.'

[2] In the revised edition, this sentence reads: 'No less than the Russian composers [. . .]'

[3] Laloy himself had heard Russian folk music performed in Paris while he was a child.

Genesis and first performances of *Pelléas et Mélisande*

Laloy discusses *Pelléas et Mélisande* at length not only in his biography of Debussy, but also in *La Musique retrouvée* and in a great many articles. The extracts which follow deal with the origins of the work, its reception at the early performances, and the beginnings of Debussyism (*le Debussysme*).

Notes for this section begin on p. 60.

Claude Debussy (1909), pp. 28–29

It was during the summer of 1892 that, walking down the boulevard des Italiens towards the end of the day, Debussy bought, at the Flammarion bookshop, a play by Maeterlinck which had just appeared: *Pelléas et Mélisande*. He began reading it that same evening, and was immediately taken with it. Only *La Damoiselle élue* had touched him to the same extent. The following day, he was determined to write music for the play; Pierre Louÿs, the first person in whom he confided about the project, in turn read the volume, and did not disguise his astonishment. But Debussy held fast, and the two friends went to Gand together to see Maeterlinck, who gave the composer full permission to treat the text in the way he understood it, to take out what he considered superfluous and, in due course, to have the work performed in whatever conditions he wished.

For ten years, Debussy worked on *Pelléas et Mélisande*. Rather he mused on it for those ten years, interrupting his reveries to write something down when he felt that the moment had come to make his thoughts concrete. The process was a slow condensing of dreams, an inveigling of the mystery, a revealing of the hidden feelings, a long and marvellous exploration of the darkness of consciousness.[1] In turn, the different episodes of the play were illuminated by music, and found their meaning, which words, like a fabric that is too loose, had not been able to retain. The duet in Act IV was written first; the rest came, as the hours went by. The ever-growing score was, for those ten years, his steady consort, and its presence alone was enough to encourage and console him. Through it Debussy was restored to himself, defended against the disturbances of life, the snare of others' advice and the danger of ill-matched collaborations.

Claude Debussy (1909), pp. 34–35

It was on 30 April 1902, at the Opéra-Comique, that *Pelléas et Mélisande* was first performed. If it had only been up to Monsieur Maeterlinck, the work would never have appeared. If one took the orchestral musicians' word for it, a failure of scandalous proportions was being prepared.[2] If the composer's contemporary colleagues were asked, they would smile wittily and their faces would glow with hope: no, certainly, a rival like this was not fearsome. People felt sorry for Monsieur Albert Carré, the director of the theatre, who was obstinately resolved; for Monsieur André Messager, the conductor, who carried out the work of the rehearsals with furious care; for Monsieur Jusseaume, who had painted scenery which was worthy of lengthy destinies; for Mademoiselle Garden, a very talented debutante, and for Messieurs Jean Périer, Dufranne and Vieuille, consummate artists, who had become enamoured of their roles. Disaster was so surely anticipated that the quasi-official programme, sold inside the theatre, enticed the public with an ironic analysis, adorned, in parentheses, with exclamation marks and reticent *hmms*; from this arose a lawsuit, which the originator of the publication was to lose.[3] The select audience at the dress rehearsal and the opening night, which was an invited one, as we know, decided in favour of the programme: they were astonished, they protested, they laughed, they made witty remarks; and people left with the pleasant certainty of having made merry at a show many would miss out on, as they did not think it would last beyond the fourth evening.[4] But they were reckoning without the Debussyists; they came, as soon as they were allowed in, that is from the third performance, and they applauded. They came back; and, as complimentary tickets are never given to musical devotees, the first consequence of their zeal was a propitious increase in the takings. 'All Paris of opening nights' was no longer there, having been called to other free rejoicings. Success was predicted and confirmed; soon there was an enthusiastic reception, the like of which had not been seen since Wagner. Six, eight, ten curtain calls after each of the acts were not enough to calm the frenzy that broke out as each person gave vent to his over-abundance of emotion. It is still the same today; but the faithful have grown more numerous. Certainly the beauty of other music is not foreign to them; but this music has reached to the very sources of their lives, which will be impregnated with it for ever. All they ask of those who do not feel the same way is to leave them free, and to go their own way.

'The miracle'[5]
***La Musique retrouvée*, pp. 103–114**

It really was a miracle. I did not know, did not believe until then that it was possible to write a piece of music without a single superfluous note, in which everything went to the heart. In all the works I had heard, there were dead spots, places where the music ceased to be new and went back over what had been said, amplified it, presented it in a different way unnecessarily, since everyone had already understood, or engaged in a series of conclusive experiments clearly proving a key or modulation, but unconnected to the subject, and with confidence abruptly betrayed in the urgency of reminding the listener that two and two make four, or in other words that G is the dominant of C. Rameau, Beethoven, Berlioz, Schumann, Franck, Grieg, Bizet - none, in the works I liked best, escaped these moments of dryness where the mind seems to be asleep, leaving musical craft to work in its place. The *Nocturnes* themselves had their repetitions, which certainly did not make for *longueur*, as the idea was so original and charming that one gladly listened twice, but already with slightly fading attention. Only Gregorian chant could, without ever running out of breath, sustain melodies whose course was impossible to guess, which were inflected at every moment by another call to prayer. But it was faith that gave it strength and it recognised no other source of inspiration.

Now a human music with the feelings of life, and disguised as nature, was equally unfettered. It yielded to the mind, but without becoming inert; without becoming rigid, it followed the mind's twists and turns, which never put it in danger of jolting or breaking; it opened out before us, incorporeal as an enchanted landscape where we walked about, attracted by the magnetism of the sound, without trampling the ground, suspended between heaven and earth. We could hear it almost without needing to listen: right from the very first notes, our attention was captivated and carried the will with it. Phrases were born like flowers and sounds were grouped by their mutual attraction with no need of any external pressure to keep them there.

I well know, and I knew it then, that the work was a production of the mind and that a detailed reading revealed premeditation. Certain melodic shapes were repeated, at long intervals, but through a very natural association of ideas and without the forced allusion of Wagner or one of his emulators. That is why these landmarks - traces of the work process which the artist omitted to rub out - passed unnoticed. The delightful chords could, if one were bent on it, have been explained by the technical words appoggiatura, suspension, inflection, auxiliary note or escape note. But the choice and use of these procedures is obedient only to feeling, which is the only master of a music that was able to conform to the rules of art without imposing the least restraint on itself.

I went to hear *Pelléas* for the first time with my friend Gallardo, who like me was under its spell, but more anxious than I to find out the cause, and I remember saying to him, 'They are not dissonances, but pluperfect chords,' meaning consonances in which a different consonance was put in to replace each note.[6] All my friends came in turn to keep me company, either in the orchestra seats where our meditation was not disturbed by the disdainful silence, or in the Gods which was chock-full of young people and where, almost always in the first row, and the first to applaud, Charles Bordes could be seen, youthful and agitated, his head even more like a round globe from the inner pressure of his enthusiasm. A young priest sat close by, his intelligent eyes and his thick dark hair motionless, looking steadily at the stage [*la scène*] which he might perhaps have called the communion [*la cène*], for his mind which had ripened in the sun of Provence delighted in witticisms and plays on words. One evening, for lack of time beforehand, he read his breviary in the interval, while walking in the corridor, as much at ease as if he had been in a cloister, and as little disturbed by the crowd, which always has respect for sincere emotion. This was the Abbé Léonce Petit, who two years later became one of my truest friends.

Those who loved *Pelléas* returned tirelessly. We recognised each other, from one performance to the next, at the box office, and without preamble we exchanged remarks about the one subject which was in all our minds. Not all those who came were young artists or students from the Latin Quarter. The audience which bought the last seats at the Opéra-Comique at that time included music-lovers of all ranks. Several who were won over by *Pelléas* had never heard of Debussy, nor even of Maeterlinck. I have since remained in contact with one of them who is a great connoisseur of music, in the rare moments of leisure which his modest position in a bank allows him.[7]

Around *Pelléas*, a party was becoming organized. It was necessary, to defend a work which had been almost unanimously condemned by music critics. Those who know how this item is sacrificed in most daily papers can ignore it. But the public does not know, and as a rule puts the same faith in everything that is printed in the paper it reads each day, from the first line to the last. The reason why the public buys newspapers is really to acquire opinions on subjects which are outside its competence or its scope of investigation; it prefers to adopt them, even if they are wrong, rather than waste its money.

And besides, those all-purpose quill-pushers who report by turns, with equal ignorance, on a performance, an accident or a Cabinet meeting, because the editor sends them, were not the only ones who ridiculed *Pelléas*. Well-known critics, whose knowledge and talent no one could challenge, were among the most severe. Monsieur Camille Bellaigue, in *La Revue des deux mondes* on 15 May 1902, had just published an article in which he recognised only noise in the music, 'and even a nasty little sort of noise.' He added indulgently, 'In the sphere which might be called verbal, Monsieur Debussy's composition might not be altogether indifferent.' But this extenuating circumstance could not prevail against the harshness of his conclusion: 'Such an art is pernicious and evil.'[8, 9]

The morality we drew from *Pelléas* was not at all lax, as the most sincere of our enemies believed. Far from delivering us up to our instincts, this morality ordered us to watch over them constantly, for it was a matter of taking the heart's impulses in their nascent state, which is also the state of grace, and keeping them there while preserving them from being turned aside by a preconceived idea or from going against the will of others. The purity of the lines produced the harmony; but this original purity had to be constantly reconquered and defended. Wagner's music offered redemption as a reward for hard exertion and as the dénouement of a drama which was dark with crimes; that of *Pelléas* effected it through an immediate and everlasting spell. 'I see nothing there,' said Arkël, 'but a great innocence.'

But man's condition is so lamentable that often innocence causes terrible misfortunes and is itself the victim of them. Then we must pity it, not condemn it. 'If I were God, I would have pity on the hearts of men.' Each note of *Pelléas* teaches forgiveness. Not the forgiveness of the puritan, who stands and bestows it by the laying on of hands thanking the Providence which has freed him from sin. Even less the prostrate forgiveness of the Russians, a legacy of Romanticism, which through an unhealthy or paradoxical taste for suffering and humiliation holds the criminal in reverence and worships the prostitute. The fraternal forgiveness offered by one weakness to an equal weakness, an act of contrition and of resignation to the inexplicable will which controls life and death.

Stravinsky later translated this impression in one of the strange, striking formulae which he spits out so cuttingly: 'What I like above all is this humble music.'[10] The great Russian composer belongs, as we know, to a schismatic church which differs from our own only in its rite, not its dogma; and that is why, even if he does not make the sign of the Cross as we do, he was able, like the faithful in France, when penetrating the sanctuary of *Pelléas*, to kneel and pray.

I tried to explain the religious atmosphere which, from the first chords of the prelude, invites us to silence and meditation, in [...] the first of [the articles] I wrote on *Pelléas et Mélisande*: it appeared in *La Revue musicale* in November 1902. And it was to bring about one of the most important events of my life.[11]

Notes

1 'Pendant dix ans, Debussy travailla à *Pelléas et Mélisande*. Plutôt il y songea, ces dix années, interrompant ses méditations pour écrire, lorsqu'il sentait le moment venu de fixer sa pensée. Ce fut une lente condensation de rêves, une captation du mystère, une révélation des sentiments cachés, une longue et merveilleuse exploration aux ténèbres de la conscience.'

2 In *La Musique retrouvée*, Laloy tells how when out walking with Jules Combarieu, he met one of the orchestral players involved in rehearsals for *Pelléas*, who said, 'The rehearsals [...] are a scandal. The orchestra refuses to play.' When the remark was reported to Debussy, he was not surprised, and commented on the 'hateful noise'. (pp. 95–96) Laloy's explanation is that the orchestral players were baffled by the 'extreme division of the parts' and that the violinists were disgruntled 'because for a whole scene, that in the underground vault, their services were dispensed with.' (pp. 99–100)

3 The quasi-official program summarized the action of the play, scene by scene. For example:

> Scene 1. Golaud, an elderly widower, father of little Yniold, lost in the forest, encounters a little girl who is no less lost. He carries her off and marries her.
>
> Scene 3. Pelléas, Golaud's brother, is walking with his little sister-in-law in the shady gardens. Hey, hey!

The full text is reproduced in R. Peter (1931), pp. 205–207. Laloy gives a brief description in *La Musique retrouvée*, p. 101.

4 In *La Musique retrouvée* Laloy comments that the *boulevard* – fashionable opinion in the street – took the failure of *Pelléas* for granted. He

also recounts a later conversation with Debussy: 'One day when I was talking to Debussy about *répétitions générales* [public dress rehearsals] and the heavy sense of boredom which usually weighs on these feasts of the Parisian spirit, he replied, "At the *générale* of *Pelléas*, I guarantee you people weren't bored."' Laloy explains, 'It seems it was difficult to hear the singers above the murmuring and laughter.' (p. 100) A fuller account of the behaviour of the audience at the *générale* and the first performance is given in *Claude Debussy* (1909), pp. 34–35.

5 This is Chapter XV of *La Musique retrouvée*, entitled 'Le Miracle'. Laloy was not in Paris for either the *générale* on 28 April 1902 or the first performance on 30 April: he was on a boat to Greece, and was involved in a shipwreck.

6 'Ce ne sont pas des dissonances, mais des accords plus que parfaits.' Laloy is referring to the pluperfect tense in French grammar, the *plus-que-parfait*, which expresses the past at one remove: 'I had done', 'We had been', etc.

7 For an account of the passionate excesses of the Debussyists, see Vallery-Radot (1938).

8 C. Bellaigue, review of *Pelléas et Mélisande*, *La Revue des deux mondes* (15 May 1902), pp. 450–455. Bellaigue's review is typical of the conservative reaction to *Pelléas et Mélisande*, and he pulls no punches: 'Of the various elements which comprise all music, there are two which [. . .] the composer of *Pelléas et Mélisande* has deliberately suppressed: one is rhythm and the other melody.' For discussion of the critical reaction to *Pelléas et Mélisande*, see Goubault (1984), pp. 375–381.

9 Six paragraphs have been omitted. They cover Laloy's admiration for Bellaigue's musical abilities and his opinion of another hostile critic, Jean Lorrain, author of the condemnatory *Pelléastres*.

10 'Stravinski traduisait plus tard cette impression par une des formules étranges et frappantes qu'il fait jaillir en traits acérés: «Ce que j'aime surtout, c'est cette musique humble».'

11 The article was the 'Exercice d'analyse' on the first four bars of the prelude which Laloy later included in *La Musique retrouvée*: see pp. 163–165. For his account of the meeting with Debussy which followed the publication of the article, see pp. 47–48.

The Légion d'honneur

After *Pelléas et Mélisande* Debussy was awarded the Légion d'honneur. The initiative came from Jules Combarieu, a musicologist and the editor of *La Revue musicale*, who held a post at the Ministry of Education.[2] Laloy, who acted as intermediary, was himself awarded the Légion d'honneur in 1920.

La Musique retrouvée, pp. 125–128[1]

Jules Combarieu was too good a musician not to enjoy *Pelléas*, and without perhaps sharing my enthusiasm he allowed me to express it as I wished in the review he edited. He was then principal Private Secretary at the Ministry of Education, which was headed by Monsieur Chaumié. When the time came to prepare the January 1903 preferment he said to me, 'My mind is made up. I will have Debussy decorated.' But at that time the composer's fame had not yet penetrated into political circles, and it was pointed out to Combarieu that the dossier he had prepared lacked one indispensable item, the recommendation of a member of Parliament.

I then contacted Debussy and, on 4 December 1902, received the following reply:

> Dear Sir,
>
> I have known only one politician in my life: that was Monsieur Wilson. It must be added that he was a charming man and one who heartily detested music. The thing is, that business took place some twenty years ago. Since then I have left it at that, the first attempt having seemed decisive. Try to come next Saturday and accept my good wishes.

Indeed Debussy, while still a student at the Conservatoire, spent a summer at Chenonceau castle, the home of Madame Pelouze, the daughter of Wilson and granddaughter of President Grévy, in the capacity of musician, to play the piano for the mistress of the house.[3]

Not only had twenty years passed since that time, but a scandal over illicit trading in decorations had occurred, forcing Jules Grévy to resign and, although the voters of Vierzon had loyally returned Wilson to the Chamber of Deputies, a recommendation from him, especially for the Légion d'honneur, would have done more harm than good. Combarieu was disconsolate. But he redoubled his efforts, worked miracles, and Debussy was awarded a decoration. Here is the letter he wrote to me:

> Sunday evening, 4 January 03
>
> Dear Sir,
>
> I had the impudent hope of seeing you yesterday and thanking you by better means than this cold paper for your cordial intervention in a business to which I only brought an attitude well designed to discourage the best will in the world.
>
> But it occurs to me you are probably not in Paris, so this letter must bear my sincere thanks for the joy you have given to my elderly parents and all who love me (this phrase sounds like something out of an old play, but excuse it, forasmuch as it vigorously translates my thoughts).
>
> Looking forward to seeing you, for which pleasure I entreat you not to make me wait too long, and sending you my warm good wishes.

Chance having brought me to his door on Saturday 24 January, while he was away, he wrote to me two days later about the same matter:

> 26 January 03
>
> Dear Sir,
>
> I can no longer apologize to you but I can lament the circumstances - as arbitrary as they are contradictory - which caused me to miss you last Saturday, it's completely deplorable.
>
> Will you please be unmindful enough of insults to tell me what must be done when one has received a letter from Monsieur Chaumié announcing the thing you know about?
>
> Yours affectionately.

He believed me to be better acquainted with protocol than I was at that time. But everything is relative, and his lack of knowledge not about good manners, which he had naturally, but about official ceremoniousness, of which he had no experience, already far exceeded my own.

Combarieu had more claim than I to his gratitude. I asked Debussy, for his part, if he did not have an unpublished piece which *La Revue musicale* could publish. After looking in vain for quite a while, he sent me this reply which gratified our wishes:

Sunday, 17 January 04

> ... There exists by Claude Debussy a symphonic suite with chorus entitled *Printemps*, which was my third *envoi de Rome*[4] and has never been played or published; if you like we could put the first piece in the musical supplement of the *Revue*? That would couple the first publication with all the historical interest that can be found in the divulgence of a 'manner' which I have never revisited ...

Thus *La Revue musicale* published the reduction for piano duet and chorus of this charmingly simple work, which has since been published by Durand and performed in concerts.[5] This *envoi de Rome*, which was presented to the Institute according to custom, was, it appears, condemned by Saint-Saëns, for an absurd reason against which there is no appeal: 'One does not write in F sharp major for orchestra.'

Notes

1 This is Chapter XVIII of *La Musique retrouvée*, entitled '*Printemps*'.

2 For details of the early *La Revue musicale*, see p. 36 n. 3.

3 Laloy is wildly inaccurate here, in that Madame Pelouze was the sister of Daniel Wilson, who was Under-Secretary of State and the son-in-law of the President, Jules Grévy. Chenonceau is one of the castles in the Loire valley.

4 An *envoi de Rome* was a composition which a winner of the Prix de Rome sent back from Rome to the Académie des Beaux-Arts, the section of the Institut de France charged with administering the Prix de Rome competition. In fact, *Printemps* was Debussy's second *envoi de Rome*; the third was *La Damoiselle élue*.

5 *Printemps* appeared as a supplement to three issues of *La Revue musicale*, on 15 February and 1 and 15 March 1904. A long article by Laloy, 'Claude Debussy. La simplicité en musique', preceded the first of these supplements: it is translated on pp. 65–72.

'Claude Debussy. Simplicity in music'[1]

This is Laloy's first long article about Debussy. He tries to correct misconceptions about Debussy's music, and we gain further insight into the reception of Debussy's works as he spells out what the misconceptions were. Laloy arranged for Debussy's suite *Printemps* to be published as a supplement to this and the two following issues of *La Revue musicale.*

Notes begin on p. 72.

***La Revue musicale* (15 February 1904), pp. 106–111**

(Prélude à l'Après-midi d'un faune)

There are some sorts of music which we admire from afar, like noble foreigners with closed faces; there are others which sometimes smile at us and sometimes distance us; others again are like ever-dear, ever-expected friends, whose cool, consoling hands we always want near us. Since I encountered it along my way, the music of Claude Debussy has been a true, unfailingly gracious companion. Where does it come from, this spell which is ever renewed, from what mysterious springs, unknown to the rest of men? That is what I must attempt to say here, as precisely and impartially as I can.[2]

When *Pelléas* appeared, almost two years ago, there was great commotion in the world of music. Critical opinion, which rarely misses an opportunity to prophesy wrongly, generally declared that the work would not go far; we heard the usual grievances, which have been employed against new music for four hundred years:[3] no melody; no clarity; harsh, tedious harmony; oh, who will give us back beautiful singing? Those who have been following the musical movement for about twenty years, and know to what extent such critical opinion is subject to recantation, paid little heed. That left the disdainful smiles of a few composers who were proud of their 'strength', the complaints of the first violins who were broken-hearted at not playing for an entire scene; and soon there came untimely admiration from a certain sector of the public which likes not to understand and goes straight to unintelligibility as a moth to a flame. Many honest people did not know what to think. Others went to see the much-discussed work, and simply found what a listener who had not been forewarned would recognize right away: music without formulae, in which everything comes from the heart, music with no idle developments, modelled on the drama, or rather on life itself, of which the words of the drama were only a pale reflection; simple, apt declamation, clear, contained orchestration; irresistible emotional power;[4] so much humanity, pity and gentle sympathy that one could not reprove any of the heroes in the tragic story, and left the theatre better people and more inclined towards forgiveness; that is what became evident to sincere minds. They understood that Maeterlinck's work was transfigured by such music and, without asking more of it, they returned to listen: thus occurred the real and lasting success of the only music drama which I, for my part, have been able to attend without ever being offended by any of those artifices which are enough to break the spell; a masterpiece of emotion and simplicity.[5]

I know the latter word runs counter to a prejudice which is still quite widespread. How many times do I hear, 'Debussy's music? It is too learned, it's beyond me.' These few words express a sincere confession and an erroneous judgement. It is perfectly alright not to understand such music at first; but let us make no mistake: what is disconcerting is not its intricacy but its very simplicity. We are accustomed to symmetrical constructions, predictable periodic recurrences of motifs, contrivances of rhythmic or modulatory distortion, and last but not least exercises in amplification which for many of us constitute the whole art of development. This rhetoric becomes necessary to our depraved taste, and we are dumbfounded at first when we encounter a work which obeys only its own inner laws and the rhythm of its own life. We do not notice that all of science, the wretched science which kills, is found in these innumerable compositions whose sentiments are vulgar, whose thoughts are pedestrian, and in which ingenuity of form tries to distract us from the poverty of the material. I know of so many fugues – and in the works which are trying to be the most modern, too – that come in the nick of time to replace an impossible development, so many of those chains of chords which carry a motif from stage to stage but do not manage to make it interesting, and those superimposed themes which 'go together' and would be better not going at all! There is none of that in the music of Monsieur Debussy: it sings, and in singing it grows animated or quietens, it grows excited or subsides, answers itself, or abruptly changes from one idea to another, just as we do when we let ourselves go with our thoughts; and it stops when it has no more to say. This last feature alone is enough to give it such a clear-cut countenance, and one which is so unusual today, that it is easy to understand the initial surprise and almost fright that many of us felt. Nature is strange in the eyes of those whom art has fed on artifice.

Nothing could be simpler, yet also more expressive, more clearly delineated, than the melodic ideas of Monsieur Debussy. This is the theme which, inscribed on the frontispiece of the drama of *Pelléas*, seems to say: 'This is a legend, an old, sad legend of the forest':

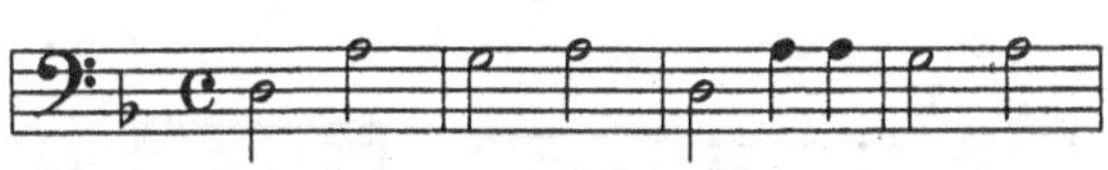

This is the graceful motif which evokes Mélisande, so frail and delicate that one hardly dares to love her, and life will crush her:

And at each step, until the end of the drama, we hear new ideas arise in this way. Some of them will not reappear, and others will come back with the faded charm of memory: thus, on the last evening when at last the grave words have been pronounced, the image of the luminous garden, witness of the first encounters, appears with these few notes:

And I know very well that I will be told, 'Short ideas, indeed! Bach and Beethoven did not think that way.' Undoubtedly, but length has nothing to do with it, concision is also a fine quality, a first-rate one when so much emotion is contained in so little space. Nor was this the place to spread out, in a drama where feelings had to be grasped and noted in passing as they appeared beneath the fabric of the words. But Monsieur Debussy is not to be judged on *Pelléas* alone. Too often people forget that he has also written absolute music,[6] and that there he did not fear to speak his whole mind. Schumann has not written anything more tender, more exalted or more sustained than the first phrase of the Andante from the String quartet:

Another phrase replies, melancholy and dreamy, as though detached from the things of this earth, and infinitely graceful:

Where would we find more consummate melodies? It is easily seen that what distinguishes Monsieur Debussy's inspiration is not a special style of writing but a personal colour: something supremely pure, first of all, ingenuous reserve and modesty, combined with an inner life which is as powerful as it is delicate; a soul which is both exalted and discreet, with a tenderness that can go as far as passion, but not as far as desire; a taste and a respect for all that is graceful, artless and touching: this is the foundation of his thought, this is its great and true originality.

These precious sentiments, which touch fibres rarely moved by real life, are developed without anything impeding their flight, not even the will of the composer who, quite obviously, listens to his interior voices, and writes only as they dictate. That is not to say that his works have no distinguishable plan, quite the contrary, but the plan stems from the very nature of things, not from the rules of a genre. Thus I could very well classify the Andante from the Quartet as a three-part song form, if I wished; but in fact it is not a song, it is a dialogue between two thoughts, with the second thought, which is resigned at first, gradually becoming stronger and more impassioned, only to fall back into the melancholy calm of the beginning. I mean there is nothing, in the whole course of the piece, that indicates a calculation, an intention to modulate simply for the pleasure of making a change, or to prepare for a return of material. It is the same in the first movement, where a first and second subject can certainly be recognised; but rather a single theme dominates, constantly enriched by subordinate ideas, and one of these subordinate ideas – the last – is more important than the others, because it is like the answer to the question that was asked: with this free ordering, Monsieur Debussy is only continuing Beethoven's manner in his last quartets; but what must be noted is that between these various developments we perceive no transitions, so great is the cohesion of the whole, so supple too the harmony which is able to shift by insensible stages from one nuance to another.

Much has been said about Monsieur Debussy's harmony: that it is new, unheard of, barbaric, impossible, or, on the other hand, magical and miraculous. I think there has been great exaggeration, in both directions, and I myself will say that it is quite simply expressive. There are several sorts of harmony. One, which without any ironic intent I will call the harmony of encounter, results when separate melodies are superimposed; the ear necessarily hears chords, since it hears several notes simultaneously, but these chords are of no importance, play no role in the musical work, which is founded solely on melody. This is the harmony of the early masters of vocal polyphony (for, from the middle of the sixteenth century, the preoccupation with the beauty of the chord for itself begins to appear). A different sort of harmony has the establishing of the tonality as its sole aim: it reigns in the seventeenth, in the eighteenth, and still in the nineteenth century in Italian opera; nothing could be more dull or more tiring than those perpetual tonic and dominant chords, when the tonality hardly changes, which is truly the case in that degenerate operatic tradition. But today harmony has learned to seek different effects; we know that a chord, by itself, is sweet or sad, painful or restful, graceful or brutal; what is more, Orlando di Lasso guessed as much, as did Bach, and Beethoven, and all the great composers. However, the harmony of encounter is still found in more than one passage in the present-day masters of counterpoint, such as d'Indy or Dukas: it is the explanation for more than one of their moments of apparent harshness. Tonal harmony is also in use, each time rapid, unexpected modulations run the risk of leading the ear astray. But the harmony of Monsieur Debussy, while always converging on very definite tonalities, is essentially expressive. There is nothing new, moreover, in the means used: appoggiaturas, inflections, pedal points, irregular suspensions. But it is a matter of the way it is done. In this as in the conduct of the development, there is nothing which is not justified by moral – that is, in the true sense of the word, musical – reasons. Monsieur Debussy paints with chords, he speaks with chords, and thus succeeds in noting down momentary nuances of feeling. It is, if you like, Impressionism, but of the best kind, for it makes the continuity of life easier to grasp, instead of interrupting it.[7] One of the passages in *Pelléas* which to me are the most moving is entirely made up of harmonies:

What is that? Quite simply two ninth chords linked together, then two others. But the E held in the low register by the violas, and repeated in the high register by the immaterial sounds of the violins, then given to the violins alone, gives the harmony a sweetness which envelops the soul: it is one of those divine moments when everything that normally holds life back vanishes, when the secret of the inner being finally appears without veils: it is an illumination. So that we do not forget to be pedants, let us also note that this E, which is a ninth or seventh in the first chord, and a third or octave in the second, makes us await and desire the descent of the fifths in the bass, and removes any ambiguity from their parallelism. A rigorous dialectic could even consider the entire first chord as an appoggiatura to the second. But the name is not important: the effect exists, it is gripping, and seems completely natural.

Naturalness! This word constantly comes back to my mind, to characterize a style which to others seems the height of refinement, even of perversity. But, as I was saying at the beginning, it is this very naturalness that surprises us today. A man who, at an assembly, decides simply to utter his private convictions, runs a great risk of being taken for a madman, or a subtle ironist, or a diplomat skilled at innuendo. The same thing happens to Monsieur Debussy. He is not understood at all at first, because his music carries us far from our towns, our houses, our closed rooms, into wild dells crowded with flowers, with thick creepers winding around tree-trunks, with a rich, fresh perfume of sun-drenched gorse. There, young sap flows abundantly, there an ardent, pure life, the memory of which we had lost, rises up on all sides, there we rediscover our feelings stripped of all calculation, in the original state of grace. I will no doubt be told that other types of music do not carry us as far from real existence, and in this way can give us more courage to face it. No doubt. But all who believe that the best part of life is what we dream of it will go often to commune with themselves in the gardens of Fantasy which Monsieur Debussy has rediscovered.[8]

Notes

1 'Claude Debussy. La simplicité en musique'

2 'Il y a des musiques que l'on admire de loin, comme de nobles étrangères au visage fermé; d'autres qui tantôt vous sourient et tantôt vous éloignent; d'autres enfin sont comme des amies toujours chères, toujours attendues, de qui l'on ne voudrait jamais quitter les fraîches mains consolatrices. Depuis que je l'ai rencontrée sur mon chemin, la musique de Cl. Debussy a été la fidèle compagne dont la grâce ne se dément jamais. D'où vient-il, ce charme toujours renouvelé, de quelles sources mystérieuses, inconnues au reste des hommes? C'est ce que je dois essayer de dire ici, avec le plus de précision et d'impartialité qu'il me sera possible.'

3 Laloy's note: 'On this subject, see Monsieur Vincent d'Indy's article

on *Pelléas* in *L'Occident* (June 1902) and his quotation from a critique of Monteverdi, which could have been written yesterday.' V. d'Indy, 'A propos de *Pelléas et Mélisande*. Essai de psychologie du critique d'art', *L'Occident* (June 1902), pp. 374–381. See p. 147 and p. 151 n. 2.

4 '[...] une musique sans formules, où tout venait de l'âme, une musique sans développements oiseux, modelée sur le drame, ou plutôt sur la vie elle-même, dont les mots du drame n'étaient encore qu'un pâle reflet; une déclamation simple et juste, un orchestre clair et contenu; une puissance d'émotion irrésistible [...]'

5 Laloy's note: 'These are precisely the two qualities which it was felt important to highlight here, after the first performance of *Pelléas et Mélisande* (May 1902). I recall it with all the more pleasure as the article was not by me.' It was by Louis Schneider: '*Pelléas et Mélisande*,' *La Revue musicale* (May 1902), pp. 196–200. Louis Schneider also published an account of an interview with Debussy, in April of the same year, in which Debussy stressed the simplicity of his approach: 'That is Monsieur Debussy's most ardent concern; he is given out to be a complicated composer, and he is more enamoured of simplicity than any composer he knows; no one has such a strong need to see clearly as he does.' *La Revue musicale* (April 1902), p. 139

6 Laloy's note:

Without being huge, Monsieur Debussy's œuvre is nonetheless already considerable; we must cite:

Printemps (1887), a suite for orchestra and chorus, unpublished until now, which we begin publishing today;

La Damoiselle élue (1888), analysed in *La Revue musicale* of 1 January 1903 [see pp. 140–144];

Six *Ariettes*, on poems by Verlaine (1888);

Five *Poems* by Baudelaire (1890), analysed in *La Revue musicale* of 1 October 1902 [see pp. 146–151];

Six *Mélodies*, drawn from *Sagesse* and the *Fêtes galantes* by Verlaine [i.e. the *Trois mélodies* of 1891, and the first set of *Fêtes galantes* from the same year];

The string *Quartet* (1893);

The *Prélude à l'Après-midi d'un faune* (1894), analysed in *La Revue musicale* of 1 November 1902 [see pp. 152–156];

A *Fantasy* for piano and orchestra, not performed as yet (1890);

Three *Nocturnes* for orchestra (1899);

Three *Pieces for piano* [i.e. the suite *Pour le piano*] (1901);

Pelléas et Mélisande (1902);

The *Estampes*, for piano (1903).

It is unclear whether this list was supplied by Debussy: compare p. 144 n. 4.

7 The phrase 'the continuity of life' ('la continuité de la vie') is a reference to the philosophy of Bergson, discussed on p. 5.

8 The first instalment of *Printemps* followed immediately after this article. Laloy introduced it:

La Revue musicale, in its Supplement, today begins publication of a

> previously unpublished work by Monsieur Claude Debussy: *Printemps*, a suite for orchestra and chorus (with the orchestra reduced for piano duet). This second *envoi de Rome* (1887), of slightly earlier date than *La Damoiselle élue*, reveals, along with a mind which is already its own master, a youthful liveliness, a naive joy of living and feeling, which have since given way to more profound sentiments. The work is of the greatest interest for those who take pleasure in following the development of a personality, and what is more, it is charming.

In *Claude Debussy* (1909), p. 18, Laloy commented that the musical language of *Printemps* foreshadowed the *Prélude à l'Après-midi d'un faune*: 'with its clear melodies and its languid chromatic passages, [it] evokes the site where later, at the instigation of Mallarmé, the Faun which desires the vain Nymphs will take form.'

'Remarks on Claude Debussy'[1]

Laloy gave this talk before a 'Soirée Debussy' organized by the singer Camille Fourrier on 6 February 1906. On this occasion, Laloy does not hesitate to speak as an enthusiast, and his tone is also sometimes witty or ironic. The programme included the first performance of *Images* I, by Ricardo Viñes, and the third movement of *La Mer* in a version for piano duet.[2]

Notes begin on p. 79.

Le Mercure musical **(1 March 1906), pp. 193–197**

Before a program which promises such rare marvels, it would be unpardonable of me to lengthen your wait. And furthermore the works which you are going to hear need no preventive exegesis in order to be felt; it is not necessary to isolate and label their characteristic motifs in detail, then bring into play in advance the mechanism of their combinations, inversions and varied disguises. Their beauty is all in themselves, not in calculation, premeditation and theory; one can enjoy them without knowing anything of their author's intentions, or his philosophical, aesthetic and social opinions, and even, I think, without knowing anything about music: a pure heart and a sincere ear are sufficient. I therefore have no pretentions to be your guide, to dictate your judgements and solicit your impressions; I only want to try to grasp, and bring out in a few words, the general spirit of an œuvre which a happy choice of examples and a happy meeting of talents is going to allow you to appreciate in its essential virtues.

This spirit can be defined in one word, which I have singular pleasure in pronouncing in these days in which we live: it is a spirit of liberty. But this word itself demands some clarification, for it lends itself to many misapprehensions. We are accustomed to confuse liberty and revolution. We willingly believe that only a struggle against a hitherto accepted obligation can attest to to our independence, and that the free man can only be a destroyer. The liberty of which I intend to speak here has no interest in defying masters it does not know, or in overthrowing an authority which it does not fear, never having been subjected to it. The music of Claude Debussy will show you nothing of the dark fervour, the protestations, provocations and demands of a Berlioz or a Hugo, two revolutionaries who spent their lives anathematizing the Classical tradition with the sole result that they could never remove themselves from its tyranny. Everything is spontaneous here; nothing is imposed, nothing is forbidden; there is no profession of faith, no absolute principle, no doctrine. And hence the first consequence, that ugliness is banned.[3]

It happens frequently indeed, in the laborious music of our time, that the author seems to say, 'I do beg your pardon; what I am doing here is not very lovely. Please believe that I am aware of it just as you are. But it is absolutely necessary that I bring in my second theme above the first here; and if they curse and swear at being together, I cannot change anything. And I know very well that the presence of this note makes a furious dissonance out of a chord that would be quite harmonious without it. Although I would very much like to be pleasant to you, I will not take it out. For then my thirty-ninth bar would be the same in every way as the seventy-seventh, and that is something my aesthetic strictly forbids.' You will not find anything like this in Claude Debussy. When two themes are not designed to go together, he lets them run on separately; and if a chord must be repeated, he does not disfigure it so as to avoid being reproached with monotony. In his eyes no rule can justify a deformity; there is no note, no melody, no sonority from which he does not demand the most perfect euphony before granting it admission into his composition. That is why his music never causes pain; it can distress hearts, not ears, and even in the deepest mourning it retains an air certainly not of joy, but I would say of happiness, meaning by the word not the happy conjunction of events but, as in the Ancients, the happy frame of mind of a well-born soul, whose suffering is still sweet and harmonious, and all the more touching for not tiring us with its cries.

Indeed, and above all, the music of Debussy is well-born. Its lot was an ingenuous grace, and its regard is that of Mélisande's eyes, those eyes which are more pure than the eyes of a lamb, in which you would say heaven's angels celebrate a continuous baptism. And it could not be otherwise, since liberty, as I have defined it, is the exclusive privilege of very elevated souls. In the same way indeed as a rigorous morality, reinforced by precise commandments, is necessary for the mass of men, and becomes unnecessary only to him who finds in himself incentives to act well on every occasion, so the rules of art, instead of impeding creative work, on the contrary simplify it, once the early apprenticeship is past, and put it within the reach of ordinary minds by lessening the role of personal intervention. To say that only a flawless sonnet is worth as much as a long poem is to repeat a solemn absurdity. Three stanzas in a personal form are capable of far higher beauties than those of a sonnet, because they give life to a new rhythm. And similarly, in music, the textbook fugue, despite its terrifying reputation, is a very easy exercise; there exist, in considerable numbers, honourable Conservatoire teachers, Directors or former Directors who have won renown in competitions with perfect fugues, and have never been able to write a single line of real music; it is because to satisfy the rules of the genre there is no need to be a musician; it is enough to possess a certain craft which works of itself and, if it is entrusted with a motif, gives back a fugue with its counter-subject, expositions, episodes and stretti in the right places. The less scholastic forms, such as the sonata, already present more difficulties precisely because of the tolerance of their laws; the general plan is still determined in advance, and it is possible, with a little taste and much work, to complete a suitable sonata or even a symphony; I mean neither better nor worse than those which are born and die almost daily around us. But what will always be impossible, except for true children of Harmony, is validly to write free music, like that of Claude Debussy; music which frolics as it pleases, sometimes in the discreet probity of the diatonic scale, sometimes in the delicate attenuations of the chromatic, or in the even light of those scales with large intervals of which the Asiatic 'Pagodes' offers you a miraculous example; music which weaves from fifths, sevenths, ninths and other, more unusual but equally natural intervals, a harmony which is very fresh and which finally, unamenable to the segmentation of Classical development, produces one motif from another as the magicians of India bring forth in a few moments, from one grain, a plant complete with flowers and innumerable boughs. What will be needed here is something other than science, and more than taste; an instinct so delicate, an intuition so certain and deep, that we can fearlessly speak of genius: such music will have to be made of genius, or not be. Its author draws directly on nature; no rule guarantees him the unity or the effectiveness of his composition, but a divining power reveals to him at every moment the secret affinity which links note to note, chord to chord, melody to melody. Thus understood, music is the art of mysterious relations and unexplained correspondences; it dedicates itself to a perpetual sortilege and assumes a magical power which Debussy indeed confers on it. No man has ever revealed himself more apt to hear the voices of nature and to unravel its vast harmonies, which are confused noises for other mortals; none has lived in closer communion with the universe.

And that is why natural spectacles are so marvellously evoked by him, even in their most fleeting appearances and their most delicate reflections; that is also why they never cause him terror. You are going to have a striking example in the third tableau of *La Mer* which will be performed at the end of today's concert. The subject of this tableau is a tempest, but notice the title: 'Dialogue du vent et de la mer' ['Dialogue of the wind and the sea']. That is because where we perceive only a gigantic, ear-splitting din, Debussy hears a conversation, a colloquy of superhuman voices which remain harmonious in their tumult, and laugh and wail in turn. We must not therefore, as has been done, reproach him for not having painted a frightening enough sea. Being afraid is not understanding; the initiate cannot know fear; the elements are his friends, and he ventures in brotherly fashion amid their apparent anger.[4]

With the same calm assurance, the same pious, familiar tenderness, you will see him go down into the darkness – which to him is luminous – of the inner world. Thrusting aside the vain magnificence of our conventions, our arbitrary reasoning and our artificial duties, he goes deep into the solitary places which are ruled by the instinct which is truer than reason, where our real soul lives, the soul whose natural language, as Maeterlinck saw, is silence; and from this silence he makes music. This, as you know, is the unique, unhoped-for and unforgettable beauty of *Pelléas*, that the composer was able to express just what could not be said, and at every point make the mystery of consciousness perceptible and present to us. You will discover this beauty in all the works in which he wished to translate human feelings. One work ['L'ombre des arbres' from the *Ariettes oubliées*] will give you the intense melancholy which seizes the soul before a very simple country scene: the shadow of the trees in a mist-shrouded river. Another, 'Hommage à Rameau', will speak of the pious admiration today's composer feels for his distant precursor, and this 'monument in music' is worthy of comparison, in its serene sadness, with the finest funerary offerings which Greek art has left us. Elsewhere, in the *Chansons de France*, you will recognize the somewhat rigid grace and the slightly constrained half-smile of souls which were still awkward, and yet very refined. The quite pagan *Chansons de Bilitis* will paint for you the voluptuousness of waiting, which is even sweeter than pleasure, or the mad, passionate dream of a carnal mysticism, designed to shake to the core any being worthy to be called living. And finally, in 'Chevaux de bois' [from the *Ariettes oubliées*], or *L'Isle joyeuse*, or the extraordinary 'Mouvement', you will be dazzled by a joy whose secret seemed quite lost to us: the joy of Fauns dancing in the sun or Nymphs gambolling, careless of the Satyr.

I believe I have said enough to show that music like this has the right to be free, and to show itself unfaithful to the conventions which have been the most highly respected up to now, including those of the diatonic scale, which is like the religious symbol of European music, traditional harmony, which represents its morality, and Classical development, which could be called its puerile, honest politeness. It has this right, because its imagination is not arbitrary at all, but expresses primordial truths, inaccessible to human understanding; through it, the life of things and our own life are revealed to us. It leads us back to a state of absolute innocence, purity and limpidity, in which even the notion of evil does not yet exist, no rule having been imposed. 'Before error' could be its motto, and this is the meaning of the musical mysteries which are going to be celebrated before you.[5] I hope that by reason of his goodwill, you will not be vexed with the indiscreet conversationalist who delayed you at the gates of this earthly Paradise.

Notes

1 'Paroles sur Claude Debussy'

2 In the 15 February issue of *Le Mercure musical*, p. 165, Laloy wrote a review of this 'Soirée Debussy'. He said he felt 'a little embarrassed' to speak about it, but 'it was so beautiful that, despite the presence of my name on the program, I want to try to tell here of the joy of the concert, in which a music of dreams was among us, miraculous and real.' He continued: '[. . .] it has been proven once again that Debussy more than any other composer today has the virtue of attracting audiences and securing, as they say, a full house: I hope our conductors and theatre directors will profit by this truth!'

3 'Tout est spontané ici; rien n'est imposé, rien n'est interdit; nulle profession de foi, nul principe absolu, nulle doctrine. Et de là cette première conséquence, que la laideur est bannie.'

4 Laloy commented on the piano-duet performance of the third movement of *La Mer* as follows:

> A good part of the day's success is certainly due to Monsieur Delacroix who, to finish, played for us, with one of his pupils, Monsieur Petit, the last tableau of *La Mer*. I am afraid of sounding

delirious, but now that I know the work's orchestral colour, I find much more pleasure in hearing it on the piano than in the orchestra, when it is performed by artists such as these, who are able to translate its moving colloquies with a sense of life, a passion, a variety and power of nuances which no orchestra will ever attain.

Le Mercure musical (15 February 1906), p. 166

5 '«Avant la faute», telle pourrait être sa devise, et tel est le sens des mystères musicaux qui vont être célébrés devant vous.'

Debussy's compositional style

This is a uniquely penetrating analysis of Debussy's musical language up to 1909, taken from the fifth chapter of Laloy's biography of Debussy. It can reasonably be assumed that at least some of the points Laloy makes derive from his discussions with Debussy. The writing style is heavier than in Laloy's reviews and articles.

***Claude Debussy* (1909), pp. 73–77**

In any Romantic work, it seems an imprisoned music is fretting, and begging to be released. Now, chains have fallen away, and chinks have opened up, allowing a glimpse of a bright world outside which poets and painters have already discovered. But other ties still bind; and the great, rectilinear walls remain standing. Claude Debussy was the saviour, because he came at the appointed time, because he had contemplated the example of the sister arts, and above all because he had listened to the voices of nature. He untied the captive, restored to her the caress of the air, and also the grace to which learned movements were doing violence. But he destroyed nothing: he brings peace, and not war. He only abolished the strictness of the commands, and asked that we find through pleasure what was formerly imposed by duty.

The melody is under no compulsion, not even to emancipate itself from the major scale; often no notes are found which Mozart would not also have allowed. Elsewhere, according to the subject and the circumstances, it allows itself irregularities which moreover are hardly noticed, because they have come from inspiration. Sometimes the melody could be ascribed to scales similar to some of our ancient Gregorian modes: thus the first motif of *Pelléas*, and the principal theme of the Quartet. Elsewhere there are the inflections of a direct chromaticism, that of the *Prélude à l'Après-midi d'un faune* or more delicate alterations: the fifth degree of the usual series lowered by a semitone, or the fourth raised by as much, as occurs in several places in the *Nocturnes*. At other times, there are successions of whole tones, shyly indifferent; and, more frequently, incomplete scales, in which the whole tone alternates only with the minor third, according to the preference of Chinese taste: it is these incomplete scales which allow 'Pagodes', from the *Estampes*, to achieve a perfect resemblance; but *Pelléas*, the *Nocturnes*, the *Proses lyriques* and the *Prélude à l'Après-midi d'un faune* are not unaware of them. It is, furthermore, improper to speak of scales, because a scale is a rule. Here the melody perpetually changes the order and nature of the intervals. This is music without scales and, indeed, a time had to come when that support would become as unnecessary as the prop of the regular line for poetry;[1] all that was required was that a composer had it within his power to sense the mutual affinity of sounds, as the poet senses the value of rhythms.[2]

Just as, for an imagination of this kind, note attracts note, idea calls up idea.[3] The Romantics juxtapose them; here they proceed one from another; and the joining points are no longer perceived. In the *Prélude à l'Après-midi d'un faune*, which is the most narrative piece, the reverie intensifies and reaches the point of despair by insensible degrees; in the second *Nocturne*, the procession, moving through the ball with its muted splendour, is bathed in the same clamour of light; the different echoes which rise up, in the evening in the streets of Granada, in the second *Estampe*, carry with them the same melancholy ardour; finally, right throughout *Pelléas*, the ideas appropriate to each situation hold together by an unknown pact, and around the fortuitous events they blend a symphony of tenderness into the unconquerable spell. That is the secret of unity which is not guaranteed by external means, does not have signposts, but relies on the natural succession of impressions. It is the unity of a character, of a landscape; in a word, it is unity of tone, if this term is taken, not in the narrow acceptation of music theory, but in the less definite sense given to it by poets and painters.[4]

The orchestration resorts to doubling at the unison only if it is necessary for reinforcement or gradation; in every other place, it prefers unblended colours; through their proximity they set each other off, react and come into play. There is a continual pulsation, a trembling light, a visible transparence, a shadow made up of reflections, a delicate effect of pure touches, placed directly on the note which requires them, or rather conceived with that very note, which is put in for the timbre of the violin, oboe or horn, and for no other. No instrument is given preference, none is sacrificed, each is placed according to its character and with a view to the ensemble. There is never any overloading, or impasto,[5] or blemish, nor any jolts, contrasts, or effects of relief that come in advance: continuous, distinct ensembles, in which the planes are organized and the objects take form by virtue of the tints and values alone.

The harmony is the image of the melody; like the melody, it is very regular on occasion, and even particularly fond of the root-position triad. But it also likes many other chords, which until then had been counted among the dissonances and which it recognises as consonant: it imposes no enforced consequence on them, no resolution; it relishes in each of them a special charm, which is enough. That is because it discovers, between their notes, relationships which the theory of the major scale could not explain, nor consequently recognize. It has been noted, very ingeniously, that a great many of these chords correspond to the harmonic series, continued beyond the sixth harmonic.[6] But they can only be reduced to it by means of the artifices of octave transposition and inversion, which alter their character; therefore no one meant to say that it was enough to know the harmonic series in order to discover valid chords. The harmony of notes, like that of colours, is not within the province of deduction, but of intuition.

Such chords will be linked by affinities of the same order as those by which the notes of the melody call to one another; instead of pointing out a key, they will form by themselves melodies which are free from all scales, and are drawn from the very wellsprings of music. Sometimes the same chord will be maintained and, with its unique, multicoloured sonority, will trace out a melodic line, which itself is capable of combining with another line; or else different chords will answer one another, bathing the melody in their unstable nuances, their waves of light.

Notes

1 Until the late nineteenth century, the most important organizing principle in French poetry was that every line had the same number of syllables.

2 In *Comment écouter la musique*, p. 62, Laloy wrote again about Debussy's free approach to modality:

> He did not study the old modes as Mussorgsky did. Much freer still, in his music it is the melody that makes the mode, and varies with it. The beginning of the prelude to *Pelléas* recalls the devout character of the first of the Gregorian modes, but does not remain in it, any more than the Quartet (1893), alternating between a scale of

G minor with an F natural and A flat, and the ordinary minor scale; and the flute line based on chromatic steps in the *Prélude à l'Après-midi d'un faune* (1894) belongs to no known mode. The feeling of tonality subsists, however, in the sense that each of these unusual scales is neatly situated in its octave, and furthermore there are frequent returns to the ordinary diatonic, but they do not take the melody captive: it comes to rest there, ever ready to take flight again.

3 'De même que la note, pour une telle imagination, attire la note, l'idée appelle l'idée.'

4 'C'est le secret de l'unité qui n'est pas assurée par des moyens extérieurs, n'a pas ses signes de reconnaissance, mais se fie à la suite naturelle des impressions. C'est l'unité d'un caractère, celle d'un paysage; c'est, enfin, l'unité du ton, si l'on entend ce mot, non dans l'acception étroite de la théorie musicale, mais au sens moins défini que lui accordent les poètes et les peintres.'

5 The *Oxford English dictionary* defines *impasto* as the laying on of colour thickly.

6 Laloy is referring to ideas put forward by the critic Jean Marnold: see p. 91 and p. 98 n. 12.

'Claude Debussy and Debussyism'[1]

This major article was published in a special issue of *S.I.M. Revue musicale*, for a festival of French music held in Munich. *Pelléas et Mélisande* and other works were performed, but Debussy did not take part in the festival. Laloy covers reception, æsthetics and musical language. Some of his remarks about Debussy's compositional technique are similar to those made in *Claude Debussy* (1909).

Notes begin on p. 97.

S.I.M. Revue musicale (August–September 1910), pp. 507–519

Music's latest progress has just been made in France, not through the effects of a reform like those of Gluck and Wagner, but by the sole and very persuasive means of the works given to us by Claude Debussy. Whatever opinion one may hold about these works, there is no doubt that they mark a date in history at least as important as that of the first Florentine operas, which allowed the vocal line to express passion and released harmony from counterpoint; for those early operas also renewed music's feeling and system simultaneously; they extended the power of music, and established it on new laws which to tell the truth had long been sought, some of which had even been glimpsed, but without the unity and the whole ever being grasped.

So great a change could not leave public opinion indifferent. Some, probably predestined, welcomed the change as the realization of their dearest and most secret hope; they recognised the promised music, because it was mysteriously prophesied in the depths of their hearts; they heard this voice; they understood this language which they had not known the day before, and they were filled with joy.

But others, close by, listened without discerning anything but a confused, strange, even painful noise. Very few had enough good faith to admit that so much innovation had caught them unawares, enough goodwill to try to become accustomed to it. A Rimsky-Korsakov was not afraid to declare that he 'did not yet understand, but was going to study and reflect';[2] he died before he finished his study, but his last score, *Le Coq d'or*, showed that he was already familiar with the new locutions. Most, envious of an enthusiasm which they could not share at once, consoled themselves by calling it affectation or madness; they took up the old sarcastic phrases which crowds have shouted, from age to age, to point out the crime of feeling what they do not feel. Lastly a few artists, while recognising the spell which captivated them, refused to abandon themselves to it, for fear of losing their reason. Among the latter we may cite Monsieur Vincent d'Indy, who publicly took up the defence of *Pelléas et Mélisande*, and enjoins his disciples to admire Debussy but not imitate him, even cautioning them against the dangers of listening to his music too often, and prescribing as antidotes the works of Bach, Beethoven or César Franck.[3]

It was not the first time these three factions had found themselves in direct confrontation. Wagner too, not to go back to Gluck, Rameau, Lully or Monteverdi, had his partisans, detractors and adversaries. Quarrels resulted, which were never lengthy, and always ended in the triumph of the new ideas: in art, as in politics, the advance parties are assured of victory after some delay. Which, it must be added, does not mean that the reactionary parties are called upon to disappear: they are necessary, since they exist.

Today we would not find, even among those who are overwhelmed with mortal boredom by *Tristan* or *Parsifal*, a man so disdainful of ridicule as to discuss Wagner. Soon Debussy will be sacred in turn. Already people have stopped boasting that they do not understand him; those who still have the courage to challenge his glory look for arguments to condemn him, and find them in the theories of Wagner, which comes down to reproaching Debussy for not being Wagner, and for being born half a century later; but most have renounced their error, either because grace has touched them, or because vanity leads them to play the connoisseur. The only ones who still resist, because they believe they are defending certain absolute principles of art, are the doctrinarians surrounding Monsieur Vincent d'Indy at the Schola Cantorum. And yet they are not beyond accepting some of the recently won liberties themselves; they only mean to restrict their use, or, as they would say, curb their misuse. Today Debussy's influence can be felt everywhere: he has enriched musical language with expressions and personal mannerisms which became necessary to him, and no artist, not only in France but in any country in the world, would wish to be without them, if he is at all concerned with being listened to by his contemporaries. The only question is what use will be made of this treasure, which was found by one individual, and is now the property of all; some would wish to retain as much as possible of the old rules, others always to move ahead, at random. However, Claude Debussy himself withdrew into self-communion after the excitement of the first discoveries, so as to be able to draw out all their potential effect. At first his glory was that of an inventor; today the artist is more apparent. The inventor, as Monsieur Jean Marnold has convincingly pointed out, had his way traced out for him; benefiting from previous searches and attempts, with a stroke of genius he drew from the darkness the new truth which had been suspected but which no one had succeeded in formulating.[4] But the artist might have had quite different taste; he might even have had none: there are numerous examples of precursors who did not have the ability to create. Claude Debussy has the privilege of being able to count himself among the composers for whom he was a precursor.

§

The innovations he has brought to music are summed up by a vocable which has already been much used, as an insult by some, as a proud motto by others: Debussyism. Debussyism corresponds to what Symbolism was in poetry, and Impressionism in painting. The analogy is not fortuitous: born in 1862, Claude Debussy's youth was coming to an end at the time when these systems were at their peak; and he was a frequent visitor at Stéphane Mallarmé's salon, which was the temple where the mysteries were reverently celebrated.

Symbolism attempts a new alliance between the senses and the mind. Our Classical poets replaced an object with an idea which they then developed logically; the Romantics converted these ideas into feelings which they manifested through images; the Parnassians returned to a detailed description of objects, taken for themselves and with no associations of ideas or feelings. The Classics are rationalists; the Romantics, spiritualists; the Parnassians, materialists. For adepts of Symbolism, on the other hand, there is no matter without thought, nor any thought without matter. Their aim will be never to separate, by deadly analysis, these two complementary aspects of all things. Under every shape, they allow an idea to show through; and there is no idea which they do not clothe with an appearance. If they were calculated and reasoned, these perpetual transcriptions would only deserve to be called allegories; they will be symbols if they are revealed by the intuition, which alone is the equal of the real. The poet will be a poet only if he is by nature initiated into the analogies which make up the universe: Symbolism is a mystical doctrine.

The word, the poet's instrument, will itself be open to two acceptations: it will have to represent a meaning, at the same time as it awakens a sensation. It is the meeting point between an idea and a sound. In the same way the line will no longer be content with a regular rhythm and harmonious rhymes: its rhythm and rhymes will not only be there for pleasure, but to represent life; the rhythm will follow the impulses of life: it will be free; the rhyme will imitate the nuances of life, it will by turns be vibrant or muted, brilliant or dark, instead of only aspiring, as the Parnassians did, to a banal richness. What the Symbolists want to draw from language, then, are the musical effects of which it is capable. Poetry, fleeing from reason, holds out its hands to music. Paul Verlaine asks for

De la musique avant toute chose.[5]

According to Stéphane Mallarmé, 'music and literature constitute the moving facet – now looming toward obscurity, now glittering unconquerably – of that single, true phenomenon which I have called the idea.'[6] And René Ghil, with words, wrote symphonic music.[7]

The Impressionist painters, too, declared war on abstract reason which wants to shut such and such a shape, a tree, a man, a house, inside a prison of outlines in order to paint it in isolation. Equally they believe that everything in the universe is constant: colours react perpetually with one another; light cannot be separated from the medium through which it passes. What must be represented, then, are not objects which have already been chosen and taken out from the whole, but the complexity of sensations as they reach our eyes; and if the representation is faithful, the mind will rediscover the objects in it by an exertion quite like that which nature imposes on it. A painting will not be a landscape, or a still life, or a historical composition: it will be a visual impression, fixed on the canvas without any sort of distortion or preconceived idea. Science, as we know, greatly helped the Impressionists to accomplish the task they had assigned themselves: it taught them that the retina had its necessary illusions, and therefore its own truth, and that any colour could be obtained by juxtaposing single colours; this latter procedure, the division of tone, is often even given as the defining characteristic of Impressionism, whereas it is only its consequence. But the lessons of science only establish a general truth; they do not point to anything, in each particular case; it is the painter who must see acutely enough to guess the reaction between colours, or to break up one of them into its first elements. As Jules Laforgue wrote, 'the visual arts depend on the eye and only on the eye'.[8] Like Symbolism, Impressionism leads to the apotheosis of sensation.

Music appeals only to sensation. The sounds it employs have no meaning, and cannot represent any object. So it seems that music must have been, naturally and from the very beginning, the most Symbolist and Impressionist of all the arts.[9] This has not been the case, at least in Europe since the beginning of history. A Chinese who is transported simply by the sound of singing stones or bells, a Hindu plucking the strings of his bamboo lute deliberately one after the other, a Senegalese who spends hours at a time caressing a little harp which is so soft that only he can hear it, are all Impressionists and even Symbolists without knowing it: they hear, they are moved, they dream. But Western man was born rational. His first concern was to classify sounds. Their pitch, which was chosen as the defining sign, disregarding timbre and intensity, assigned each of them a determined place in a pre-established series which is called a scale: this invention dates back to the ancient Greeks; it has endured to our day. Thus the sound ceases to be a sound and becomes a note, that is a serial number; on hearing it, one experiences no particular impression, but recognizes it as the first, the third or the sixth degree of a certain scale, and asks oneself if one or another of the neighbouring degrees is going to follow. The Western mind, frightened of anything which escapes reason, wanted to make music inoffensive by transmuting sensation into notion. It succeeded better and better in the course of time. Greek music still has different scales called modes and, as I have attempted to show elsewhere,[10] one mode cannot be reduced to another, as each has its own intervals. The modes of Gregorian chant, which derive from these, are already no more than pieces of one and the same scale, which has been cut in different places. From the seventeenth century onwards, this scale itself only admits of one regular cut, one normal mode: the major scale, and the minor scale, the only vestige of the former diversity, only counts as an accidental alteration of the major. By the eighteenth century, music is only a game between different major scales, which are exactly the same as each other, but transposed to different pitches: these are what are called keys; a change of key is a modulation: the whole interest of the music called Classical is in modulation. The business of the melodies it uses is to represent a key; of the accompanying harmony, to state it more definitely, through affirmative formulae called cadences. Music reaches a point of total stylization, of geometric abstraction. Or rather it would reach that point, if composers did not have an indomitable instinct; in spite of everything, sensation slips through the rigour of the system, and life, which we thought had been destroyed, reappears. What gives the works of Couperin and Rameau, of Haydn and Mozart, of Bach and Beethoven, an unsullied quality of youthfulness, is the imagination they brought to them: the melodic inflection not called for by the scale, the chord progression which is not explained by the logic of the key, the charming and unexpected modulation.

The Classics tolerated the rules because the expression of their rational mentality did not require great freedom. The Romantics rose in rebellion against the rules, to carve out a course for the torrent of their passions. Indeed they did open up large breaches, but they did not bring down the walls completely. Eager for the space it has glimpsed, their music wants to rush towards it, but the impulse is dashed, for the space is still surrounded. Hence in all their works there is a struggle: we hear cries of appeal, shouts of defiance, victories, despondency, regrets, despair. Berlioz, Chopin, Schumann, Liszt, Wagner: none is an exception; in the last of these, the struggle even takes on a epic grandeur, with all the new forces ranged against the old fortress which solidly resists. Only with Debussy did deliverance come; it was sudden and effortless; as if touched by a magic wand, the ramparts vanished instantly into thin air, and nature was opened up, quivering, rustling, radiant and unlimited.

This ease only seemed miraculous. It had been foreseeable since 1880. On the other side of Europe, composers had already escaped from the fortress and run freely about the countryside: Balakirev, Rimsky-Korsakov, Borodin and Mussorgsky; the first two were picturesque, smitten with sonority to the point of intoxication, and they invented a type of orchestration in which every note is a colour; the other two had the gift of a lively, tender, generous sensibility, which they wanted to be able to put whole into their music, without any concern for rules; and above all the last, preserved by ignorance from correcting happy mistakes in his harmonies, succeeded in doing so. In his songs and in *Boris Godunov*, Mussorgsky is Debussy's nearest precursor.

The principle of the new music which has been given to us is that note attracts note directly, without the justification of a scale; similarly chord attracts chord without a cadence; idea attracts idea with no need for contrast or modulation.[11] Everything is linked together, and nothing is done to order: it is a music which obeys no precept, only the laws of sensation: a purely auditory music, just as Impressionist painting is entirely visual. It has no preconceived ideas, and frequently its melodies use no other notes than those of the major scale, and its chords are those of a definite key: thus it revisits the Classical system, but with no deliberate intention of conforming to it, and only because this arrangement is the very one dictated by its imagination. Equally it revisits quite different systems; sometimes we think we hear an echo of the ancient modes, those of Gregorian chant or Greek music, sometimes the Chinese scales without semitones, also the chromatic scales consisting entirely of semitones, scales of whole tones, and others still, with previously unknown alterations of the fourth, fifth and seventh degrees. But this is only an illusion: this music, which seems to employ so many different scales, does not use any. It does not have scales: it only has melodies.

Its harmony does not have necessary progressions: it only has chords. That is to say that it knows only consonance, not dissonance. A dissonant chord is an unstable, provisional chord, which must be resolved to a consonance. The chords in this harmony all have, within themselves, their reason for existing: therefore they are all accepted as consonant. Monsieur Jean Marnold has shown irrefutably that through the ages a larger number of chords was admitted to the number of consonances, and that this progressive accession followed the same order as the harmonics: the fifth became consonant before the third.[12] Today it is the turn of the seventh and ninths, and even the elevenths and thirteenths, which stand for the harmonics of the same number. There is more: we are reaching a period in which every chord, whatever its composition may be and even if it cannot be reduced to harmonics, can count as a consonance. A chord no longer has to furnish any proof of its legitimacy; it is a sonority which, when used well, will fully satisfy our ear, and therefore be justified. From the combination of sounds, a different total sound results, as a different colour from the juxtaposition of colours.

Such chords will follow one upon another as do aspects of the sky or the emotions of our heart. And the whole work will have just this unity: melodies will be linked by a secret kinship and, instead of playfully fighting among themselves, as in Classical music, they will appear one after another like sisters holding hands, different of face and yet inseparable. The work will only be justified by itself; it will carry within itself the inner reason for its details and accidentals; it will be the creator of its own form.[13]

In such music, nothing is put in for the sake of symmetry, contrast or embellishment. Every note is sensation; everywhere life breaks through. But Symbolist poetry taught Debussy respect for mystery: it would be ashamed to yield itself up. His melodies will not stand out clearly and frankly, a cloud of harmony will protect them; and immediately they have appeared, they will vanish, fearful that, in an instant, they have given themselves away. This is music of allusion, of indication, itself like the symbol of a different music, which will forever be ineffable, as it would uncover the very roots of existence.

Such is the extraordinary delicacy to which Debussy gradually led his art, illustrating the *Ariettes oubliées* (1888) and the *Fêtes galantes* (1891) of Verlaine, the *Proses lyriques* (1893) on his own text, the *Chansons de Bilitis* (1898) of Pierre Loüys, writing the String quartet (1893), the *Prélude à l'Après-midi d'un faune*(1894), inspired by Mallarmé's poem. The masterpieces of the genre are the *Nocturnes* (1899), and the drama *Pelléas et Mélisande*, on Maeterlinck's text, performed at the Opéra-Comique on 30 April 1902. The *Nocturnes* are three orchestral tableaux such as had never been attempted: 'Nuages', 'Fêtes' and 'Sirènes' are evoked not by themselves, but simply by the vibrating air, the trembling light; all that is retained of objects is the envelope; nothing material, opaque, or motionless is left: changing reflections, passing glimmers of light, at the borders of dream and reality. In *Pelléas et Mélisande* the composer extends the poet's thought well beyond the illusory words and brings out the unknown desire hidden in the depths of our hearts, a desire which knows nothing of reason or duty.

The destiny of the work is well known: the critics were almost unanimously ironic, there were protests and laughter at the final rehearsal and the early performances, then, when finally the public which loves music and is never invited was allowed in, came attentive listening, self-communion, deep emotion, endless applause and the success which has not been contradicted to this day. Debussy's victory was conclusive.

§

But as it happened, at that time the unchallenged reign of Symbolism and Impressionism was coming to an end: artists were beginning to realize that art had become a marvellously delicate instrument, but that something better than exactitude could be asked of it. The first, Gauguin, subjugated nature instead of competing with it, by the authority of his detailless figures with their summary outlines, and his pure colours whose harmony is richer for suppressing nuances. So proud an example was not to be lost: henceforth what was asked of a painter was not so much to capture the chance aspect of a moment as to establish stable relationships, which do not depend on resemblance. The artist has regained his right of interpretation; he has nobly affirmed it: today he would push a preconceived idea to the point of absurdity, rather than abdicate when confronted with the object.

Literature too refused to submit to all the whims of feeling. It wanted to eliminate that which belongs only to the history of an individual consciousness, and on the contrary retain that which manifests a law of life. Our young poets' mentor is now not Mallarmé but Paul Claudel, whose direct style with its phrases of hard stone they rightly admire. But the more general truth which is being sought in this way is not a truth of reason, as in the centuries of Classicism: it is a truth of intuition, of the intuitions which Symbolism was able to attain, simply disentangled from the appearances which were veiling it.

Music could not escape this tortured search for the essential. The *Nocturnes* and *Pelléas* are works which will forever be dear to us because, better than all the poets' lines and all the painters' canvases, they convey the youthful enthusiasm of the times when unknown regions of existence were being discovered; what makes them even more dear to us is that they will never come again. The feelings they brought to us will not be lost, but the confusion and uncertainty of the first moments will not return. This world which at first we hardly dared contemplate is now to furnish the artist with the material to construct a different world, more solid and more definite. This is what Claude Debussy has ventured to do.

Since 1904 there has been a perceptible change in his manner. In that year there appeared three songs on poems by Verlaine, which form the second set of *Fêtes galantes*; in the second of these songs ['Le Faune'], the piano, instead of enveloping the vocal line in a vibration of chords, is content to toss off a melancholy ritornello, in imitation of a flute, to the muted rhythm of a distant dance; in the third ('Colloque sentimental'), the harmony accompanying this dialogue of forgetting reposes on a single, constant note, whose dismal beating bespeaks more eloquently than any modulation the sadness of what is no more. In the same year, three *Chansons de France*, on words by Charles d'Orléans, attained the poet's proud, strong grace by means of even simpler lines. The following year, there was a set of three piano pieces, called *Images*, the first two of which show a style as supple and florid as the *Estampes* of 1903; but the last

('Mouvement') is satisfied to combine perpetual triplets with a brief, savage theme. In 1905 *La Mer* also appeared: these are three symphonic sketches, for which the first idea dates back to 1903; here the melody is unreserved, and the harmony forms its chords by combining definite motifs, according to the principle of counterpoint; but the first of these is no more tied down to the major scale, than the second to the perfect cadence: their will alone directs them.

In 1907 there appeared a second set of *Images* for piano, the second of which achieved what was believed forbidden in modern times: an entirely melodic music. Here, there is no longer a tune resting on chords, as in the Classical and Romantic periods, or emanating from them, as in Symbolist art. Under the title, 'Et la lune descend sur le temple qui fut', a vast, sleeping landscape, caressed and consoled by intermittent rays of moonlight, is evoked by a melody so sustained that it can do without any external support. A melodic line rises up and continues, isolated in silent, listening space; but this line is itself marked outlined by chords; it is no longer a line, it is a three-dimensional figure into which the composer, a sculptor of sounds, has condensed all the dispersed life around him.

Finally, in 1908, the little set for children, *Children's corner*, sketched out delicate miniatures with melodies of this type, and some new *Chansons de Charles d'Orléans* created choruses from them, with the same sinewy grace as the Renaissance models, but more tenderly so.

These works were the messengers of a new form, a more solid form than that used by Debussyism; but the artist was not yet fully master of it. He divined it, came close to it, at times found it only to lose it again. Whence came a certain sense of diligence which contrasted with the earlier ingenuousness, and also from time to time a slight unevenness of style, which was surprising in such an infallible composer, giving hope to some, and to others the anxiety that his genius might be about to lapse; but a few understood that after leaving the sure refuge of the manner he had established, which was already being zealously imitated, he was seeking to realize an idea of beauty which had been ripened in his mind; and they put their faith in him. Their hope has not been misplaced, for this very year, one after another have come compositions which are wholly quickened by this beauty, with no hint of confusion or hesitation, no retouching or repentance: the two symphonic poems, *Ibéria* and *Rondes de printemps*, the twelve *Préludes* for piano, and the *Rhapsody* for piano and clarinet.

Ibéria is divided into three parts, the last two played without interruption, and the three are linked together by the return of a few melodies. For this work contains melodies which are not only complete, but are developed, productively generating different melodies around them which interlace without masking the main melody, which is like the strong trunk of a luxuriant tree. And for this reason they are repeated, and have a new appearance each time: two of them, except for the secondary recurrences, suffice to occupy one of the pieces entirely. In this work we find the opposite of indication: the tune in relief throughout, the affirming phrase, the sweeping rhythm. And yet the central episode, 'Les Parfums de la nuit', shows the suppleness of which this clean, clear writing is capable: it is a sweet, contemplative piece in which ideas emanate from the diffuse distance, draw nearer each other, become clearer, evanesce, and return, transfigured by an inner variation which changes all their details without losing their feeling. By a secret instinct for order, these ideas are arranged as in a couplet between two refrains, but they are linked together by a constant forward movement and, when the first idea reappears, everything has taken on a new accent of voluptuous sadness: thus life always accompanies equilibrium, or rather engenders it of itself, as in a supernatural world in which harmony is an attribute of existence.

The *Rondes de printemps*, which are even more bold, develop a single idea which runs and trips through clear melodic foliage, a breathless dance is reached which whirls for a moment, then quietens and disperses into the tender air; and, as the orchestra itself has rejected the brilliance of the brass, the effect is – though with more luminous tones – like the misty but precise grace of a landscape by Corot.

The *Préludes* are imaginative pieces which can evoke, for example, 'Danseuses de Delphes' ['Delphic dancers'], 'Le vent dans la plaine' ['The wind on the plain'] or 'Des pas sur la neige' ['Footsteps in the snow'], though these assimilations are in no way necessary, and each prelude associates its ideas by reasons which are above all musical; and that is why the titles are, very ingeniously, placed at the end: what one hears first of all is a musical composition; afterwards one can take pleasure in illustrating it with such and such an image. These preludes differ from what has been written under this title up to now in that they are not content to meditate on a single motif: their construction is more complex, and in each one we can distinguish a principal melody, which is stated and returns, even sometimes more than once, after being answered by other melodies. These are the most perfect works the composer has written for the piano to this day: they do not have the exuberant ornamentation of the *Estampes*, nor the sometimes slightly anaemic bareness of the second *Images*; this music is entirely emotional, and does not deny itself broad chords or rapid, varied figuration, always stopping exactly at the point before which the expression would not be complete, whereas beyond it would be the beginning of virtuosity.

Finally the *Rhapsody* for clarinet is an incomparably rich piece, in which one idea is born from another, by turns dreamy, caressing, passionate and sadly playful, all warm, in accordance with the character of the instrument, and as though they all sprang from the same immortal source.

These compositions will be followed by others: we can already cite two songs on fragments from Tristan Lhermite,[14] and three others on ballades by Villon, all gravely and restrainedly beautiful. The time has come for Claude Debussy, having made music capable of conveying impressions which had been impossible to express until now, to arrange these elements according to his mind's will. So today, now that all the extraordinary things he brought with him have been sorted out, we can decide to which race of artists he belongs: the purest of all, the race whose art is capable only of love, and knows nothing of hatred, combat, contrast, violence or ugliness. Among composers, Josquin des Prés, Palestrina, François Couperin, Handel and Mozart were of this race, and Debussy is close to the last of these especially, through an equal gift of innocence and clarity: both have the power to spread a limpid serenity over everything they touch, and their minds rise spontaneously towards peace and joy. Those who speak of the divine Mozart could well apply the same praise to Debussy; needless to say most of them indignantly refuse to do so. And not only these short-sighted defenders of a tradition which they believe is dead but which lives again, not only the Wagnerians who pronounce their mentor's theories like articles of faith, or the disciples of Monsieur d'Indy who wear austerity like armour, but even a number of Debussyists, hold back admiration which it would seem easy to give to music that was much more regular and explicit than that of the early works; one would think they hold a grudge against Debussy, as if he had betrayed them, for having exceeded the definition of him that they had given themselves: they made an initial effort to understand him – a considerable one; henceforth we will get nothing more from them. They are sticking to the *Nocturnes*, and think they are quits with Debussy when they have written that title on one of their programmes. The *Nocturnes* are indeed marvellous poems, but they come at the beginning of a career which is fertile both in the number of works and because each of them, compared with those which preceded it, is new. How easy it would have been for the composer, after his early successes, to achieve popularity and spend the rest of his days copying himself! He must be forgiven: in him, sincerity is not a virtue, but a necessity.

Notes

1 'Claude Debussy et le Debussysme'

2 This would have been during a conversation with Laloy, in Paris in about 1907. Laloy said Rimsky-Korsakov 'showed himself to be the most courteous of men, without however making the slightest concession to me out of politeness'. *S.I.M.* (15 July 1908), p. 740

3 D'Indy published an article on *Pelléas et Mélisande* soon after the first performances: 'A propos de *Pelléas et Mélisande*. Essai de psychologie du critique d'art', *L'Occident* (June 1902), pp. 374–381. In *La Musique retrouvée*, p. 102, Laloy says that in spite of defending *Pelléas et Mélisande* against accusations of disorder or artifice, d'Indy was careful to protect his students against 'what he called "a technique of illumination" ["un procédé d'enluminure"], meaning by that, I suppose, touches of colour, without supporting lines.'

4 J. Marnold, *Musique d'autrefois et d'aujourd'hui* (Paris, 1911), p. 80

5 'Music before all things', the first line of the *Art poétique* (1875) by Paul Verlaine. In the first two stanzas of this poem, Verlaine advises poets to create a musical effect by writing lines with an uneven number of syllables (rather than the conventional even number). He also says that words should be chosen 'somewhat inadvertently' so as to blend precision and vagueness into the 'grey song' which he values so highly:

> De la musique avant toute chose,
> Et pour cela préfère l'Impair,
> Plus vague et plus soluble dans l'air,
> Sans rien en lui qui pèse ou qui pose.
>
> Il faut aussi que tu n'ailles point
> Choisir tes mots sans quelque méprise:
> Rien de plus cher que la chanson grise
> Où l'Indécis au Précis se joint.

6 B. Cook, ed., *Mallarmé: selected prose poems, essays and letters* (Baltimore, 1956), p. 50. The French is: '. . . la musique et les lettres sont la face alternative, ici élargie vers l'obscur, scintillante là avec certitude, du phénomène que j'appelai l'idée.' Laloy also quotes this passage in an article on the *Prélude à l'Après-midi d'un faune*: see pp. 154–155.

7 The Belgian-born Symbolist poet René Ghil (1862–1925) wrote a *Traité du verbe* in 1886. In it he emphasized the qualities common to certain vowel sounds and emotions, and also established equivalences between vowel

sounds and musical instruments. Some examples are: 'O' - organ; 'E' - harp; 'I' - violins; 'O' - brass; 'U' - flutes. *Traité du verbe*, ed. T. Goruppi (Paris, 1978), p. 60

[8] 'Les arts optiques relèvent de l'œil et uniquement de l'œil.' The poet Jules Laforgue (1860–1887), famous as one of the creators of *vers libre*, was also an art critic for *La Gazette des beaux-arts* and other reviews. The quotation is found in his *Mélanges posthumes* (repr. Geneva, 1979), p. 142.

[9] 'La musique ne fait appel qu'à la sensation. Les sons qu'elle emploie n'ont aucun sens, ni ne peuvent représenter aucun objet. Il semble donc qu'elle dût être, naturellement et dès l'origine, symboliste et impressionniste entre tous les arts.'

[10] Laloy's note: '*Aristoxène de Tarente et la musique de l'antiquité*'. Paris, 1904, repr. Geneva, 1973

[11] Laloy first mentions this idea in the fifth chapter of *Claude Debussy* (1909): see p. 82.

[12] J. Marnold, 'Les *Nocturnes* de Claude Debussy', *Le Courrier musical* (1 May 1902), pp. 129–133. Also see p. 83.

[13] 'De tels accords se suivront comme se suivent les aspects du ciel ou les émotions de notre cœur. Et l'œuvre entière n'aura pas d'autre unité: les mélodies y seront unies d'une parenté secrète, et, au lieù de lutter entre elles par jeu, comme dans la musique classique, elles paraîtront l'une après l'autre comme des sœurs qui se tiennent par la main, différentes de visage et pourtant inséparables. L'œuvre ne sera justifiée que par elle-même; elle portera en elle la raison intérieure de ses détails et de ses accidents; elle sera créatrice de sa propre forme.'

[14] *Le Promenoir des deux amants* (pub. 1910) consists of three settings of Tristan Lhermite. Laloy must be referring to the second and third songs, 'Crois mon conseil, chère Climène' and 'Je tremble en voyant ton visage', which both date from 1910; the first of the set, 'La Grotte', was composed in 1904.

'Claude Debussy's works for the theatre'[1]

La Revue musicale, **vol. 1, no. 2 (1 December 1920), pp. 151–154**

On 30 April 1902, the Opéra-Comique first produced *Pelléas et Mélisande*; a date to remember, for on that day we heard for the first time an opera in which, by a sort of miracle, the most apt expression of feelings accorded constantly with the most perfect harmony.

Since its origins, which go back, as we know, to sixteenth-century Italy, opera had tried to reconcile these two necessities, without ever completely achieving its aim. Monteverdi was the only composer before Debussy who succeeded in uniting what all intervening composers would separate; yet is it not without some sacrifice of one of the two compositional elements: in his first works, such as *Orfeo*, expression, in the last, like *The Coronation of Poppea*, harmony. After him, no other means of adapting the music to the drama was found but to divide the work into two parts: in one the music would be dominated by the words, in the other it would be free of them. On one hand, recitative, under whatever name it was given; on the other, arias or orchestral items in forms as fixed as if the composer had intended them for a concert, not for the theatre. Neither Rameau, more of a symphonist, nor Gluck, more dramatic, rid himself of this division, any more than Mozart, Beethoven, or any nineteenth-century composers, until Wagner.

Wagner was tormented by the concept of unity, and as soon as he began to reflect on his art, he strove to dissolve and weld the different parts together, with great difficulty and great exertion, like Siegfried forging the pieces of his father's sword together in the fire. He did not always succeed, because his impetuous genius sometimes escaped from the prepared moulds and interrupted the flow for edifices which rise up, in isolation, right in the middle of the work and can easily be detached from it: the Ride of the Valkyries, Siegfried's funeral march, the Valkyrie's love duet, the Magic Fire music, the Good Friday music. *Tristan und Isolde* is almost the only place where poetry and music are united, as the composer wished, in a formidable, indissoluble embrace. In spite of the difference in means and the contrasting styles, it can be said in this sense that Debussy is the successor to Wagner, whose influence on modern music he nonetheless had to destroy, and that from afar Pelléas and Mélisande can recognize Tristan and Isolde, even though they are of another time, of another race, and are not innocent.

Wagner's example was certainly not without its uses for Debussy who sets himself the same problem, but resolves it through a procedure which did not occur and could not have occurred to Wagner. Wagner has an organizing mind: materials are furnished to him separately, he selects them, fashions and assembles them, in such a way that for example a vocal line which only obeys the words is inserted into an orchestral texture rich in vigorous motifs, where music reclaims all its rights. Debussy is intuitive: an unaccompanied melody, an unprepared chord contain all the complexity of the thoughts he was able to amass in them as a result of patient retouching, like the Far Eastern worker crouching over a piece of jade which he scoops out, thins, hollows, reduces in size, using its very resistance to give it the luxurious suppleness of living bodies or flowering stems.[2]

Debussy had forerunners. The French composers who wrote for the theatre towards the end of the nineteenth century, notably Gounod and Massenet, had been able to free themselves from the rigid cadences of recitative and produce a vocal line which, following the natural inflections of speech more closely, also lent itself to delicate modulations. But they still only used this new form as recitative, between the arias, which they constructed in the old way. The Russian composers went much further. One of them, Dargomïzhsky, composed an entire opera, *The Stone Guest*, on the prosody of the words, without ever putting in a definite melody. Mussorgsky started from the same principle, but his profound musical instinct led him to find inflections which were both the most apt and the most melodious, and *Boris Godunov* certainly is, as the delightful Charles Bordes said to me one day, 'the grandfather of *Pelléas*'. *Boris Godunov* is unfortunately uneven, and one act, the one which takes place in Poland, does contain undeniable banalities. Were it not for these weaknesses, and quite a number of oversights in the writing which Rimsky-Korsakov clumsily corrected, *Boris Godunov* would be the equal of *Pelléas et Mélisande*, which it surpasses in the grandeur of its characters and its lofty religious sentiments.

After *Pelléas*, what could Debussy have given us? Another *Pelléas*? That is what he was being asked for on all sides, and success would have been assured. He refused, or rather he declared that he was incapable of repeating himself. He had worked for ten years on *Pelléas*, from 1892 to 1902. As soon as it had been performed, he undertook to set two tales by Edgar Allan Poe for the stage: *Le*

Diable dans le beffroi and *La Chute de la maison Usher*. The first gave rise to a disorder of gesture allowing expression of the comic imagination which would later inspire 'Minstrels' or 'General Lavine' in the volumes of the *Préludes*. The second was presented by the storyteller himself in the form of a symphony of forebodings, which is constantly reinforced until the catastrophe restores calm along with mourning. Interrupted then taken up again in turn, neither of these projects was to be completed; only the scenarios were written, the music was never drafted.[3]

Debussy then intended to compose a music drama on the romance of *Tristan et Yseult*, as he had come to understand it through Monsieur Joseph Bédier's admirable book. For the two tales of Edgar Allan Poe, he had wanted to do without collaborators. This time, he had too many. Joseph Bédier and Claude Debussy were enough. Other personalities intervened, years were wasted checking their abilities and discussing their rights, so that writer and composer both lost patience, and the work which had barely been sketched was abandoned.[4] It is a great pity, for it would have been good to see Debussy measure swords with Wagner, and give our nation's music a legend which Monsieur Bédier had already reintegrated in his poetry.

Le Martyre de saint Sébastien, by Monsieur Gabriele D'Annunzio, was produced for the first time on the stage of the Châtelet on 22 May 1911, with music by Claude Debussy. The Italian poet, who was at the time receiving the hospitality of French literature, could not have paid more worthy homage to our country's musical art. Why did the play, organized by an artist whose taste is not at all French, have to sink under pomp and excessive length?[5] It was only the following year, when the new score, extricated from the exuberant poem, was performed by itself at a concert given by the Société Musicale Indépendante, that we were able to appreciate its pure, sublime beauty. However, as this was only incidental music, the composer had written a special piece, as free of contours as it was exact in proportions, for each of the episodes reserved for treatment by him, and this may be why some of his former admirers, who were always waiting for another *Pelléas*, were disappointed. The truth is that the music of *Le Martyre*, which is more accomplished than that of *Pelléas*, is no less animated, and radiates a celestial clarity which was foreign to the entirely human and earthly *Pelléas*.

In the last years of his life, Debussy intended to transform *Le Martyre de saint Sébastien* into an opera. The new management of the Opéra encouraged him in this, and Monsieur D'Annunzio very gallantly gave *carte blanche* for the revisions and cuts. The rather thankless work on the text was interrupted by a relapse of the illness which was to take the great composer's life. We will never know in what form or style Debussy would have composed his second opera: it remains shrouded in the same mystery that surrounds Beethoven's tenth symphony.

He also gave the stage two ballets: one, whose title is *Khamma*, dates from 1912 and belongs to an English dancer, who has never danced it; the other is the ballet *Jeux*, written on a scenario by Monsieur Nijinsky and produced for the first time at the Théâtre des Champs-Elysées on 15 May 1913. The music of these two works is delightful, but is related more to the symphonic poem than to ballet properly so called. Finally, the Théâtre du Vaudeville produced last year, in its all too brief lyric season, *L'Enfant prodigue*, *La Damoiselle élue* and *La Boîte à joujoux* as a 'ballet for children', which was not the composer's original intention.

Notes

1 'Le théâtre de Claude Debussy'

2 'Debussy est intuitif: une mélodie sans accompagnement, un accord sans préparation contiennent toute la complexité des pensées qu'il a su y accumuler par l'effet d'un patient travail de retouches, pareil à l'ouvrier d'Extrême-Orient penché sur le morceau de jade qu'il évide, amincit, creuse, amenuise, utilisant sa résistance même pour lui prêter la molle souplesse des corps vivants ou des tiges fleuries.'

3 Debussy himself wrote the libretto of both *La Chute de la maison Usher* and *Le Diable dans le beffroi*. Musical sketches do in fact exist for both works: a few pages for *Le Diable dans le beffroi*, more substantial in the case of *La Chute de la maison Usher*. In *Claude Debussy* (rev. ed. 1944), pp. 109–110, Laloy writes about Debussy's work on these two Poe projects: '[He] was thinking, he told me one day, of the piano with no keyboard known as the cymbalon to characterize the mocking demon in the first tale. But the second tale, divested of any lineaments of intrigue, could not engage a dramatic plot. Debussy understood, and abandoned both.'

4 Debussy wanted to write a work based on *Le Roman de Tristan* as adapted by the eminent medievalist Joseph Bédier in 1900. (In 1908 he signed a contract with the Metropolitan Opera in New York for this project, together with *La Chute de la maison Usher* and *Le Diable dans le beffroi*.) It seems to have been Laloy who introduced the two men: 'I was on friendly terms with Bédier, formerly one of my masters at the Ecole Normale Supérieure, and I informed him of the project, which pleased him greatly. The scholar and the composer became acquainted; each as discreet and sensitive as the other,

they understood one another immediately.' *Claude Debussy* (rev. ed. 1944), p. 110

Debussy began work on the *Tristan* project with Gabriel Mourey in 1907, but an associate of Bédier held the theatrical rights and when no compromise could be reached it was abandoned. See *La Musique retrouvée*, p. 175.

[5] The 'artiste dont le goût n'a rien de français' mentioned here was the Russian-Jewish dancer Ida Rubinstein, who played the part of the saint. The performance lasted over five hours: see p. 225.

Debussy and Satie

There was a strong antipathy between Laloy and Satie. Laloy described him as 'very thin-skinned and touchy' and 'one of my surest enemies.' However, despite the bitterness of Satie's insults, Laloy's writings about Satie are mostly quite balanced.

La Musique retrouvée, pp. 258–262

Debussy, at this time [1913], made him known to me, and we met from time to time at his table, exchanging bitter-sweet remarks and side-long glances which I really think Debussy enjoyed. An angry yet indissoluble friendship linked him to Satie. Or rather, it was one of those family hatreds which are exacerbated by repeated stubborn clashes, but without destroying the sympathy between the characters, which is due to their common origin.[1] It was like seeing two brothers, placed by the events of their existence in very different conditions, one rich and the other poor; the first welcoming, but proud of his superiority, and ready to make it felt, the second unhappy beneath a joking mask, paying his share in pranks to amuse his host, hiding his humiliation; always on the alert with each other, but unable to stop loving each other dearly. Brothers in music, rivals as musicians.

Usually only one copy exists of a man and especially a of great man. But at times nature makes a mistake and makes the same negative do double service. Then the proofs are different in their degree of clarity; one is overdeveloped and dark and the other is transparent; here, all the lines are distinct; there, they vanish into a blur; sometimes there are even gaps or smudges which still do not prevent us from recognising, in the sacrificed proof, the resemblance to the other, so charming in its delicacy and nuances. Debussy and Satie received the same genius. The nature of the former, like a favourable leaf-mould, gave him rich nourishment and produced an abundant flowering. In the mind of the latter, genius was in difficulties, reduced to growing on stony ground and barely finding a way up to the light, producing fruit which had no pulp but was permeated with a rare flavour, which would one day be the subject of discussion among connoisseurs.

Satie had a deep admiration for Debussy which made him determined to lie low, or if he risked attempting something musical, to make it seem like a joke. Jean Cocteau, in *Le Coq et l'arlequin*, dating from 19 March 1918, reports a remark of his that Debussy reported to him: 'Take care, a tree in the scenery does not bend because a character comes on stage.' He meant that music, like scenery, can keep its balance, and thereby only become more touching because it is more musical. 'That,' adds Jean Cocteau, 'is the aesthetic of *Pelléas*.'[2] It would have been the aesthetic of *La Princesse Maleine*, if Erik Satie had carried out his project of setting to music this other play by Maeterlinck, and then, by role reversal, he would have been the one to speak gratefully of advice given by Claude Debussy. The two friends were in agreement about what must be done, because an identical instinct pushed them to it, and that is why their words, which had no effect on anyone else, were fruitful for them alone, and served to clarify their shared understanding and intentions.

But Satie, once he knew Debussy was working on *Pelléas* and had obtained the author's permission – which he had not realized – cast aside *La Princesse Maleine*. 'Old fellow,' he said to himself, 'all you can do now is keep quiet.' He did indeed keep quiet for nearly twenty years. But when he dared, still very cautiously and modestly, to risk expressing some of his thoughts in public, certain choice minds were astonished by them and, won over to his cause, lavished encouragement on him. Georges Auric, who had just left the Montpellier music school for the Paris Conservatoire and the Schola Cantorum, expressed his admiration in a letter to him, and became the first composer of his generation to approach him.[3] Jean Cocteau made his acquaintance at about the same time, immediately discerned the quality of his art, and wholeheartedly devoted himself to his success through one of those spiritual adoptions which are not the only, but one of the finest claims to the gratitude of artists by this poet who was doubly creative, in both his own works and others', which he inspires and loves – as I have witnessed – more than his own: a privilege of the highest intelligence and which always, even before he realized it, made him a Christian.

Debussy was not a Christian, any more than Satie. The only difference is that he did not conceal his pride. Moreover, in the years when Satie saw the first rays of glory, which were also the years of the war, Debussy was sorrowful, overwhelmed by events, consumed by an illness whose slow poison nothing could stop, absorbed in bitter thoughts and less capable than ever of an effort of goodwill or a kind word of praise. When concerts devoted to his own works were being organized for Satie, Debussy could not go, as he was already confined to his room, and stories of their success left him suspicious, believing that there had been intrigue and perhaps a practical joke. Satie understood the feeling which Debussy intimated to him, and was embittered by it to the point of writing him a letter which was almost offensive. Debussy received it in bed, where he had remained for several weeks and was soon to die. His unsteady hands crumpled the paper on the coverlet and suddenly tore it up. 'Sorry,' he murmured like a child about to be scolded, with tears in his eyes. I held a grudge against Satie for causing such distress, though he probably did not foresee that it would be so cruel. It was only after his death, which occurred seven years later, that I forgave him, having learned from his friends how much he himself must have suffered when others were fêting him and the approval which mattered most in the world to him was withheld. This, through the fault of both, was the lamentable end of their friendship.

Notes

1 'Debussy, à cette époque, me l'avait fait connaître, et nous nous sommes parfois rencontrés à sa table, échangeant des propos aigres-doux et d'obliques regards dont je crois bien que Debussy s'amusait. Une amitié rageuse et cependant indissoluble l'unissait à Satie. Ou plutôt, c'était une de ces haines familiales qui s'exaspèrent par le choc répété de travers incompatibles, sans détruire pourtant la sympathie des caractères, due à la communauté de l'origine.'

2 Cocteau said that Satie was warning Debussy against Wagner: 'Il prévint Debussy contre Wagner. «Attention, lui disait-il, un arbre du décor ne se convulse pas parce qu'un personnage entre en scène.» C'est l'esthétique de *Pelléas*.' *Le Coq et l'arlequin: notes autour de la musique* (1919), p. 57. Laloy's attitude to Cocteau is complex: one aspect of it is that in an article entitled 'Ce que je pense d'Erik Satie' ('What I think of Erik Satie'), *Le Courrier musical*, vol. 28, no. 11 (1 June 1926), p. 301, he takes Cocteau to task for overstating Satie's influence on Debussy's æsthetic. Laloy also thought that Satie's friends, including Cocteau, talked too much to him about Debussy, 'thus creating a sort of rivalry between them in which Satie was beaten in advance'.

3 It has not been possible to find this letter, which is likely to date from about 1913.

Advice on playing Debussy's music

This is the last chapter, complete, of Laloy's biography of Debussy: it deals with performance practice. Laloy evidently asked Debussy to approve what he had written, for in a letter dated 27 July 1909, Debussy wrote: 'There's no need to alter anything in the advice you've given for playing my music. It remains simply to read and understand.'[1]

Claude Debussy (1909), pp. 95–98

The various recommendations which follow are addressed to performers – virtuosi or otherwise – who might be puzzled by the innovativeness of an art which as yet cannot be learned from a teacher. The brevity of these remarks will be their excuse.

The first requirement for playing such music is that it should not be considered difficult. Those who hear only dissonances in it, or search fruitlessly for the melody which is so obvious to others, must be advised to continue with their meditations until they receive grace, or else to give up, and abstain.

When the performer has sensed what is there, he must not exert himself to put in what is not there, and particularly not 'effects'. The quality which matters most is unity of tone.[2] Anything which disturbs it, *portamenti*, interruptions of the rhythm, arbitrary retardations or *accelerandi*, is not only unnecessary, but disastrous. Moreover, it would be better to mistake completely the spirit of a piece, for example to play 'Pagodes' playfully, or 'La Soirée dans Grenade' in the manner of a bullfighter on guard, than abruptly to break the spell with a jab or a grimace.

Conductors will do well to forget Berlioz and Wagner as completely as this can be done; no contrasts here, and, above all, none of those sentimental outbursts in which our instrumentalists – corrupted by their repertoire – unfortunately indulge as soon as they are asked to be expressive. Equally it is unnecessary to seek to modify the perspective, as one so willingly does for the Classics; brandishers of the baton draw out at will such and such a timbre from the orchestral mass into the foreground: one conductor prefers the French horn where another favours the 'cello; a third takes it into his head to seek out the clarinet, which has only one note to play, and thus he in turn has become a master. We must persuade ourselves that here, as, it must be added, in any properly orchestrated work, each detail is in its place and must remain there; each detail has been calculated for the total effect, and the effect would be compromised by the slightest alteration of the balance.

Pianists must give up the presumption of 'bringing out the tune'; when thoroughly understood, the melody will take on by itself the slight prominence which is needed; to insist would be to fall into Romantic affectation.[3] But pianists must no more draw attention to what they quite wrongly call runs, that is those rapid figurations whose function is to envelop the main tunes, to trace a harmony for them with lines, according to the very character of the piano, and to give vivacity to the background. It would be better to blur these patterns, even to let slip some wrong notes, as amateurs do, than to overcome the difficulties they present in a triumphant manner, and look for applause by preening like a gymnast. What is true of Debussy is, moreover, just as true of Schumann, Chopin and Bach, and of all who wrote for the keyboard. But one thing is more particular: often notes are accompanied by a sign which was quite rarely used up to now, which is a small dash. Some people think they must detach these notes, others think they must intensify them; but what is asked for is a transparent sonority; it can be achieved by a clean and never harsh attack, which is prolonged by the pedal, with the finger leaving the key immediately.[4]

Singers must, first of all, be concerned with singing. As is well known, they have lost the habit. A very widespread prejudice would have it that, in all modern music, it is only necessary to 'speak', with as little voice as possible, without even observing the correctness of the intervals. This is an absurdity. A melody is not to be called formless because it breaks away from Classical squareness, does not fall back onto the equilibrium of a cadence every two bars, follows the rhythm of the text and does not distort the accent of the words. Even when the melody remains motionless on one note, the purpose is not to imitate the intonation of speech, which is endlessly variable. It is to paint the half-light of contemplation and silence by means of a thoroughly musical metaphor. The character of these lines persists, even if the support of the words is removed. Far from obliterating them or breaking them into pieces, care must be taken to sustain and nurture them.

Finally, euphony is required throughout: care must be taken that bows do not grate, that reeds do not snap, flutes do not rasp, the brass does not blare out, piano strings are not ripped out, vocal cords not worn bare. In order to guard against such failures of charm, it is advisable that the artist develop the habit of listening to himself; that orchestral rehearsals be held in a hall where the acoustic is not too stern; that the pianist, paying attention to his touch, should feel the sound in his fingertips; that the singer never distort his voice; that they all, in short, maintain softness in strength, and strength in softness. Everything must follow on and hold together. This music must be bathed in harmony; it will not tolerate any ugliness, even intelligent ugliness.

Notes

1 Several paragraphs from Laloy's chapter are incorporated without acknowledgement in Long (1970), p. 20. However, the same passages are acknowledged in Long (1960), pp. 37–38.

2 See p. 82, where Laloy explains what he means by unity of tone.

3 A review Laloy wrote of a performance by Harold Bauer is revealing in this connection. Laloy said that he thought Bauer's interpretation of the quieter movements of the *Estampes* and *Children's corner* was 'somewhat weighed down by excessive contrasts, by melodies unnecessarily brought out, by untimely pedal points, memories of a Romanticism which is familiar to the artist, but out of place here.' *S.I.M.* (January 1909), p. 72

4 'Mais voici ce qui est plus particulier: souvent des notes sont accompagnées d'un signe dont l'emploi était assez rare jusqu'ici, et qui est une petite barre. Les uns croient devoir les détacher, d'autres les renforcer; mais ce qui est demandé, c'est une sonorité transparente; on peut l'obtenir par une attaque franche et sans dureté, que la pédale prolongera, le doigt quittant la touche aussitôt.'

Though some ' – ' markings in Debussy's piano music must certainly just mean an accent, in the majority of cases Laloy's explanation fits. Not only is it often possible to do what he describes, but the technique produces a memorable, ringing sound. It seems appropriate to apply the technique to octaves and chords as well as single notes, as in these passages from 'La cathédrale engloutie' and 'Jardins sous la pluie':

*R: the passage as played by Debussy in a recording on Welte-Mignon piano roll (Durand-Costallat Edition)

'La cathédrale engloutie', *Préludes* I, bb. 5–13

'Jardins sous la pluie', *Estampes*, bb. 147–157

After Debussy's death

No substantial obituary by Laloy has come to light, but this short paragraph was published in the month after Debussy died. It appeared in the polemical Italian periodical *Ars nova*, founded by the composer Alfredo Casella.[1]

Ars nova (April 1918), p. 4

Today we can determine to what race of artists he belongs. To the most pure of all, that which in its art is capable only of love, and is unaware of hatred, combat, violence and ugliness. Among composers, Josquin des Prés, Palestrina, François Couperin, Handel, Mozart were of this race, and Debussy is particularly close to the last of these, through an equal privilege of innocence and clarity: both have the power to cast a limpid serenity over everything they touch, and their minds spontaneously rise upward towards peace and joy.

A year after Debussy's death, Laloy published a longer tribute in *Excelsior*, under the title 'Un anniversaire. Claude Debussy.' This is an extract from it.

Excelsior (25 March 1919), p. 4

That he was a great composer, no one disputes today. But he was more, because his mind maintained subtle analogies with the visual arts and contemporary poetry, and fulfilled beyond all hopes the wishes of a period which was anxious about the future. No artist was more strongly opposed to preaching and dogma. None led an existence which was more withdrawn from the world, more contemptuous of all annunciation, explanation, even discussion. None, however, had more fervent disciples, whom often he did not know; none exerted greater influence over minds; none, although he gave no tuition, better deserved the name of master.[2]

Notes

1 Laloy's paragraph appeared at the end of an article by Alfredo Casella, 'Claude Debussy', *Ars nova* (Rome, April 1918), pp. 1–4. Casella commented: 'It seems to me that this opinion, which I unreservedly share, admirably defines the "human" value of the great French composer's work . . . ' Casella's article and Laloy's tribute appeared some years later in *The monthly musical record*, vol. 63 (January 1933), p. 3, in an English translation by R. Capell.

2 The day after this article appeared, on 26 March 1919, *Excelsior* carried an account of a gathering to mark the first anniversary of Debussy's death, on which occasion Laloy gave a short speech.

> Debussy's friends gathered yesterday before the tomb of the great composer, at Passy cemetery, to commemorate the anniversary of his death. Among the deeply affected and contemplative assembly: Messieurs Alfred Bruneau, Théodore Dubois, Paul Dukas, Mesdames Marguerite Carré, Croiza, Messicurs Florent Schmitt, Roger-Ducasse, André Caplet, Ruhlmann, Francelle Albers, Vieuille, Arturo Vigna, André Hellé, Inghelbrecht, Samazeuilh, Pierre de Bréville, Gabriel Grovlez.
>
> Our distinguished collaborator Louis Laloy thanked Debussy's friends and followers in these terms:
>
> 'I am charged by Madame Debussy with thanking you for coming loyally to our sad meeting-place. That is the extent of my mission. If it were a matter of pronouncing the funeral oration of the great artist who has left us, or even simply of telling of the admiration and regret which he inspires in us, other voices better authorized than mine should be heard here. What would I tell you, moreover, that you do not already know, and is not the emotion which unites us before this tomb one which is to be collected piously in meditation and silence?
>
> Last year, at the same time, in circumstances which further aggravated the misfortune of losing him, we accompanied him to an abode which was not even the final one. It is only quite recently that he has been able to find rest here, in the place chosen by him from the first signs of the illness which was to take him away. As you see, no monument yet marks his burial-place. At least, we have heaped flowers there, a very modest tribute to his glory, but the very simplicity of which was designed to please him. Once again, gentlemen, thank you!'

A year later, Laloy published another commemorative article: 'Un anniversaire', *Excelsior* (29 March 1920), p. 4.

'The Debussy monument'[1]

In 1932 two monuments were erected in tribute to Debussy, one in Paris and the other at his birthplace, Saint-Germain-en-Laye. (See Plates 5–7.) They were inaugurated on 17 June, when a Claude Debussy Festival was held. Laloy's article discusses that concert and the monument in Paris, which was constructed by Jan and Noël Martel after the death of the sculptor Antoine Bourdelle. The monument's site is a square called the *Jardin Claude Debussy*, close to the Bois de Boulogne and the house where Debussy lived.[2]

Notes begin on p. 121.

***La Revue des deux mondes*, vol. 102, no. 10 (15 July 1932), pp. 460–467**

On 29 March 1918, a few friends[3] accompanied the mortal remains of a great musican from the avenue du Bois-de-Boulogne[4] to Père-Lachaise cemetery. On 17 June 1932, in the presence of the official representatives of Paris, of France and foreign nations, the Claude Debussy monument was inaugurated.

The dead move away from us rapidly. But we have the power to bring them back to us. We might think they are hiding in the early days, as if they were ashamed to have died. More than anyone else, Debussy escaped us, because our hearts were troubled. News of the war was bad. If the breach opened up by a massive attack on our battlefront was not healed, the capital would be in danger. So that we would feel it, a long-range cannon from time to time sent shells which fell at random, on a tram shelter, a garret, a hospital ward, on children in the street, before burying worshippers under the ruins of a church where they had gone to listen to Good Friday Vespers and the Chanteurs de Saint-Gervais.[5]

As in a bad dream I notice the coffin near the piano, I recognize, beneath their uniform, recruited musicians who are surprised at my own uniform. The door was opening and closing all the time. People did not know where to put their flowers.

Once the procession was formed, the Minister of Education took his place at the head. In front of me, side by side, the two conductors of our great symphonic societies, Camille Chevillard and Monsieur Gabriel Pierné, walked in silence, after so many concerts where Debussy's music had found inflection and harmony through their attentive care. The sky was overcast. Was that rumbling in the distance a storm, a projectile exploding, army cannon? Along the broad avenues, we met only military vehicles, and the passers-by, on the footpaths, hurried past without a glance. But the uphill streets of Montmartre were alive with people as usual. Children, in order to make room for us, lined up along the gutter, their eyes wide. Shopkeepers made inquiry of each other, on their doorstep, and read the pennants attached to the wreaths: 'It seems', they said, 'he was a musician.'

At the cemetery, there were not more than about thirty of us,[6] but crowded, squeezed together by the graves; the opening of the temporary tomb could barely be seen between the headstones.[7] It had seemed superfluous, considering the circumstances, to deliver any address. There was one, however, in the name, I think, of the Societé des Auteurs. I could not listen to it, as I was busy collecting my unmanageable thoughts which were flying to bid a last farewell to the friend who did not reply.

French in taste, in mind and in heart, the war had not made him, as it had other 'intellectuals' of that time, assume a blazing patriotism that was new and slightly awkward. He had not, like Saint-Saëns, had to return a decoration to the German Emperor, nor like Anatole France spectacularly abjure the error of international socialism. 'Long live Rameau! Down with Gluck!' This enthusiastic cry was hurled long ago, not far from me in the courtyard of the Schola where Charles Bordes had just introduced us to the French composer's exquisite *La Guirlande*.[8] How many learned music-lovers had not criticized this cry as an outrage! How many others, up to the time of the war, had scolded or lectured him, because he lacked respect for Wagner! In art, he was a nationalist and was to be so to the point of intolerance. He loved Rameau as a spiritual father. He defended the territory where he had his ground, despite the recriminations of these bad neighbours, unwitting accomplices in the foreign invasion.[9]

Detained at first a long way from him, I had been struck, when I had been able to see him again at the end of 1915, by his extremely dejected mood, the sad look in his eyes. He had just completed his *Noël des enfants qui n'ont plus de maison*,[10] a heart-rending lament of the innocents after the fires and massacres with which Belgium had been punished for its loyalty. We made no other allusion to the crime that day: his music sufficed. Neither did we speak of military operations, but of Reims cathedral, and Joan of Arc. The idea had come to him for a cantata in which her pity, her courage, her pain would be heard, and in the flames of torment her prophetic faith announcing for the future, after other ordeals, the salvation of the country. He asked me to write the poem for him, and from then on this was the principal, if not the only, topic of our all too rare conversations. He would read in a deep voice, reflect, make a note about orchestration or tempo in the margin of the manuscript, ask me for a different rhythm, a repetition, often retracting one of his own ideas, changing course after an experiment, walking around the draft and looking at it from every angle, faithful to this method of patient conjecture and progressive accommodation which finally resulted in the most precise adherence between thought and style. It was during one of these periods of study that he came to say to me, about a strident trumpet call which he had first suggested then abandoned: 'I mistrust the exceptional.'[11] That was the last piece of advice I received from him. I would like to convey it to posterity.

But the war went on. He suffered from it as from a wound which would not heal. This enduring grief most certainly contributed to the change in his health, which was no doubt secretly brewing, but only manifested the following year in symptoms which were serious and soon alarming. He left Paris, in search of a milder climate, and when he came back he was only capable of receiving me lying down, not moving, not complaining, responding in a scarcely audible voice or with a pale smile to our reassuring lies; he was already half drowned by the darkness and silence into which he would soon disappear.[12] I was not present for the inventory of his manuscripts and was only to learn ten years later that he left a sketch, for voice and piano, of our *Ode à la France*.[13]

Never since he passed away had I felt him as close to us as on the luminous afternoon when the whiteness of that votive marble glittered for the first time. The previous day, in the meeting-rooms of the Ministry of Arts, he would certainly have thanked Monsieur Paul Léon with all his heart and congratulated the artists, Monsieur Krettly and his three companions of the bow, Madame Ninon Vallin, Messieurs Alfred Cortot and Jacques Thibaud, for this select programme which brought together, in a perfect performance, two works not of his youth, but from the beginning of his mature period, the elegiac and whimsical String quartet, the *Chansons de Bilitis* in their subtle tenderness and the Sonata for piano and violin, written in the last years of his life, which was even more delicately graceful in its crystal clarity.

The Martel brothers' monument is very noble in conception. It seeks to celebrate the œuvre, not the man, through the two figures of female musicians, one carrying the lyre and the other lightly bowing the strings of the violin, stationed on either side of the central panel, whose bas-reliefs can be deciphered like hieroglyphics: Saint Sebastian in his armour, Mélisande's hair, the Faun with his slanting flute, the waves of the sea engulfing the cathedral. To lessen the rigidity of the stone, a mirror of water repeats the image, softening it with faint reflections. A happy, and necessary, allusion to a music which was on intimate terms with springs, grottos and the sea.

The city ends there, on an esplanade separating it from the Bois de Boulogne, not far from the house where he lived, sheltered from material cares, between the garden where he used to walk and read his newspaper at the end of the day, and the study where he kept his Japanese etchings, his favourite faience. The window had a view of the slope of the rampart, the clouds of steam indicating that a train was passing in the cutting of the Ceinture.[14] They brought noise with them, but he had grown used to it, stopping for a moment, if he was at the piano, without losing his train of thought. He was a home-lover; did not like voyages, because the best travelling could be done in his mind.

Javanese dancers from an international exhibition inspired his 'Pagodes'. Between the stalls and thickets of a country fair, beneath a cloudy sky, listening to the echoes of distant fanfares, he dreamed his *Nocturnes*. From a beach overrun with crowds of bathers, he brought back the poem of *La Mer*. Spain sings in his *Ibéria*, although he never went further than Saint-Jean-de-Luz.[15]

The landscape surrounding his monument is like the one he discovered when he left off from his reading or his music paper, and I believe he would have been pleased to choose it for an even longer stay. From the rostrum on which his friends took their places, having become members of the Committee magnificently organized by Monsieur Gabriel Astruc, he would, beside us, have relished the fresh breeze which shook the dark curtain of trees with a pleasant murmur and, on the other side, the almost seaside-like gaiety of the houses decked with yellow blinds and even, in front of us, that stonemasons' building-site on a vacant lot, recalling the suburbs. Nature was there, but near to the city, in the form of a wood which invited strollers. A surface luxury decorated, but did not erase, the meagre ground of wretchedness and toil where genius thrusts down its most solid roots.

An official monument is occasionally well placed. An official speech can depart from banality. Monsieur François Latour, President of the Municipal Council, laid claim for the Ile-de-France not only to the composer, who was born in Saint-Germain-en-Laye, but also to his music, worthy of a noble, serene land.[16] Messieurs Paul Léon, the Director of the Arts, and Jean Mistler, the Under-Secretary of State, one more philosophical and the other more literary, were able to define their admiration in apt words. The President of the Republic honoured the ceremony with his presence and, better still, Monsieur Albert Lebrun took the liveliest interest in it, equally attentive to the words and the music: clarinets of the Republican Guard, as agile as the violins of a symphony orchestra in that vibration of light around the ascension to Paradise in *Saint Sébastien*; choruses from the *Chansons de Charles d'Orléans*, gathered up by the passing wind; and, above all, also heralding *Saint Sébastien*, those melancholy fanfares.

In the evening, at the Théâtre des Champs-Elysées, the composer's glory was celebrated through his works, and again this time, amidst members of the Government and foreign diplomats, the highest magistrate of our Republic stayed until the end of the concert, which he appreciated as a connoisseur. Five conductors, one of whom was far away, succeeded one another. From Basel, indeed, by radio telephony, came the *Prélude à l'Après-midi d'un faune*, conducted by Monsieur Weingartner. The intention was excellent. I must admit that the result was disappointing. Such delicate vibrations cannot with impunity be plucked out of the air, to be put back later, after a journey over waves of a completely different nature. The flute shelled off reedy sounds such as would put even the memory of the nymphs to flight, the violins grated, the horns disappeared.

Monsieur Ph. Gaubert, at the beginning of the evening, gave us a most supple and musically intelligent reading of another part of that unfinished cathedral, *Le Martyre de saint Sébastien*: it was the first tableau, with its doleful prayer, the insidious menace of the fire without flames, the pure faith which subdues it, the miracle and his cries of joy, as if the sky were opening: lofty music bursting forth in white pillars which reach up to a gently radiant rose-window.

I did not listen to it without remorse. After the first performance, in 1911, in which Madame Ida Rubinstein had such a fine success of expressive gesture and living imagery, Claude Debussy remarked like all of us that the music was too short in comparison to the recited poem and was not well adapted to it, and he formed the idea of revising his work so that everything in it was sung. The text had to be abridged and revised. We were to carry out this work together. With his customary generosity, Gabriele D'Annunzio gave us full discretion. Through my fault, the work had scarcely begun when war broke out.[17] We were far from expecting war, and even further from anticipating that one of us would not see the end of it.

How touching Monsieur Gabriel Pierné was to see as well as to hear, conducting the *Nocturnes*, drawing out the right sonority with an attentive arm, effortlessly detaching the phrase from its envelope of chords so as to let it expand freely, and later, during the applause at the end of the piece, motionless in front of his music stand, with his black coat hitched at the shoulders and his head bent, caught up in an emotional state where the applause did not reach him, because it was at the same time the emotion of a musician and a friend! They were, in 1901, a revelation which charmed some people from the outset, but surprised others to the point where they suspected heresy, these three landscapes suspended between earth and sky and dematerialized, singing clouds, imaginary fairs, elusive sirens, mirages of music. Thirty years later, it is still this strange, delicious excitement, of a dream one dared not hope for.

Likewise *Pelléas*, where Monsieur Inghelbrecht, at the head of the excellent orchestra, was able to highlight the inflections with intense fervour. It was the fourth act, which was missing only the scene where the child Yniold smiles at some sheep being led to the abattoir; it is omitted in the theatre to avoid, I think, a change of scenery; it is a great pity, for the music is charming, and between Golaud's furious jealousy and the confession made during the nocturnal assignation beside the fountain, it consitutes a necessary diversion with its sense of frightened innocence and evil foreboding. The interpreters were those of the first performance, except Monsieur Bourdin who, despite his fine voice, cannot erase the memory of Jean Périer in the role of Pelléas. It is a great absurdity to fall to his knees with his hand on his heart and yell to Mélisande, 'I love you!' In spite of himself, these words escape from Pelléas, and she replies, so softly that he hardly hears her, 'I love you, too'. It is a secret which they dared not admit to themselves and is finally torn from them by this last, collusive, dangerous night. At this spot Madame Mary Garden was able to find the murmur, as though astonished to be heard, that the composer wanted in agreement with the poet, but made the mistake, in the preceding scene, of sobbing out loud, without regard for the music, and making Arkël carry her off, convulsed and weeping, as if to detract attention from his phrase, which is the only one that should conclude the scene: 'If I were God, I would have pity on the hearts of men.' Monsieur Vieuille, in this role, and Monsieur Dufranne, in that of Golaud, remain what they always were, one admirable for his wisdom and pity, the other for his naive anguish and rough goodness.

Pelléas, like the *Nocturnes*, was and remains a revelation, not of another world but of ourselves, like a sudden flash of lightning in the night of our hearts. Except for the first attempts and later a few pieces of work done on commission, each Debussy work remains unique in its genre, because it always has a firm objective, chosen through thought, observed, studied, meditated on, macerated to the point of complete dissolution and transmutation of the substance into musical form. After which, there was no reason to return to it.[18]

When this drama, defended by Albert Carré and saved by André Messager, carried off a victory which surprised Debussy more than anyone, for several years those who applauded this success besieged his door, asking him to give them another *Pelléas*. But he turned a deaf ear: 'If I wanted to,' he said to me in a weary, plaintive voice, 'I wouldn't succeed.'[19]

The disappointment was keen, for these petitioners, when three years later a symphony concert introduced them to *La Mer*. They did not recognize the author of *Pelléas*, did not acknowledge that he might break his word to them at that point, rejected this work because it exceeded the expected density. Their excuse, if yet they were not capable of reading the score, is that the conductor, himself caught unawares, could not extricate himself from this closely meshed net, in which he could not open up any chinks or call up air.[20]

This time, thanks to Monsieur Toscanini, *La Mer* received the honours of the evening. He is an infallible musician and a virtuoso of the orchestra. Well proportioned in his costume, with an imperious profile but a smile on his lips beneath the fine, downy crown of his grey hair, he walks deliberately onto the stage, simultaneously thanks and calms the cheering audience with a friendly, courteous hand, then, turning towards the instruments, imposes his lucid will on them, with no discussion possible and as though he were playing a game. For the first time, between dawn and midday at sea, the cellos' triplets did not take on the rocking of a barcarolle; they were strictly reduced to an eddy as far as the eye can see, letting the glaucous lustre of the clarinets and horns float to the surface. For the first time, the waves at play did not interrupt their dance for a moment, its joyful, tender refrains twisting round and round. For the first time, the whining of the flutes, like seagulls, soared unceasingly above the storm of the double basses. To these powerful thoughts, presented in an order that was finally clear, the audience responded with a unanimous ovation and since then *La Mer* has been rehabilitated.

This composer is a poet, and his music is pure as poetry can be, with no external constraints and no formulae for its laws, which can only be judged by taste. This is a very French tradition, born of Gregorian chant, the joyful piety of which he revived in his *Le Martyre de saint Sébastien*. The composers of our Renaissance, whose chansons for several voices he studied, Rameau to whom he never stopped paying homage, Couperin whom he adored, these are his direct ancestors. In the last century, Gounod and Massenet are of the same family, but in a collateral line and not without misalliances with the painted beauties of the theatre and with worldly elegance. Debussy is of unalloyed nobility. His music is never frivolous. Lying for him is not forbidden, but impossible. His incorruptible genius refuses all concessions. Whence his magical power. As in the tales that he loved, one would think that he received it from a fairy which had come to his cradle without being seen. There have always been fairies in France leaving their magnificent gifts, if that was their whim, in the most humble dwellings.

Fifty-two French cities and seventy-four foreign cities have their names engraved in the stone of the monument, as they were set down in the lists of subsidies. In countries throughout the world, committees were formed, to give concerts and collect subscriptions. Such is the fame today of 'Claude Debussy, French composer.'[21] This designation, which can be read on all sides of the bas-relief, is certainly the one he would have wished for as the finest of eulogies.

Notes

1 'Le Monument de Claude Debussy'

2 Laloy also wrote a short article about the monument at Saint-Germain-en-Laye, in the commemorative program for the Debussy Festival in 1932. Completed after Bourdelle's death by Aristide Maillol, this monument depicts a young female figure in a meditative pose, and the pedestal is inscribed with a few bars of the *Prélude à l'Après-midi d'un faune*: see Plate 7.

In Saint-Germain, beneath the gentle sky of the Ile-de-France

> [. . .] this expressive figure will be raised on a stele, bearing as its only motto the illustrious name, and the two dates which summed up too brief an existence. The monument will be placed [. . .] on a low rise, around it, shady trees, and a spring: it is a site which he would have liked.

The monument, entitled 'La Musique', is now in the town hall at Saint-Germain-en-Laye.

[3] The friends present included Henri de Régnier, Paul Dukas, André Caplet, Gustave Samazeuilh, Gabriel Pierné, Camille Chevillard and Pasteur Vallery-Radot.

[4] From October 1905 until his death, Debussy lived with his wife Emma at 80, avenue du Bois-de-Boulogne (now avenue Foch). Some sources incorrectly state that Debussy moved there in 1908: the error arises because the street numbering changed in 1907. (The old number was 64.) To add to the confusion, the address can also be given as 24, square du Bois-de-Boulogne.

[5] Les Chanteurs de Saint-Gervais (the Saint-Gervais Singers) were a choir devoted to performing early music. The conductor was Charles Bordes, one of the founders of the Schola Cantorum. Laloy discusses their performances in *La Musique retrouvée*, p. 69.

[6] In *La Musique retrouvée*, p. 229, Laloy recalled:

> In the garden at [Debussy's] home, about fifty people had come, but most slipped away en route, and when we arrived there were only about twenty of us. Through the streets of a Paris which one sensed was anxious, in spite of its brave face, Camille Chevillard and Gabriel Pierné made the whole journey on foot, thus paying composer and friend the most loyal homage.

[7] Debussy's body was buried in Père-Lachaise cemetery on 28 March 1918. In 1919 it was removed to Passy cemetery, for which Debussy had expressed a preference as he found it less depressing than the other cemeteries in Paris, with its trees and birds.

[8] The first two acts of Rameau's opera *La Guirlande ou les fleurs enchantées* (*The garland, or the enchanted flowers*, 1751) were performed on 22 June 1903 in the courtyard of the Schola Cantorum, where a stage had been specially constructed. Laloy describes the audience's enthusiastic reaction in *La Musique retrouvée*, p. 83. Debussy wrote a review of the performance: see Debussy (1987), pp. 89–93.

[9] Debussy and Laloy shared an interest in Rameau, whose music underwent a revival in France in the early decades of the century. Laloy says that Debussy's 'great faith' in Rameau, whom he saw as embodying the true virtues of the French tradition, dates from the performance of *La Guirlande* mentioned here. In 1906, when Laloy stood in for Romain Rolland at the Sorbonne, his course of lectures on music history was to start from eighteenth-century opera, and that was the beginning of his interest in Rameau. It was in connection with these lectures that Debussy wrote his well-known letter, on 10 September 1906:

> I'm delighted about your enthusiasm for Rameau. He deserves it for

all the qualities in his music which ought to have protected us against Gluck's deceitful grandiloquence, Wagner's bombastic metaphysics and the old Belgian angel's [César Franck's] false mysticism; all of which we have clumsily adapted to a manner of understanding [which is] the exact opposite of what that music demands, while we continue, like vain children, to ignore the perfect taste and strict elegance which make up the consummate beauty of Rameau's music. And, unfortunately, where there are signs that we're turning to him again, it's only out of idle curiosity. It's almost impossible for us to realize what we've lost in paying him so little attention, proud as we are of knowledge which was never intended for us and which might even be described as the negation of music . . . I feel a serious revolution is the only thing to get us out of this cosmopolitan stew.

Lesure and Nichols (1987), p. 172

Words in square brackets have been added by the present writer. Debussy's admiration for Rameau was lasting, and he wrote a number of articles about him. Laloy's researches resulted in an article, 'Les Idées de Jean-Philippe Rameau sur la musique', *Le Mercure musical* (15 November 1907), pp. 1144–1159, and the book *Rameau* (Paris, 1908).

10 Here and in *La Musique retrouvée*, probably because he is writing from memory, Laloy gives several incorrect versions of the work's title, which have been corrected in the present volume.

11 'Je me méfie de l'exceptionnel.'

12 In *La Musique retrouvée*, p. 228, Laloy recalls: 'We saw his features become hollow, his eyes grow dull. He was forced to keep to his bedroom, then to stay in bed. "Oh! this bed! this bed!", he would say to us despairingly.'

13 See Laloy's article, 'La Dernière œuvre de Claude Debussy: l'*Ode à la France*' ('Claude Debussy's last work: the *Ode to France*') which is translated on pp. 231–235.

14 The Ceinture (*le chemin de fer de Ceinture*) is the railway line encircling Paris, on the site of the ancient fortifications. The section in question still exists, as part of the RER network.

15 French seaside town near the Spanish border, on the Bay of Biscay. Debussy gave his last performance there in 1917, playing the Sonata for violin and piano with Gaston Poulet.

16 The Ile-de-France, the geographical region lying at the centre of the Paris basin, is famous for its rich artistic heritage, including the palaces of Versailles and Fontainebleau. The region also prides itself on having inspired numerous paintings by Corot, the Barbizon school and the Impressionists.

17 Compare p. 15.

18 '*Pelléas*, comme les *Nocturnes*, était et demeure une révélation non pas d'un autre monde mais de nous-mêmes, comme un éclair soudain dans la nuit de nos cœurs. Sauf les premiers essais et plus tard quelques travaux faits sur commande, chaque œuvre de Debussy reste unique en son genre, parce qu'elle a toujours un objet déterminé, choisi par sa pensée, observé, étudié,

médité, macéré jusqu'à dissolution complète et transmutation de la substance en forme musicale. Après quoi, il n'y avait plus à revenir.'

[19] 'Mais il faisait la sourde oreille: «Quand je le voudrais, me disait-il d'un ton las et plaintif, je n'y arriverais pas.»'

This comment recalls a letter Debussy wrote to André Messager in 1903, saying that if he found himself continuing in the same style he would 'immediately set about growing pineapples at home, taking the view that certainly the most annoying thing is to repeat oneself.'

[20] See Laloy's review of this first performance, which was conducted by Camille Chevillard (pp. 191-193).

[21] 'Claude Debussy, musicien français' was the signature Debussy chose in the last years of his life, as a statement of his patriotism and his loyalty to the French musical tradition.

'Recollection'[1]

Written in the year before World War II began, this short tribute was included in a special issue of *La Revue musicale* entitled 'Autour de Debussy et de Satie' ('Around Debussy and Satie').

La Revue musicale, vol. 19, no. 183 (April–May 1938), pp. 244–245

Claude Debussy died during the war, and it can truly be said that he died of the war. Certainly, twenty years on he would now be in his seventies, and there would be no great chance of his still being of this world. But he could have lived longer, much longer with us, in the full maturity of age and genius. The war is guilty, among so many other crimes, of his premature end. He could not bear that great outburst of violence, nor the threat of seeing not only beings and things destroyed, but also the most precious wealth of our spiritual heritage. This great French composer was a good and true Frenchman.

There was nothing aggressive, blustering or jingoistic about the feeling that bound him to his country. It was, as for his friends and relatives, who still remember and miss it to this day, a discreet, delicate, suspicious and profound friendship.

Overtaken by the outbreak of war during his customary stay in the country, near Arcachon, he returned in December 1914 to the home in the avenue du Bois[-de-Boulogne] where he had spent so many happy days. That is where I saw him again, less frequently than had until then been our custom, because I was otherwise employed. With his mind still just as lucid and rigorous, he worked when he was able to overcome the dejection brought on by thoughts of the calamity, which never left him. From the constant effects of grief, his health, hitherto so robust, suddenly deteriorated. A serious illness declared itself, and forced him to stay in his room, then in bed, after a brief remission followed by an aggravation which soon left no room for hope. The last sound of this world which reached his ears was that of the shells which were bursting over Paris, in a bombardment which began three days before he died.[2]

At the start of the war, the invasion of Belgium and the destruction of its villages inspired the *Noël des enfants qui n'ont plus de maison*. Two years later, he conceived the idea of a more significant work, of which he left us only a sketch, entitled *Ode à la France*.

His whole œuvre deserves this fine name. That is why we must honour it, and assemble around it today, more closely united than ever.

Notes

1 'Souvenir'

2 The first shells (Big Bertha) were launched on Paris on 23 March 1918. Laloy says that in the last days of his life Debussy was disappointed not to be able to attend Rameau's *Castor et Pollux*, which was being performed complete for the first time since its première in 1737:

> The Opéra [. . .] was preparing the revival of *Castor et Pollux*, the *générale* of which was given on Thursday 21 March 1918, in the afternoon, for there were fears of air-raid signals in the evenings. It was one of [Debussy's] last regrets that he could not attend. Trying to smile, he said to me in his faint voice as he saw me leaving, 'A very good day to Monsieur Castor!' Two days later, on the Saturday morning, the bombardment of Paris with long-range cannon began. He heard, in his last days, the lugubrious sound of the explosions, and his suffering ceased on Monday 25 March.
>
> *La Musique retrouvée*, pp. 228–229

Plate 1: Louis Laloy.
Photograph in possession of M. Vincent Laloy. Reproduced by permission.

Plate 2: Debussy and Laloy flying a kite.
Photograph in possession of M. Vincent Laloy.
Reproduced by permission of Bibliothèque Nationale de France.

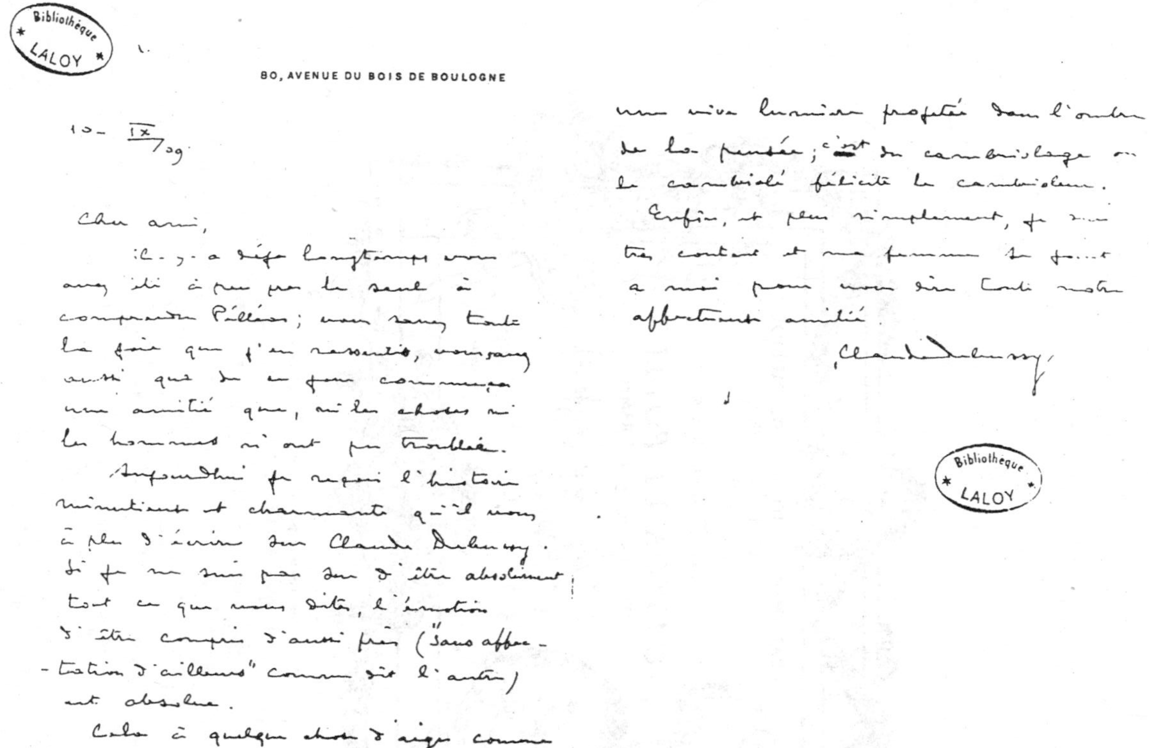

80, AVENUE DU BOIS DE BOULOGNE

10 – IX/09

Cher ami,

Il y a déjà longtemps vous avez été à peu près le seul à comprendre Pelléas; vous savez toute la joie que j'en ressentis, vous savez aussi que de ce jour commença une amitié que, ni les choses ni les hommes n'ont pu troubler.

Aujourd'hui je reçois l'histoire minutieuse et charmante qu'il vous a plu d'écrire sur Claude Debussy. Si je ne suis pas sûr d'être absolument tout ce que vous dites, l'émotion d'être compris d'aussi près ("sans affectation d'ailleurs" comme dit l'autre) est absolue.

Cela a quelque chose d'aigu comme une vive lumière projetée dans l'ombre de la pensée; c'est du cambriolage où le cambriolé félicite le cambrioleur.

Enfin, et plus simplement, je suis très content et ma femme se joint à moi pour vous dire toute notre affectueuse amitié.

Claude Debussy

Plate 3: Letter from Debussy to Laloy, 10 September 1909.
Part of the text of this letter is transcribed on p. 40 n. 50, and translated on p. 16. In possession of M. Vincent Laloy. Reproduced by permission.

Carte d'invitation pour la reprise de *Castor et Pollux*.

Plate 4: Invitation to the revival of Rameau's *Castor et Pollux*, 1918.
Reproduced in Rohozinski (1925).

Plate 5: The Debussy monument in Paris.
Reproduced in Rohozinski (1925).

Plate 6: The Debussy monument in Paris (detail).
Reproduced in Rohozinski (1925).

Plate 7: The Debussy monument at Saint-Germain-en-Laye.
Coll.: Ville de Saint-Germain-en-Laye, Musée municipal Claude Debussy.
Reproduced by permission.

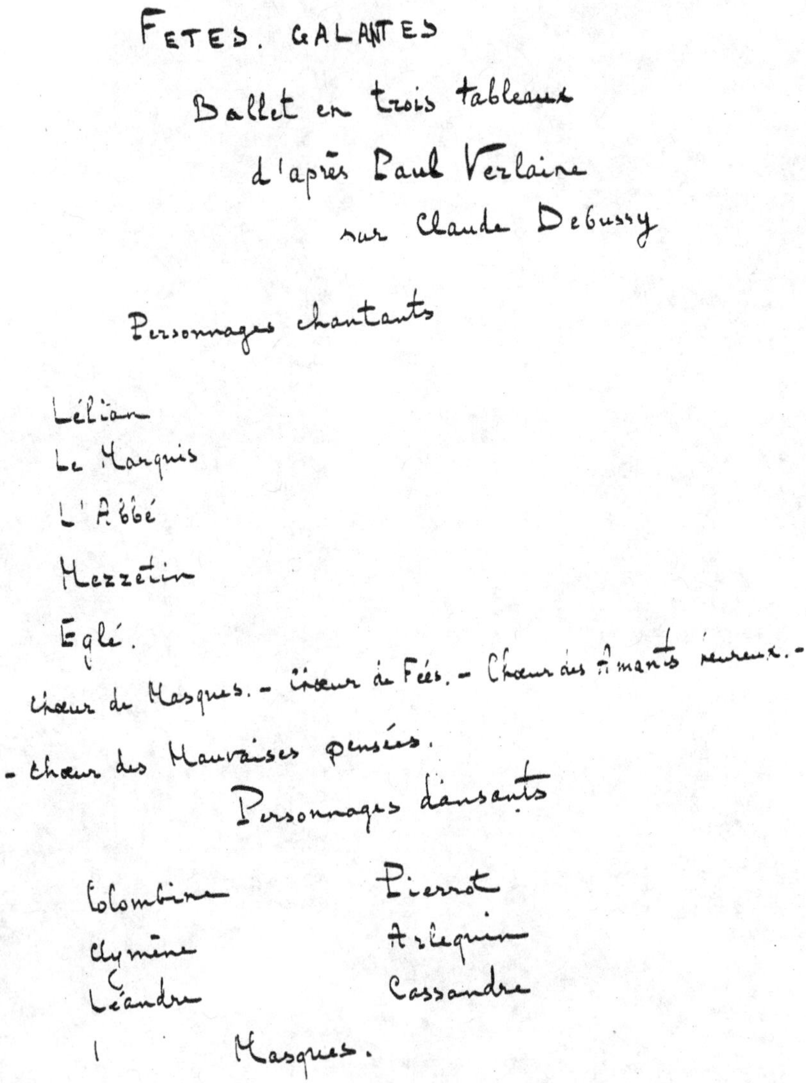
FETES. GALANTES
Ballet en trois tableaux
d'après Paul Verlaine
par Claude Debussy

Personnages chantants

Lélian
Le Marquis
L'Abbé
Mezzetin
Eglé.
Choeur de Masques. – Choeur de Fées. – Choeur des Amants heureux. –
– Choeur des Mauvaises pensées.

Personnages dansants

Colombine Pierrot
Clymène Arlequin
Léandre Cassandre
Masques.

Plate 8: Debussy's projected *Fêtes galantes*. First page of libretto. In possession of M. Vincent Laloy. Reproduced by permission.

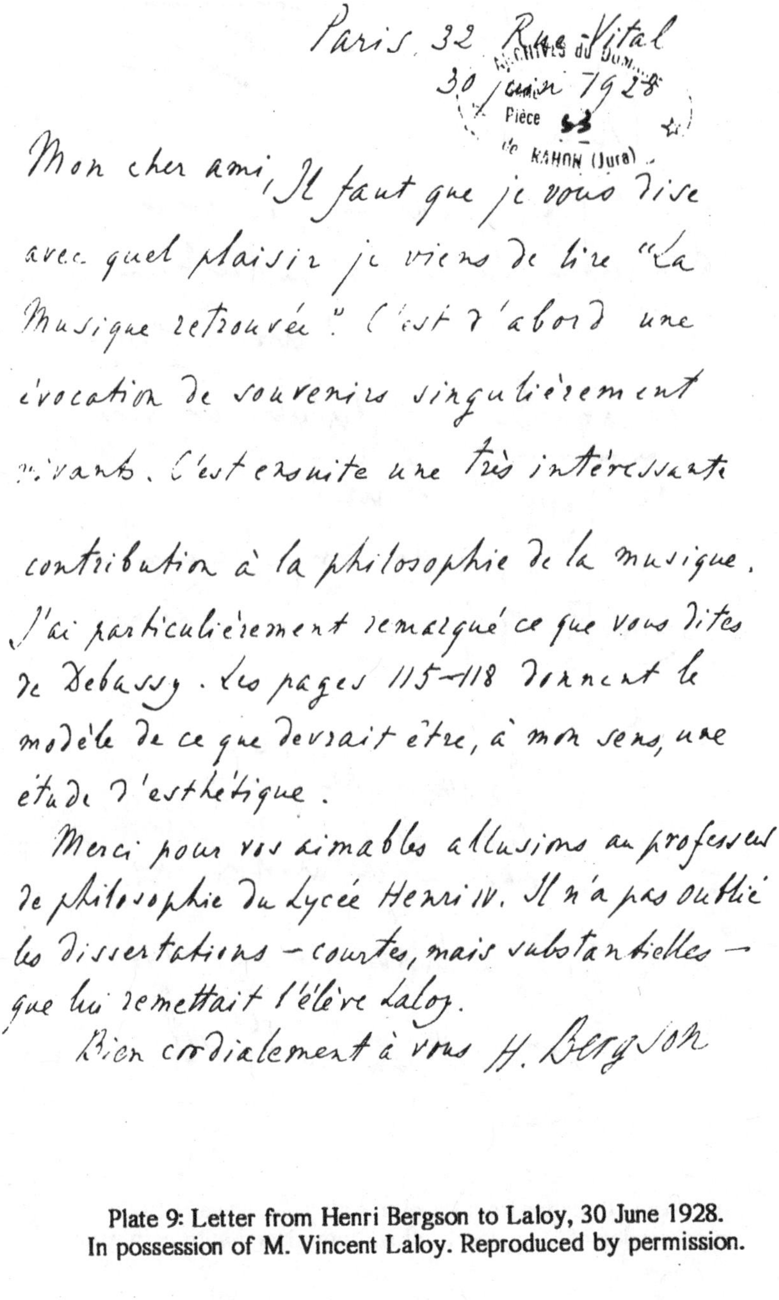

Paris, 32 Rue Vital
30 juin 1928

Mon cher ami, Il faut que je vous dise avec quel plaisir je viens de lire "La Musique retrouvée". C'est d'abord une évocation de souvenirs singulièrement vivants. C'est ensuite une très intéressante contribution à la philosophie de la musique. J'ai particulièrement remarqué ce que vous dites de Debussy. Les pages 115–118 donnent le modèle de ce que devrait être, à mon sens, une étude d'esthétique.

Merci pour vos aimables allusions au professeur de philosophie du Lycée Henri IV. Il n'a pas oublié les dissertations – courtes, mais substantielles – que lui remettait l'élève Laloy.

Bien cordialement à vous H. Bergson

Plate 9: Letter from Henri Bergson to Laloy, 30 June 1928.
In possession of M. Vincent Laloy. Reproduced by permission.

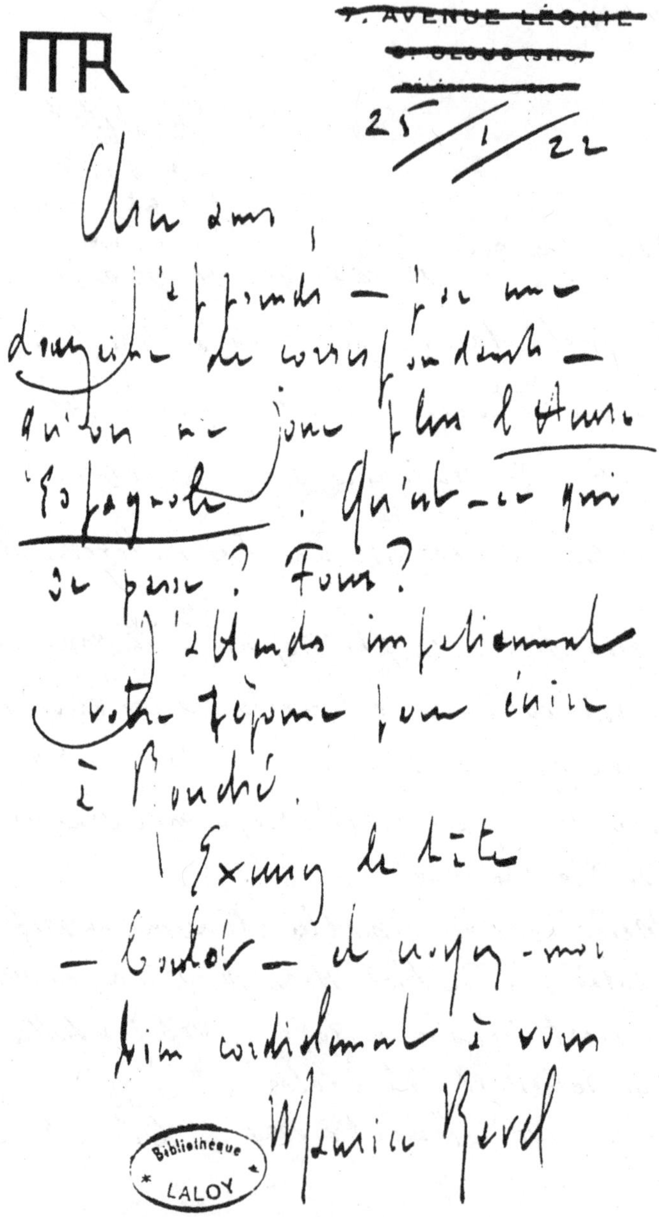

~~7. AVENUE LÉONIE~~

25/1/22

Cher ami,

Maurice Ravel

Plate 10: Letter from Ravel to Laloy, 25 January 1922.
In possession of M. Vincent Laloy. Reproduced with permission.

Plate 11: Louis Laloy, Mme Susanik Laloy (far left), Diaghilev (back row, second from left), Serge Lifar (front row, second from left), Stravinsky (front row, third from right), Jacques Rouché (far right), *c.*1920. In possession of M. Vincent Laloy. Reproduced with permission.

Plate 12: Stage design by V. Barbey for Laloy and Roussel's *Padmâvatî*, 1923. Reproduced in Rohozinski (1925).

La Damoiselle élue

Laloy wrote two reviews of *La Damoiselle élue* after performances in December 1902, in which Mary Garden sang the title role. The work had been composed in 1888, as an *envoi de Rome*,[1] and was first performed in 1893.

Notes begin on p. 144.

La Revue musicale (December 1902), pp. 532–533

Ever active and vigilant, Monsieur Colonne put Debussy's *La Damoiselle élue* on the programme. By doing which he seems to want to inform us of two things: the first is that *envois de Rome* can, on occasion, be interesting; in which case they run the risk of not being well received by the competent section of the Institute; the second is that Monsieur Debussy, before he was the author of *Pelléas*, was already a composer.[2] Even though he did not encumber dozens of virginal pianos with romances, even if he did not, year in year out, write his three dozen *Gavottes* or *Characteristic pieces*, his œuvre before *Pelléas* was very respectable, for respect must be given, not to the number of blackened sheets, but to the wealth of an inspiration which is always sincere and spontaneous. Monsieur Debussy wrote nothing which he did not think through; equally, he is unaware of occasional works, articles for current consumption, products for export, and cut-price work. One can count on one hand the composers, even famous ones, for whom this is the case. So the list of his principal works will appear not over-long but singularly abundant, if we think that each of these works has within itself its reasons for existing and represents a moment, a happy moment in the life of its author:[3]

Six *Ariettes* (poems by Verlaine), published in 1888;
Five *Poems* by Baudelaire, in 1890;[4]
Four *Proses lyriques* (1893);
Chansons de Bilitis, by P. Louÿs (1898);
Trois mélodies (*Sagesse*, by Verlaine) [1891];[5]

Trois mélodies (*Fêtes galantes*, by Verlaine) [1891];
String *Quartet*, performed at the Société Nationale and the Exhibition of 1900;
Fantasy for piano and orchestra (1890), not performed as yet;
La Damoiselle élue, for soloists, chorus and orchestra, an *envoi de Rome*, performed for the first time at the Société Nationale in 1893;
Prélude à l'Après-midi d'un faune, first performance at the Société Nationale on 22 December 1894;
Three *Nocturnes* for orchestra; first performed at the Concerts Lamoureux on 9 December 1900;[6]
Pelléas et Mélisande . . .

La Damoiselle élue, which returns to us today (dedicated to Paul Dukas), is a lyrical poem, whose words were provided by a very Pre-Raphaelitistic Italian poem by D.-G. Rossetti; Monsieur Gabriel Sarrazin is the author of the translation. The story is simple, and takes place in paradise: the Blessed Damozel is waiting for her beloved, and promises herself that she will ask the Virgin and Christ for the grace to continue to live with him and love him, as hitherto on earth. But the beloved does not return; and she weeps. The music is exquisite in freshness, in pure tenderness, in plaintive, resigned melancholy; and we feel that everything is going on very far above us, and that luminous air envelops this figure, who is still human through her hope and longing. What the divine simplicity of the angels' chorus is, what sweet music is the stars', which chords accompany the names of the five servants of Mary, these names which are 'sweet symphonies', and which inflections translate the sadness of the Blessed One (Mademoiselle Garden), I will shortly tell. Let us be content today to quote the first phrase,[7] to congratulate Monsieur Colonne on his intelligent performance, and the public on the emotion and admiration with which it listened.

La Revue musicale (January 1903), pp. 33–35

This lyric poem[8] dating from 1888, it can easily be concluded that it is one of the first works by a master who is now famous. Since then the critics' attitude has come naturally: discreet reserve, pitying respect, an indulgent smile at this youthful work: 'To think that he wrote that in 1888! Hasn't he come a long way! What progress he's made! Who would have thought it? Who would have believed it?'[9] And it does not occur to people that this composition by a twenty-five-year-old musician must have revealed singular originality and a very decided turn of mind, since it had the good fortune to displease the delegation from the Académie des Beaux-Arts which was charged with examining the *envois de Rome*; and the Institute is never wrong.

From the very first notes, indeed, no doubt was possible: a free, pure mind was escaping the grip of rules and formulae:

All Monsieur Debussy's spontaneous grace, all his profound, refined ingenuousness were already revealed in this calm phrase which opens paradise to us. *Pelléas* begins similarly, with a slow succession of root-position triads; but the tone is very different; here we find none of the mysterious atmosphere, the religious solemnity which we recently attempted to analyse.[10] No church vault weighs down on our eyes and invites us to go within ourselves: all wishes are fulfilled, the other life is won, an azure sky opens out before us, and a soul rises up into it, hands joined in prayer; among the serene clarity of the heavenly regions this legend will unfold.

There is nothing more difficult than to evoke dream landscapes disappearing from view, in which shapes dissolve into light and feelings into happiness. Neither Dante nor Monsieur Sully Prudhomme[11] has, in a subject which seems to exceed human powers, completely avoided monotony or embarrassment. Schumann and Franck are almost the only composers I know of who succeed in transporting us effortlessly into the abode of happiness. We must add to these names that of Monsieur Debussy, with this difference however that his paradise cannot be won: it is not the reward promised and given to the merciful, the humble and the suffering. Nothing speaks to us of the Blessed Damozel's virtues, of her merits or labours; but everything tells us that she is Blessed, by reason of the innate grace which presides over her life and justifies all her feelings, and even her love. Let us not be astonished: Margaret did commit a crime, and Goethe sends her to paradise. It is because there are virginal souls, whose innocence is proof against their own actions, and whom heaven attracts quite naturally to itself.

Into this gentle, spontaneous ascension we are initiated by music in which nothing betrays effort, in which the old rules fade away before the happy imagination of a mind which is sure of itself, which no longer needs to be guided towards beauty, as a soul which is freed from sin no longer needs to obey laws in order to act well. For the apparent irregularity of these harmonies and developments is in reality only a more perfect order, just as a morality without obligation would perhaps (if we could attain it) be a superior morality. And let us not think there is anything strange for us in this supraterrestrial music: for it is made with our everyday feelings, purified and ennobled. A hopeful tenderness and suppliant melancholy make up the soul of the Damozel, a soul of prayer and longing; this tenderness and melancholy are known to us, familiar, and we rediscover them here, simply removed from the uncertainties, the hesitations, the egotistical twists and turns, in short the thousand defilements which life inflicts on them:

This heavenly purity, joined to a broad humanity, is certainly the most precious, the newest and the most enchanting quality in Monsieur Debussy's art. By this means the music seizes us and raises us up, by this means it is great and goes far beyond factional quarrels and professional debates. That is what the good secular public also feels, taking no notice of parallel fifths or unresolved dissonances. And from *La Damoiselle élue* or the *Cinq poèmes de Baudelaire* to *Pelléas*, this special quality of mind is revealed and must assert itself. There is in Monsieur Debussy's œuvre an unswerving continuity: we sense that he is a man who has never betrayed or distorted, even for a moment, his own interior music. And the reason why he has been able to grasp it, fix it, translate it into notes and chords, is precisely that he has only ever listened to it, and not vain precepts or prejudices.

But do not jump to the conclusion, however, that I claim to find all of *Pelléas* in *La Damoiselle élue*. On the contrary, the work is very different, in the detail of the conception as in the style: here the melodies are more developed, the declamation is not modelled exactly on the shape and rhythm of the speech, and we would look in vain for chords like those accompanying the two brothers' descent into the subterranean vaults of the castle. What can we say, except that in this subject which is more lyrical than dramatic the music could follow more stable emotions less closely, that a Blessed One did not have to speak with the familiar rapidity of a mortal, and that lastly there are no subterranean vaults in a legend of light? A personality is not affirmed in such details; and variety is precisely the characteristic of a rich and independent talent. But rather than pursue pedantic discussions here, I want to conclude with a word, a single word, from the Blessed Damozel: the name of one of the five servants of Mary, one of the names which are five 'sweet symphonies'.

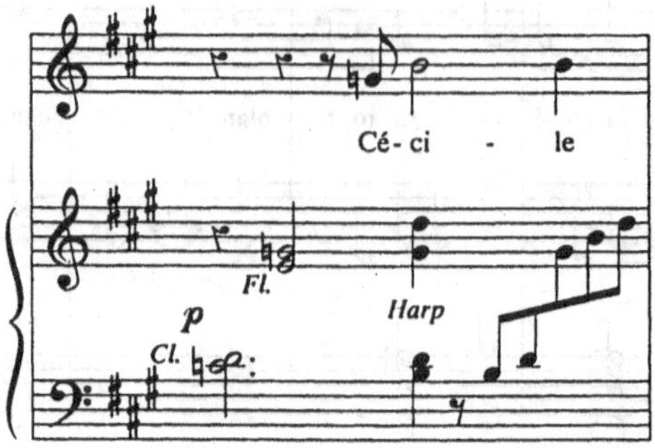

I cannot adequately describe the charm of this detail: the sweet, timid timbre of the clarinets, the two sounds very near to one another, above which comes the flutes' winged chord, and the serene rising line of the harp, it all transports us beyond heaven.

Notes

1 See p. 40 n. 51.

2 Laloy was later to write briefly about Debussy's winning Prix de Rome cantata, *L'Enfant prodigue* in *Revue musciale S.I.M.* (15 January 1909), p. 71:

> *L'Enfant prodigue*, of which we heard two fragments on 6 December, dates from 1884; it is a cantata like other cantatas, with the three obligatory characters, the recitatives and arias. But the music is by Claude Debussy, or, if you like, Claude-Achille Debussy. Already, despite the tyranny of traditional forms, the work manifests a freshness of sentiment and a purity of taste which were unknown until that time, especially in the Prix de Rome competition. And the dance tune has a delicately archaic grace, with that almost Chinese-sounding flute, which moves lightly down a melody that is not delayed by any semitones.

3 It seems likely this list was supplied by Debussy, because in a letter dated 11 December 1902, he wrote to Laloy: 'Attached is a list which I think is more or less correct and complete. It isn't an admirable record, but one does what one can – life is very short and art so difficult.' It is conceivable that a list which was only written on 11 December could have been published in the December issue of *La Revue musicale*, because the dates of concert reviews in certain issues show that the periodical must have appeared not on the first of the month but some time later in the month.

4 Laloy's note: 'Reprinted in 1902 by Durand. See the article on this subject which appeared in our October issue ('Musique moderne').' The article is translated on pp. 146–151.

5 These three songs, published under the title *Trois mélodies*, were 'La mer est plus belle', 'Le son du cor s'afflige vers les bois' and 'L'échelonnement des haies'.

6 Only the first two *Nocturnes*, 'Nuages' and 'Fêtes', were performed on this occasion: compare p. 159.

7 In fact there are no musical quotations in the article as published.

8 Laloy's note: 'Vocal score by Durand. We know that *La Damoiselle élue* was performed at the Concerts Colonne on 21 and 28 December 1902, and achieved resounding success.'

9 In *La Musique retrouvée*, p. 132, Laloy comments on a resemblance to Wagner:

> *La Damoiselle élue* [. . .] is the only Debussy work in which we notice, in certain slow harmonic transitions and the orchestration which is a little shrouded in places, a recollection of Wagner, and particularly *Parsifal*. But elsewhere in the work we find a mystical fervour which, less constrained, was to radiate in the last of his great compositions, *Le Martyre de saint Sébastien*, in 1911.

10 Laloy's note: 'November 1902 issue ('Exercices d'analyse').' The article is translated on pp. 163–165.

11 Laloy must be referring to Dante's *Paradise*, the third part of the *Divine Comedy*, and, no doubt with ironic intent, to the French poet Sully Prudhomme (1839–1907). Sully Prudhomme was awarded the Nobel prize in the year before this article was written; Laloy might have had in mind certain poems from his *Les Solitudes* (1869) and *Les Vaines tendresses* (1875).

Cinq poèmes de Baudelaire

La Revue musicale (October 1902), pp. 404–408

Debussy's *Cinq poèmes de Baudelaire*[1] are, after *Pelléas et Mélisande*, the most significant work this young master has written for the voice. It will be noticed that the words Romances, Vocal Pieces, or Songs, are banished from the title. And indeed these terms are incorrect, in that they give the idea of music written in connection with the text, and not dependent on the text alone, but on a certain musical genre whose laws it follows, whether the words wish for it or not. Monsieur Debussy, on the contrary, wanted everything in his composition, melodies, harmonies and rhythms, to be the image and almost the musical reflection of the poem; he wanted to follow the words exactly, in their physical outline as in their deep meaning: in a word, he rewrote Baudelaire's poems in music, as he had rewritten Maeterlinck's play. Numerous examples, among which one can cite Gregorian chant, polyphonic compositions of the sixteenth century, the chorales of Bach and the dramas of Gluck, show that it is in this voluntary self-effacement that music, a true queen-slave, finds the secret of its omnipotence. The case of Monsieur Debussy must be added to the preceding: for his musical transpositions, which are so faithful, at the same time exceed their object, compensate for imperfections in the language or the style, light up the darkness of the words and let us hear their mysterious echoes. Monsieur Maeterlinck's prose is transfigured, Baudelaire's lines take on colour and become charged with all that the poet was unable to say. They are indeed *Pelléas et Mélisande*, 'Le Balcon', 'Harmonie du soir', or 'Le Jet d'eau', but more emotional, more alive, more eloquent, closer to our soul, more beautiful and also clearer than we knew them. There is no more cheering sight in the world than the triumph an artist owes to his sincerity, to his profound faith in the thoughts he wishes to translate, to the seriousness he has put into getting them thoroughly into his mind, devoting himself to them; for it is a victory of the heart as much as of the spirit.

I said that Monsieur Debussy's music was clear, clearer than the words on their own. I know that I am thus going against a still quite widespread prejudice: Monsieur Debussy is reproached with the disconcerting boldness of his harmony, the freedom of his rhythm and the variety of his melody. Monsieur d'Indy has replied very wittily to this censure, quoting,[2] after a few phrases gathered from our newspapers, another quite similar phrase, in which the same grievances are expressed, at the beginning of the sixteenth century,[3] about one of the founders of opera. And in fact pedantry is eternal. For it is pure pedantry to seek to know whether or not a work is consistent with the rules of Aristotle, Quintilian or Reber,[4] instead of simply letting oneself go with the feeling, and taking it as the author intended it. It is in music above all that this pedantry is practised with the highest degree of concentrated frenzy or calm assurance (as the case may be), for it possesses a word which, through the ambiguity it creates, becomes a formidable weapon, and that word is *obscurity*. Inasmuch as a work, through the learned superposition of melodies, the breaking-up of rhythms or the rare quality of its harmony, escapes elementary analysis to some extent, inasmuch as, when listening, one cannot immediately nod one's head on the strong beats, hum the 'tunes', predict a modulation to the relative or the subdominant key, people conclude that the impression itself is, or rather *must* be confused and vague. That is wantonly to confuse two things which have no connection: the means employed by the composer concern no one apart from the composer himself, those who wish to educate themselves in his school and, later, music historians. There is nothing simpler, more consistent with all the rules, or easier to analyse than a harmony exercise or a student fugue: there is also nothing less musical, emptier, and consequently more obscure for the listener who is seeking a meaning. By contrast, multiplication of appoggiaturas, inflections and auxiliary notes can produce the composition which is most rich in emotion, which has the greatest effect on the soul, and which by that very fact is the clearest and simplest. Now Monsieur Debussy's music rightly has the privilege of imposing itself on the unbiased mind, of possessing it to the point where it completely forgets reality. Of what importance, in consequence, are chromatic accidentals, parallel fifths and the chord of the ninth (which must not be confused with the ninth string)?[5] One can read and reread, play and replay the *Cinq poèmes*, and not grow tired, finding them each day more intimate and dear; Schumann's lieder are almost the only works I know which become friends for life in this way; so penetrating and deep is the feeling!

This deep feeling is certainly found in Baudelaire; but mostly it is buried beneath a pile of curious, precise images, very elaborate in their detail, encircled with strong outlines like the figures Manet paints: there is nothing less amenable to music than these lines which are loaded down with concrete reality. Fortunately it also happens, although much more rarely, that for a time the poet renounces that machinery of over-elaborate symbols and showy emblems, and is content to follow, with the help of the words and the rhythm, the flight of the ideas in his brain, whether it be excited or out of sorts, and ceases to be a Parnassian[6] in order to become an Impressionist. And then we sense in him those vague, powerful emotions, which sum up a soul's whole life, and which only music can easily translate: this is the character of the five pieces Monsieur Debussy has gleaned from the collection *Les Fleurs du mal*:[7] 'Le Balcon', 'Harmonie du soir', 'Le Jet d'eau', 'Recueillement', 'La Mort des amants'. The exquisite memory of a too-intense happiness, the unexplained melancholy of evening, the tender pity which mingles with love, the sensual delight of pure suffering, the joy of a death with brings release, these are the subjects which the composer has treated after the poet, or rather with him: for it is impossible to imagine a closer union. No violence is done to the words: the melody is varied or repeated with them, as was the rule of the masters of the motet. And by turns, according to whether the words are more or less emotional, the melody makes from them a coherent line, or a simple rhythmic declamation. The latter mode of translation prevailed, we remember, in *Pelléas*; it is also the one which suited the voluntarily simple, familiar prose of Monsieur Maeterlinck. To apply it in the same measure to lines which often carry within them a latent music, would have been the error of a systematic mind. Monsieur Debussy did not commit it, and we find in his new composition phrases which have an outline as precise as it is noble and pure:

Harmonie du soir

Le Jet d'eau

A descriptive line will, on the contrary, almost be spoken:

Le Balcon

But then the accompaniment reveals all the emotion contained in these simple words:

Do not these descending chords, full and compact, speak of the perturbing sweetness of the closed room, the 'sickly exhalation of heavy, warm perfumes',[8] and the languid intoxication of the senses?

In this way the music at times transmutes the words themselves into melody, at times weaves melody around them, always gives them a more intimate meaning. And let no one believe that this rather frequent passing from voice to instrument disturbs the work's unity. Monsieur Debussy's music is free, but there is nothing fantastic or incoherent about it. Although the written laws of fugue or sonata are not observed in it, the unwritten, eternal, laws of musical thought are wholly represented. A logic presides over the sequence of ideas, a logic of sentiment which is perhaps more eloquent than that of reason. In this way, in 'Harmonie du soir', a certain alternation of meditative, rocking chords (on the line, 'Le ciel est triste et beau comme un grand reposoir') derives from the rhythm announced from the second bar, a sort of musical cell which multiplies and runs throughout the whole work, a perpetual, changing refrain. And again the melody we quoted a moment ago ('Tes beaux yeux sont las') is later brought back in chords, beneath the arpeggio which has all the quivering grace of water:

And this return is all the more striking for not being prescribed. But even more often a spiritual relationship, for which analysis cannot account, links the motifs together; one only senses that they all derive from a single sentiment of which they are almost the different musical aspects, and that the slightest change in the order would rob the work of its whole meaning. The first and second ideas in a Beethoven sonata only hold together, in most cases, by a bond of this kind, and yet we know how closely unified they are. Monsieur Debussy, who exceeds the number of two ideas, arrives nonetheless, by the same means, at a perfect unity of impression; for he possesses the precious gift, perhaps the rarest of all, of associating musical ideas. Let there be no mistake: a singular power of mind is revealed in these constructions which seem so airy and fragile, which are not supported by any framework; and what must perhaps be praised above all in Monsieur Debussy is the quality of a mind which is as free and spontaneous as it is sustained and coherent.

Notes

1 Laloy's note: 'Durand et fils, publishers'

2 Laloy's note: 'About *Pelléas et Mélisande*, in the review *L'Occident.*' V. d'Indy, 'A propos de *Pelléas et Mélisande*. Essai de psychologie du critique d'art', *L'Occident* (June 1902), pp. 374–381. On p. 379 d'Indy quotes Artusi on Monteverdi, and comments, 'There is nothing new under the sun of Criticism!'

3 As the passage is about Monteverdi, Laloy must mean the seventeenth century.

4 Laloy is ironically mentioning a minor French musician in the same breath as a philosopher and a rhetorician of Classical Greece. Henri Reber (1807–1880) was a professor of harmony and composition at Conservatoire, and was best known for his *Traité d'harmonie* (*Treatise on harmony*, 1862) which went through many editions. In an anecdote in *La Musique retrouvée*, p. 78, Laloy tells entertainingly of wanting to study harmony while he was a student at the Schola Cantorum, where he was enrolled in counterpoint and composition courses. A friend lent him Reber's treatise, with the additional notes written by Théodore Dubois: these were 'forbidden books, and I remember the amused precautions with which he took them out of his briefcase for me, one evening when we were dining together [. . .]'

5 In French this is a pun between *l'accord de neuvième* (ninth chord) and *la corde neuvième* (ninth string). Laloy might just be playing with words, or perhaps he has in mind an ancient practice which he describes at the beginning of 'La Musique de l'avenir', *Le Mercure de France* (1 December 1908), p. 419: 'The rigorous magistrates [. . .] in Sparta [. . .] cut off the eighth or ninth string of a lyre which was guilty of having added a note or two to the scale of the ancestors: it seemed there could be no question of progress in music, but only of models, rules and traditions.'

6 The Parnassians (*les Parnassiens*) were a group of nineteenth-century French poets whose aim was to save poetry from the excesses of Romanticism. The Parnassians included Sully Prudhomme and Heredia, and their models were Baudelaire, Théophile Gautier, Leconte de Lisle and Théodore de Banville. They believed in *l'art pour l'art* ('art for art's sake'), and placed a high value on technical perfection.

7 *Les Fleurs du mal* (1857) was Baudelaire's famous volume of poems.

8 'la maladive exhalaison de parfums lourds et chauds'. This rather Baudelairean line is in fact by Verlaine. It appears in Verlaine's poem 'Crépuscule du soir mystique' from the collection *Poèmes saturniens* (1866).

Prélude à l'Après-midi d'un faune

Laloy, who was only twenty in 1894 when the work was first performed, wrote this review in 1902. He also reviewed the ballet version which was staged in 1912 by the Ballet Russes, with choreography by Nijinsky.

Notes begin on p. 157.

La Revue musicale (November 1902), pp. 454–456

This Prelude is not a new piece in the absolute sense, since it was performed as early as 1894 at the Société Nationale, and taken up again soon after by Messieurs Lamoureux and Colonne. But the work was not appreciated, nor probably listened to, with all the requisite calm, seriousness and impartiality for, at that far-off time, Monsieur Debussy's name was still a standard around which noisy battles were being fought. It was evident, at one of the recent Concerts Chevillard, that sweet Mélisande has stilled these evil passions and calmed violent quarrels. So the time has come to say a few words about a work which we are beginning to be able to appreciate in peace.

Mallarmé's 'eclogue'[1] is only distantly related to the eclogues of Virgil: this faun does not know the tender ballads of a Meliboeus or a Corydon;[2] his double flute, which soon becomes a syrinx, 'instrument of flights', evokes, in the mirage of a scorching afternoon, delectable figures and successful pursuits:

> Ces nymphes, je les veux perpétuer.
> Si clair,
> Leur incarnat léger, qu'il voltige dans l'air
> Assoupi de sommeils touffus.

> [Those nymphs, I want to make them permanent.
> So clear
> Their light flesh-pink, it hovers on the atmosphere
> Oppressed by bushy sleeps.]

But this lustrous vision might only be a dream:

> Réfléchissons . . .
>
> ou si les femmes dont tu gloses
> Figurent un souhait de tes sens fabuleux!
>
> [Let's think . . .
>
> might not the girls you are describing be
> Wishful figments of your mythopoetic senses?]

The doubt vanishes: after all, what do these subtle distinctions between illusion and reality matter? The faun is going to sing of the images which memory, or desire, presents to his eyes: the surprised nymphs, diving among the loving waves, or the way they sleep beneath the roses, and wake in the arms of the seducer:

> . . . arcane tel élut pour confident
> Le jonc vaste et jumeau dont sous l'azur on joue:
> Qui, détournant à soi le trouble de la joue,
> Rêve, dans un solo long, que nous amusions
> La beauté d'alentour par des confusions
> Fausses entre elle-même et notre chant crédule;
>
> . . . .
>
> Je t'adore, courroux des vierges, ô délice
> Farouche du sacré fardeau nu qui se glisse
> Pour fuir ma lèvre en feu buvant, comme un éclair
> Tressaille! la frayeur secrète de la chair:
>
> [. . . whatever
> The secret was, it chose for its safe vehicle
> The spacious double reed I play under the blue,
> Which, taking to itself my cheek's hot agitation,
> Dreams in a long soliloquy that we did entertain
> The beauty all around us by deceitfully
> Confusing it with that of our credulous song;
>
> . . . .
>
> O holy wrath of virgins! I adore you, O
> Wild tang of lovely naked burdens gliding to
> Evade my fiery lip that sucks as thrilling as
> Lightning! the secret creeping of the flesh:]

Resentment follows this rapture; but evening is falling, and indifference returns, bringing peace with it.

> Tant pis! vers le bonheur d'autres m'entraîneront
> Par leur tresse nouée aux cornes de mon front:
>
> . . . .
>
> A l'heure où ce bois d'or et de cendres se teinte
> Une fête s'exalte en la feuillée éteinte:
>
> . . . .
>
> Couple, adieu: je vais voir l'ombre que tu devins.
>
> [Ah well, too bad! Toward happiness there will be others
> To draw me on by their hair caught up on my horns.
>
> . . . .
>
> At twilight when this wood turns gold and gray a rite
> Is celebrated in the dying foliage:
>
> . . . .
>
> Couple, goodbye; I'm going to see the shadow you became.[3]]

This *diminuendo* ending must have been seductive to a composer; besides, it would have been apparent that the whole poem is musical, both in the way it moves and in its subject matter, for one impression follows another without the involvement of reason, returning in the unexpected yet natural ways which belong to feeling and also to music; and besides, the poet does not claim to be doing more than illustrate the flute's tune, being powerless by himself to give the images shape; for the composer, the flute will immediately become the main character, its appearances and reappearances ensuring the unity of the work.

As an artist of equal discretion and refinement, Monsieur Debussy did not set Mallarmé's poem to music, but gave it a Prelude. He seems to have wanted to let the poet speak after him, as if he too believed that 'music without literature appears as a very subtle cloud; it, as such common coin', or that its charm is 'useless until language, retempered and purified by the flight of song, has given it meaning', or lastly that 'music and literature constitute the moving facet – now looming toward obscurity, now glittering unconquerably – of that single, true phenomenon which I called the idea'.[4, 5] But it turns out that in fact, because the composer willed it so, his Prelude is an independent work, clearer than the poem, and slightly different in character, although the large lines are retained. The flute begins by sounding this gently inflected tune, which will be the main theme:

We feel ourselves immediately transported to a better world; everything wild and grimacing in the flat-nosed countenance of the faun has been erased; desire still speaks, but it is veiled in tenderness and melancholy. The chord sounded by the woodwind, the distant horn call, and the wave of limpid sounds from the harps accentuate this impression. The call is reinforced, becomes more pressing, quietens almost immediately to allow the flute to sing again. This time the theme is developed, the oboe intervenes, the clarinet soars up in turn, quite a lively dialogue takes place, and a clarinet phrase leads to a new motif, which tells of satiated passion, but conveys the sweetness of a shared emotion rather than ferocious victory:

The first theme returns, slower, and the croaking of muted horns obscures the horizon; the theme comes and goes, lustrous chords are heard, finally a cello solo joins the flute, and mirrors it (an effect of this sort is found in the Andante of the *Pastoral* symphony), and all is dissipated in feathery clouds, like a mist 'hovering on the atmosphere'.[6]

The most striking quality in this charming work, as in everything

Monsieur Debussy composes, is unity of style, and it is more palpable by very reason of the freedom of the development. It is also the quality which is most lacking in Mallarmé's poetry, where the most quintessential affectation is placed next to a very Classical strictness, in which a half-amusing, half-solemn jumble is suddenly lit up by a very beautiful line that is more surprising than everything else. There is nothing like that here, everything is linked and holds together. And the pleasure of not having to weigh the meaning of a word, or scrutinize the syntax of a sentence! For there are certainly more obscure pieces than this one by Mallarmé; and still it takes more than one attempt before we know where we are with it. The composer does not inflict a similar task on us. By a spell which he was to use again in the *Cinq poèmes de Baudelaire* and *Pelléas*, he has delicately drawn out the timid emotion which was hidden, tried to find itself and became lost among the vain mass of words and syllables. Or rather he has re-thought and re-felt the poet's work, and by that very act has increased its level of emotion; which comes down to saying that he has purified it. We no longer sense, in the Prelude, what might have shocked us in *L'Après-midi*: the perverse curiosity of the man of letters amusing himself, playing with the ardent sensations of a primitive, suspect sensuality. The ardour has remained, as has the naive tenderness; the vice has disappeared along with the affectation, the Nymph has triumphed over the Faun; all the blemishes in the picture have been erased, and innocently voluptuous lines play out in one of those pure lights that only music can create. And I do not need to say how much I prefer, to Mallarmé's two-horned Faun, the Elysian Faun of Monsieur Debussy.[7]

***La Grande revue* (25 June 1912), p. 847**

This year, the *Prélude à l'Après-midi d'un faune* was staged through the good offices of Nijinsky. It is a hazardous undertaking to incarnate a piece of music which is evocative of elusive yet precise forms, the delights of the inward eye. Moreover, the mythological definition of the subject set a dangerous trap. All the adepts of antique gesture, not excepting Isadora Duncan, a pastoral Greek, and Régina Badet, a sugarplum Tanagra figurine,[8] have made the mistake of transferring to the stage appearances which they copied from bas-reliefs or vases, not sparing one art any of the conventions peculiar to the other. Similarly Nijinksy felt obliged always to show himself in profile and with hands outstretched. But for a great artist, a fixed viewpoint, even an absurd one, is profitable by reason of the constraint which confines his inventiveness. From these forced positions his instinct deduced bold, realistic attitudes, as a skilful poet finds in the required rhyme the germ of a thought. We cannot forget that body, partially mottled in memory of the primeval fur, those limbs bending in the lassitude of an unnecessary strength, that elemental cupidity which is deflected by an animal timidity. The only fault in this plastic poem is that it has such a remote relationship to the music that one cannot follow both at once. As for the young women representing the nymphs, their efforts are less happy: it would not matter that the telegraphy of their arms remains unintelligible to the spectator, if it were not manifest that they themselves attach no meaning to it, and pay attention only to the agreed signal. And besides, the Faun's fruitless desire was only meant to pursue chimeras.

Notes

1 Laloy's note: 'Published in 1876.'

2 Characters in the first two of Virgil's eclogues

3 Translation by William Austin in Norton Critical Score of *Prélude à l'Après-midi d'un faune* (New York, 1970), pp. 22–29. I have made a change to the last line, in accordance with Austin's invitation to his readers to join the translation 'committee' for this poem.

4 Laloy's note: 'S. Mallarmé, *La Musique et les lettres*, Perrin, [Paris,] 1895.' Also see H. Mondor and J. Jean-Aubry, eds, *Stéphane Mallarmé. Œuvres complètes* (Paris, 1945).

5 'En artiste aussi discret que raffiné, M. Debussy n'a pas mis en musique le poème de Mallarmé, mais lui a donné un Prélude. Il semble avoir voulu laisser parler le poète après lui, comme s'il croyait, lui aussi, que «la musique sans les lettres se présente comme très subtil nuage; elles, une monnaie si courante», ou que son charme est «vain, si le langage, par la retrempe et l'essor purifiant du chant, n'y confère un sens», ou enfin que «la musique et les lettres sont la face alternative, ici élargie vers l'obscur, scintillante là avec certitude, du phénomène que j'appelai l'Idée».' The English translation of the second and third quotations is from B. Cook, ed., *Mallarmé: selected prose poems, essays and letters* (Baltimore, 1956), pp. 49, 50; the translation of the first is by the present writer. Laloy also quotes this passage in an article, 'Claude Debussy et le Debussysme': see p. 88.

6 'qui voltige dans l'air': from the third line of the poem

7 In a later review, Laloy said he observed a resemblance between the *Prélude à l'Apres-midi d'un faune* and the fortieth symphony of Mozart:

> [I]n spite of differences of construction and orchestration, they reveal minds of the same family, in the candid grace of their

inspiration, the natural logic of their thoughts (more discursive in one, more continuous in the other) and finally the quality of the sound and the colouring of an orchestration which is made up of light, in which not a single note is lost, in which everything stands out and charms the ear before it speaks to the heart: divine games, visions of paradise, music of sun and enchantment [. . .]

Le Mercure musical (15 December 1905), p. 628

[8] Isadora Duncan (1878–1927) was a pioneer of modern dance who drew her inspiration from Ancient Greece. Laloy wrote an article about her: 'Isadora Duncan et la danse nouvelle', *La Revue musicale* (15 May 1904), pp. 249–253. It has not been possible to find any information about Régina Badet.

Nocturnes

The *Nocturnes* were first performed complete on 27 October 1901 at the Concerts Lamoureux, conducted by Camille Chevillard. The first two had been heard in December of the previous year. Laloy's review is consistent with the tone of reviews by other critics, and gives an insight into the reception of Debussy's music at the turn of the century.

La Revue musicale (November 1901), p. 411

These nocturnes are exquisite: a harmonic thread of artless, subtle fifths provides support for a plaintive cor anglais recitative; then the flute sings in turn, sweeter, calmer, and, if you like, *clouds* mass and disperse or fade; above all it is fine, penetrating, distinguished music. An agitated motif depicts a *Festival*, through which runs an unexpected, graceful fanfare. And finally, to an almost unseizable rhythm, *Sirens* sing: baffled by the chromatic inflections, these enchantresses produced augmented semitones and diminished whole tones which I did not find unpleasant; I think of the 'soft diatonic' and 'hemiolic chromatic' dear to the contemporaries of Pericles . . . [1] This reverie is interrupted by cheering, mingled with a few exclamations. I really do not know what Monsieur Debussy is reproached with. With not developing his themes? But that is the law of pictorial music. With surprising the ear by irregular chord progressions? I noticed nothing in these small pieces that was not perfectly musical; and as for the rules of harmony, everyone knows that they have only ever existed to be broken on occasion: Bach is the proof of this. An obliging neighbour pointed out the real reason to me. Monsieur Debussy is an innovator, and an innovator he will remain. It is a matter of common knowledge that his music is obscure, learned, laborious, bristling with difficulties. But then why come to hear it?

Le Mercure musical (1 March 1906), pp. 211–212

At the concert on the 18th, Monsieur Chevillard restored to us the three *Nocturnes* by Debussy ('Nuages', 'Fêtes', 'Sirènes'); and he is even promising them to us again for the 25th. This is a case of unaccustomed generosity, and we should go down on our knees and thank him; moreover the public abundantly repaid him with its applause, to which Monsieur Chevillard replied by bowing to right and left; then, as the enthusiasm did not abate, and a large number of listeners asked for the second of the masterpieces to be repeated, he sat down, unconcerned, among the orchestra, as if to say, 'Children! Are you going to stop soon?' Taciturn pastor of the flutes and violins, thrifty superintendent of music, morose but fundamentally good-natured captain of the regiment of sounds, you musn't be angry that, after such delights, we were out of our senses. These *Nocturnes* are not comparable to any other music: they are poems of celestial light[2] which have effortlessly, almost without our being aware of it, opened to us the invisible doors of the dream world; freed from the chains of the material world, divested of our body, we travel the pathways of the sky: the white clouds are our brothers, and their melancholy soul takes on the voice of the cor anglais, cradled by the violins. Then there are festivals, wilder and at the same time sweeter than any on earth: a round dance comes and goes, beneath a joyous light that trembles like stars; the imaginary dancers don't shake the airy floor, and now they spring forth with sparkling leaps; but a mysterious procession moves through the ball, and seems to draw the rays of light into the dull folds of half-glimpsed purple robes and golden brocades ... And finally, beneath the transparent night sky, there is the shifting mystery of the sea, and the melodious roar of the waves with the languidly inflected calls of the distant Sirens. Here I really must say that the Sirens sang much too loudly, more like Rhinemaidens than the voice of the Ocean: what was needed was a dispersed murmur, coming from no one knows where, perhaps from the moon-veiled horizon, which we excitedly watch for, and which vanishes just as we think we have grasped it? There are other details to mention, too: some harsh effects in 'Fêtes', which were interpreted too concretely, and thus robbed of the tenderness which subtly blends with their joyful quality; and, in 'Nuages', perhaps a slightly fast tempo, and a string section which was notably too energetic.[3] But this music is so beautiful, and it is written with such happy, fresh sonorities, that its charm will always be triumphant: even supposing it was approached with ill will, these melodies could not be robbed of their accent, these harmonies of their persuasive breadth, nor this orchestration of its colours which are both delicate and clearly defined. And, from the very first notes, we will always be caught up and entranced: a fairy comes to us, and takes hold of our life without our even thinking of defending it, for she makes it divine in her own image.

Notes

1 Laloy is being ironic about the Sirens' intonation and also airing his knowledge of Ancient Greek music theory. At least as far back as the fourth century BC, the three basic genera of the tetrachord - i.e. a group of four notes comprising the interval of a fourth - are separated into shades, one for the enharmonic, three for the chromatic and two for the diatonic. In the 'hemiolic chromatic' shade, the intervals of the tetrachord in ascending order are three-eighths of a tone, three-eighths of a tone, and one-and-three-quarters of a tone. In the 'soft diatonic' shade, the intervals of the tetrachord in ascending order are a semitone, three-quarters of a tone, and one-and-a-quarter tones. Laloy has more to say about the out-of-tune Sirens at this performance in *La Musique retrouvée*, p. 95.

2 Later Laloy wrote of '[. . .] these tableaux where all that subsists of things is their envelope of changing light.' *Claude Debussy* (1909), p. 50

3 Both Laloy and Debussy were critical of Chevillard's interpretations of Debussy's music. Laloy recounts an anecdote from the time of the rehearsals for the *Nocturnes* which reveals something of Chevillard's approach, and is consistent with Debussy's complaint at the time that Chevillard was 'as charming as a cageful of bears':

> Later I was told of this dialogue [. . .] between the author, invisible at the back of the darkened hall at the last rehearsal, and the conductor who, hearing his faint but ringing voice, had just stopped his musicians with a dry tap on the desk, and turned round to listen: 'I'd like that hazier.' 'Faster?' 'No, hazier.' 'Slower?' 'Hazier.' 'I don't know what you mean. Let us recommence, gentlemen!'
>
> *La Musique retrouvée*, p. 93

Laloy records that, in spite of his professed incomprehension, Chevillard did make a change for the performance.

Pelléas et Mélisande

This is an extract from an article Laloy wrote for the London periodical *The listener*. With the English musical public in mind, he is careful to explain the Symbolist nature of the play.

Notes for this section begin on p. 187.

The listener (19 May 1937)[1]

This play called for music and, of all possible music, that of Debussy. It called for music because in the play not everything is said. Music found its place in prolonging the meaning of words which were left suspended, but without hardening the meaning too much as it would shatter. Friendship, tenderness, jealousy, fear, longing, pity, remorse, everything rises up from the depths of the soul and the darkness of the unconscious, beneath the complicit incantation of the impassable forest, the sunlit terrace, the crystalline forest, the stagnant water at the bottom of the abyss, the park at night or the bedroom where Mélisande wants the window opened and does not know that she is going to die. Nothing is explained. Everything is understood. As our great Christian philosopher Pascal said: 'The heart has its reasons which reason knows nothing of.'[2] The music, too, on pain of breaking the spell, had to let the heart speak.

Laloy was not in Paris for the *générale* or the first performance of *Pelléas*. He wrote this article in November 1902 after the second series of performances. He analyses the first four bars of the prelude, making comments about their harmony and modality that were unique at the time. It was in response to this article that Debussy first invited Laloy to visit him.

'On two chords'
***La Musique retrouvée*, pp. 115–118**[3]

This is the sweet, solemn tune which rises from the orchestra at the beginning of *Pelléas*, heralding an ancient legend. How is it that such simple notes stand before us like a door opening on a peaceful sanctuary?

This movement by ascending fifth, from the D to the A, is perhaps the most natural of all the movements to which the human voice is accustomed: a great number of Gregorian Introits, and several popular songs in older style like *Le Roi Renaud*, *La Pernette*, *Le Roi Loys*, *Voici la Saint-Jean*, use this progression to move to the note which will be the axis of the melody; this note is called the dominant. Dionysius of Halicarnassus recognised the interval of a fifth in the Greek language between the accented syllable and the other syllables.[4] Smaller than the octave and almost as consonant, the interval of a fifth is as easy for the ear to grasp as it is for the voice to reach. Which explains its important role in the music of all ages and all countries.

The two notes of this fifth are supported by a single chord. It is a root-position chord built on the D, but stripped of the third which would be an F sharp or F natural and would make it major or minor. Between these two modes, modern music must make it choice. But here we would think they do not yet exist. The mind is in suspense, the ear is fully satisfied, for the consonance of the fifth is more blended than that of the third: it is more difficult to distinguish the A from the D than the F from the D. This is why Classical antiquity and the Middle Ages ranked the fifth among the perfect consonances, and considered thirds as imperfect. Until the beginning of the sixteenth century, it was forbidden to put thirds into the last chord of a piece. The last chord was to contain only octaves and fifths. Conversely, in our day the third is required, because we prefer precision to euphony.

The second bar brings two chords of consecutive fifths, on the D and the C. Harmony textbooks forbid these progressions which are called parallel, for much the same reason that the hiatus was proscribed in poetry.[5] But here the second fifth does not sound abruptly against the first, because the G is only heard as a provisional note, and the phrase is only finished, the meaning is only complete after this G resolves to an A. There can be no doubt. Musical discourse has a syntax. Two root-position chords built on the D and the C cannot be linked, because there is only a very remote key relationship between them. It is not done to stop there. We go on; the C chord disappears and is replaced by a sixth chord, which itself, if the order of the notes is inverted, represents the root-position chord of A. The A is the upper fifth of the D. It is what is called the dominant note of the key, if the D is the tonic. To pass from the tonic to the dominant is a natural movement, for the harmony as much as for the melody. That is why, at the slightest indication, we are quite prepared to believe in it. Music indeed is not written only for the ear, but for the mind, and a series of notes or chords, even if harmonious, would only be a pleasant noise, if the order of the series seemed arbitrary to us.

This four-note phrase, which will be repeated with a more marked rhythm in the next two bars, thus rests on two chords, the first of which, built on the D and without a third, can be understood equally as major or minor, until the second chord appears and is clearly minor. Then the ambiguity is dispelled straight away and we perceive that the first chord, still present in our memory, could also only belong to the minor mode. In this way the composer is able to give the feeling of mystery without being obscure, using extraordinarily simple means.

But our D minor scale permits of a C sharp, which is its last note or leading note. Here the C, very conspicuous in the bass, is not altered. A D minor scale without a leading note is the first mode of plainchant, the most solemn of the eight principal modes among which the music of the Middle Ages, more varied in its theory than our own, was divided. It is therefore not without reason that this short phrase suggests solemn thoughts to us. Unconsciously, we recognize in it sounds which for centuries have echoed in cathedral vaults, inviting us to resignation, to obedience, to forgiveness. The composer did not need long calculations to achieve this effect; he did not examine the value of the chords, the meaning of the accidentals, he did not go through old Graduals or meditate on the mystical value of the different modes. It sufficed for him to look within himself: the soul of our ancestors was reawakened, and along with it the memory of their songs. That may be the reason why this music, which is so moving to us who have not denied our ancient liturgy, has some difficulty in opening up a path through a spirit which has been touched by the Reformation and informed by the Lutheran chorale.[6]

Laloy gave lectures on 'Le Drame musical moderne' at the Ecole des Hautes Etudes Sociales in Paris in March-April 1905. Transcripts were published in *Le Mercure musical*, and this one is the last of the series.[7] Debussy wrote appreciatively to Laloy on 13 September 1905:
'While I was in Paris I saw an issue of *Le Mercure musical* which contained an essay on *Pelléas*. In all humility I found it remarkable: I don't see how understanding of a work could go further. Reading it was a real pleasure and comfort; the *Pelléas* lovers were beginning to make me wonder a little what my intentions had been, their comments were all so reductive and fatuously prosaic. All the same, rest assured that I shall not forget the friendship of the man who wrote these words, and whom I already regard with an affection no letter can do justice to.'[8]

'Modern music drama: Claude Debussy' *Le Mercure musical* (1 August 1905), pp. 233–250

Pelléas et Mélisande is a legend, but a deeply human legend, with a dreamlike sweetness which is both familiar and fraternal.[9] Beneath their golden crowns and the fine embroidered robes which lend their gestures such solemn breadth, these kings and princes of a kingdom not of this world harbour thoughts similar to our own: they speak as we do, and suffer in the same way, simply, not cursing the fearful, cunning destiny whose playthings they also are. The love that unites them and creates their unhappiness is not the unexplained, violent, stupid love that precipitates the heroes and heroines of so many novels, tragedies and operas towards each other; it is not the brutal, declamatory love which inspires Louise and Julien[10] to utter the delicate words you know; neither is it the ignorant, rudimentary love which seizes Siegfried when he sees the Valkyrie, or Fervaal at Guilhen's side,[11] love that is a revelation, an education, which is taught, with solid lessons, like a philosophy course in a German university, and which I will call didactic love. No, this is a love born of life itself, which has grown day after day, through domestic conversations; which has slowly, like an elusive cloud of mist, moved away from fraternal tenderness, given an unavowed charm to all the routines of an everyday intimacy and woven invincible links between two souls which are not equal but alike; which invades the whole being like a sweet, deadly poison; which is already the absolute master when its existence is barely perceived; – in short, and in a word, a true love.[12]

The story of this love and its reverberation on the other souls nearby is told in a series of tableaux, each showing a characteristic or critical moment in this irresistible development. This story is known and dear to us all, and I will not insult Maeterlinck by retelling it here in detail. Suffice to recall that Prince Golaud, grandson of Arkël, the old king of Allemonde, is a very strong, good man, but a little heavy and rough, who does not know how to go about things, and handles life with hands that are too accustomed to brandishing his heavy hunting spear. One day he meets Mélisande, who like him is lost in the forest; she has come from afar, she was greatly frightened, she fled, and her golden crown, an accursed gift, fell into the fountain. Golaud marries this Mélisande who is too gentle, whose anxious, loving, childish soul he will never understand. Pelléas is Golaud's brother; he is young, sensitive and melancholy. He knows how to talk to Mélisande, she stops trembling when she is with him. They watch the day close in over the ocean, from the castle terrace, as the vessel which brought Mélisande sails off, never to return. Pelléas is due to go away, but each day he allows himself one more day's grace. He leads Mélisande through the empty places in the immense park to the old, abandoned fountain, and she plays, – 'a transparent symbol', – with the wedding ring which Golaud gave her. The ring falls into the water, and, at the same moment, Golaud sees his horse bolt for no reason in the forest; he has a terrible fall, and we next see Mélisande at his bedside, very attentive, quite distressed by an unknown illness. It is then that, while consoling her with all the tenderness he has, Golaud sees that the tiny hand he is pressing between his own is bare of the wedding ring. And Mélisande, instinctively, does not dare say where she lost it; she invents a different story. Caught in her own ruse, she must go and look for the ring, straight away, in the grotto by the sea. Pelléas goes with her, the sound of the sea is vaguely threatening, clouds gradually reveal the moon, and we see, asleep against the rocks, three old paupers who have come to spend the night there. Mélisande is afraid of this deep, ordinary misery, afraid and a little ashamed of herself: when they are leaving she refuses Pelléas' hand.

But here I am, in spite of my promise, following every step of the enchanting tale. I am straying. I won't be able to get out of this forest of complicit perils.[13] I must hurry on, and yet I would like to tarry longer in the garden where night is falling, while Mélisande combs her hair, her long hair that falls down to reach Pelléas' lips, like an emanation, a radiance from herself, and a desire of which she is unaware. I would also like to tell of the disquiet that eats at the heart of Golaud, the secret desire for vengeance which slumbers in him like the stagnant water in the underground vaults of the castle, the fatal thirst for knowledge which devours him to the point where he interrogates the innocent little Yniold and his great, frightened eyes about the evil they might see. But why recall scenes which are engraved today in every memory? Let us simply express regret at the subtly melancholy episode where Yniold is seen playing all alone near the fountain; his golden ball is trapped under a stone which cannot be raised; some sheep go past, and bleat 'because that isn't the way to the stall': and once again, two light touches serve to indicate the all-powerful destiny which fastens on its prey, and drags us where we do not want to go. And then Pelléas arrives, quite anxious about having to say farewell, and Mélisande joins him, 'out of breath like a bird being pursued,' and only then, in the emotion of the impending departure, does the confession of love escape from their lips, almost in spite of themselves, like a spring overflowing. How far we are from the dissertations of Tristan and the literary lyricism of so many lovers in the theatre! And how deeply those simple words which Mélisande murmurs, 'I love you too', touch our hearts![14]

In the last act, Golaud has killed Pelléas and wounded Mélisande, who was running away, cowardly in the face of death. She is dying, however, watched over by Arkël, who loves her and has understood everything, and Golaud, who is still tortured by the insane desire to know what happened. But Mélisande cannot answer him, she is already too far from life, she is no longer aware of anything. She dies, soundlessly, with the mystery of her soul; and Golaud will die after her, desperate that he could not understand; an immense pity descends on these unhappy creatures who have all suffered too much to be considered criminal: what happened is not their fault, the fate of their own nature and of treacherous circumstance willed it thus. And we, the spectators of this cruel and very tender drama, have recognised the marvellous image: it is the story of our very own hearts, and we leave more moved and more compassionate towards the troubles of our brothers, really better people.

What! people will say, no unintelligiblity? No symbol in need of exegesis? No moral idea to elucidate, with any amount of commentaries, rapprochements and etymologies? No theogony to establish, no collapse of superseded Valhallas, no dawn of new times, no final conflagration, in the blazing glory of a newly founded religion? No, none of that. Certainly, along the way, we have acquired more than one symbol. But they were all connected to this idea which is not moral, social, or religious, but simply philosophical, of inescapable Destiny. Nothing is being proved in *Pelléas et Mélisande*, we are simply reminded that we cannot change the order of events, that forces within and outside us guide us and push us along, or rather, if you like, that our deep-seated instincts and what seem to be external accidents are but one and the same thing, one same Unconscious, one same Non-self which lives its own life and imposes it on us, with no concern for the illusions of our intelligance or the fantasies of the poor Self which believes itself to be the master. Mélisande's hair and the ring which escapes from her fingers, and the stagnant water, and the golden ball and the sheep signify nothing other than this sovereign dominion of Fate. But we see that these symbols, which moreover are perfectly clear, do not encroach on the personality of the characters, and do not in any way alter the course of the action. We can fail to understand them or suppress them with our mind, and believe that Golaud's falling at the moment the ring fell is mere coincidence, that the stagnant water in the underground vaults is only there to justify Pelléas' fright when he feels his brother's hand tremble, and that the scene with Yniold at the fountain is only a pretty tableau of troubled innocence, such as life offers in the middle of its gloomiest ventures: we, can, in a word, fail to recognize all Destiny's warnings, and see only chance or whim where others will recognize the work of a mysterious, tenacious Will: the play will be just as clear, just as coherent, just as irresistibly logical and natural. In the same way, for positive minds our daily life is only a thin fabric of material events and clear actions, whereas others think they can hear mysterious calls, and almost the words of a figurative language spoken by Nature. The symbolism in *Pelléas et Mélisande* is not systematic, it does not determine the events, it is added to them and responds to them like an echo from the depths of things. Far from giving the play a rigorous, abstract aspect, it brings it closer to life by making it ambiguous like life: the play includes both sides of existence, the dark and the light; the most inconsequential acts and ordinary proceedings suddenly awaken secret forebodings and distant analogies which fade as soon as our mind tries to grasp them. This really is a total image of life, since it shows reality thoroughly suffused with dreams.

Very simple is the language in which these emotions, intentions and apprehensions are expressed. They are words everyone uses, words we utter daily ourselves; it is only circumstances that confer a gravity on them which we did not think they had. It is the same in real life: the most ardent emotions, the cruellest pain, or the delights of ecstasy, bring to our lips a few words which are barely linked together, and in them the soul is revealed. As Mélisande goes into the grotto with Pelléas to look for the ring that is not there, she cries out:

> Oh! – What is it? – There are . . . There are . . . – Yes, I saw them too . . . – Let's go, let's go! – They're three old paupers who have fallen asleep. There is a famine in the land. Why have they come to sleep here? – Let's go, let's go! – Take care, don't speak so loudly . . . Let's not wake them. They are still sleeping deeply. Come. – Leave me alone, I prefer to walk by myself. – We will come back another day.

Mélisande's fright, Pelléas' pity, the disquiet both of them feel on seeing these three paupers whom they scarcely dare to name: these feelings become ours precisely because the words are familiar to us. And further on, when Pelléas, standing at the foot of the tower, coils Mélisande's hair in his hands and carries it to his lips, what does he say to her? Is he going to burst forth with excited protestations or lyrical apostrophes to the night, is he going to attach a metaphor to each of those blond hairs? No, he will only speak very simple, almost childlike words, like the words we murmur to ourselves when we are living a dream:

> Oh! oh! What is that? Your hair, your hair is falling towards me! All your hair, Mélisande, all your hair has fallen down from the tower! I can hold it in my hands, I can hold it in my mouth. I can hold it in my arms, I can put it around my neck . . . I'll keep my hands closed all night!

And that suffices to make this scene, in its melancholy chastity, a pure marvel of true poetry, I mean of a poetry which is not in words, but in things themselves; and there is not one of us who does not share the divine emotion quivering in these vague speeches, and does not think he recognises a memory from his own life.

Only now and then an image crops up, always new and full of meaning: one of those unforeseen rapprochements, which we do not look for, and are like a flash of lightning illuminating our inner darkness. On the evening he is to say goodbye, which will be the fatal evening, Pelléas arrives at the fountain quite agitated, as if he had just woken from a dream:

> This is the last evening ... the last evening. Everything must finish ... I played like a child around a thing I had no inkling of. I played in a dream around destiny's snares. Who woke me all of a sudden? I am going to run away, yelling in joy and pain like a blind man running away when his house burns down. I am going to tell her that I am going to run away ... It is late, she isn't coming. I had better go away without seeing her again ... I must look at her properly this time. There are things I can't remember ... at times it's as though I haven't seen her for a hundred years. And I haven't looked into her eyes yet ... There is nothing left for me if I go away like this ... And all these memories, it's as though I was carrying a little water in a muslin bag. I must see her one last time, right to the bottom of her heart. I must say everything I haven't said.

This is just the way we feel regret for a past made of enchanted dreams, which cease being culpable because they are going to end, and which we would like to look at, for the last time, more closely than ever. And it is in just this way that images rise spontaneously from the bottom of our heart and glow amidst our confused words like roses in the night.

§

Maeterlinck's play is already, in itself, a masterpiece. But its beauties are solemn, discreet and profound; in order to experience them in all their fullness, leisure and meditation are needed. It is in reading, not on the stage, that the work makes its full effect. And I even ask myself if this effect would be as notable without the constant memory of the music. Perhaps I have praised Maeterlinck's text too highly, and attributed to him what belongs exclusively to Debussy. Indeed it is worth remarking that *Pelléas et Mélisande* seems to me today the most moving of Maeterlinck's plays, and that I even prefer it, by far, to

Alladine et Palomides or the formidable *Mort de Tintagiles*. Why so? Is it not because now the words will only come to my mind enveloped in the melodies and chords which clarified their outlines and revealed their hidden meaning? It is possible. Never has any music so closely followed all the impulses of the words, been as intimately united with them, and at the same time prolonged them in wider, more shifting or more coloured reflections. It is not surprising that, as they leave the harmonious wave of the music, the words are still impregnated with a glimmering light, or that *Pelléas et Mélisande* seems to be ringed with a magical brightness, whereas Maeterlinck's other plays are blurred in Flemish mists.

It is unique, this work on which two poets of genius laboured, each thinking it out in turn; and the poet in sound deserved the name of creator no less than the other poet for having come after him: he made each word, each gesture, each detail of the action his own, putting his whole soul into it, and his soul is more vibrant and more lyrical than that of the first inventor. He loved everything about the work which was handed over to him, and so he enriched it with an energy which it did not possess. He penetrated the mystery, unveiled the arcane, gave brightness to the shadows and a voice to the silence. And his music drama made us forget the prose drama which inspired it. Today the author of *Pelléas et Mélisande* is Claude Debussy, not Maeterlinck.

Very simple, like the words it overlays, is the declamation. No melodic rules, no portamentos, rounded phrases, or prepared cadences. Nor any of those great gestures, those upward leaps modelled on the rough accentuation of German, which more than one French composer has imitated inappropriately. A line which is often quite level, and inflected only at phrase endings, as in ancient psalmody: an exact image of spoken Latin and French. But these slight impulses can, by their very rightness, disclose the deepest and most restrained emotion. An example is the celebrated letter from Golaud to his brother Pelléas, which is read to old Arkël so that he may decide what must be done:

How could a composer better convey the fearful, moving sense of pity inspired by a fragile being, for whom even tenderness risks being too harsh? And yet we are quite close to small talk here.

When the emotion is stronger and more direct, the accents are more marked and more expressive. What melancholy grace there is in these simple words of Mélisande to Pelléas, on the terrace by the sea:

or in her reply to old Arkël, who tells her that the bad times will come to an end, whereas she feels she is already guilty and will not confide anything about herself:

And listen to Pelléas singing, when Mélisande's hair has come to him:

This is a true melody, but its shape and rhythm are the very motions of the impassioned words; it is a melody that palpitates with controlled emotion, and takes up again, and becomes elated, and improves on itself, in a sweet, impetuous frenzy.

Also listen to the entreaty from Golaud, who does not wish to die without being pardoned by the woman he judged, and killed:

And I would very much like to go on and tell of Mélisande's reply, sweetly indifferent, and unaware. But let us stop at these supplicatory accents which are so simple and sad. Through these few examples, it will have been seen that each emotion, and consequently each personality, is expressed in the very line of the vocal part, with miraculous precision, rightness and intensity, and that is only achieved by virtue of a free melody which is modelled on the spoken word and is, at the same time, profoundly musical.

And everything that the characters do not say, all the reasons in their hearts which they do not confess to themselves, all the suggestions of things that they undergo without understanding them, everything that is hidden in the depths of their consciousness, is revealed and realised by the orchestra's living symphony. In that way, if you like, *Pelléas* is related to the Wagnerian dramas, but with such profound differences that really an entirely new style of symphonic drama has been born.

We can recognize, in the course of the work, a certain number of motifs which reappear at different points and ensure unity. But first of all these motifs do not designate, as happens in Wagner, a definite object, a helmet or a ring, still less a definite situation, a curse or a spell, nor even one character to the exclusion of all others. They are not those tag-motifs with headings, placed at intervals by a provident composer in the midst of an abstruse score, like the signposts along the paths in a Germanic forest pointing to the *Schöne Aussicht* or the *Restauration*.[15] Here each theme applies only to a feeling and only comes back when summoned by that feeling.

For example, here is a motif which at first seems to belong to Golaud, since it is most often heard at his entrances and is marvellously suited to his harsh, sad form:[16]

But a derivative of this same motif will later depict the muffled, threatening sound of the sea:[17]

It is because in reality the theme does not denote Golaud particularly: it expresses disquiet. In the same way, the sea's agitation[18] will also, later, be Golaud's anxiety:[19]

Similarly again, do not think that this flute tune, which accompanies Pelléas' entrance,[20] will be exclusively devoted to him:

For you are going to meet it again, slightly modified, at the start of the fountain scene,[21] where it expresses the melancholy tenderness of things, not of a being:

We understand the role of these motifs: to manifest hidden feelings, to make the soul transparent, to let us see to the bottom of it, almost to weave, around the unreliable words, an embroidery of the revealed Unconscious. Thus, when Mélisande replies to Golaud, who is worried at seeing her so unhappy, 'No, no, it isn't Pelléas, it isn't anyone,' involuntarily the faded memory of the sweet hours by the fountain arises in her heart:[22]

And when at last the solemn words have been spoken, and the confession of love has escaped from their lips, for an instant the sunlit garden appears to the soul's eye, as in the days of hope when everything seemed to be smiling:[23]

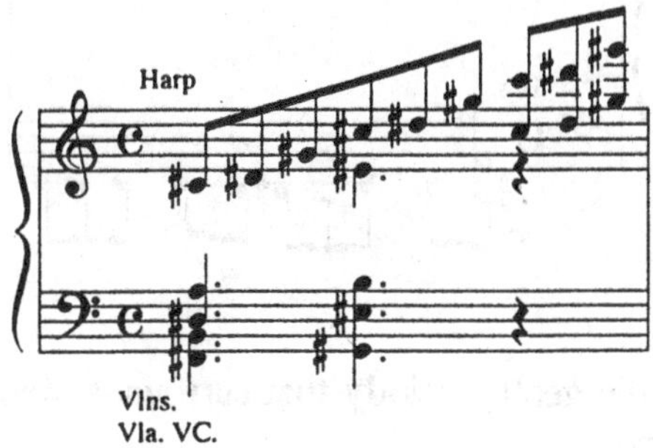

These motifs are all very short. They are not, as in Wagner, complete phrases which are developed and end peremptorily. They are extremely expressive, harmonious accents, but they only last as long as emotion itself when it passes in the depths of the soul, like a shadow that vanishes as soon as it is glimpsed. And thus we come to notice not only some set feelings, given once and for all, and therefore conventional, but the finest and most intimate nuances of our moral life. Furthermore, the motifs are also perpetually modified, and never reappear in the same form, imitating in this the instability of our feelings, which never have the same flavour or aspect at any two moments of our lifetime. But these transformations never result from the application of some law or formula: they are quite spontaneous, impossible to predict, and yet so natural! Each of these musical ideas seems to live for itself, and to open out freely under the eye of its creator; it has a germinative energy and so branches out in all directions; we see it appear, then become lost among the bushy foliage and luminous mists of the harmony, only to reappear further on; and it is still the same, and it is not the same: it is a new flower, different in shape, colour and smell, blooming on the same stem.

We have already seen the theme which at first accompanied Pelléas languish beside the fountain, and become shrouded with regret deep down at the memory of Mélisande.[24] Here it is back again, but this time Golaud is dreaming of the tentative intimacy, with bleak jealousy; in this way he becomes sinister, in the image of the threatening theme that accompanies him:[25]

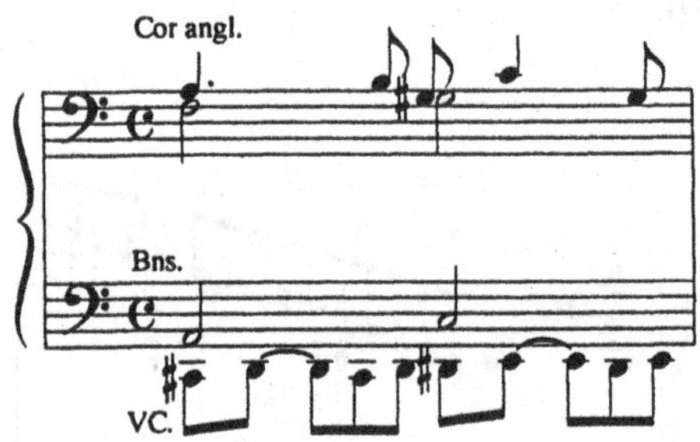

Everyone knows the gentle melody that surrounds Mélisande's timorous grace like a lover:[26]

Here it is again, much changed and very sad, at Golaud's bedside:[27]

And now Mélisande is sleeping the sleep of near-death, and the melody folds painfully back on itself:[28]

Mélisande has woken up, and is looking in astonishment at those around her, already uncomprehending:[29]

And finally here is the approach of very sweet, very peaceful death: the melody too breathes its last; all that remains of it is a fragment floating in a vague rhythm, apparently following its own course like a cloud ready to vanish:[30]

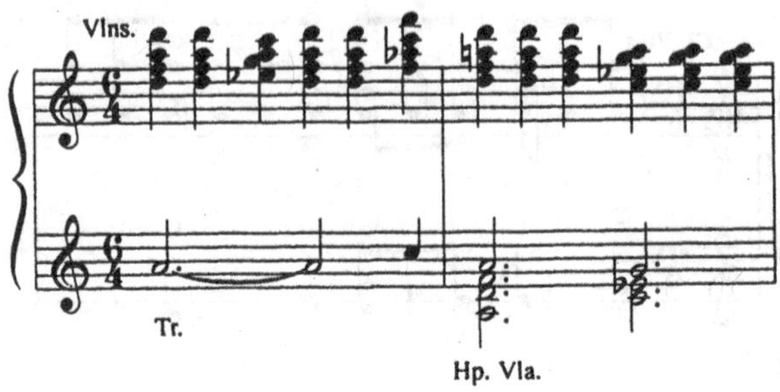

There could be nothing more clear-cut, more limpid, or more unreservedly melodic than all these thematic evocations; and yet we have noticed along the way that they are often combined, with each other or with themselves:[31] but that is a natural counterpoint which highlights the contours of the blended melodies, and produces no harshness or obscurity of any sort. It is the same with the harmony which almost always envelops and suffuses these motifs: it cannot be said that it derives from them; it lives alongside them, and colours them with its reflections, yet accords with them as a sky accords with a landscape.

Very harmonious, and definitely very consonant - that is how I would describe the harmony of Claude Debussy. And straight away people will talk to me about sevenths, ninths and altered fifths. But that is the language of music schools, not of our senses. A chord is consonant when it charms us by itself, and does not urgently call for another to follow it. Conversely, aggregations of notes must be called dissonances when the harmony is not enough to justify them, and they are only excused by the movement of the parts, which introduces suspensions, auxiliary notes, appoggiaturas and other liberties. In this sense, the harmony of Wagner and his disciples is very dissonant: so it always has a rigorous, authoritarian, implacable quality; we feel that the ear's pleasure will always be sacrificed to the treatment of the counterpoint and the interests of the tonality. Each note is justifiable by what precedes and responsible for what follows. The impression of the moment does not count at all; it is a harmony of context and connection. Claude Debussy's harmony is completely free. Each of the chords which comprise it is a consonance - a new consonance certainly, richer and more harmonious than all the consonances we used to know, gathered from among nature's vibrations with marvellous judgement, but ultimately a consonance which carries within itself its reasons for existing, and satisfies the ear to the point where we do not ask for anything after it. The chord progressions will therefore be entirely at the will of the composer. No cadential formula, no resolution of the leading note will govern the way they proceed. Each chord will be chosen only for its colour and its sonority; in this way the composer will gain new and unprecedented means of expression. For by means of a chord, even more than by a motif, no matter how short it might be, he will be able to convey instantaneous nuances of emotion.[32] Debussy is a master of this, whether he is spreading the delicate resonance of thirteenth and ninth chords around a melody,[33]

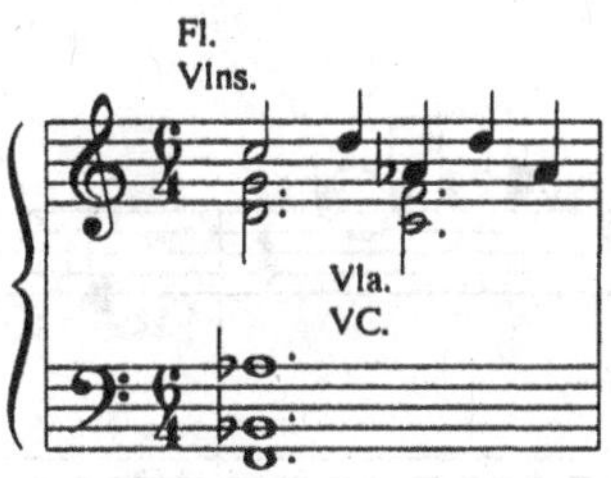

whether he is content with the chord alone, without melody, to depict the calm, somnolent water:[34]

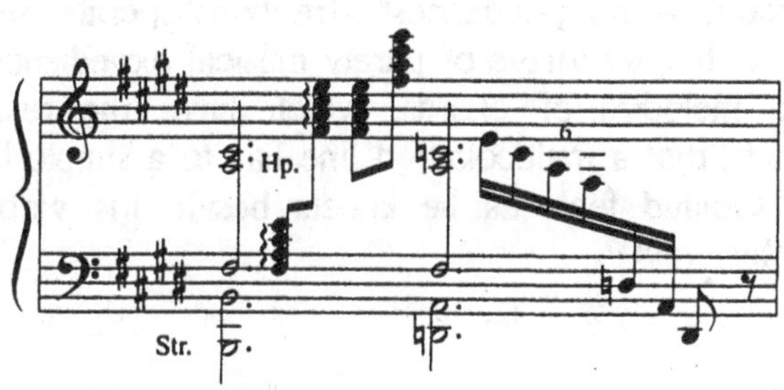

or the oppressive sensation as though the whole forest is pressing down on Golaud's chest:[35]

or Mélisande asleep, gentle and weak:36

And at other times, instead of being isolated in this way, the chords are juxtaposed against one another, but according to quite different laws than those governing cadences: attractions operate between them as with single notes, by virtue of purely musical expediencies; and this gives rise to melodies of chords, which have the relationship to ordinary melody that a multicoloured line has to a simple black stroke. The anxiety Golaud feels as he kneels beside his victim's bed is conveyed in this way:37

and so is the delicious intoxication of feeling that the barriers have fallen between souls:[38]

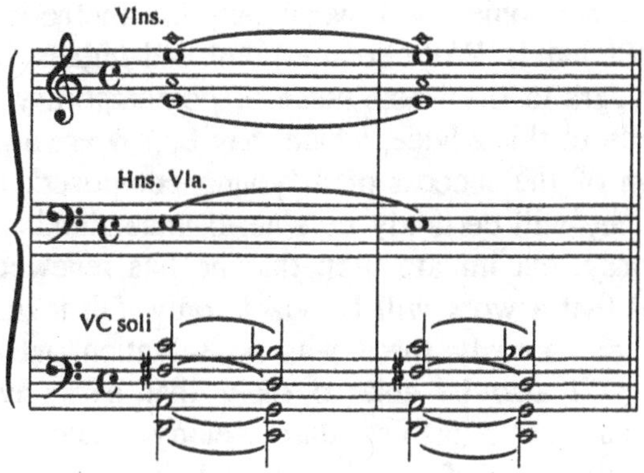

Add to this an orchestration of which no idea can be gained except by listening: a sober, clear orchestration, which is always coloured, the enemy of the thickening, the heavy mixtures of timbres, in short the whole grisaille of Wagner; an orchestration that proceeds by pure tones, in the French manner, which is also the manner of Berlioz and d'Indy, but it has a delicacy of nuance and a lightness of touch which is not the case with either of these two masters: a subtle, bold orchestration, which can make the oboe play above the flutes and the horn above the string section, and only ever uses just as many notes as are needed to make its effect. And then you will understand why *Pelléas et Mélisande* is the indisputable masterpiece of modern music drama, and why its charm is all-powerful: no preliminary study or metaphysico-musical initiation is necessary in order to experience this art of light and life. We can wander without a guide in the forest where every element sings: myriad fresh breezes blow, and an eternal dawn frolics among the tropical creepers. No word of human language can convey this magic which takes possession of all our senses at once.

Is there still a need for a conclusion? We have seen heroic legend culminate in a very generous and noble work which is slightly affected and not only lofty, but haughty. We have seen realism fail piteously, and only give us works which are ill-formed or odiously insincere. Human legend and free music have created an immortal masterpiece. We must not hesitate to plunge into the way that is now open. And I know full well what young composers are being told, what the most intelligent teachers in the official schools – the teachers who hear some music from time to time – will tell them over and over for a long time to come: 'Admire Debussy, but do not imitate him. Crown him with flowers and banish him from your thoughts. He succeeded, but it was by chance. His harmonies will wear out, his methods will appear ridiculous in your hands. Write counterpoint and fugues, build cantatas and close your ears to the whole noise of contemporary music.' They will listen silently to this advice, which may be sincere and inspired by other fears than of the success of a 'young composer'; but they will not follow it. They will certainly be able to understand that they must not copy Debussy, but imitate him; that he has renewed both music and drama, and that a work will be viable only if it is inspired by his principles, just as formerly there was no salvation outside Wagner's reforms. They will also be able to reply that harmony is no more changeable or subject to fashion than melody, since the same rules prevail over the grouping of sounds and over their juxtaposition; that if Mozart's chords have lost some of their freshness, his themes scarcely fare better today, and finally that as music, like everything else, is subject to constant change, it is better to please one's own time than to write in a language no one listens to any longer. More especially as in this way one has the greatest chance of pleasing posterity: it has always been the works which were the freshest and most daringly modern when they first appeared that have later become the glorious masterpieces in whose shadow future generations will rest.

La Revue musicale (15 April 1905), p. 244

A triumph: capacity audience, four, five and six curtain calls after each act, shouts of enthusiasm. Evenings when a fine work is revealed are good evenings; those when we return to a masterpiece, even more beloved than on the first occasion, are better. More than a masterpiece, *Pelléas et Mélisande* is a unique work, the only one, as far as I am concerned, that I can listen to in the theatre without finding anything to grate on me, to betray the author's intentions, his complacency towards himself or his heavy artfulness (as so often happens in Wagner): there is no word which is not both everyday and profound, all the gestures are natural and noble, the scenery harmonious and true; there is not an unnecessary or unexpressive note, not an insignificant chord; everywhere is life, most candid in its beauty. No effort is necessary to understand the subject, hear the words, or discern the melodies;

the work acts as a whole, its charm is immediate and irresistible like a spell; from the first chord to the last, we sail along as in a dream, but a human dream, in which we encounter ourselves again and discover ourselves. [. . .]

Fortunately the interpretation has not greatly changed. Mademoiselle Garden, Messieurs Périer, Dufranne and Vieuille are equally excellent as artists and singers. Mademoiselle Passam (Geneviève) sings her role too much and does not *say* it enough.

Comœdia (11 June 1914), p. 2

And I saw again the only child . . .[39]

The child of our dreams, *Pelléas et Mélisande*, the work of salvation which by delivering music from all that was not itself made it weightless as light and free as thought. The spell is still working, and today it is safe to predict that it will be immortal. Silent are the prophets of doom, who when faced with our enthusiasm took up Madame de Sévigné's maxim about Racine and coffee.[40] The success is a lasting one; fashion had nothing to do with it; familiarity, far from dulling the impressions, revives and refines them.[41, 42] Each note is known to us; we wait in full certainty for the question, the reply, the involuntary confession, the hidden anxiety, the lament, the threat, the forgiveness; we are on the look-out for the flute, the clarinet, the harp, the divided violins, the muted horns, the distant trumpet and the trombones of destiny. Our hope is fulfilled at every moment; our emotion, which does not succumb to initial surprise, swells into joy as if through a language which enables us to grasp directly the most subtle allusions and the implicit relationships.

In this way we discover, in this imponderable art, an unfailing solidity, and it is pure music, in the true sense of the word: music which does not rely for support on any external apparatus of repetitions, reminders or developments. It will no doubt be objected that the situations and words of the poem inspired it. This observation is undeniable, but irrelevant, since the music can sustain itself if the situations and words are omitted: in the same way, we do not need the dedication to the moonlight, nor the epigraph *muss es sein* [sic] in order to appreciate the inner logic of a sonata by Beethoven, or the finale of one of his quartets.[43] The music, in *Pelléas et Mélisande*, superimposes on the literary drama a musical drama whose impulses are analogous but independent. Which of us has not had the experience of playing the score at the piano, without pronouncing a word and, captivated, following its course which is more varied but also more necessary than that of Classical symphonies, which are always deduced point by point like exercises in oratory?

The orchestra, which gives the music its colours and perspective, often crushes or clogs the lines. That was not the case this time, thanks to the devoted intelligence of a conductor[44] who was able to bring out each detail without being at all insistent: the melodies which rise up by turns would perish if they were detached from the harmony which bathes and nurtures them; the rule of this music is continuity, not a continuity obtained after the event, as often happens in Wagner, by interlacing separate layers, but an inborn continuity which unites very precise, distinctive forms according to their origin. That is why there is no place for any artifice of enlargement or expression; it is sufficient to allow the notes their value. But precisely these qualities of exactitude and moderation are, among musical interpreters, the least widespread, for it is far easier to exaggerate an accent than to hold it within its limits.[45]

I will not speak of the singers, for many reasons, one of which is that I am afraid of already being like the old music-lover who has so often taken pity on us, saying, 'Oh! if you'd heard Grisi!'[46] But the scenery and production this time seemed far removed from the character of the drama, and especially of the music. They have not changed since the first performance, and it is they which are at fault, for our taste is now more informed, and has changed. We did not know, in 1902, that there was a better way to represent a forest than by cluttering the stage with silhouettes of trees, or that a bedroom, even in a palace in a legendary kingdom, was imaginable without all its furnishings. Today, thanks to what we have learned from research carried out in Berlin, in Moscow, in London, thanks to the results which the Russians, led by Monsieur de Diaghilev,[47] have shown us, and thanks lastly to the experiments at our Théâtre des Arts,[48] we understand that theatrical works, similarly to music and poetry, gain in power and harmony to the extent that mind is made to prevail over matter. If ever the principles of simplification were applicable, it is in a work like this, which is careful only to define each of the characters by the emotions he feels, and assigns to the action itself a location which favours these feelings, without any regard for ordinary verisimilitude. The spring is only there to receive Mélisande's tears; the gardens look out over the sea so that the lights of a ship give rise to thoughts of Pelléas' departure; the grotto is muddy like a bad conscience, the three paupers who have come there to sleep are a reproach, and the underground vault beneath the castle is nothing other than the refuge where murderous doubt lurks. Too much reality, in objects which are meant as signs and figures, shocks and offends us. We dream of a forest reduced to an evocative tree, of a garden fading into the evening mists, of a grotto with only deep blue shadows for walls, of an underground vault with the light of the lantern trembling in the thick darkness. Of what use are these green paper leaves, these craggy outlines of boulders and, in the sky over the sea, these gentle clouds which seem to have been brought straight from Dieppe or Trouville?[49] Monsieur Jusseaume, a very talented painter and a delicate artist, is certainly as sensitive as we are to these errors, and if it were given to him to redo this scenery, today he would conceive it quite differently.[50]

Notes

1 '*Pelléas et Mélisande*', written in French, is reprinted in F. Aprahamian, ed., *Essays on music: an anthology from 'The Listener'* (London, 1967), pp. 74-77.

2 'Le cœur a ses raisons que la raison ne connaît point.' Blaise Pascal (1623-1662), *Pensées* iv, 277. In fact, Laloy modernizes the quotation, giving it as 'Le cœur a ses raisons que la raison ne connaît pas.'

3 This article first appeared in *La Revue musicale* (15 November 1902), pp. 471-473, under the heading 'Exercices d'analyse'. The translation is of a revised version which appears in *La Musique retrouvée*, pp. 115-118, as a chapter called 'Sur deux accords (novembre 1902)'.

4 In Ancient Greek, accent was created by means of pitch rather than stress. Dionysius of Halicarnassus wrote in the first century AD: '[. . .] the melody of speech is measured by a single interval, approximately that termed a "fifth", and does not rise to the high pitch by more than three tones and a semitone, nor fall to the low by more than this amount.' *De compositione verborum* xi, p. 40ff

5 The hiatus, a discontinuity produced by the occurrence of two vowel sounds in succession, was generally forbidden in French poetry from the seventeenth to the early twentieth century.

6 Elsewhere in *La Musique retrouvée* (p. 110) Laloy says that he thinks a Protestant upbringing - at least of the Calvinist form which Protestantism took in France - would be a barrier to enjoying *Pelléas*. He explores the idea of the contrast between the Roman Catholic and Lutheran traditions in 'Le Chant grégorien et la musique française', *Le Mercure musical* (15 January 1907), pp. 75-80.

7 'Le Drame musical moderne.' I: 'La Légende héroïque: *Fervaal*';

II: 'Les Véristes: Zola-Bruneau'; III: 'Les Véristes français: Gustave Charpentier'; IV: 'C. Debussy.' *Le Mercure musical* (15 May, 1 June, 1 July, 1 August 1905), pp. 8-16, 75-84, 169-176, 233-250

8 Lesure and Nichols (1987), p. 160

9 The first paragraph, which looks back over the previous articles in the series, has been omitted.

10 Principal characters in Charpentier's *Louise*

11 Principal characters in *Fervaal* by d'Indy

12 'Non, c'est un amour né de la vie même, qui a grandi au fil des jours, au gré des entretiens familiers, qui lentement, comme une molle vapeur insaisissable, s'est dégagé de la tendresse fraternelle, qui a donné un charme inavoué à toutes les habitudes d'une intimité quotidienne, qui a tissé des liens invincibles entre deux âmes non pas égales, mais pareilles, qui envahit l'être entier comme un poison suave et mortel, qui est déjà le maître absolu lorsqu'à peine on s'aperçoit de son existence; - enfin, et pour tout dire, un amour véritable.'

13 'Je ne pourrai sortir de cette forêt': the first words, sung by Golaud, of Debussy's *Pelléas et Mélisande*. (In Maeterlinck's play, they occur at the beginning of Act I Scene ii.)

14 Elsewhere, Laloy wrote about the similarities between *Tristan und Isolde* and *Pelléas et Mélisande*:

> Debussy could vilify the *Ring*, *Die Meistersinger* or *Parsifal*, which he admired and no longer loved. He always loved *Tristan*. Whence the care he took to fight against its charm, which was poison to his nature. Having drunk from the philtre, he had to find the antidote and exorcise the spell. His *Pelléas* is another *Tristan* which suggests without explaining, feels compassion instead of cursing, is lit up by tenderness and finds in pity its absolution.
>
> *Claude Debussy* (rev. ed. 1944), pp. 38-39

Later he commented that 'forty years apart, [Tristan and Pelléas] are two brothers, the elder more heroic, the younger more a dreamer, dedicated to the same fate by love's poison.' '*Tristan* et *Pelléas*', *La Joie musicale*, vol. 6 (16 May-15 June 1930), p. 6

15 *Schöne Aussicht*: fine prospect. *Restauration*: restaurant.

16 Laloy's note: 'Page 2 of the vocal score, page 1 of the orchestral score.' All references to score pages in the remainder of this article are by Laloy.

17 Pages 92 (vocal) and 132 (orchestral).

18 Pages 92 and 134.

19 Pages 253 and 375.

20 Pages 30 and 40.

21 Pages 48 and 70.

22 Pages 75 and 109.

23 Pages 221 and 333. Compare 135 and 206.

24 'Nous avons déjà vu le thème qui d'abord accompagnait Pelléas s'alanguir au bord de la fontaine, et se voiler de regret au fond de la mémoire de Mélisande.'

[25] Pages 187 and 277.
[26] Pages 34 and 46.
[27] Pages 69 and 102.
[28] Pages 243 and 363.
[29] Pages 249 and 371.
[30] Pages 278 and 403.
[31] Other examples: pages 125 and 185 (Mélisande's grace and Pelléas' tenderness); pages 58 and 84 (the theme of Golaud's roughness in its original form and inversion simultaneously); pages 201 and 309 (a motif by imitation).
[32] A year before this article was published, Laloy gave a lecture in Brussels on 'L'Ecole française de musique contemporaine' ('The French school of contemporary music') and notes taken by M. Hébert were published in *Le Guide musical* (3 April 1904), pp. 309–311. Laloy compared the harmony of *Pelléas et Mélisande* to that of César Franck:

> In Franck, the harmony is always connected, dissonance is resolved; in Debussy, juxtaposition of chords without justification by the movement of the parts. Combination, for example, of two juxtaposed root-position triads (like the strokes in Pointillism; it is for the listener to make the synthesis). In this way one obtains, in music and painting, extraordinary effects.

[33] Pages 75 and 109.
[34] Pages 48 and 70.
[35] Pages 68 and 101.
[36] Pages 243 and 366.
[37] Pages 261 and 384.
[38] Pages 220 and 332.
[39] The first line of a poem in Verlaine's collection *Sagesse* (1881), which begins:

> Et j'ai revu l'enfant unique: il m'a semblé
> Que s'ouvrait dans mon cœur la dernière blessure,
> Celle dont la douleur plus exquise m'assure
> D'une mort désirable en un jour consolé.

[40] The writer Madame de Sévigné (1626–1692) did not in fact say that Racine, like coffee, would go out of fashion, but it is a common misapprehension among French *littérateurs* that she did.
[41] In 1908, in an article on that year's musical budget, Laloy had reported that *Pelléas et Mélisande* achieved the highest takings of any modern work at the Opéra-Comique. He then noted bemusedly that the government official who wrote the report, one Monsieur Buyat, could not understand this success, as he found the music 'particularly difficult'; he could only put it down to 'the perfection of the staging [...] and [...] the superiority of the main performer, Mademoiselle Mary Garden.' *S.I.M.* (15 January 1908), pp. 2–3
[42] *Pelléas et Mélisande* reached its hundredth performance in 1913, the year before this article was written. Of that occasion Laloy wrote: 'A most Parisian supper celebrated this anniversary; friends appeared in their numbers, much greater numbers than on the already distant day of the

première, but it is apostolic to welcome, even belatedly, all who are interested.' *La Grande revue* (10 February 1913), p. 623

43 *Muss es sein? Es muss sein! Es muss sein!* (*Must it be? It must be! It must be!*) is the fatalistic comment written above the last movement of Beethoven's String quartet in F, op. 135. The title *Moonlight* sonata did not, of course, originate with Beethoven.

44 The conductor was François Ruhlmann, Director of Music at the Opéra-Comique from 1906 to 1913, in which capacity he also conducted the first performances of Dukas' *Ariane et Barbe-Bleue* and Ravel's *L'Heure espagnole.*

45 Detailed criticism of the orchestral balance has been omitted.

46 The Italian soprano Giulia Grisi (1811–1869) gave operatic performances in Paris and London from the 1830's until her retirement in 1861. She was famous for the perfect placement and evenness of her voice.

47 As pointed out in Buckle (1979), p. 16, Diaghilev had 'minimal nobility' on the side of his paternal grandfather. Accordingly some French sources refer to him as 'Monsieur de Diaghilev'.

48 See p. 2.

49 Popular seaside holiday spots in France

50 Two paragraphs about the staging have been omitted.

La Mer

Laloy was staying at his family estate in the Jura in October 1905 when he learned that *La Mer* was to be performed for the first time. He caught the train back to Paris to hear it. The audience was hostile after the scandal over Debussy's divorce and his relationship with Emma Bardac, and most critics disapproved of the work. Laloy's was one of the few favourable reviews.

Notes for this section begin on p. 204.

Le Mercure musical (1 November 1905), pp. 487–489

Our great concert series, besieged by a public long deprived of good music, reopened their doors on 15 October; and as early as that first day, they gave us a new work by Claude Debussy which is among the loveliest, the most harmonious, the most captivating, and at the same time one of the broadest and most powerful not only in music, but in the whole of art, and I would almost say in nature, so near the elements does one find oneself in this work, as though close up against things. Once again, the great Initiate has lifted the veil of Isis, and this time not only her languid smile has appeared, as in *L'Après-midi d'un faune*, but her lustrous eyes, pensive, pierced with none knows what serene melancholy and as if closed, over a world of unknown tenderness. Never has the entire mystery of the world so nearly been revealed to us.

This impression, which is my own, and took hold of me violently and almost painfully, was not shared, I know, by some of my colleagues, and not the least of them. Debussy has been reproached with having portrayed not the sea as a whole, but a single aspect of it, and this aspect also seemed to some to be too sunny and smiling. Despite the most admirable efforts on my part, I cannot understand these critics. It goes without saying that, like the painter who establishes a landscape at a precise time of day and in a fixed lighting, Claude Debussy only wanted to express a single moment and a single impression in each of his tableaux; to include all the sea's appearances, his composition would have had to fill all eternity. But in each of these three episodes, entitled 'De l'aube à midi sur la mer', 'Jeux de vagues' and 'Dialogue du vent et de la mer', which have an infinite existence, he has been able to create enduringly all the glimmerings and shifting shadows, caresses and murmurs, gentle sweetness and fiery anger, seductive charm and sudden gravity contained in those waves which Æschylus praised for their 'smile without number'.[1] Let us not be too romantic. Let us not seek to hear, in the roaring of the waves, imprecations which are of little concern to them; let us not curse the wrecker who cannot hate us, since she is not aware of us; and let us love things naively, as friends who are too great ever to know us, but so much more beautiful than we!

About the musical form which realised this marvellous feat of evocation, it also seems to me that no one has said exactly what needs to be said, since no one has said exactly what I think. Debussy is upbraided for not having written three new *Nocturnes*. Certainly in *La Mer* we do not find the trembling colours which constitute the somehow virginal charm of 'Nuages', 'Fêtes' and 'Sirènes'. *La Mer* has a different character, and almost a resplendent maturity. It is larger and broader, firmer in its foundations and richer in its contours. This is no longer Pointillism, but it is still Impressionism, through the unaltered freshness of the emotions which are translated into melodies and harmonies unique in the world, some of which I cannot restrain myself from quoting: here from the first movement is one of those tenderly poignant chromatic phrases of which only Debussy knows the secret:

And this melancholy call, which reappears in the first and last movements, instantly raises up before our eyes the sterile wastes which are the kingdom of the wind:

And this solemn phrase in the trombones, horns and trumpets, which concludes the first movement, and also plays an important role in the whole work, seems to be a breath from the depths of the abyss:

I will stop here (and moreover I will return to the work), for I would need to quote many other, equally sublime passages, which grip the throat as everything superhuman does: in my view, only Debussy's music and the sights of nature cause such pain by dint of joy and the very excess of their beauty.

The work was conducted with much feeling and precision: I could certainly criticize points of detail (the brass were often too strong); but I do not have the heart to, so grateful am I to Monsieur Chevillard for offering us such a fine program,[2] which also included Beethoven's Symphony in A, the fourth Beatitude of César Franck [...], the sparkling Symphony for piano and orchestra by Vincent d'Indy [...], and the *Carnaval romain* overture by Berlioz.[3] Thus one could follow the growth of French music throughout a whole century, up to its last, wonderful bloom.[4]

Le Mercure musical (15 November 1905), p. 546

I must begin with a most painful confession: I was not at the concerts on 29 October. I had escaped to my distant estate,[5] taking with me *La Mer*, like treasure which was stolen perhaps,[6] but made mine by right of love. Touched by the first hint of cold, the forest flamed with yellow and russet, a biting wind blew across the drenched meadows, one could sense in the distance the imperceptible white snow on the plateaux of the upper Jura, and all around, from the swollen, damp tillages to the darkened thatched roofs, a sad calm foreshadowed the winter (I dedicate this alexandrine[7] to my Franc-Comtois[8] friend Henri Gauthier-Villars). It was there, in that contemplative, inward-turned, almost dying world of nature, that I came to understand even better the masterpiece of life, light and strength which Debussy has just given us; above all I better grasped the powerful, free logic which gives rise to the melodic efflorescences and links them one to another: the logic of a beautiful tree whose branches are dissimilar yet harmonious, a logic directly opposed to all scholasticism, being directly inspired by nature; a musical logic, if ever there was one, opening up for our art, which has for so long been a prisoner in our houses, our salons and our concert halls, a dizzying view of the universe, which is its true model, its true kingdom.

Claude Debussy (rev. ed. 1944), pp. 88–90

The symphonic poem, *La Mer*, which was first performed by Camille Chevillard at his concert on 15 October 1905, was begun in 1903. The long delay is explained by the period of agitation through which the composer had just passed, traces of which can be found in the work, recognisable not in some transport of indiscreet passion, but on the contrary in a sense of order which is more apparent and more studied than usual. In these three 'symphonic sketches', entitled 'De l'aube à midi sur la mer', 'Jeux de vagues', 'Dialogue du vent et de la mer', and arranged like the three movements of a Classical symphony,[9] we also find, in the Classical manner, textual transpositions of the same idea into different tonalities, over a tied harmony, at times even interleaved with intermediary inflections. However, the ideas are strong and free, joyful, serious, light or plaintive in turn, all drawn from the springs of nature, but it seems that the composer, too often disturbed in his work, was unable to rediscover their first freshness, and was then obliged to treat and manipulate them, instead of letting them live and blossom: sirens caught in the net, still breathing.

The work was one of importance and imposed itself authoritatively. However, more than one listener, remembering *Pelléas* and the *Nocturnes*, was worried at not recognising the persuasive sweetness which had so moved him. Was a reaction being foreshadowed, a return to former laws? Such fears were unnecessary. This solid frame was only a safety measure, dictated by exceptional circumstances. Even the luxuriant detail offered by the *Estampes* was not to last. The works were going to progress in quite another direction, far removed from all eloquence, towards pure lines and strong relief. Already two works of more modest dimensions, which had just appeared,[10] brought proof to those who knew how to read and listen.

At the Concerts Colonne on 19 and 26 January 1908 Debussy conducted *La Mer.* It was his conducting début. The performance was a great improvement on Chevillard's in 1905, the scandal over Debussy's private life had been forgotten, and the work was given a rapturous reception. This article analyses the change in Debussy's compositional style which had occurred with *La Mer.*

'The new manner of Claude Debussy'[11] *La Grande revue* (10 February 1908), pp. 530–535

The concert on 19 January, at the Châtelet, introduced us to a new work, *La Mer*, and a new conductor in the person of Claude Debussy, taking up the magic baton, that moderator of the powers of sound, for the first time.[12] His authority, his imperious succinctness and his power surprised only those who had not so far understood the hidden solidity of a music in which the imaginative quality is never arbitrary. Since François Couperin, we have never had a composer in France who was more the master of his art, more capable of making the notes say what he wanted, of directing his thoughts in the only order that was appropriate to them.

So his first works are not youthful works, in the usual sense of the word, since their form is already pure, and completely independent.

They are young works, though, in the quality of emotion: that charm that seems to flee, that quivering grace, those murmurs, those appeals rising and vanishing, that restless taste for pleasure, that joy which is so light that it dissolves into a dream or becomes lost in chimeras, above all that poignantly intimate melancholy, that tenderness which life does not encourage – all of that is youthfulness, and of the type that arose around the 1890's: ardent, tormented, quick to feel disgust, a seeker after the impossible, wanting to change a too harsh reality into symbols, falling in love with lily-like mysticism and at the same time with an aggrieved paganism. Baudelaire, Verlaine and Mallarmé were its masters; and Claude Debussy owed his first inspirations to their poems, as also to the Pre-Raphaelite subtleties of Rossetti and, a little later, to one of those Maeterlinck plays which have the sweetly disturbed quality of a fever or a rainy sky. Far be it from me to think of disparaging the music which transfigured the visions – the at times slightly laborious visions – of literary men in the throws of 'speaking of the best'.[13] It was only through the intervention of music that blemishes, awkward passages, artifices and untruths were removed from these visions; through music they were given feeling. First read the text of *La Damoiselle élue*, or 'Le Balcon',[14] or *Pelléas et Mélisande*, then their translation into music, and you will see how these works, conceived afresh by the composer, were created for a second time, and only then found their perfection.

But this very perfection did not have to put us on the wrong track. Youth must pass, and Claude Debussy's latest works evince a maturity, a balance and a reconciliation with life. I am speaking of the second set of *Fêtes galantes*, the first and especially the second volume of *Images*, and this symphonic poem *La Mer*, whose splendour is finally apparent to us.

Until recently, it was an art of indications, nuances and allusions; an evocative art, which found an echo in the listener's soul to a quality of thought which was not indecisive but deliberately unfinished, and was able to sketch deliciously impressionistic pictures – all vibrations in the air and effects of light – with almost no prominent lines, above all with no impasto:[15] remember the *Estampes*, or the enchanting miracles in the *Nocturnes*. Today, while renouncing none of the sensuous delicacy which is perhaps unique in the world, the style is tight, determined, affirmative, full; in a word, Classical. This evolution was as necessary as it was fortunate, as the adjacent examples of literature and painting demonstrate; a feeling for construction and integrity of design allowed Claude Monet and Gauguin to risk bold colours without making a motley; the Greek Muses saved Henri de Régnier and Jean Moréas; and many a literary journal, remaining faithful to the idolatrous cult of the word, dies of pedantry and boredom. Always protected by a natural distaste for excess and incoherence, Claude Debussy still could not, at the time he when he was avoiding clearly outlined contours, attain either a sense of fullness – that beauty of power which produces a wholesome joy and almost the intoxication of living – nor, on the other hand, that bare, pure concision which can express a personality or a complete scene in a few strokes. He was devoted to the exquisite, the ineffable, the unreal; today he is leaving his fields of dreams and his imaginary kingdoms; the enchanting coulours he brings back with him will hereafter be sustained and in relief. I would be very surprised if his future orchestral compositions were not large and strong like *La Mer*, or if he did not employ voice and piano for those authoritative miniatures of which we have the model in 'Le Faune' from the *Fêtes galantes* or in the unforgettable *Image*, 'Et la lune descend sur le temple qui fut'. And no one doubts that the adventurous love story of Tristan and Isolde[16] will call forth different vocal writing than the melancholy attraction between Pelléas and Mélisande.

Every part of the work evinces a new spirit. The melody, rather than remaining suspended or dissolving into the air, is now explicit, strong and self-contained. Witness that phrase, right at the beginning, which stands out from the murmuring background that is as yet undefined: it is a muffled cry from the lonely places where dawn spreads its first reflections:

It is so distinct, however, that we will always recognize it and it will be able to return, sometimes bathed in sunlight, in the course of this first movement ('De l'aube à midi sur la mer'):

or else whipped and dilated by persistent squalls in 'Dialogue du vent et de la mer'.

Similarly, that two-part phrase which shows the play of light and water, mirroring them first joyfully then tenderly:

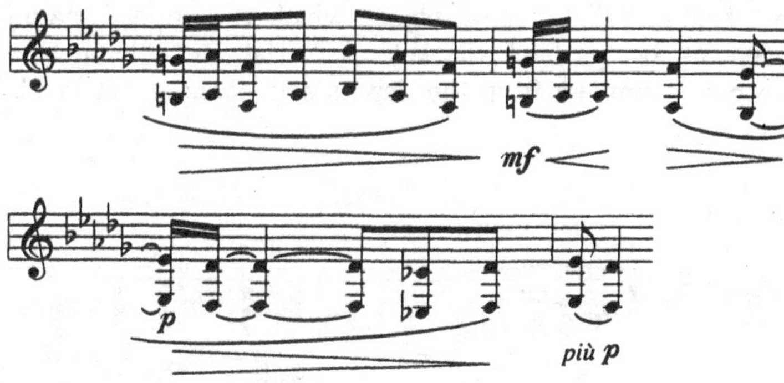

It alone, after the prelude is over, forms the first section of the piece, broadly developed, not by textbook procedures, fragmentation, augmentation or inversion, but by a natural fecundity which makes the melody spring up on all sides: the oboe's sadness, the flute's delicate flight, the violin's caress, all voices awaken. Truth to tell, Claude Debussy has never conceived a developmental passage except by association of musical ideas; but, until now, he had not constructed one on such a broad scale, or in which his controlling conception was as evident.

These developments follow one other by virtue of a very clear plan, and the work's three parts have the role and the form of a symphony first movement, scherzo and finale. It will be said that the laws of the symphony are not those of a symphonic poem; which is true if one is thinking of certain particular laws, such as the enforced modulation for the second subject; and false if one is speaking only of general rules of equilibrium, which are the very condition of art.[17] Elsewhere[18] I have attempted to show that 'programme music is valid only if it can dispense with the programme', and that 'the difference between the most detailed symphonic poem and the most abstract symphony is one of degree, not of nature'. The music of *La Mer* can, if necessary, be explained by itself; its descriptive power is in no way diminished for that, quite the contrary. The only total realism is that of bad photography; a work of art always supposes an inner harmony which makes it stable for, within the infinite continuity of nature, it isolates certain forces which must form a closed system. These are elementary truths, but the Romantic revolt, by its doctrines more than its products, has made us forget or scorn them. Thus it is further praise of this new work to point out that the first movement includes two subjects which are developed at the same time as they are stated, one in D flat, the other in B flat, and that a third subject, which will appear again in the last movement, brings back the key of D flat: the solemn trombone and horn call, rising up from the depths and opening out in glowing triumph:

And do you know how the return to the main key is announced? By a dominant pedal point, that is, by a series of harmonies over a sustained A flat in the bass, which our ear waits to hear resolve down a fifth. But these harmonies vibrate with warmth, and they are heard around a slumbrous, torridly voluptuous tune:

It is the midday hour, when the eyes close and the body grows drowsy. Thus, with one of those chords of which this artist possesses the secret, reason is satisfied at the same time as nature is observed; and the composition of the picture adds to its brilliance.

These unambiguous tonalities are not at all overbearing. They gently guide a melody which retains the freedom to avoid semitones, in the Chinese manner, or to bring them together in chromatic progressions, to imply a note, to alter another, and to burden the key of D flat with a G natural and a C flat: the curious are able to recognize in these antiquated structures the vestige or image of some scale from Gregorian chant or ancient music. Really, these are not restorations, but inventions which foreshadow the imminent fall of our two poor diatonic modes, major and minor, and the advent of a music with no fixed scales, which is based directly on harmonic relations.

The harmony, which is present everywhere, prevents any misunderstandings and resolves any uncertainties, assigns a definite function to notes which are linked not at all randomly, nor in view of pictorial effect alone. This harmony, which is as fine and as rich as ever, is realised more broadly here, and is more figured. Instead of being presented in the primitive form of chords and being entrusted to one instrumental choir, the harmony is distributed across the whole orchestra, passes from one group to another, swells out then falls back, and above all is translated into lively accents, into resolute motifs, even into complete melodies, which bring life to the backgrounds that have hitherto been motionless, dividing them into successive planes and giving them movement. This symphonic poem has an agile polyphony which is always clear because it is the flowering of the harmony, and it awakens the rhythm from the summit to the depths of the orchestra.

Claude Debussy's music has always had a rhythm, in the sense that it has always conveyed a gesture or an attitude in the most poetically faithful way: perhaps the feeling of dance was always present. But he used to write stylised dances, reduced to a candid simplicity of lines, of waving veils or quivering effects of light: dancing clouds or evanescent sirens, dancing spirits of the air or antique shades, with diaphanous bodies that are unembraceable. Today they are true dances, pursuits, responses, intertwining rhythms rising, calling to each other, forming brilliant roundelays, processions which break and re-form endlessly, or harmonious confusion. All of space trembles with the joy of movement, all forces enter into action, carrying each other along, and we feel surrounded, bathed and almost rolled about by soft waves which we cannot resist, on the sea's vast bosom, which is swollen with life.

Power: that is the striking and perhaps surprising thing in this new art. This power was already present in the works which were lightest in appearance, but it remained latent: it could only be guessed at in the sureness of gesture, the assurance of bearing and that exquisite reserve, which is the sign of a singular dominion over oneself. It blazes out today, as it did already in certain places in *Pelléas* – the most dramatic places: for example, the scene of anguish and pity in which Golaud, altered by knowledge, interrogates the child and makes him a witness. But these were isolated signs, and perhaps they stand out too much amidst a sweet music in which all will is unravelled. Many people misunderstood them, to the point of wishing in their hearts that Claude Debussy would keep repeating those tableaux in the garden or at the fountain: the languid charm of those passages was prescribed by the subject matter, chosen some years previously, but perhaps at the time the work appeared it no longer satisfied a vigorous mind which aimed to leave life whole, instead of perfuming it with a saddened sensuality. At that time it was not seen that the future of music lay in strength; not the brute strength of a Richard Strauss, a disciplinary composer who too often force-feeds the listener or canes him on the soles of his feet. We have nothing to fear: strength is always harmonious in those who have received the gifts of the Muses. And if we doubted it, we would have only to recall that passage in the middle of the second movement ('Jeux de vagues') where a sweet, lustrous melody is lashed by waves of tingling spray like calm pathways traced across the mirrored expanse of the sea:

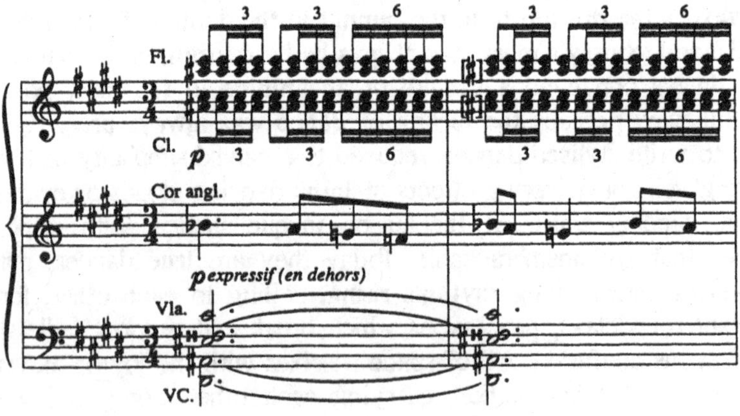

or else the very tender reply the sea makes to the wind's assaults, in the Dialogue which concludes the poem with tremendous energy and emotion:

Notes

1 Æschylus, *Prometheus bound*, line 90

2 In 1908, just after Debussy conducted *La Mer*, Laloy wrote that the 1905 performance would have been better postponed (*La Grande revue* (25 February 1908), p. 373). It was generally acknowledged that Chevillard's 1905 performance was unsatisfactory, and in fact Debussy wrote beforehand to Jacques Durand, 'Chevillard is bound to dismember *La Mer* unmercifully.' However, when Chevillard conducted the work again in 1908, Laloy thought the interpretation was 'much more controlled and coherent' ('beaucoup plus surveillée et suivie'): see *S.I.M.* (15 December 1908), p. 674.

3 Remarks about the performers have been omitted.

4 Debussy wrote to thank Laloy for this article three days later, on 4 November 1905:

> I am too well aware of the delicacy and rigorous comprehension in you to congratulate you or even thank you.... At the very most I'll think it valid to tell you the emotion I feel at seeing you follow me step by step with a power of divination that derives from something I cannot name accurately enough. And with words as simple as flowers, chosen with such infallible taste which, moreover, you seem to wear on all occasions.
>
> When do you return?... Be sure to let me know, for I must see you; I have so many things to tell you! among others that a few days ago I became the father of a little girl – the joy of that has overwhelmed me slightly and still frightens me.
>
> Hoping to see you soon ...

It is interesting to compare this appreciative letter with one Debussy had written to Pierre Lalo on 25 October 1905, in response to Lalo's unfavourable review of *La Mer*:

> There's no problem in your not liking *La Mer* and I've no intention of complaining about it. I shall perhaps suffer regret that you haven't understood me and astonishment at finding you (though one such occasion doesn't establish a habit) in agreement with your fellow music critics. [...] You say [...] 'that you do not see or smell the sea throughout these three sketches'! That's a large claim and I don't know who is going to evaluate it for us ... I love the sea and I've listened to it with the passionate respect it deserves. If I've been inaccurate in taking down what it dictated to me, that is no concern of yours or mine. You must admit, not all ears hear in the same way. The heart of the matter is that you love and defend traditions which, for me, no longer exist or, at least, exist only as representative of an epoch in which they were not all as fine and valuable as people make out; the dust of the past is not always respectable. If in the future we are no longer able to understand one another, I shall not forget all that *Pelléas* owes to you for your warm and unstinting support ... Indeed, it's the main reason for my writing this letter.
>
> Lesure and Nichols (1987), pp. 163–164

5 The Laloy family estate is at Rahon par Chaussin, between the towns of Dôle and Poligny in the Jura region in eastern France.

6 Laloy's note:

> See what is said of me, over 'A cup of tea', by the famous composer R.-N., with whom I ask only to become better acquainted; for he has a sense of humour.

This is a reference to a light-hearted article, earlier in the same issue of *Le Mercure musical*, by Emile Vuillermoz. It was one of his occasional series called 'Une tasse de thé', in which fictitious characters discussed musical issues of the day. On this occasion the subject of conversation was the reception of Debussy's music, and in particular the music critics Louis Laloy and Camille Mauclair. 'The famous composer R.-N.' condemns both critics in the following terms (pp. 508–509):

> They are both pettifogging amateurs, nothing more. Their views are of absolutely no importance to me. [...] The first glories in counting [Debussy] among his friends, the second replies that these things must be concealed carefully 'like a secret'! One swings him about his head like a bludgeon, the other hides him in a deep vault, like stolen treasure ... no one thinks of simply embracing him!

7 In French poetry, a line containing twelve syllables is called an alexandrine. It is predominant in Classical French poetry and drama and therefore carries a certain prestige. Laloy's alexandrine is: 'Une sérénité triste annonçait l'hiver'.

8 Laloy and Gauthier-Villars (the music critic known as 'Willy') were both natives of the area of eastern France which is sometimes called the Franche-Comté.

9 The French Classical symphony, unlike the German, normally had three movements.

[10] *Fêtes galantes* II and *L'Isle joyeuse*

[11] 'La Nouvelle manière de Claude Debussy'. The article was also published in *S.I.M.* a few days later, slightly reduced and with score examples which have been added here: '*La Mer*. Trois esquisses symphoniques de Claude Debussy', *S.I.M.* (15 February 1908), pp. 209–214.

[12] In a review in *La Chronique des arts et de la curiosité* (1908), p. 30, Laloy wrote:

> Monsieur Claude Debussy's first appearance before an orchestra, on 19 January, was a great event. Monsieur Colonne has given an example which deserves to be followed: it behoves authors to show first of all how they themselves understand their works. We had already heard the three symphonic sketches of *La Mer* at the Concerts Chevillard, two years ago. Or rather, we did not hear them, so lacking were the qualities of movement and life, essential to the new work, in the person who marked the beat. Monsieur Debussy showed himself to be a vigorous, precise conductor, and the great, moving rhythms finally unfolded before us.

[13] The French phrase is 'dire du mieux' ('to speak of the best'). It is an obscure reference to the title of a treatise by the Symbolist poet René Ghil, *Dire du mieux* (1889–1895).

[14] The first of the *Cinq poèmes de Baudelaire*

[15] The *Oxford English dictionary* defines *impasto* as the laying on of colour thickly.

[16] Laloy's note: 'We know that the next drama by Claude Debussy will be on this subject, after the poem which has been so artistically restored by Monsieur J. Bédier.'

[17] Laloy later commented again on the symphonic structure of *La Mer*: 'Here the symphonic poem joins the symphony, as also in the *Nocturnes*, and the *Prélude à l'Après-midi d'un faune*; but as the work is more weighty and richer in detail, its large lines are also simpler and more marked.' *S.I.M.* (15 December 1908), p. 674

[18] Laloy's note: 'L. Laloy, *Rameau*, p. 236'

Images II

Laloy reviewed the first performance, and later told how he gave Debussy the idea of the first piece in the set, 'Cloches à travers les feuilles'. This account was confirmed by Debussy's step-daughter, Dolly Bardac. Debussy dedicated the second piece in the set to Laloy.

La Grande revue (10 March 1908), pp. 180–181

On 21 February, at the Cercle Musical, Monsieur Ricardo Viñes presented to the public, for the first time, the new *Images* by Claude Debussy, which were published six weeks ago: his performance, interesting as always, nevertheless felt the effects of such a brief period of study, and will become better as he better penetrates the meaning of pieces which – especially the last two – mark a veritable revolution in the art of writing for the piano: never had a composer ventured such pure lines, a style so simple and bare, a form which is at once so natural and so sustained. These are works to which one cannot listen without abandoning one's soul to them; and for that reason, in spite of the great success which welcomed them, they are perhaps less well suited to the undifferentiated crowd at a concert than to an intimate, invited audience.

Claude Debussy (rev. ed. 1944), pp. 95–96

A second set of *Images* for piano appeared in 1907. I was in the habit at that time of extending my stay in the country until the beginning of winter and, writing to my illustrious friend who had long since returned to Paris, I told him about the touching use of the knell which sounds from Vespers on All Saints' Day until the Requiem Mass,[1] ringing from village to village, across the forests with their yellowing leaves, in the silence of the evening. Thus the idea came to him for the first piece, with its diffuse but vibrant softness, whose title is 'Cloches à travers les feuilles'.[2]

The second piece transports us to a different land, where distances and letter post do not exist, a dream country where we would go together, 'Et la lune descend sur le temple qui fut'. More so than in 'Pagodes', in a less torrid, more serious Far East, the mind retires within itself and the music becomes condensed, pure of any egotistical mixing, a translucent, compressed gem, born of space and silence.[3]

But the third piece, to bring a brilliant ending to the set, returns from over the seas to the inhabited isles and firm lines of the Japanese etching in which these 'Poissons d'or' were drawn.[4] Rebelling against all systems, and in this much closer to Couperin than to Rameau, he is guided by taste, and the world, known or unknown, belongs to him; as the mood takes him, he sets off on a voyage of discovery or revisits, no less joyfully, a familiar landscape. However, even if he does not retrace his steps, he is no longer the same man. What has changed are not his features, but his bearing, which has become more assured. Thus this etching [*estampe*] in music does not return to the same ground as those of 1903 but follows on from them, the flower of a different season.

Notes

1 The Feast of All Saints occurs on 1 November; the Requiem Mass is held on the following day, All Souls' Day.

2 'Un deuxième recueil d'*Images*, pour le piano, paraissait en 1907. J'avais coutume alors de prolonger mon séjour à la campagne jusqu'aux approches de l'hiver et, en donnant des nouvelles à mon illustre ami depuis longtemps de retour à Paris, je lui disais le touchant usage du glas qui sonne depuis les vêpres de la Toussaint jusqu'à la messe des Morts, traversant, de village en village, les forêts jaunissantes dans le silence du soir. Ainsi lui vint l'idée de ce premier morceau, d'une douceur diffuse mais vibrante, qui a pour titre: "Cloches à travers les feuilles".'

In *La Musique retrouvée*, p. 196, Laloy elaborates: 'At that time we used to extend our stay until the first week of November, so as to hear [. . .] the distant bells answering each other across the forests which muffled everything but an echo from beyond the grave.' ('Nous prolongions en ce temps-là notre séjour jusqu'à la première semaine de novembre, pour entendre [. . .] les cloches au loin se répondre, par delà les forêts qui ne laissent passer qu'un écho d'outre-tombe.')

3 Laloy says that although the piece received bad press, 'My feeling is that never had [Debussy] attained a similar hollowing of the sound material, which is scooped out like a jade flower with translucent petals [. . .]' *La Musique retrouvée*, p. 177

4 Laloy is referring to the lacquered panel Debussy owned, also

entitled *Poissons d'or*. In *La Musique retrouvée*, p. 177, Laloy confirms: '[. . .] the last piece had the splashes of light and zig-zag strokes of the Japanese etching which inspired it.' The etching is reproduced in Lesure (1980), p. 181.

Children's corner and *Trois chansons de Charles d'Orléans*

Laloy observed a marked change in Debussy's style in these two works, both of which were first performed in 1908. The first of the two reviews presented here also highlights the reception of Debussy's music in the middle part of his career.

S.I.M. (15 November 1908), pp. 1205–1206[1]

The titles of the individual movements will be given further on; the first work, named *Children's corner* (*Le Coin des enfants*),[2] is an album of fantastic, gentle images. The other is a homage to one of our purest French traditions, believed lost. These three *Chansons de Charles d'Orléans*, written for unaccompanied SATB voices, are not an imitation of but a continuation from Janequin, Costeley and Orlando di Lasso, masters of French song in the sixteenth century. This is clear-cut music, not corrupted by Italian loquacity or Germanic grandiloquence, with mouldings as delicate as they are firm, yet modern in its richness of colour, and personal in its emotional smile. The other collection runs a great risk of incensing that faction, growing more numerous in France from one day to the next, which jibs at irony because it feels itself the victim of it. These serious minds will be all the more offended by this irony because it is light and amicable: to those people I deem it useless to explain the learned arpeggios in 'Doctor Gradus ad Parnassum', which are cut off by joyful frolics, or the muted grace of the serenade, or the tender, peaceful melancholy of the pastoral reed-pipe; and to them the ungainly rhythm of the cakewalk would be a scandal. But will there be men to whom the 'Elephant's lullaby',[3] a dark music, worthy of Rudyard Kipling, will not show the primeval forest and the serious beasts dandling their young in such an attentive, imperfect and touching manner? Will there be some who, as they listen to the snow dancing, will not see the astonished, sad face of the little girl watching that eddying whiteness? There will surely be some such, but they will hardly be men: they will be critics.

Finally, the whole spiteful chorus of former friends who discovered

Pelléas will cry out, 'This isn't him!' This is their way of acknowledging the progress of an art which today has attained confidence, affirmation, richness too, and a clarity which would reconcile all tastes in a country which was not as divided as ours, not such a slave to the partisan spirit and not so preoccupied with personal quarrels.

But there are beauties in these two works to console us for all our troubles.

La Grande revue (25 April 1909), pp. 817–818

These names [Claude Debussy and Charles d'Orléans], which both belong to the highest nobility of art, had already come together for two *Rondels*, refined, sinewy, tender and haughty, melancholy and exquisitely discreet in their grace: *Le temps a laissié son manteau*, and *Pour ce que Plaisance est morte*.[4] These were songs accompanied by piano. Increasingly enamoured of the beauty of the voice, this time the composer has written unaccompanied choruses, like his sixteenth-century ancestors. Several experts, without having either read or heard them, uttered the word pastiche: one might as well say that a string quartet cannot be written without copying Beethoven, nor the tuba used without aping Wagner. There is nothing in these compositions which is put in for the sake of resemblance, nothing which does not translate what is in the author's mind with the strictest accuracy. But it must be added that this mind, not being a slave to modern regimentation, effortlessly makes the forms of the past its own. Thus, the scale without a leading note, which appears in the first *Chanson*, is just as familiar to the Renaissance masters; but a long time ago Claude Debussy rediscovered it, by instinct, and put it in many places where he cannot be suspected of archaism, for example in his Quartet, and in *Pelléas*.[5]

He had not given us anything, up to now, in a style so accomplished, so compact, so full and vigorous within the most firm delicacy.[6] Everything stands out in relief, in these vocal ensembles which have no support and no envelope; and melody is a requisite throughout. That is why it was a very daring act to strip away all the veils of the orchestra in this way; it was bound to succeed for a composer who owes the richness of his harmony to the strength and freedom of his lines. We did not at first recognize, beneath the touches of such clear, sweet colours, the solidity of the lines and their rigorous connections. These features stand out today, in the full bloom of their nakedness;

and we recognize that this artist's design contains perhaps even more of lighting effects than of painting. A little over a year ago in this same publication I foresaw, I also expressed a wish to see that design become more and more apparent. I did not know then to what extent I would be justified in the event.[7]

It is very difficult to express in words the fervent adoration of the first song (*Dieu! qu'il la fait bon regarder!*), the nonchalance of the lazy voice in the second (*Quand j'ai ouy le tabourin*), above the gentle tumult of the dancers on their way to the maypole, or the contrast of the imprecations against winter (*Hyver, vous n'estes qu'un villain*) with the sweet memory of summer: the harmonic or textural lay-outs can be analysed, not the beauty of the melody, in which truly all the music lies. When these songs appeared, at the Good Friday concert on the stage of the Châtelet, conducted by the author, a religious silence developed in a moment, as with works which are not comparable to what we usually hear. After each of them, there was the unusual spectacle of unanimous applause, so enthusiastic that the last two had to be repeated. It must be said that it was an evening audience, much more cultivated than that of matinées, which recently put me so badly out of temper, but its opinion is only the more significant for that. Could this music, which grows more and more pure every day, have the privilege of reconciling the different tastes which quarrel so bitterly in France? That is too fine a hope to dare delude oneself with it.

The choir was excellent, each detail in its place, and the intonation almost perfect. We must give thanks for its goodwill, for the author's decisive conducting, as also for the intelligent pains and devoted tenacity of the young musician who conducted the early rehearsals, Monsieur André Caplet.[8]

Notes

1 The title of the article is 'Deux ouvrages nouveaux de Claude Debussy' ('Two new works by Claude Debussy').

2 *Children's corner* was published under its English title, the connection being that Debussy's daughter Chouchou, to whom the work was dedicated, had an English governess. Laloy translates the title into French as an explanation to his readers.

3 i.e. 'Jimbo's lullaby'

4 These are two of the *Trois chansons de France*, written for solo voice and piano in 1904. The other song was 'La Grotte', set to a text by Tristan Lhermite.

5 In *La Grande revue* (10 November 1908), p. 190, Laloy stressed that although the work 'marks the resurrection of a genre dear to our sixteenth-century composers', it was a question of 'resurrection, not imitation: for the form of vocal counterpoint here lends itself to music of a modern, personal sentiment.'

6 In *Claude Debussy* (rev. ed. 1944), p. 98, Laloy wrote: 'It was a great surprise, to those who thought [Debussy's music] was devoted to chords and resonances, to find it reduced to four decisive lines [. . .]'

7 See Laloy's article, 'La Nouvelle manière de Claude Debussy' ('The new manner of Claude Debussy') which is translated on pp. 195–204.

8 It is interesting to note Laloy's contribution to the *Trois chansons de Charles d'Orléans*. When Debussy decided to set 'Quant j'ai ouy le tabourin', as a companion to the two songs of Charles d'Orléans he had written ten years earlier, he wrote to ask Laloy's help with the fifteenth-century French. The letter is dated 16 June 1908:

> It would be very kind of you to tell me the exact meaning of the words I've underlined in the following *Rondel de Ch. d'Orléans*:
>
> Quant j'ai ouy le tabourin
> Sonner, pour s'en aller en may,
> En mon lit n'en ay fait *affray*
> Ni levé mon chief du coissin;
>
> En disant: il est trop matin
> Ung peu me rendormiray
> Quant j'ai ouy le tabourin
> Sonner, pour s'en aller au may
>
> Jeunes gens *partent* leur butin;
> De nonchaloir *m'acointeray*
> A lui je *m'abutineray*
> Trouvé *l'ay* plus prouchain voisin
> Quant j'ai ouy le tabourin.
>
> I find this little piece so full of sweet interior music that – naturally – I cannot restrain myself from 'exteriorising' it – as our friend Victor Segalen would say – May good Charles d'Orléans kindly forgive me.
>
> I prefer to tell you straight away that I am waiting on your reply so that I can set my colours?

Trois ballades de François Villon

La Grande revue (25 April 1911), pp. 847–848

The *Trois ballades de François Villon*, set to music by Claude Debussy, were published for piano and voice some months ago. But the author only wanted to produce them in public with orchestra: so wait we must.[1] In exchange, we were granted two hearings: the first at the Concert Sechiari, with makeshift resources which did not really permit of a sane appreciation, except for those who had already prepared by reading the score; the second, at the Cercle Musical, had a much better fate, thanks to the experienced instrumentalists and the terse precision of Monsieur Jean Périer. The response of the audience was unanimously enthusiastic, and had the quality that, among today's composers, only Claude Debussy can command: gentle, pious, and poignant in its reflections on our unworthiness. For these are beautiful compositions which reach to the heart, and which each of us would like to take as the rule of his life. Nothing is put in to attract attention, to provoke curiosity, to intrigue, seduce or surprise; and even analysis is powerless to discover the reason for the marvel. There are no sudden outbursts, no hazardous blendings, no learned inaccuracies: a simple, smooth style, which appears only to use the common vocabulary. With an inflection of two notes, we feel the resigned desolation of a heart which is too proud for condemnation:

> Fausse beauté, qui tant me coûte cher.
>
> [False beauty, which costs me so dearly.]

A most naive melody accompanies the litany:

> Dame des cieux, régente terrienne.
>
> [Lady of the heavens, earthly regent.]

And the challenge of the women of Paris owes its energy to no singular modulation:

> Il n'est bon bec que de Paris.
>
> [Good chatter is only found in Paris.]

But the choice of the expression is such that it seems to be at one with the ideas. Right from the time of his first works, Claude Debussy has been searching for this adherence; at first he obtained it through the insubstantial pliancy of a form which was amenable to any impulse; today, the form dominates, contains and checks: every note is vibrant with prolonged echoes; and the line, when it curves, is clearly taut with inner strength. Such firmness is only possible on condition that everything accidental is resolutely sacrificed. That is why today we are seeing the composer who, better than the poets themselves, fulfilled the wishes of Symbolism, abandon Baudelaire and Verlaine for texts from the Middle Ages: Charles d'Orléans, François Villon, even the romance of *Tristan et Yseult* which he intends to set for the stage according to the artistic reworking of Monsieur Joseph Bédier. It is because in a modern author, despite all the trouble he takes only to speak in figures, personal emotion always breaks through, quite near to the words. By a different excess our Classicists hold it at a distance and keep only the idea of it. But those who came before the Renaissance are able to paint it as though in outline, by means of a clearly delineated language free of retouching or overworking. In this way, they too reach a general, but concrete, truth, one which is thoroughly prepared for music, provided that the composer is able to find the spirit, very much on this side of the letter; he will feel his freedom of invention increasing with the distance to be crossed; a precious poet, like Tristan Lhermite, will not tire him with events as much as our contemporaries; Charles d'Orléans will be even more discreet, and above all Villon, whose wrought-iron style only responds to the impulses of life with fixed aggregations: this is a natural symbolism, no longer studied, but constrained and necessary. In revealing the deep meaning of these poems, Claude Debussy confers on Villon the same blessing as formerly on Maeterlinck; what is more, he is taking up a tradition the break with which is unanimously lamented today.

Notes

1 The version for voice and piano was published by Durand in 1910, the orchestral score in 1912. In fact the version for voice and piano had been performed twice: Laloy's sister-in-law, the singer Marguerite Babaïan, gave the first of these performances on 16 January 1911.

Ibéria[1]

Laloy reviews the first performance, which was conducted by Gabriel Pierné. The critics were divided, though Ravel was among those who wrote a favourable review. The *Images* for orchestra were not performed complete until 26 January 1913, at the Concerts Colonne.

La Grande revue (10 March 1910), pp. 192–194[2]

The new work which the Concerts Colonne have just introduced to us, on 20 and 27 February, dates from 1909. It is the second of three *Images* for orchestra: the first, *Gigue triste*,[3] is as yet unpublished; the third, *Rondes de printemps*, will very shortly be performed at one of the concerts which the house of Durand is devoting, in memory of its founder, Auguste Durand, to the authors it has published.

Why *Ibéria*? Simply because one day the composer felt nostalgia for the Spain he had dreamed of.[4] His composition is not a document; it is an 'image', shaped first of all in his mind, and contemplated with an inward eye before being manifested outside. This is what we might have expected from an artist who has never abdicated before nature and, far less an Impressionist than a Symbolist, has only prized appearances for the emotion they reveal. But, until the last few years, this emotion trembled beneath floating veils, afraid of being discovered. It does not hide away now; not that it is naked: it is connected to the external world by the bonds of analogies; but it imprints, onto the fabric of sensations enveloping it, decisive accents and tempi which, though it does not yield itself up, let us guess at it.

This stylistic progression has been defined in this same publication, in relation to another symphonic poem by Claude Debussy written in 1905, *La Mer*.[5] But that work, admirable for its power, has now been exceeded in simplicity. Already, there, Symbolism's vapours of sound were resolved into settled lines; but the lines were many in number, and wove together to form a close-textured fabric. Here the melodies stand out in high relief, succoured by everything that hitherto was scattered or dispersed around them: the orchestra sings, and its colours, which are brighter than ever, are its very voice, not an adornment. This work is cast in a single block: nothing can be detached. Emotion fills it and makes it wholly vibrant.

So we would search in vain for picturesque effects or amusing details, let alone the national themes that have allowed so many composers to quote rather than invent. Spain furnished no other elements than certain dance rhythms, and two characteristic instruments: castanets and Basque drum. Nothing more was needed: it was not a matter of imitating the music of the Spanish people, but of conveying the feelings to which it was able to give rise; one might say, taking up a grouchy remark of old Beethoven, of setting it to music.[6]

The first piece is entitled 'Par les rues et par les chemins'. There is a sense of joyful eagerness, as of a crowd hastening up, and the soul of a waltz whirls round and round; it is not one of those motifs taken directly from reality, or composed on a realistic model, such as we find, for example, in the *Capriccio espagnol* by Rimsky-Korsakov; it is the idea without anything material: it is purely musical. The waltz goes round and round, and other ideas arise, and reply to it, plaintive, gentle, playful in turn; the last of these ideas is affirmed in a victorious spirit; the waltz reappears again, fades away, evaporates like a memory: all is quiet. It is, if you like, the old form of the rondeau, dear to French composers in the eighteenth century: it even has the more broadly treated episode in the last couplet, which might be considered as a 'second subject'.[7] But there is the difference that the motifs are not derived from one another by means of variation: a perfect agreement unites them; each motif, when it appears, brings with it the surprise of another which we did not know, but which had to come.

'Les Parfums de la nuit': a night in which we feel, rather than see, the quivering of vague shadows, a night in which sweetly pungent scents rise up, sighs float on the air, and faint echoes of a festival linger. Human desire, incited by this mystery, rises up, grows sad, sobs with ecstasy, grows calmer and weeps softly. As if freed by this voice, the darkness slips away; and it is then that we hear a murmur beginning in the distance, so vague that at first we take it for the wind rustling the branches. But it comes closer, and gradually swells: suddenly light is everywhere. It is 'Le Matin d'un jour de fête', with sounds of awakening, an irresistible march, songs, calls, a sense of gladness overflowing in dazzling waves.

Nothing can be compared to the action of this music which takes hold of the senses as much as the heart, which envelops, bathes and transports us, which secures, without ever a commanding gesture, the acquiescence of the whole being, and gives us confidence at the same time as enthusiasm. Pleasure is everywhere, but everywhere, too, tenderness accompanies it, embalms it and consoles it for not being capable of enduring; the greatest agitation gives rise to no commentary, and touches us all the more because it holds back and is not expansive. This is Classical moderation, united to the charm of an art which is no longer afraid to feel; the soul and the body, long separated, and often hostile, here have the same joys and desires, the same regrets, the same love.

The orchestration of this new work is extremely rich; but it is even more remarkable for its exactitude. Each instrument is used in its most distinctive register, and comes at the place where any other would be impossible; none plays a helping role; none is ever subordinate. And there is no question of priority between them: the strings no longer think all the tunes must be reserved for them; but they are chosen for their penetrating sweetness when the tune of the second tableau is born. On the contrary, the horns, trumpets and trombones introduce the 'second subject' of the first movement. The cor anglais, at the beginning of the same piece, has a more inscrutable sound in its high register than the oboe. In the last piece, the pizzicato string chords make the march ring out across the air. The xylophone and celesta pierce the evening shadows with subdued and then brilliant points of light; the bells evoke the first rays of golden dawn. Performing such precise music is not without its difficulties: at the first concert, it was manifest that the preparatory work was not finished; but Monsieur Pierné took his revenge at the second concert: perhaps he is a little too tranquil in the first and third movements, but he understood the second very well, and followed the progression of the sentiments. It is only regrettable that the xylophone is so dry, and that the celesta, which is the small model, transposes an octave higher.[8]

Notes

1 Laloy himself always writes the title '*Iberia*' without an acute accent, in the Spanish spelling; Debussy wrote '*Ibéria*'.

2 This article is partly reproduced in *La Musique retrouvée*, pp. 184-186.

3 Debussy's original title for the first of the *Images* was *Gigues tristes*, but he later changed it to *Gigues*. Laloy wrote briefly about the piece in *Claude Debussy* (rev. ed. 1944), pp. 101-102, saying that it 'can be compared, in sentiment and construction, to the first of the *Nocturnes*. However,

these are not "Nuages" using the solemn, plaintive voice of the cor anglais, but *Gigues* tossed off, amid the light mist, by the oboe in A, known as the oboe d'amore because of its sweetness.'

4 Laloy frequently stresses the connection between Debussy's music and the world of dreams. This particular remark recalls a comment Debussy made about Spanish folk music in an article dated 1 December 1913: '[. . .] that admirable folk music, in which so much of dream mingles with so much rhythm, making it one of the richest in the world.' ('[. . .] cette admirable musique populaire, où tant de rêve se mêle à tant de rythme, qui en fait l'une des plus riches en ce monde.') Debussy (1987), p. 250

5 Laloy's note: '"La Nouvelle manière de Claude Debussy"' ('The new manner of Claude Debussy'), *La Grande revue* (10 February 1908). See pp. 195–204.

6 Perhaps Laloy has in mind the comment found in Beethoven's sketches for the *Pastoral* symphony: '[. . .] without titles the whole will be recognised as a matter more of feeling than of painting in sounds.' G. Nottebohm, *Zweite Beethoveniana* (Leipzig, 1872), p. 375

7 In France in the seventeenth century a rondeau was an instrumental form which alternated a refrain with a variable number of couplets. In the late eighteenth century, the rondeau developed into sonata-rondo form.

8 The celesta, invented in 1886 by Auguste Mustel, originally had a compass of five octaves from C below middle C, but the bottom octave was abandoned because of its poor sound quality. This must be why Laloy talks about the 'small model'. However, the rest of his comment is inaccurate, in that all celestas transpose an octave higher.

Rondes de printemps

La Grande revue (25 March 1910), pp. 397–400

The four 'Concerts of French music' organised by the house of Durand gave the fine testimonies which one might have expected: we know the perspicacious attention with which these musicians and publishers, Auguste Durand and his son Jacques Durand who today succeeds him, have always observed the progress of music, adopting the youngest and boldest of our authors from the time of their first successes, not with the great public, but with the small number who know how to listen. Thus we see assembled here almost all who have contributed to this progress, from Camille Saint-Saëns, who retains the credit for restoring the taste for Classical form in France, to Vincent d'Indy, Claude Debussy, Maurice Ravel, [Jean] Roger-Ducasse[1] and André Caplet. Only César Franck and Gabriel Fauré, who remained faithful to other publishers, were missing from this tableau of history.[2]

The works were, with only one exception, known; but it was instructive to hear them together; they were conducted either by their authors, or by Monsieur Rhené-Baton, a very painstaking and fervent conductor who, in order to become excellent, only needs to be less worried, and that will certainly come with practice. Already, he has given just the right nuances to Ravel's *Rapsodie espagnole*, but without managing to adapt the orchestral sound to the exiguity of the Salle Gaveau; and to the three tableaux of *La Mer*, by Claude Debussy, he has given a very well-judged though as yet slightly too studied suppleness of movement.

The new work was by Claude Debussy: the *Rondes de printemps* are the third of the *Images* of which we have just heard the second, *Ibéria*. The author himself took the baton, and was precise, rigorous, attentive to contain, moderate, curb any outpouring or infringement, any ill-timed expansion; and this discretion, by playing down the detail, immediately made manifest the pure certitude of the lines and the equal strength of a sentiment which, like the breeze, carries us along and sustains us. So the audience found itself effortlessly, unthinkingly and almost without realizing it, transported by an enthusiasm which, when the magic was over, exploded in endless applause: and it required very firm circumspection on the part of the author to refuse a second playing.

Ibéria was the poem of the passion for life, dreaming of dance rhythms, shedding, beneath the night's caresses, the tears of desire, then letting itself be enveloped by joy.

The *Rondes de printemps* sing of the joy of a tender renewal; there are no tears here, no obsessive whirling, nor any of those great calls of the flesh twisting and sighing: a more than virginal innocence, puerile, divine: the innocence of flowers opening and branches giving themselves up to breezes from the heavens. In *Ibéria*, there was the dazzle of bright colours; the shadows were fresh and cool, and the light glowed with golden reflections. However the momentary outbursts and the contrasts were never detached from the emotion, which was not only their basis, but their principle. Here, the emotion comes to us, direct, but it retains within itself the vibration of the air, and the filtered light that passes through the foliage. Thus the two works, with different characters and proportions, achieve the union of sentiment and sensation which Claude Debussy has always sought, which he alone can give us, and which he has succeeded today in putting into a more clear-cut form than ever.

Music which is all about sentiment is abstract; music which is all about sensation has no continuation.[3] It is the constant, natural union of the two that makes Josquin des Prés, François Couperin and Mozart pure musicians: Claude Debussy is of their lineage. This latest work brings him close to Mozart especially, thanks to the ingenuousness of the subject-matter, which allowed him to display a similar aptitude for drawing the music from itself, with no circumstances intervening, no fuss and no drama. But in Mozart, who was restricted to development and symmetry, inventiveness only appears intermittently. Here it provides everything: the melody continually germinates and springs up from the melody, and the order, which is more necessary to an art without fixed forms than to any other, is itself a created order. It is not the unvarying progression, traced out in advance, of such and such a sonata or symphony movement; but a harmony of lines, a laying-out of planes, a proportion, conformity and equilibrium, which henceforth are to be discovered for each new musical work, as for works in the visual arts: it is a rhythm.

Claude Debussy had long been infallible in determining this rhythm of the whole; but never had he sustained its graceful effect with such rigorous firmness. The work is traversed by a single idea which is constantly varied, from which it blossoms as from a supple tree-branch. This idea, almost imperceptible at first, gradually breaks away from all the life pulsating around it, but one by one it is surrounded by new motifs which it nourishes with its sap, and which at times are parted so that it can be seen, and at other times cover it with their abundant profusion, while still permitting us to divine its invisible course. This idea is related to an old children's song, which had already appeared in the third of the *Estampes*, 'Jardins sous la pluie'; its words are: 'Nous n'irons plus au bois' ['We won't go to the woods any more']. But the transfiguration is such that we cannot speak of borrowing, and we need to be told in advance if we are to find the notes of the round in this airy dance whose sudden impulses and fluid movements only Corot's nymphs, with their vaporous bodies, could follow: a very musical dance, which contains its gestures in itself, and does not call for help from any physical movement; a dance of sounds, like them impalpable, diaphanous, carrying off thoughts with an irresistible power. You would think that through its magical spell the soul of the forest was awakening all around us and singing its own song, which we did not know, for it is neither that of the birds, nor even the rustling of the leaves or the tinkling sound of the springs: here everything is revelation, not imitation.

It can be said that the *Rondes de printemps* are the murmuring of the French forest. The comparison is not to be feared: the Germanic forest which Wagner depicted in all its swaying luxuriousness will keep its vastness; but this delicacy will not be crushed, being made of a very differently textured fabric. In the famous Siegfried episode, a constant undulation, taken rather directly from nature, acquires through its very monotony an overpowering strength; and the fateful bird's song, which comes to rest on this moving thread, does not melt into it, but contrasts with it, as the legend with reality. In the French work, everything holds together and evokes, completes and follows on from everything else; no detail is put in for picturesque effect; no melody has the mission of signalling a particular person; through the artist's meditations, the tableau is entirely transmuted into music; no insoluble fragment of reality subsists. We discover the unblemished limpidity of a sound-world in which all existence is immediately translated into melody. This is one of the paradises of music, such as only the greatest masters have been able to open up for us; it has an eternal serenity.

Thus Claude Debussy, in each new work, seems to leave himself behind, in search of a purer beauty. He was his own precursor. He kept in store for us, perhaps for himself also, this great surprise, after the feverishness, agitation and melancholy of Symbolism, of an art of plenitude and joy. All who loved the *Nocturnes* and *Pelléas* sincerely, without either fraudulence or vanity, thus see their hopes exceeded through the proud independence of an artist who will never be a prisoner of his fame.

Notes

1 Though Laloy is remarkably accurate about most names, he repeatedly makes mistakes about Jean Roger-Ducasse's: here he gives 'Roger Ducasse.'

2 The concerts were given in the Salle Gaveau, with the orchestras of the Concerts Lamoureux and the Concerts Colonne. They took place at weekly intervals from the end of January 1910. The start of the series almost had to be postponed because the Seine flooded, but the water level went down and light was restored to the Salle Gaveau in time. The program for the four concerts also included Debussy's 'Le Jet d'eau', d'Indy's second symphony and *Jour d'été à la montagne*, conducted by the composer, Saint-Saëns' *Organ* symphony, Dukas' *L'Apprenti sorcier* and works by Roger-Ducasse, Aubert, Pierné, Witkowski, Caplet and Rhené-Baton.

3 'Une musique toute de sentiment est abstraite; une musique toute de sensation n'a pas de suite.'

Le Martyre de saint Sébastien

Funded by Ida Rubinstein, and with decor by Léon Bakst, *Le Martyre de saint Sébastien* was first performed on 22 May 1911. Here, Laloy not only discusses the work but also gives his impressions of Gabriele D'Annunzio, the author of the text.

La Musique retrouvée, pp. 206–210

Gabriele D'Annunzio is a poet and a charmer. I had long admired his novels with their splendid visions. From the moment I met him, I realised that neither Debussy nor anyone else could refuse him anything. Bald and pale, with yellowing teeth and heavy eyelids, this man who from a distance is almost repulsively ugly captivates and fascinates whomever he wishes, by the elegance of his politeness and the brilliance of his conversation which is rich not only in images, but in science, intelligence and wit, all bound together in a sheaf and offered as a magnificent tribute. I remember one evening when in his company and that of Monsieur and Madame Debussy we heard a mediocre performance of *Pelléas*, which he restored with his praise and brightened up with his sarcastic remarks for the benefit of the performers. When we left, he took us, my wife and I, to his home near the Etoile,[1] a furnished appartment which he had made his own with the help of screens which followed him everywhere. A light refreshment had been prepared, perhaps in anticipation of a more tender tête-à-tête, and he set about serving us with a lordly air and a magician's surprises. Another evening, we took him out to dinner, with our friends the Debussys, at a Chinese resaurant I knew. Debussy remained on his guard, having a stomach crammed with prejudices.[2] D'Annunzio told us that evening how Isadora Duncan, who had just lost her children,[3] had approached him to repair this damage, but without success despite all the hope which the cooperation of a dancer and a poet could give. He did great justice to the swallows' nests, the carp with mushrooms, the sea-cucumbers, and above all the gallant ginger.[4] Another day he came to see us at Bellevue,[5] bringing us as a present a perfume of his own composition, in a bottle blown by this gentleman glassmaker, and bearing the name *Aqua nuntia.* And he found the prettiest compliments to commend our house, which was very poor beside the luxury which surrounded him.

But he has never had any sense of theatre. Carried away by his lyricism and erudition, he constantly immobilises the characters for rejoinders which are all monologues, often very beautiful to read, but interminable on stage. The *répétition générale* started at half past eight. At two in the morning, we came out into the place du Châtelet with no car on the horizon. We were overwhelmed by declamations, suffocated beneath the abundance of words as Saint Sebastian beneath the flowers, and set even more on edge by our impatience finally to hear the music, all through scenes in which the conversation took up again when one thought everything had been said, always passing from one character to another like a ball; and, when finally the orchestra or chorus raised their harmonious voices, our immense relief was spoiled by the fatigue which left us without the strength to match so much emotion. I understood the deep meaning of the music much better on reading the score, and in concert the following year. But then, what a revelation it was!

Religious music, like that of *Pelléas*, but in a very different way: no longer that diffuse piety and compassion in an undertone, but sublime confidence, and from a basis of steadfast faith prayers are raised up to heaven in ribbed arches and glittering rose-windows. Debussy, as Wagner with *Parsifal*, built a cathedral for *Saint Sébastien*. It is unfinished: a transept, a tower are lacking. Pressed by time, he was only able to sketch the nave and the apse. He was intending to complete the construction when death surprised him, and it was his monument.

In the first act, the prelude raising up its chords like hands joined in prayer, then the resolute song of the two brothers who are ready to die, and at the end, when the music takes up again for the miracle of the inferno, the chorus in which the voices one after another, on three notes, shine out like beams of light piercing through fog, then the muted sparks of the fire in the middle register of the orchestra, the sudden freshness brought down form heaven by limpid chords; and lastly the illumination of the divine witness with the root-position triads hesitating a moment before growing still in ecstasy.

In the second, the supernatural prelude auguring the subterranean darkness which glows with the light of stars under a Chaldean spell, then the song of the virgin Erigone which certainly is, as D'Annunzio intended, 'the golden crystal of a virginal voice bending over the soul like an August sky', and then changes, by the saint's authority, into the lament of the Christian virgin and her heavenly consolation.

The prelude to the third act, roaring with pride, the song to Apollo with its hard, proud lyres, and the music accompanying the florid narration of the Passion, which is sad unto death.

In the fourth act, the prelude breathing out its thrilling lament beneath the cold sky, and the slow procession which is softened by pity in the uncertain dusk which suddenly opens up to reveal a radiance from beyond the earth. And the apotheosis is complete. The song of the blessed rises up: the song of the martyrs, full-toned as an organ, but an aerial organ, with no mechanism, detached from the earth: the song of the virgins, precise and artless, the affirmative song of the apostles, the bright song of the angels. Like four shining clouds, the four choirs support the voice that is the soul of Sebastian, which rises in a series of leaps like wings beating more and more assuredly, while the triumphant chorus of the saints of Paradise bursts out in welcome, praising the Lord with the full strength of a rising scale which adds a final florid curl to a jubilant *Alleluia*, than which Gregorian chant never knew anything more graceful, and whose flight is even more lively in its transcendent sweetness.

When the score was finished, D'Annunzio was the first to declare his admiration. Since then he has named Debussy 'Claude de France', and again recently he recalled the marvellous day 'when for the first time he felt the revelation of the melody rising up from the depths of the drama.'

Notes

1 D'Annunzio was living in the avenue Kléber near the place de l'Etoile, which is now the place Charles de Gaulle.

2 Jacques Rouché gives a similar account of a Chinese meal, and Debussy's reaction to it. He tells of a luncheon at Laloy's home, where he, D'Annunzio and Debussy were guests. One of the dishes was 'a fish, expertly prepared, covered with a sauce which gave the appearance of lacquer. Gabriele D'Annunzio exclaimed joyfully, "Delightful, amusing, how marvellous!" Debussy lost all sense of proportion, and rejected the skin and the small bones: "What I wouldn't give for a *sole meunière*!"'

3 Isadora Duncan's children were accidentally drowned in the Seine in 1913.

4 This is a reference to ginger's supposed aphrodisiac properties.

5 Laloy lived at 17 bis, rue des Capucines, Bellevue. Bellevue is just outside Paris, near Meudon.

Various piano works

Laloy did not write many reviews of Debussy's piano music. He may have wanted to avoid a conflict of interest as his wife, Susanik, was a professional pianist who had lessons with Debussy.

Notes begin on p. 229.

Estampes
Claude Debussy (rev. ed. 1944), pp. 33–34

[The collection] *Estampes* brings together visions, which date back to impressions from the International Exhibition of 1900 and have been ripened by time: Javanese dances in 'Pagodes', Spanish night in 'La Soirée dans Grenade', Parisian thickets in 'Jardins sous la pluie'. But here the style of drawing, as befits *Estampes* [*etchings*], is more sustained, and the colouring more constant. The idea settles in, ready to be admired. Yet there is nothing, in the way the idea has adorned itself, which owes anything to fashion or has been made especially with fashion in view:[1] the glissandi on black keys reflect the liquid sonority of a Far-Eastern orchestra; the melody of the chords with their mingling vibrations makes us think of invisible guitars; the zigzagging arpeggios whip sun and rain across the glossy foliage of a well-raked gravel garden, adorned with variations on two French folk-songs, for here, as a rare exception, a piece of music which is destined to listen only to itself uses borrowed themes. And all this rendered wonderfully, down to the last detail. But who would have ventured to pay such a compliment to the preceding works?[2] The passage from the implicit to the explicit is manifest. Is this the beginning of another age?

La Revue musicale (1 February 1904), p. 96

Mademoiselle Selva[3] interprets the *Estampes* with great intelligence; the first two pieces of this new set, 'Pagodes' and 'La Soirée dans Grenade', in no way resemble the fake, adulterated Spain and East of our musical bazaars: for they have the fresh, slightly wild flavour of natural fruit; the last piece, 'Jardins sous la pluie', recalls with greater breadth the Toccata for piano: we observe, here and there, the same very Classical turn, despite the novelty of the language. We will soon have the opportunity to return[4] to this collection which is worthy of the master to whom it is dedicated: Monsieur J. Blanche.

Préludes
Claude Debussy (rev. ed. 1944), pp. 104–105

Since the time of Louis XIII,[5] when the lutenists of France, having established the variable pitch of their instrument, checked its tuning and sought out the coming melody amongst a cloud of harmonies, the prelude has always retained its musing freedom, even in the more clear-cut forms imposed on it by the keyboard. Chopin's *Preludes* owe their title to this freedom alone, for no sarabande or fugue follows after them; meditations in music, preludes to silence, they are not intended for the public forum of concerts, which Chopin gave only under duress, but for the intimacy of a salon where people know how to be silent. It is the same with those of Debussy, except that Chopin, in memory of the *Well-tempered clavier*, arranged his in a key order[6] which will not be observed here, and also that this time, after each piece, when listeners are about to discuss their thoughts, the composer forestalls them, but quietly, indicating by a mention in parentheses how he had the idea of writing it: 'Le vent dans la plaine', 'Les collines d'Anacapri', 'La puerta del vino' (which he had never seen, except on a postcard sent to him by Manuel de Falla), 'Les tierces alternées'. 'I always had an object,' said Couperin in the preface to his first book of *Pièces de clavecin*, 'in composing all these pieces: different occasions have provided them. Thus the titles correspond to ideas I have had; I will be excused from giving an account of them.'[7]

Préludes II
La Grande revue (10 July 1913), pp. 179–180

We heard [. . .][8] the *Préludes* of the second series, in which the music in defiance of æsthetics and its classifications simultaneously attains its supreme purety and its liveliest representation, because the harmony of the notes and lines grows so rapturous that it merges with the original emotion. Very different from the vague series of chords with which seventeenth-century lutenists announced mode and key, these preludes have a clear-cut form which however only follows the composer's thoughts; this is because the thoughts are born musical, or rather born music, and by analogy alone evoke some scene from the world or from dreams. Frédéric Chopin showed the way; it was given to Claude Debussy to discover its unique and radiant end.

Etudes
Claude Debussy (rev. ed. 1944), p. 105

The twelve *Etudes* were dedicated, in the summer of 1915, 'to the memory of Frédéric Chopin', who was most worthy of this tribute, for, even better than Liszt and Schumann, he was able to extract from a problem of execution the most pure essence of music, in this new genre brought into favour by the Romantic progress of virtuosity. In the same way, and even more strictly, each *Etude* by Claude Debussy is devoted to thirds, fourths, octaves, chromatic steps, repeated notes, contrasting sonorities, chords, and from these technical themes the composer, precisely because he isolates them and fashions them at leisure, draws out effects in which certainly we find the whole spirit of his music, but which he had never taken to this degree of inexplicable emotion and elemental depth.

Notes

1 This passage works particularly well in French because *idée* (idea) is feminine: 'L'idée s'installe et se laisse admirer. Rien cependant, dans la toilette qu'elle a faite, qui tienne de la mode et ne soit ajusté spécialement pour elle [. . .]'

2 It is clear from the context that Laloy means the piano pieces *D'un cahier d'esquisses* (1903), *Masques* (1904) and *L'Isle joyeuse* (1904), which he says were 'conceived at the time of *Pelléas*.'

3 Blanche Selva performed the *Estampes* on 16 January 1904, as part of 'a musical program devoted to the works of C. Debussy' arranged by Laloy at the salon of the Princesse de Cystria.

4 No later review of the *Estampes* has come to light.

5 That is, in the first half of the seventeenth century.

6 Each volume of J.S. Bach's *Well-tempered clavier* contains twenty-four paired preludes and fugues, organized by key in ascending chromatic

order: C major, C minor, C sharp major, C sharp minor, etc. The twenty-four Chopin *Preludes*, op. 28, are organized according to the circle of fifths: C major, A minor, G major, E minor, etc.

7 F. Couperin, *Pièces de clavecin* (*Harpsichord pieces*) Bk I, ed. K. Gilbert (Heugel, Paris, 1972), p. xiv: 'J'ay toûjours eu un objet en composant toutes ces pièces: des occasions différentes me l'ont fourni. Ainsi les Titres répondent aux idées que j'ay eües; on me dispensera d'en rendre compte.'

8 A list of the other works on the program has been omitted. The concert's venue, and the name of the pianist, are not known.

Ode à la France[1]

Laloy describes his collaboration with Debussy on this patriotic work, which was left incomplete when Debussy died. The article appeared in 1928, just before a completed version was performed by the Société des Concerts du Conservatoire. Writing a number of years after the event, Laloy makes some slips: these have been corrected in accordance with the score.

***Musique*, vol. 1, no. 6 (15 March 1928), pp. 245–249**

The *Ode à la France* is Claude Debussy's last work, unpublished until now. He asked me for the words towards the end of the year 1916, after the harsh battles of Verdun and the Somme, which left us with all the less hope as they had on the whole gone to our advantage but had not perceptibly increased our chances of success, and above all had not brought it any closer. I was all too well placed to know this, working at the Information Office of the Ministry of War, in daily contact with General Headquarters in Chantilly.

Although not wounded either physically or emotionally by the calamities of the war, Debussy felt them profoundly. When I met up with him in Paris, around the middle of the previous year, I had been struck by the sadness in him, from which nothing could distract him. Before then, in the course of our long friendship, I had more than once seen him gloomy or anxious, but always able to come out of himself for the sake of an interesting idea, a joke to cut sympathy short, a memory or an artistic project which would change the direction of his thoughts. His robust genius would break the chains and chase away clouds with a flash of lightning. But this time he seemed disheartened. Our conversations, which were fewer because of my activities, had no other subject than the country's suffering.

His health problem was surely not unrelated to the extreme dejection he felt. But it was the effect, more than the cause. The shock of terrible events which he, like almost all French people, had been far from foreseeing, certainly triggered off the sudden progress of the illness, which had been latent until then, and was to carry him off before the war ended.

He was a good Frenchman, but again like most of our fellow-countrymen it had taken the war to make him aware of it. In the deceptive calm of the preceding years, arriving sometimes in summer a little before dinnertime, I would come upon him in his garden, working his way through the major evening paper. At my approach he would fold it up, and we would speak of other things. We did not make much distinction between politics and news items, and if we did it was rather in favour of the latter, since they were a better source of insight into people's idiosyncracies. In July 1914 we were among the great number of people for whom the event of the day was the trial of Madame Caillaux,[2] not Austria's largely unnoticed ultimatum to Serbia.

His music, however, asserted convictions that are easily applied to politics: without hating any nation in particular, his music loathed tyranny. Debussy reproached Wagner not with his German nationality but with his abuse of strength, comparing him to the generous integrity of another German, Beethoven, whose 'severe, loyal mastery', he wrote, 'easily bested that high-helmeted claptrap which lacks any clear mandate.'[3] It has been pointed out that Wagner had no part in the 1914 war, having ceased to live in 1883. That is the evidence. Evidence must always be mistrusted. Wagner's music is that of a conqueror who will not suffer any resistance, and forces the listener into passive obedience, under the combined authority of notes and words which are each other's accomplice and, jealous of any particle of attention that might escape him, uses the cement of his orchestration to stop up the slightest fissure in the fortified double enclosure. It is useless for him to preach the vanity of power, the holiness of renunciation, the illusion of existence and the attraction of nothingness: the instinct which his reason wishes to subjugate triumphs in his music, a monument to pride, a Titanic construction, a challenge to the heavens.

Debussy, in his period, was the only composer not to be afraid of Wagner. Without needing to rebel, he was able to free himself from his obsession, and instead of amassing material as Wagner did, he knew how to hollow it out further and further, until it became transparent, open to all plays of light, all movements of the spirit. Whence his admiration for Bach, Rameau and Chopin, who were quite different from him in the quality of their serious, contemplative or passionate emotion, but like him were gifted at surrounding the outline of an idea with the most fitting passage, without filling in the gap, leaving the imagination free to be attracted to the space in the design. Equally remote from despotism and anarchy, he wished for authority, but one which was voluntarily accepted, for duty, but carried out by inclination, it being moreover understood that each of these notions was used with a different meaning from the usual, and only came into its own in an artistic sense.

The fracas of the war, waking him as from a dream, forced him to turn his thoughts back to the external world, or rather to leave behind the reality of his meditations and his music so as to live out a bad dream in which he did not understand anything. The vibrations from the first German cannon-shot against the fortresses of Liége were enough to overturn the balustrades of his earthly paradise, and deliver him defenceless into the appalling cataclysm that was bursting on our lands. I do not think he would have taken the time, nor found the strength, to ask himself on which side reason lay or to seek out those responsible. Violence being odious to him, from the very first he was on the side of those who were its victims.

It is possible that, if the fortunes of war had favoured us at the early encounters and allowed us to invade Germany, we might have exacted a high price, perhaps repeated the burning of the Palatinate, which was, moreover, as we know, ordered by Louvois, in spite of Turenne's protestations and against the will of Louis XIV.[4] But in fact, the opposite occurred: the conflagration of Belgium is at Germany's account, as was the devastation, a little later, of our northern provinces. I agree that by rights the guilty party was not Germany, but the war. Neither Claude Debussy nor I at that time had the serenity of mind necessary to reach this level of impartiality, above the mêlée. I do not believe that even today I have to find excuses for a natural reaction of indignation and pity.

The *Noël des enfants qui n'ont plus de maison* and the *Berceuse héroïque* bore witness, right from the beginning of the war, to Debussy's feelings.[5] But soon he was musing on a more significant work. The situation was untenable and yet, from day to day, and from communiqué to communiqué, it was prolonged beyond all expectations. The uninterrupted series of calamities was a slow death, the obsession of thinking about them an asphyxiation. The only means by which Debussy could regain the music he had lost was to start from these misfortunes and this obsession.

I cannot say which of us first had the idea of taking Joan of Arc as an image of France in its sufferings, a victim offered up to the injustice of fate so as to avert it, and save future generations. Did he suggest it to me? Did I propose it to him? Both, I suppose, during one of those conversations in which we were following the same thought, passing it round and round so as gradually to bring out every aspect of it with our alternate replies.

I wrote quite rapidly and, if my memory is correct, at the beginning of January 1917 I was able to show him the Ballad, which begins 'La pitié du royaume de France.' He declared himself completely satisfied with it, and set to work straight away. The ensuing lines, where Joan lifts up the wounded body of France, calls the warriors to help, and invokes the end of the heavens, were brought to him a few days later, and likewise accepted. The rest gave us both much more trouble. Two versions were tried and abandoned, because they made the work too long: one version had a dialogue between Joan and the warriors, in answering verses, the other had a chorus of supplicants. Claude Debussy had the idea of a soldiers' song, on a march tune whose rhythm he gave me on some sample words. But for Joan's answers and those of the heavenly voices, I drafted several more versions, and only much later found out which one he had chosen.

In the spring of 1917, a stricter discipline and quite a number of transfers on special duty left me no free time at all, and I only saw my poor friend again in December of the same year, lying on his bed of pain, which was to be, which was already, and he knew it as well as we, his deathbed. I did not dare speak to him of the *Ode à la France*, fearing that he might not have been able to finish it, and he said nothing to me about it, waiting for me to ask, perhaps not thinking about it any longer. His suffering ended on 26 March 1918; one of the last sounds of this world to reach him was the explosion of the shells which had been falling on Paris for five days.

His manuscripts were deposited in a safe, without being examined or classified, for they had to be put somewhere away from the destruction as soon as possible. Only a few months ago, after much searching, Madame Emma Claude-Debussy[6] found the *Ode à la France*, and immediately told me the good news. It was not a sketch, but a fair copy, for piano and voice on fifteen very closely written leaves. He had only written out the words in full for the Ballad and the three following stanzas, and quickly marked in the words of the soldiers' song, so that at first we thought he had set only the first part of the poem to music. A closer examination soon showed us other passages obviously intended for voices. The manuscript pages which I had given him were not all there. But I had kept my rough copies. By referring to them I was able to reconstitute from the shape of the melody the implied text, which gives the work a coherent meaning and brings about its conclusion.

The *Ode à la France* is a cantata for soprano solo, chorus and orchestra. The chorus represents in turn the voices of heaven and earth. Throughout the vocal score, the entries of characteristic instruments are indicated. In one place, the percussion rhythm is marked on an extra staff. The directors of the house of Choudens, which is going to publish the *Ode à la France*, have entrusted the orchestration to Monsieur Marius-François Gaillard, with the agreement of Madame Debussy and the author of the text, who are both acquainted with the talent, taste, feeling and dedication of this young musician.[7]

Claude Debussy's last work flows from the same inspiration as *Le Martyre de saint Sébastien*, in as pure a style and with even more poignant feeling. This will soon become evident: the first performance will be given on 2 April, in the Salle Pleyel, in a concert which will also include other unpublished works by this great composer, but from an earlier period, and the proceeds will contribute to the cost of the Debussy monument.

Notes

1 'La Dernière œuvre de Claude Debussy: l'*Ode à la France*'

2 Henriette Caillaux, the wife of the Minister for Finance, was afraid that the newspaper *Le Figaro* would publish letters concerning her private life which had the potential to cause her husband political embarrassment. On 16 March 1914 Madame Caillaux shot dead Gaston Calmette, the paper's editor, in his office.

3 '[. . .] Beethoven, de qui, écrivait-il, «la sévère et loyale maîtrise eut aisément raison de ces boniments haut casqués et sans mandat bien précis».' Laloy is quoting from from Debussy's article on the Ninth Symphony, in *La Revue blanche* (1 May 1901): see Debussy (1987), p. 37. In fact, Laloy changes the passage slightly, though without altering the sense. The original is: 'La sévère et loyale maîtrise du vieux Beethoven triompha aisément de ces boniments haut casqués et sans mandat bien précis.'

4 In 1674, as punishment to the Elector Palatine for his defection from the French cause, French armies under Turenne razed the Palatinate, burning towns and villages and butchering peasants. It was the systematic nature of this barbaric destruction, and the fact that it was carried out on the authority of the Secretary of State for War, that made these events such a source of shame to the French people. The Palatinate was burned again by France in 1689, in accordance with Louis XIV's claim to territory there after the death of the Elector.

5 In *Claude Debussy* (rev. ed. 1944), p. 106, Laloy wrote briefly

about the sonatas Debussy composed during the war. He saw them as sonatas in an older sense:

> The fly-leaf sets out the title as for a volume of Couperin or Rameau, and the address of the publishers is given, as was done then, 'at No. 4 in the place de la Madeleine, near the *grands boulevards*.' This is no amateur's whim, but a deliberate resolution to affirm that, more than ever in these troubled years, he was faithful to the fine examples of yesteryear. And the word sonata here does not have the strict meaning implying oratorical development and symmetrical returns, which it only took on in the second half of the eighteenth century. Before becoming specialised, it meant simply the linking of the successive movements, in a concertante style which came from Italy and from the end of the preceding century, acclimatised in France through the tender care of François Couperin, took on the flavour of the soil.

[6] This is a (rather unusual) way of writing the name of the wife of a 'great' man, and is no doubt intended as a mark of respect for Debussy.

[7] Marius-François Gaillard (1900–1973) was a pianist, conductor and composer. He performed the complete cycle of Debussy's works for piano.

On Ravel

Ravel and the Prix de Rome in 1905[1]

In 1905 Ravel was excluded after the preliminary stage of the Prix de Rome competition. As he had an established reputation, a scandal ensued, and it reached the general press. Laloy and many other critics, including Jean Marnold and M.-D. Calvocoressi, strongly supported Ravel, who did not himself make a protest. The culmination of the scandal was that Théodore Dubois resigned as Director of the Conservatoire and was replaced by Gabriel Fauré.

Le Mercure musical (1 June 1905), p. 85

Once upon a time, in the official music College of a great capital, there was an old composition teacher. How had he reached this position? No one knew, for he was only known through lamentably puerile works, one of which, dedicated to a national heroine who died at the stake, was a new torment to her memory, and more refined than the first: the torment of ridicule.[2] One day this respectable old man said to one of his disciples who handed him a passage he had orchestrated, 'But, my young friend, there is a serious error here; you want a soft effect and you are using trombones.' – 'But, Maître, I have marked them *pianissimo*.' – 'No, my friend, no trombones, keep them for loud passages.' So spoke the old teacher, unaware of what Monteverdi knew at the beginning of the seventeenth century: that the timbre of the trombone in *pianissimo* is more mysterious than that of the muted violin, and that nothing can replace it. And he also said, 'No arpeggios in the flute, nor in the clarinet, if you please; you have the harp; why not use it?' And so he went on, preaching his limited science and his childish wisdom. But the pupils who braved the boredom of similar advice were well rewarded.

Towards the beginning of the month of May 1905 the preliminary competition for the Prix de Rome opened. Nineteen competitors presented themselves; they belonged to the classes of Messieurs Fauré, Lenepveu and Widor. The jury was composed of Messieurs Th. Dubois, Paladilhe, Massenet, Lenepveu and Reyer, as regular members, and Messieurs Leroux, Hillemacher and Duvernoy, as co-opted members. The competition took place, each competitor wrote his fugue, and did his best with the chorus which was to be inspired by Monsieur Guinand's text.[3] The result: *the only six accepted were pupils of Monsieur Lenepveu, the only teacher who was also a member of the jury.*

Among the rejected candidates were Mademoiselle Fleury, a pupil of Monsieur Widor, and Monsieur Ravel, a pupil of Monsieur G. Fauré, both second place-winners in one of the previous Prix de Rome competitions.[4] I do not speak of their talent, nor of their works, nor even of Ravel's String quartet or songs. I know that the Conservatoire does not enter into these considerations and only takes diplomas into account. How can it be that two second place-winners in the Prix de Rome are not even judged worthy to compete? And does not the jury's composition make it suspect? And does not the result of the competition confirm these suspicions, with a sort of artlessness that is naive and stup . . . efying? Is it not time, if ever, to revise a judgement which complacently smacks of the most flagrant injustice?

Notes

1 The article was entitled 'Le Prix de Rome. Une révision nécessaire' ('The Prix de Rome. A revision needed').

2 Laloy is alluding to Charles Lenepveu (1840–1910), and his opera *Jeanne d'Arc* (*Joan of Arc*, 1886).

3 In the preliminary competition, entrants were required to compose a four-part fugue and a chorus for four or more voices with orchestra.

4 In fact, Ravel was never awarded second place. For an account of Ravel's attempts at the Prix de Rome, see Orenstein (1975), p. 33ff. Hélène-Gabrielle Fleury studied at the Conservatoire between 1899 and 1905, after which her career seems to have ended.

Ravel's works for music theatre[1]

The great composer who has just been stolen from our imagination by a painful and premature end has his place marked out in the history of music theatre in our time, not by the number of his works or by the scale of their proportions: their interest suffices.

This artist, whose refinement was well known right from the beginning of his career, was not afraid to write for the theatre. Those who were astonished were wrong. They forgot that dramatic music is not unremittingly dedicated to grandiloquent language, nor to exuberant forms of which the nineteenth century provided too many examples. Between the vocal display of historical opera and the symphonic overflow of Wagnerian drama there is room, fortunately, for a purer and therefore more intense sort of music - that of Rameau, Grétry, Mozart, Weber, Beethoven in *Fidelio* and this tradition, rediscovered, when they are not forcing their talent, by Gounod and Massenet in France, leads after them to Bizet, Chabrier, Fauré and Debussy, to mention only the deceased. Maurice Ravel is part of this line, with particular qualities and a personal accent which we must attempt to define.

As early as 1895, while still a student at the Conservatoire, at the age of twenty, he dreamed of the theatre, sketching a fairy opera whose subject he intended to take from the *Thousand and one nights*. After abandoning this project, he became interested in the tales of Hoffmann, and in Gerhart Hauptmann's play *La Cloche engloutie*,[2] finally settling on *L'Heure espagnole*, a comedy by Franc-Nohain which had just been given at the Odéon. That was in 1906. Ravel had already become known through works as characteristic as the String quartet,[3] *Miroirs*, *Shéhérazade*. Claude Terrasse, who was not only a good composer, but the most obliging of friends,[4] took on the task of notifying Franc-Nohain, and Monsieur Roland-Manuel, in his remarkable book on Ravel's dramatic works,[5] reports the surprised, if not anxious, reaction of this poet of fantasy, when he learned that his light muse had had the good fortune to please a composer he knew nothing about: he almost declined the honour.

A victim of the same prejudice, Rameau also defended himself against it in a letter to an academician who was very famous in his own time, and has been very obscure ever since: 'He who speaks of a learned composer usually means a man whom nothing escapes in the different combinations of notes but he is thought to be so absorbed in these combinations that he sacrifices everything to them: feeling, spirit and reason.'[6]

While a pupil at the Conservatoire, and a brilliant pupil, like most of our great composers, Ravel passed in the usual way from harmony to fugue, and from there to composition, successively in the classes of Pessard, Gédalge and Fauré. Through assiduous study, he perfected the gift nature had given him of an exceptionally subtle ear. Not only do none of the combinations of notes which are already known escape him, but he is capable of discovering others, as yet unknown, but no less legitimate. No one has pushed the art of substitutions, alterations and unexpected convergences as far as he – to the farthest limit where the chord, at the point of breaking apart, still remains in balance, and always obeys the rational principle of tonality: everything is surprising and everything can be explained. But he does not make a show of this unequalled skill and it is only useful to him for making explicit what is in his mind. There is not a single phrase that does not have a definite direction, not a note that does not add a necessary detail to it. He is a composer of character, and that is why he was always attracted by the diversity of characters and situations the theatre could offer.

His music is always expressive, but not at all in the manner of Gluck and Wagner, nor of Gounod or Massenet, nor even of Fauré or Debussy. The feeling which finds its perfect form in his music is of a very subtle essence, into which nothing sensual or even sentimental enters. With no voluptuous agitation, with no need of effusiveness, with no impulse and no desire, it is a contemplative feeling which could be described as Cartesian, because, following the order assigned by Descartes in his treatise on *Les Passions*,[7] its principle is admiration. An admiration which feels pity, rather than tenderness, at the games and the sufferings of the innocent lovers brought to the stage in the ballet *Daphnis et Chloé* (1912), and melancholy rather than sadness at the evocativeness of the sweet *Pavane pour une Infante défunte* (1899) or *La Valse* (1920) which recalls a vanished elegance.

Of the feelings which are particularly dear to him, one arises from the familiarity with Spain which came to Ravel not by birth (for his mother was Basque, not Spanish, and his father of French Swiss origin) but through good neighbourly relations established at an early age and always maintained during vacations, which he regularly spent at his birthplace, Ciboure near Saint-Jean-de-Luz. Spanish music thus became so familiar to him that he was able, without being disrespectful, to make gentle fun of its bombast and disdain its frenetic sensuality, only retaining its secret ardour which was precious to him in a different way. This is the character of the miniature Spain he shows us in 'L'alborada del gracioso' (1905) and the *Rapsodie espagnole* (1908), this is one of the greatest attractions which *L'Heure espagnole* offered him.

The comedy by Franc-Nohain did not claim to do more than present a conventional Spain, in the style of Lesage or Beaumarchais,[8] in the easy manner of a slightly licentious tale. One of those big-bellied clocks which we identify with the Franche-Comté or Normandy becomes Catalan for the occasion and serves in turn as a hiding-place, in the husband's absence, for the poet and financier who are paying court to the clockmaker's beautiful wife. The Spanish hour is what we call the shepherd's hour,[9] which will not sound for them, for in the circumstances the shepherd will be a robust muleteer. That is the plot of this modern *fabliau*[10] whose greenness is seasoned, as the characters sing in their final couplet, 'with a bit of Spain around it'.

Of this bit of Spain, Ravel did not increase the dose, but gave it a different flavour by blending in the authentic rhythms of the habanera, the malaguena and the bolero, adding to that the accent of the melodies, imitating the vibrant sonority of guitars in the orchestra; and all of it without insistence, without taking anything seriously, through furtive allusions which are lightly touched with a mocking smile. Then again the setting suggested to him the symphony of clocks and mechanical toys, favourable to an emotion which is all the more delicate for not being able to retain anything carnal. The waggish lines which he had to translate into music are brought out by a declamation which follows the accent of the words, but by means comparable to those of the harmony, also imprints on the melody inflections and alterations which deliberately deform it while pushing it slightly towards the baroque. Ravel was right to choose this work: he knew what he wanted, what he could make of it. From a summary sketch, which had a certain amount of precision, but was always full of jokes, he drew out a tableau of charming verve and delightful colouring.

L'Heure espagnole had its first performance at the Opéra-Comique on 19 May 1911, with Madame Geneviève Vix, Messieurs Périer, Coulomb, Delvoye and Cazeneuve in its five roles, and received a favourable welcome from the public, but the performances, interrupted soon after by the theatre's annual closure, were not continued. In 1921, the Opéra-Comique surrendered the piece to the Opéra, where Monsieur Rouché gave it an interpretation of choice, bringing together Madame Fanny Heldy, Messieurs Couzinou, Fabert, Huberty and

Dubois, and with lively, joyous scenery by Monsieur André Marc. The success was complete and still continues.

There is a different sentiment in which Ravel takes equal delight: that is the attentive, delicate, friendly and discreet sympathy he is able to show towards beings, and especially small beings who are not or are not yet men: toys singing a *Noël* (1905), animals in the *Histoires naturelles* (1906), children for whom the great composer, who had kindly become their playmate, translated for piano duet, in 1910, *Les Contes de la mère l'Oye* [*Mother Goose tales*], which were transcribed for orchestra and, two years later, became a ballet on the stage of the Théâtre des Arts.[11]

Madame Colette knew it well. That is why she wrote for him the text of the fairy comedy which later took the title *L'Enfant et les sortilèges*: here we see a little terror, who at first becomes very angry, and then very vexed, who has a fairy who consoles him, pieces of furniture which come to life and animals which are in revolt but are sensitive to pity. This is the subject which was proposed to Ravel, in 1917. Despite the interest he immediately took in it, he delayed a little in setting to work, detained by *Le Tombeau de Couperin*, published in the same year, in which a funerary tribute to friends who died in the war is hidden beneath the cenotaph of a great musical ancestor. And despite so many favourable themes, he took a long time to finish his task, leaving it and taking it up again many times, so that the score was only ready in 1924, and was given, in March of the following year, at the Opéra in Monte Carlo, with Madame Gauley, Messieurs Fabert and Warnery in the three leading roles, and in 1926, at the Opéra-Comique, where this time Madame Gauley's partners were Messieurs Bourdin and Guénot.

This slowness in composition arose from the change which was then taking place in Ravel's style, and is seen in his works of the same period such as the Duo for violin and cello (1922),[12] the Sonata for piano and violin (1927), the *Chansons madécasses* (1926); he wanted, in one last effort, to reduce this music which was so elaborate and so filled with accidentals to its simplest expression, and rather than writing in all the notes of a chord, to suggest them by the movement of the melodious lines. This purification was accomplished in the last work Ravel destined for the theatre, giving it a direct and penetratingly intense accent which up till then had only been achieved by Mussorgsky in *The nursery*. Unfortunately, a plot in which so many animals or domestic objects have be made to dance or sing poses very difficult problems for the director. That is why this *Enfant* [*Child*] surrounded by too many *sortilèges* [*spells*] was never able to remain on the stage for long. But the music is immortal.

Notes

1 'Maurice Ravel' in P. Lalo et al., *Histoire du théâtre lyrique en France depuis les origines jusqu'à nos jours* (Paris, n.d.), vol. 3, pp. 229–233

2 *Die versunkene Glocke* (*The sunken bell*), translated into French by A. F. Hérold

3 Laloy later wrote of the Quartet as 'seductive music, clear, full of games and graces, in which from time to time we think we recognize a new Fauré.' *La Grande revue* (25 February 1908), p. 375

4 Claude Terrasse (1867–1923) was a prolific composer of light music, especially *opéra bouffe*. He and Laloy were friends in the early years of the century: Laloy, Terrasse and Paul Mazon collaborated on a opera based on Homer's *Odyssey*, which was never performed.

5 *Maurice Ravel et son œuvre dramatique* (Paris, 1928)

6 Rameau, 'Lettre à M. Houdart de La Motte, de l'Académie française pour lui demander des paroles d'opéra', 25 October 1727, in J.-G. Prodhomme, ed., *Ecrits de musiciens* (Paris, 2nd ed. 1912), p. 323ff.

7 Descartes, *Les Passions de l'âme* (1649)

8 Both these eighteenth-century writers were famous for using Spanish settings and references, with the purpose of satirizing French life and manners. Lesage (1688–1747) is best known for his satirical novel, *Le Diable boiteux* (*The devil on two sticks*), and Beaumarchais (1732–1799) for his plays *Le Barbier de Séville* (*The barber of Seville*) and *Le Mariage de Figaro* (*The marriage of Figaro*).

9 The auspicious hour for lovers

10 A *fabliau* is a short, bawdy poem in medieval French literature.

11 Laloy reviewed the 1912 performance of *Ma mère l'Oye*. He was critical of some aspects of the staging, for instance that 'the Beast is not as monstrously ugly as the music gives us to hear'. He continued:

> But these details are readily forgotten when we listen to the music, which looks on and smiles in amused compassion. The divided orchestra, while asking each instrument for its most characteristic – sometimes its strongest – sounds, allows them to play mutually without merging into one; a clear outline encloses these sparkling colours which we might think had been laid down by some geometer-magician.'
>
> *La Grande revue* (10 February 1912), p. 624

12 This work is now more commonly known as the Sonata for violin and cello.

Shéhérazade

The song cycle *Shéhérazade* was first performed at the Société Nationale on 17 May 1904. Ravel said it showed the influence, at least in spirit, of Debussy, and that he had 'yielded to the profound fascination the Orient had had for me since childhood.'

La Revue musicale (1 June 1904), p. 290

As for the three songs by Monsieur Ravel on verses by Tristan Klingsor (*Shéhérazade*), I must say they delight me: the imaginative quality of 'La Flûte enchantée', the melancholy beauty of 'L'Indifférent' and the spiritual picturesqueness of this dreamlike 'Asie' are conveyed with such exquisite finesse and lightness of touch that each listener immediately thinks of Debussy. Undoubtedly these two are minds from the same family, but the analogy should not be exaggerated, nor should the disdainful epithet of imitator be flung at Monsieur Ravel: his music is not an imitative music; it has a personal accent and, in particular, shows evidence of a taste for pictorial detail which is not encountered in Monsieur Debussy. It cannot be disputed that the influence of the latter is obvious, but the greatest geniuses began by having masters and models, and one could choose worse.

Histoires naturelles

There was uproar at the first performance of the *Histoires naturelles* on 12 January 1907. This was at the Société Nationale, where the conservative spirit of the Schola Cantorum was strong. There was a spate of polemical articles in the press over the work's simplicity and humour. The critics were divided: Pierre Lalo wrote dismissively of 'café-concert music, with ninth chords,' but Laloy was extremely enthusiastic and thought Ravel was most truly himself in this work.

Notes for this section begin on p. 252.

Le Mercure musical (15 February 1907), pp. 155–157

'Natural histories? Ha! not so natural!' I do not know why these spiteful words of Voltaire came back into my mind, and made me a little wary. However, it is a long way from Buffon to Monsieur Jules Renard, who wears neither cuffs nor a wig, but probably mud-spattered trousers in the style of Monsieur Lepic, the father of Poil de Carotte, and, I suppose, smokes venerable pipes as he watches his chickens skilfully pecking up grubs in the open furrows.[1] For he is a true countryman, who knows the precise names of things and beasts, as well as their colours and their habits; who is not afraid to hunt for eggs in the places where the hens have taken a whim to lay them, or himself to supervise the scattering of mounds of dung in his fields. But make no mistake: his dissembling smile is not that of a peasant, but of a retired psychologist who still observes, and is secretly amused, and caresses everything around him with a tender irony. I feared this irony, which is present almost throughout, enveloping every emotion so that it can only be foreshadowed or guessed at, and stopping it at the point where in revealing itself it would lose its subtlety; I feared this exquisite modesty, which is to all appearances the enemy of any melodic outpouring; and above all I feared words which only give a literary pleasure: the guinea-fowl, the hunchback of the yard, who 'is always ready for a fight because of her hump';[2] or the peacock's gown, 'quite heavy with the eyes of those who couldn't stop looking at it'. But in fearing all that, I was reckoning without Maurice Ravel, whose ingenious, fantastic music has been able delicately to capture all the genuine emotion these little poems contain, without losing any of the mocking grace which always goes with it. And they are five little tableaux of a finesse and intensity of character unequalled by anything except certain Japanese landscapes which show, as here, speckled birds stretching their wings above the setting sun which is obscured by a pensive reed. Here is the peacock, lifting his small feet to a proud rhythm, in his wedding garb, and crying out at great length: 'Léon! Léon!' (that is what he calls his fiancée). And here is the cricket, returning to his humble hole; can you hear the cry of the door, almost inaudible because it is so high-pitched? 'Then he winds his tiny watch', and plunges deeply, climbs down an invisible chain that creaks a little, to the depths, to the centre of the earth where finally he feels reassured, while up above only the poplars rise up and dream beneath the moon. This little piece seems to me to be the most poetic of all, the one in which we most feel that tenderness, to the point of tears, which only tiny, defenceless creatures can inspire in us. I would certainly say that all the spirit of Mussorgsky's *The nursery* is there, but combined with what sureness of taste and what prodigious skill! The swan is most graceful as well, with the great rings in the water so well described by the harmony, and the floating clouds, and the brusque ill-humour of the final disillusionment: 'He is getting as fat as a goose'. Then the kingfisher, whom we feel we are following in silent flight, as he alights on the fishing rod almost without bending it, and unhurriedly departs. Lastly the guinea-fowl with her harsh cry, the furious charge of her dry feet, and the delightful contrast of the fowls' peaceful chirping, when she isn't there. All this described by a few expressively and singularly coloured chords, inserted here and there like unerring brush strokes, and evoking the whole landscape around a melody which adheres so closely to the words that we hardly think we are listening to a vocal line: it is a story, amiably told, with all the vocal inflections and all the rhythmic nuances of colloquial language.[3] Here again Mussorgsky showed the way, but had neither the courage to follow it to the end, nor the talent to envelop such free narration with music – real, pure music. Madame Jane Bathori set out these slight poems with the admirable sureness of diction for which she is known, and an emotional, slightly childlike grace which makes them very touching: a little girl looking at the beasts and laughing at their comical appearance or the antics they get up to, but feeling very fond of them just the same. As for the author, seated at the piano, stiff and impassive, he was the only person in the entire hall who betrayed no emotion; but his fingers were able to find the sonorities – enveloped and veiled, or light and sparkling – which were in his mind. Soon there was real delirium, and I do not know whether such a frenzied success has ever been entered in the annals of the Société Nationale, which is a fraternal society, and therefore usually a little reserved in its admirations. The last piece was encored and, even more unusually, supernumerary listeners were seen to invade the stage of the Salle Erard! Nothing could have been better deserved than this enthusiastic appluase, nothing could have brought more joy to the musicians' hearts. For we received in this work, better in my opinion than in any other of Maurice Ravel's works, the revelation of an artist of the most refined kind, who is now the master of his style and sure of a talent which is unique in its genre, an exquisite genre. I also owe him, on my own behalf, a debt of gratitude for having made me better realize to what an extent our modern-day fabulist is a delicate poet and a true friend to the beasts which brighten, and also soften, his rural solitude.

La Musique retrouvée, pp. 162–167

In February 1907,[4] one of the concerts of the Société Nationale gave the *Histoires naturelles* of Maurice Ravel, on texts borrowed from the book by Jules Renard. Madame Jane Bathori was the performer, accompanied by the author. The choice of this prose which is artful and contracted by irony seemed to be a challenge to the music, so much so that some listeners, insensitive to the charm of the chords, supposed that the composer wanted to make fun of them. They protested, while the rest of the hall increased its cheering; and Gustave Sérieyx, a passionate disciple of the Schola Cantorum, announced, in a journal for which he wrote, his intention 'mercilessly' to combat a form of art which seemed to him an insult to his dignity.[5] I then returned to the work, which I had reviewed the previous month, to take up the defence of the author in the review *S.I.M.* on 15 March:[6]

> I wrote previously that the *Histoires naturelles* are in my opinion the work which best reveals Maurice Ravel's personality, his particular vision of nature, and the facility for writing down subtle nuances of sound which was a precious gift from a good fairy. This impression is confirmed today, after a comparison.

The Quartet has exquisitely fresh passages and a youthful sound which are well liked: but the work is not constructed to an appropriate plan, and the periodic return of the first subject, intended to ensure unity, seems artificial in places. As for the piano pieces (*Pavane*, *Jeux d'eau*, *Miroirs*), they are of prodigious technique and rare colour; but here again everything does not flow from one source: and at times one senses a slight overload of ornamentation. That is why I have never been able to raise myself to the heights of enthusiasm with regard to these works that some of our friends reached in a single bound; even the magic of Ricardo Viñes was not always enough to hold me under the spell and ward off the hint of arbtirariness which arises from time to time. I am too interested in Maurice Ravel, and I know his conscientiousness and his artistic integrity too well to hesitate even for a moment to give him my full opinion, particularly now when I am able to find in his latest work everything that was missing in the earlier works: clear construction and a close linking of all the sections, a sober style which is always precisely expressive and, as the guiding principle of all this, an inspiration which is always sustained, an emotion which is ever-present. The emotion is sharpened by a hint of irony, undoubtedly, but this is precisely why it so eminently suits a man who, like his poet, Jules Renard, will always remain an observer. We must not believe, as some seem to, that transports of passion and Romantic fire are always the mark of sincerity. A person might be lying if he burst forth in loud transports of feeling, but reveal himself entirely by a few calm, well-chosen words.

Maurice Ravel's thought is naturally circumspect, penetrating, and inclined to make fun of whatever moves him. A mocking hobgoblin[7] lives in his mind, singing and playing bells, for Ravel discovers in the blink of an eye the unexpected comedy and as it were the secret grin inside all things. And this light ironic touch, far from lessening the emotion, on the contrary quickens it and makes it more poignant; nothing is closer to tears than this smile, which was that of Cervantes and Dickens before it belonged to Jules Renard or Tristan Bernard.[8] Maurice Ravel is a humorous composer; he was born thus, and now I can explain to myself why I prefer the 'river god laughing as the water tickles him' shown to us by *Jeux d'eau*[9] or the lovelorn jester who sings his 'Alborada' in *Miroirs*, to the slight hint of sentimental affectation which mars, for my taste, the *Pavane* or 'La Vallée des cloches'. A man like this is not completely himself when he is not secretly poking fun. And that is why the *Histoires naturelles* are an accomplished work, and as unique as the

> meeting of two such well-attuned minds. And what exquisite tenderness appears beneath the transparent veil of the smile! What delicate solicitude for the cricket, the 'negro insect', so small and fearful! What pure grace in the swan who 'glides over the lake like a white sled, from cloud to cloud'. Can you hear the soft wash of the water as he parts it and pushes it before him? And what caressing chords surround the kingfisher, sitting 'like a great blue flower at the end of a long stem'! The peacock himself, in spite of his ridiculously proud bearing, becomes touching in his illusion of eternal betrothal; and how could we be vexed with the guinea-fowl for the evil practical jokes which she does with such wit? How long until we have 'The water-fly', or 'The tree family', or 'The bats', or so many other masterpieces of observation and subtle poetry, to which the composer could bring a life and movement of which literature is incapable?[10, 11]

This article, as many I wrote at that time, did not have the good fortune to please either of the two camps which were quarrelling over the supremacy of French music. The Schola was offended and condemned me as a heretic, although Vincent d'Indy continued to treat me kindly, hoping for my return to the fold and perhaps even believing in his heart that I had not left it. Those who styled themselves 'Debussyists' were more severe with me. They had put all their hopes in Maurice Ravel, of whom it was beginning to be said: 'You will see that he will go further than Debussy'. As if music were a science whose progress down the ages would be marked by the discovery of a chord, in the laboratory where the composer carries out his experiments, using ruled paper for his calculations and the piano as a test-tube. As Ravel had indeed shown a subtle shrewdness for this sort of research, people concluded that he would be the greatest composer of modern times, running the risk of finding that he had been outstripped by another who, by adding a few extra sharps or flats to his sound combinations, had enriched the nomenclature of musical chemistry and thus made even more beautiful music. Indicating to Ravel what I thought to be his way, I was accused of leading him into an impasse, by mistake or even by treachery, to protect Debussy from imminent danger, because those who had taken Ravel as their champion expected nothing less, and especially nothing more, from him than symphonies worthy of Beethoven and dramas as colossal as those of Wagner.

I was always on very friendly, but not intimate, terms with Ravel. He never told me exactly what he thought of himself. However I have every reason to think that he was rather embarrassed by the huge ambitions people wanted to impose on him and the plan for his career which they traced out in advance. He knew and very sincerely admired Debussy. I did all I could to prevent a misunderstanding between them, but too many hare-brained busybodies seemed to take pleasure in making it inevitable, for example sacrificing Debussy's quartet to Ravel's, or else raising absurd questions of priority between the 'Habanera' and the second of the *Estampes*. The two composers then stopped seeing each other; as their esteem was mutual they both – as I can vouch – regretted the rupture.

As for my advice to listen to the 'mocking hobgoblin', perhaps it was not so bad, since after the *Histoires naturelles* Maurice Ravel wrote *L'Heure espagnole*, on the comedy by Monsieur Franc-Nohain, and quite recently, with Madame Colette, *L'Enfant et les sortilèges*.

Notes

1 It has not been possible to trace the quotation Laloy attributes to Voltaire: 'Histoires naturelles? Eh! pas si naturelles!', referring to the celebrated eighteenth-century naturalist Georges-Louis Leclerc, Comte de Buffon (1707–1788). Buffon published a thirty-six volume *Histoire naturelle* between 1749 and 1788. The French word *histoire* can mean either history or story: Buffon's work was a natural history, whereas Renard's *Histoires naturelles* are stories. *Poil de Carotte* (*Carrot-top*, 1894) was a novel also by Jules Renard (1864–1910), about the sufferings of an unfortunate young boy who lives with his family on a farm.

2 '[. . .] la pintade, bossue de la cour, qui «ne rêve que plaies à cause de sa bosse»'. This is a play on words: *bosse* is a hump, and *tomber sur la bosse de quelqu'un* means to assail or go for someone.

3 'Tout cela décrit par quelques accords d'un coloris expressif et singulier, piqués de ci de là comme des coups de pinceau infaillibles, et qui évoquent tout le paysage autour d'une mélodie si adhérente aux paroles, qu'à peine croit-on entendre un chant: c'est une histoire, aimablement contée, avec toutes les inflexions de voix et les nuances de rythme du langage familier.'

4 This seems to be a slip: the first performance took place on 12 January.

5 Laloy must mean Auguste Sérieyx (1865–1949), a composer and musicologist who taught at the Schola Cantorum and was a close friend of d'Indy. In his article in *Le Courrier musical* (1 February 1907), p. 77, Sérieyx spoke of protecting music and musicians from 'similar undertakings in "musical decomposition"'. It is interesting to find an ironic mention of Sérieyx' name in a letter from Debussy to Laloy, on 17 April 1904 when Laloy had the flu: 'You may be sure that the Sérieyx sonata has a lot to do with your

indisposition.' This would have been the Sonata for violin and piano (1904), which Laloy must recently have heard.

[6] 'Maurice Ravel', *Le Mercure musical* (15 March 1907), pp. 279–282. At this date the review's full title was *Mercure musicale et bulletin français de la S.I.M.*: see p. 36 n. 4.

[7] 'un farfadet moqueur': a mocking hobgoblin, goblin or sprite. Interestingly, there is a fragment of a sketch by Ravel for piano called *Farfadets*, in the collection of the Robert Owen Lehman Foundation: see Orenstein (1975), p. 244.

[8] The novelist and playwright Tristan Bernard (1866–1947) was known for his slightly grotesque characters and his deadpan humour, for example in a very funny play, *L'Anglais tel qu'on le parle* (*English as it is spoken*, 1899).

[9] Ravel's *Jeux d'eau* bears a quotation from a poem by Henri de Régnier: 'Dieu fluvial riant de l'eau qui le chatouille'.

[10] The last sentence in this paragraph appears only in the original article, not in *La Musique retrouvée.*

[11] In the last paragraph of the original article Laloy reviews another Ravel work, composed in 1905:

> The concert finished with the first hearing of an *Introduction et allegro* for harp and small orchestra. An occasional work, no doubt. The idea is very pretty, a little in the taste of the *Sonatine*, and the two wind instruments, flute and clarinet, blend delightfully with the strings. But I did not clearly grasp the role of the harp. The performance no doubt had something to do with it: the pedal instrument was out of tune, and Mademoiselle Micheline Kahn made the mistake of pounding out *glissandi* which could have been turned to better effect. Nonetheless the harp part consists entirely of passage work; virtuosity in itself is not a bad thing, I know; yet it must have a meaning. It seemed to me that the piece would gain more than it would lose if the harp were absent. But [. . .] it may be that a dry interpretation has led me astray. And then there are the *Histoires naturelles*, which make Ravel pale before Ravel.

Rapsodie espagnole

The first performance of the *Rapsodie espagnole* took place at the Concerts Colonne on 28 March 1908. The work was an immediate success with both public and critics.

La Grande revue (10 June 1908), pp. 397–399

The *Rapsodie espagnole* by Maurice Ravel is not an entirely new work: at least one part of it, the 'Habanera', was written for the piano some twelve years ago. The author did not think he had to disown passages which were already of respectable antiquity, considering his age, and he did well: the orchestral suite he drew from them is not only a feast for the ears and the mind; it affirms, as decisively as the *Histoires naturelles*, a personality which can be loved or hated, but whose independence and interest cannot fail to be recognised.

Spain exerts a singular attraction on our composers today: in the same way as Nietzsche by the 'African' *Carmen*,[1] they feel themselves seduced by a burning sky, an expansive melody, dominating rhythms. But it is no longer opaque Wagnerian metaphysics which needs to be dispelled; rather that in order to deliver music from the stale smell of holy water with which César Franck afflicted it, it is being torn away from the shadow of the church, or the darker one of the school, and given up to the perfumes of an Andalusian night, moulded to the undulations of languid dances and, in case of need, exposed to the bustle of a 'feria' in a square vibrant with sunlight and dust. This contrast between Spanish taste and a certain type of French, or rather Gallo-Belgian, taste is quite strangely exemplified by Albeniz' *Iberia*; for we find in these piano pieces, alongside harsh, biting ideas which the composer owes to his race, long developments of a simultaneously abstract and sentimental character, whose origin is also recognizable, and which go with them more or less as the colours of Puvis de Chavannes would go with a landscape by Gauguin.[2]

Monsieur Ravel's *Rapsodie* is very far from these incongruities: the unity of the style and the way it is adapted to his thinking are most remarkable, and yet here we will not find the melancholy reverie, the shimmering light and the lost echoes of 'La Soirée dans Grenade' by Claude Debussy, nor the jerking – more bestial than lascivious – of another habanera, that by R. Laparra (I say this in no way to reproach him).[3] This is a very well-observed Spain, but observed by an eye which is mocking, and will gladly overdo or deform: the Spain of Cervantes or Goya, with more artificial lines, more distorted forms, and more fantastical caprices; a Spain tending a little towards the Japanese style, full of piquant details, winks, grimaces, and unexpected, almost impossible contortions, striking in their accent. All this translated into a very select, very invented language in which the furious taste for the new never leads to vain complexity or unintelligibility: this is a privilege which only belongs to artists gifted by nature, and on which other composers would do well not to pride themselves too much. The small proportions of each piece, the absence of any development, did not seem to me a deficiency, quite the contrary: a rhapsody is not a symphony, and the art of Monsieur Ravel, all concise indications and delectable windfalls, revolts at the solemnity of great constructions. The value of a work is not measured by volume, nor by weight: an ivory figurine can give an impression of beauty which is denied to a giant statue of Liberty bringing light to the world. How many operas, or more or less musical dramas, would we not sacrifice in exchange for the *Histoires naturelles* or the *Rapsodie espagnole*!

I only have a few reservations about the orchestration, which seemed to me a little slender and tart at times; I do not know whether the author's relative inexperience is to blame, or the boorishness of an orchestra which continually, at the rehearsals and almost at the performance, gave signs of discontent or irony, which in truth are quite unnecessary: the opinion of a second or even a first violinist does not matter to us; we only ask this instrumentalist to play his part, which, it seems, is already not so easy. Monsieur Colonne was able to find, on this as on many other occasions, the necessary words to quieten these extemporaneous critics: and, in three rehearsals, he took the study of the work far enough for the general character, if not the last detail, to emerge accurately: we must give thanks for the devoted efforts of this excellent conductor.

Notes

1 Nietzsche wrote at some length about Bizet's *Carmen* in *Der Fall Wagner* (*The Wagner case*, 1888):

> With [Bizet's composition] one bids farewell to the *damp* north and to all the fog of the Wagnerian ideal [. . .] This music is gay, but not in the French or German way. Its gaiety is African; fate hangs over it, its happiness is short, sudden, without reprieve. I envy Bizet for having had the courage of this sensitiveness, which hitherto in the cultured music of Europe has found no means of expression - of this southern, tawny, sunburnt sensitiveness . . .
>
> *The complete works of Friedrich Nietzsche*, ed. O. Levy (New York, 1974), vol. 8, pp. 3-4

2 The fresco-like paintings of Pierre Puvis de Chavannes (1824-1892) employed subtle colours which would certainly be incompatible with the bolder, more vibrant canvases of Gauguin.

3 The music of Raoul Laparra (1876-1943) reflected his strong interest in Basque and Spanish folk music. Laloy is referring to his opera *La Habanera*, which had recently had its first performance.

Gaspard de la nuit

La Grande revue (25 January 1909), pp. 395–396

The first concert of the Société Nationale began sadly with a very posthumous trio by Guillaume Lekeu,[1] rich in souvenirs of Beethoven and Schumann, heavy, awkward, and tiresome [. . .][2] But the three poems for piano, inspired in Monsieur Ravel by the same number of proses of Aloysius Bertrand,[3] dispelled all the clouds. Let us first of all thank the pianist, who triumphed while making light of some exquisite and very interesting difficulties. Never perhaps have a composer and his interpreter found themselves more perfectly in agreement than Monsieur Ravel and Monsieur Viñes: these elaborate works, in which every detail has its value and must stand out, needed these sinewy fingers, these intelligent hands, and even this smile behind the moustache, which links the performer to the mischief of the composer. For there is, and probably always will be mischief in Monsieur Ravel: his mind is a conjuror which, even when it is emotional, still enjoys a prestigious skill. The *Histoires naturelles* showed us a friendly irony which by no means everyone understood. Here, as in the *Miroirs*, emotion prevails, but it is more direct: nothing could be simpler than this 'Ondine', with its doleful melodic line surrounded only by the fleeting shiver of the waters; and certainly there is a quality of great pity in this plaintive, monotonous 'Gibet'; the last piece, 'Scarbo', keeping rather the character of an entertainment. But in each of the three the workmanship is so dense, so highly finished, so ingenious, that each note brings with it surprise and joy. Monsieur Ravel is a stylist; and this virtuosity of expression does not damage, in his latest piece, either the strength of the feeling or the logic; this is an advance which ends the charming, uncertain period of his experiments. He is the master of his art, which may be loved, or condemned, but no longer discussed.

Notes

1 Guillaume Lekeu (1870-1894) was a Belgian composer who died of typhoid fever at a very early age. The work Laloy mentions was probably the Piano trio (1890).

2 Remarks about the performance of the Lekeu work have been omitted.

3 The collected prose poems of the French writer Aloysius Bertrand (1807–1842) were published posthumously under the title *Gaspard de la nuit*.

L'Heure espagnole

The 'lyric comedy', *L'Heure espagnole*, was first performed at the Opéra-Comique on 19 May 1911. Critical reaction was mixed, with discussion as to whether it was valid for French composers to use the Spanish idiom. Laloy, Marnold and Fauré were among those who wrote positive reviews.

La Grande revue (10 June 1911), pp. 627–628

L'Heure espagnole, by Monsieur Franc-Nohain, is a comedy not of manners, still less of characters, but of movements and words. [. . .][1] Analogous to the text, the music makes fun of the subject and itself: the vocal line alternates lyrical portamenti with simple parlando; the imperturbable symphony[2] is augmented by the untimely cries of automata; an intemperate growling underlines the charge of an imaginary bull; the financier, made joyful by love, dresses up his imposing theme as a waltz; the muleteer is anounced by brutal fifths, and disturbing eddies underline the swinging of the clock on his shoulders with Gonzalve inside; the five voices come together for a last quintet in which one by one, to a habanera rhythm, they make ornaments of chords from their parallel trills, or else take over a motif from each other and transpose it, but the double bassoon comes to the aid of the bass who can sing no lower. The mockery, in all that, is of such and such a contrapuntal figure, such and such a progression or modulation, orchestral effect, or compositional form. Wholly musical pranks, plays on notes similar to the plays on words and which, similarly, require a certain perception of the procedures if they are to be understood. But Monsieur Ravel is such a pure musician that he never exceeds the limits of beauty; in his style, even when he disguises it intentionally, harmony is innate; and if we smile on hearing it, we are also moved by a tenderness whose object is none other than the music itself. Already the charm of the *Histoires naturelles* arose from this sweet soul which could be guessed at through the external irony. It is a much more significant work this time: never has the author shown himself to be more inventive, nor more the master of this genre which he has made his own, and whose principle is to accord equal though opposite satisfaction to intellect and sensibility.

Notes

1 A paragraph discussing the characters, and the burlesque element in Franc-Nohain's writing, has been omitted.

2 The word *symphonie* had a wider range of meanings in Laloy's time than it does today. Here it refers to the orchestral accompaniment in an operatic work.

Daphnis et Chloé

Ravel had not completed the score of *Daphnis et Chloé* in time for the planned first performance by the Ballets Russes. In fact he took three years to write it, interrupted by work on the *Cinq mélodies populaires grecques* and the *Valses nobles et sentimentales*. The work was eventually performed on 8 June 1912. Laloy and most other critics observed a new maturity and solidity in Ravel's style, though not many besides Laloy and Willy (Henri Gauthier-Villars) admired the orchestration.

La Grande revue (25 April 1911), pp. 846–847

The last concerts in the winter season were, as is customary, the most worthy of interest, as if the artistic rivals had saved their strength for the final test. Thus we had the privilege of hearing, at the Châtelet, a few extracts from the ballet commissioned from Monsieur Ravel by the Russian venture, the performance of which was postponed. The subject, chosen and arranged by the dancer Fokine, is that of *Daphnis et Chloé*: it is evident what advantage the staging will draw from this subject in terms of light draperies and feigned artlessness. The composer is less helped by it, as he finds only shadows of feeling, and lustreless colours. But Monsieur Ravel is not among those who are rebuffed by difficulties or discouraged by paradoxes; he accepted the challenge; success seems assured for a score which is lively with rhythm and most ingeniously varied. But the episodes which worked best for him were, as we should have expected, those with a fantastical character which allowed him to develop the particular resources of his imagination. An explorer in the world of sound, he likes nothing better than to travel its borders; we follow him with both anguish and rapture, for at every moment we are trembling lest he cross the borders; and indeed he does cross them, but in order to annexe forbidden regions, and win them for harmony; thanks to a facility which has something of sorcery about it, he knows how to soften and pacify to the point of the strangest delight chords which, handled by anyone else, would be harsh to the ears.[1] Others recommend themselves to us by greatness of thought or strength of emotion; as a creator after his own manner, he has the satisfaction of exercising his powers with greater guarantee; for future generations may repudiate our conception of art: they will be far from refusing the benefits of his discoveries. In his new work, it was the first fragment that best fulfilled our expectation of the marvellous: a nocturne trembling with unseen terror, in which the most confused echoes result simply from a certain layout of the string section, while in another place an instrument hitherto employed to imitate wind directly is blended with the orchestra, achieving that union of sound and noise which the music of the future is called on to exploit. The choruses of fright which follow will no doubt make more of an impression on the stage than in concert, and the dance of the pirates has a picturesque ferocity, but lacks mystery.

La Grande revue (25 June 1912), p. 848

Maurice Ravel is a magician in sound, who at birth was given the secret of capturing sounds with subtle threads, and assembling them despite their resistance in unstable states of balance which do not seem to arise from the laws of this world. That is why his music is ravishing and disconcerting; rarely can a definite image be associated with it; or when it is close to nature, it only touches the farthest boundaries: fountains, whims of light, childish expressions of tenderness, chimeras of exoticism, melancholy birds, wary insects. The seriousness of human feelings, and especially the simplicity of antique feelings, are outside his domain. Sooner would butterflies or cicadas dance to these slight rhythms, than these shepherds in floating tunics. But we marvel at this symphony[2] in which we guess at supernatural presences amid the rustlings of night; and dance tunes, though it is not easy to bring a bodily cadence to them, abound in delicate lines which we would wish to savour at leisure.

Notes

1 'Explorateur du monde sonore, il n'aime rien tant que d'en côtoyer les limites; on le suit avec angoisse et ravissement à la fois, car on tremble à tout instant qu'il n'aille les franchir; et il les franchit en effet, mais c'est pour annexer par delà des régions interdites, et les gagner à l'harmonie; ces

accords qui, par tout autre maniés, rudoieraient les oreilles, il sait, à la faveur d'une habileté qui tient du sortilège, les adoucir et pacifier jusqu'au plus étrange délice.'

[2] See p. 260 note 2.

Adélaïde and *L'Enfant et les sortilèges*

Adélaïde ou le Langage des fleurs (*Adelaide or the language of flowers*) was a ballet based on the orchestral score of the *Valses nobles et sentimentales*, with an argument written by Ravel. It was first performed in 1912.

La Revue des deux mondes vol. 109, no. 52 (1 August 1939), pp. 699–703

For several years, the Opéra has retained in its repertoire [Ravel's] *Daphnis et Chloé*, first performed in 1912 by Diaghilev's Ballets Russes, and *L'Heure espagnole*, which was surrendered by the Opéra-Comique where it appeared in 1911 and was not able to continue. In order to pay fuller homage to the author's memory, the Opéra has just acquired the ballet *Adélaïde* and the 'lyric fantasy' entitled *L'Enfant et les sortilèges*. Thus it has been possible to present evenings wholly devoted to the music of Ravel, and they were fine commemorative celebrations, emotionally melancholy and penetrating. Far from detracting from one another, the works were mutually sustaining and enlightening, and there was no risk of monotony, for they transported us by turns, each in its own way, into that new world to which Ravel introduced us, and being given permission to remain there made us happier still.

A new world of sonorities and chords, as was understood from the very beginning, but also, and first, as we now realize, a new world of feelings and thoughts. Because Ravel had a horror of bombast and because he was able to discover affinities between notes or sounds that but for him would escape us, he was accused of dryness and artifice. That was a great mistake.

Written first for piano, in 1911, the waltzes whose title pays homage to Schubert were transcribed for orchestra the following year, at the request of Madame Trouhanova who was giving dance entertainments at the Châtelet, and that is when they received a scenario which caused them to take a new title: *Adélaïde ou le Langage des fleurs*. In Schubert's time, which for us was that of the Restoration, the proud

Adélaïde hid and confessed her feelings for the tender Loredan, despite the jealousy of a noble duke, using the daisy, the iris and the ranunculus as go-betweens.[1] The idea was pretty, and it was in this guise that the ballet made a brief appearance on the stage of the Opéra in 1916, in one of the Thursday and Sunday matinees which the management was then succeeding in giving, not without difficulty. Now that it has just taken its place in the repertoire, Monsieur Serge Lifar, entrusted with the choreography, could not resist philosophizing a little on the subject, making Loredan a poet, Adélaïde a muse, and taking away the duke's noble rank, making him simply a dancer; two female dancers also have roles, and I confess that I understood nothing of the plot; but no matter, since the dances retain their alternate character of playfulness, languor, restlessness, hope and joy. Monsieur Serge Lifar, who was the poet, achieved his customary success, worthily surrounded by Mademoiselle Chauviré, who is so graceful and witty, Madame Darsonval, who knows everything that can be learned about her craft, and Monsieur Paul Goubé, who is a magnificent dancer.

No matter especially because the music is there, intervening, dispelling the shadows of the performance, and clearly transmitting to us the coded message of the gestures or flowers. One to another the waltzes are joined, in changing keys, but in a friendly relationship; in triple metre, each one sets out with a different step, and the melody springs up, bends, and just as it is about to touch the ground it rises up and starts again, revived by the modulation which lies in wait for it. At first our curiosity was aroused by the sound, which is so odd; it remains unique in its genre, but no longer intrigues us, and we better perceive how singing this music is. It is a delicate song, exquisitely sweet, and more touching still because there remains nothing of carnal emotion in it: it is the song of the spirit, lavishing its pensive tenderness and its incorporeal caress on ideal creatures, in a landscape of dreams. The harmony which was born with it is no less sure of its bearing, no less rigorous in its connections: that is what allows it constantly to avoid brutal affirmations and to form complex chords which hold fast to one another, linked to the direction of the phrase, clarifying and completing it by adding nuances and reflections.

Ravel's *Valses* are one of the works in which he attains, with a simple, refined technique, the most marvellous effects of that style which is simultaneously light and sustained, airily graceful, staunchly solid. Not a single chord but which is made strictly with the necessary notes, and nothing more. And the melody bends to the rhythm so naturally that we experience its charm before we have noticed its evocative undertone. These virtues are even more apparent in the transcription for orchestra, where chords break up the better to re-form, with the notes judiciously distributed between flutes, oboes, clarinets, bassoons, horns or violins, each instrument having a distinct part, separated from the others by an empty space; there is no confusion or heaviness in this harmonious concert which, through the good offices and intelligence of Monsieur Philippe Gaubert,[2] took on its precise colouring and its true balance.

§

L'Enfant et les sortilèges is a different kind of enchantment. [. . . It consists of][3] two very different, almost contrasting, sections, one ironic and domestic, though broken up by the appearance of the Princess, by a touching episode and almost by a love duet, the other set in the open air, where the voices of nature breathe out the secrets of the night. Both sections call on the realm of the fantastic - insinuating and unexpected, free of any element of incantation - in which Ravel has always excelled.

Here his music is in the same style as that of the *Valses*, but more direct and concise. Other works from the same period, such as the Duo for violin and cello,[4] the Sonata for piano and violin, the *Chansons madécasses*, show evidence of a similar direction: not content to reduce a thought to its simplest expression, he goes further, into ellipsis and allusion, and rather than pronouncing all the notes of a chord succeeds in suggesting them through the movement of the melodious lines. To use technical language, the counterpoint henceforth suffices to evoke all the subtleties of the harmony. It only takes two oboes, playing together, to open the nursery to our eyes, and only a flute to surround the imaginary princess' farewells with tender-hearted sweetness. The melody too is contained, shorter and concentrated; less graceful no doubt, it touches our hearts with a sharp blade. This laconicism is more pronounced in the slightly burlesque scenes of the first section. The second, which is less tight, is steeped in poetry as intense as it is discreet, announced by a brief prelude which recalls, without resembling it, the marvellous introduction to the third tableau of *Daphnis et Chloé*. And the violins, until now almost completely excluded from a sharp-edged orchestration, raise their sweet voices, and the melody softens. This is the construction of the work, in which Ravel smiles at a child whose sorrows he knows, and at innocent beasts who confide in him, for he knows how to listen like a trusted grown-up friend, who enjoys himself, who laments and consoles at the same time, always careful not to move too suddenly or speak too loudly, lest he cause alarm. Whence this brief, fleeting, intense emotion, of which Schumann and Mussorgsky before him gave the most striking examples. Ravel deserves to be likened to them, in this aspect of his talent, which also has other aspects, and that is no faint praise. Monsieur Gaubert, who was responsible for the musical performance, once again showed his ability to know and to love music, and the stage presentation does the greatest honour to the informed, infallible taste of Monsieur J. Rouché.

Notes

1 Schubert's song *Adelaïde* (1814) was less well known than Beethoven's to the same text by Friedrich von Matthisson. For the lover in the poem, the natural world reflects the name and image of the beloved: petals will bear her name, and when he dies a flower will blossom on his grave.

2 Philippe Gaubert (1879–1941) was a flute virtuoso and composer, and also conducted at the Opéra from 1920 onwards. He won the Prix de Rome in 1905, the year in which Ravel was excluded after the preliminary round.

3 Four paragraphs have been omitted. The first two discuss the difficulties of staging a work of such intimate proportions in large theatres, and the merits of the performers; the third and fourth duplicate material from the article on Ravel's works for music theatre which appears on p. 244.

4 This work is now more commonly known as the Sonata for violin and cello.

On Stravinsky

Le Sacre du printemps

The first performance of *Le Sacre du printemps* was given by the Ballets Russes on 29 May 1913 at the Théâtre des Champs-Elysées. It was greeted with outrage and uproar by audience and critics alike. Camille Bellaigue thought the work was 'something barbaric, an effort against, or rather an overthrowing of musical civilisation', and other critics referred to it ironically as '*Le Massacre du printemps*'. Even though the musical language was radically new, it was Nijinsky's choreography that aroused the greatest hostility: at a concert performance the following year, the work was more favourably received. Laloy was in a unique position to write about *Le Sacre*, because he knew the composer and because Stravinsky and Debussy played a piano-duet version of the work at his home in 1912. The extracts begin with an advance review; there is a small amount of duplication between the other reviews.

Notes for this section begin on p. 281.

La Grande revue (25 June 1912), p. 850

At the same time as *Petrouchka*, Stravinsky this year brought us an almost completed work, the performance of which is promised for next year, *Le Sacre du printemps*. It is a religious ballet, based on the rites of Slavonic paganism, but they are made new, and unconstrained by erudition. Everything is invented, even the themes, and it is not monuments or texts, but the earth's eternal liveliness that inspires this music and carries the triumphant frenzy to the point of terror; then in the restless silence of night, there is the long pursuit in the darkness, the capture, the homage to the chosen victim, and finally the meditation preceding a liberating sacrifice. A superhuman music, a revealing of the elemental powers, labyrinths, whirlwinds, clamourings, distant voices, the breath of living things, the thrills of space, agitation, ecstasy, fright, cruel initiations and mysterious celebrations: the cult of nature finds its liturgy.[1]

The author of these prophetic revelations is a slender young man, with a kind, curious face. Sitting at the piano, he is transported by passion, his hands run dizzily across the keyboard, unleashing unknown sounds; he rises, staggers, but he smiles, happy with his composition, and a short while later, resting in that leafy garden, bows his head: 'Oh! that blackbird's song, how it flows through the air!'

La Musique retrouvée, pp. 213–219

On a bright afternoon in the spring of 1913,[2] I was strolling in my garden at Bellevue with Debussy: we were waiting for Stravinsky. As soon as he caught sight of us, the Russian composer ran, with arms outstretched, to greet the French master, who glanced over his shoulder at me in amusement and fondness. Stravinsky had brought the piano-duet reduction[3] of his new work, *Le Sacre du printemps*. Debusssy agreed to play the bass on the Pleyel piano which I still possess. Stravinsky asked permission to remove his collar. With his gaze immobilised by glasses, his nose close to the keyboard, and at times humming a missing part, he drew his companion's soft, agile hands into an explosion of sound. Debussy followed without a hitch and seemed to enjoy the difficulty. When they had finished, it was no longer a question of embraces, or even of compliments. We were struck dumb, overwhelmed as by a hurricane springing up from the depths of the ages to take our life by the roots.

A few days later, we attended the first performance which, as is well known, was one of the most tumultuous ever. The contradictory shouts of the public and also the systematic distortions in the dancing might not, perhaps, have allowed me to appreciate the music fully, had it not been for this first impression, since confirmed by score-reading and concert performance. I conveyed this impression in an article published by the newspaper *Comœdia*:[4,5]

> The sage Tzu-ch'i, of Nan-kouo, sat leaning against the table; turning up his head towards the sky, he gave a great sigh and appeared dead in body and soul. His disciple Tzu-yu, standing in front of him began to speak: 'Why, master, would you endeavour to make your body like dry wood, your heart like dead cinders? The being that I see leaning against the table now is certainly not the one which was leaning there to begin with.' Tzu-ch'i replied, 'You speak more wisely than you know. I have

just entombed myself. Do you understand? You have listened to the organs of man, not those of the earth. You have heard the organs of the earth, not those of heaven.' Tzu-yu asked for an explanation. Tzu-ch'i continued, 'The breathing of the universe is called the wind. Sometimes, the wind is inactive. When it rises, all the cavities in nature are set in motion and they reverberate. Have you never heard those long owls' cries? The rugged outlines of the wooded mountains, the enormous hollows of great trees, then become like noses, like mouths, like ears; they are only transoms, cups, mortars, swamps, marshy hollows. The wind springs up, whistles, shouts, sighs, calls out, weeps, groans, chirps. It gives the note, and everything tunes up. It is light or powerful, and the harmony grows weaker or stronger. Then it stops, and all the cavities empty immediately. Have you never experienced these outbursts of sound?'

The disciple replied, 'I see that the organs of the earth are composed of all the cavities of nature, and that the organs of man are measured tubes. Can I ask you what the organs of heaven are?' Tzu-ch'i said then, 'These infinitely varied sounds, in order that each of them have its independence, and that each of them can be produced, must there not be a cause?'

Thus, in the second chapter of his work, wrote Chang Tzu, one of the most profound philosophers and one of the boldest poets, not only in ancient China but in the world, and of all time.[6] We have just heard the organs of the earth, not at random in the wooded mountains and the uneven wind, but captured by industrious man and placed at our disposal in the comfort of a concert hall. Since music became an art, I do not think it has celebrated a more splendid victory over nature.

Nature, to tell the truth, is the only model. In the same way as poetry or painting, music is inspired by nature, but with so much reserve and by such remote transcriptions that several theorists have mistakenly believed that music only proceeded by arbitrary rules, like those in the game of chess. It is very clear, however, that the first savage who bent his bow, not with one string, but with four or five, to shoot sounds and not arrows, wanted to rival supple branches waving in the breeze; that drums, timpani and gongs are the image of horses galloping or of thunder; in short that the organs of man were only invented on the example of the organs of the earth. Man only had his voice; the natural function of the voice is words, not song. Instruments give the fixed, definite note which is the first element of music. The voice conforms after a fashion to instruments. Instruments imitate, though not closely, the noises of nature.

In certain primitive tribes, we encounter instruments which try to reproduce the complexity of these noises. Some African harps have metallic rings which add a dull clanking, evocative of elytrons[7] rustling in the forest, to the vibration of the strings. Other nations, already induced by the progress of analysis to allow only pure notes, enrich them through timbre: Chinese, Cambodians, Siamese and Javanese in this way produce symphonies by a judicious mix of strings and pipes with metal or wooden blades, bells and even resonant stones; these symphonies have in recent years been revealed to Europe, and have become her joy and despair. For Europe, having learned reasoning from the Greeks, abused it to the point of conceiving a sort of ciphered music, in which the note only represented a note of a scale, and kept its value even when it did not correspond to a sound of any sort.

Modern music's great progress is to have reintegrated the sound, alongside the note. This progress, moreover, had long been foreshadowed, and there is not one true composer who, even during periods of the most excessive abstraction, and even without being aware of it, did not take sounds into account. Lully, François Couperin, Rameau and Mozart did not write a note or chord without mentally hearing its effect. But the Romantics dreamed of music which yielded to impressions of the soul or the senses. The Russian composers ventured combinations whose only guarantee was the resulting charm. Claude Debussy joined the logic of sounds to that of notes.

A few innovators today are trying to reproduce directly the sounds of everyday experience with appropriate machines. Their research may bring some interesting discoveries, always on condition that it is used to musical ends. If precision alone is intended, no machine will equal the phonograph, in the same way that for this purpose no drawing can bear comparison with photography. Art cannot do double duty with nature; it borrows elements from nature, out of which it creates a separate world.

The condition of this world is harmony, understood not in the narrow sense of our conservatories but as the principle of unity: the parts must be linked to one another and to the whole by relationships which are not defined, but perceptible. Now noise, if it is not mixed with music, is only disorder. Therefore it can only occur as an accident which disturbs the composition but does not detroy it. A symphony of noises is inconceivable.

But it is even better to imitate noise, or rather to transpose it into music. That is what Monsieur Stravinsky does in his *Le Sacre du printemps*. He employs neither the wind machine in which Mahler rejoiced, nor the grumblers or gurglers of the Italian Futurists,[8] nor the sheet of metal which in the wings of our theatres plays the role of thunder. He writes with notes which he entrusts to the ordinary instruments of the orchestra. But the choice of these notes and these instruments is such that one would think one was witnessing the most fierce altercations of the elemental powers. There are the terrors of the night-time, the light touch of wings, the cries, the murmurs, the wailings of outer space, there are the roars of monsters, implacable gallopings, animals crawling, leaps of surprise, starts of agony, fights, anguish, delirium, prostrations, bloody triumphs, and there is the indissoluble union of life and death. Nature appears to us here in her terrible blindness, with neither the attenuation nor the interpretation which our cowardice inflicted on it for so long. This is nature's rough language, which is only completed, reinforced and clarified at times when she can only stammer confused syllables. These are the organs of the earth, but a composer is a keyboard.[9]

The effect is prodigious. It is an intoxication, an ecstasy, an annihilation, and when the music stops, the audience is beside itself: people clap their hands, stamp their feet, and cheer, in the grip of an enthusiasm which could only better be described as panic.

'I have,' said Monsieur Stravinsky, 'completed a work of faith.'[10] He has communicated this faith to us. With him we have celebrated the mysteries of the Great Mother; we have contemplated human sacrifice without horror and we have shared out the slaughtered flesh.

Yet we cannot forget another music, the daughter not of the earth but of heaven, which brings us peace, calm, rest and the imperceptible echo of the eternal silence. Of this music, that of the earth is the material projection. In it alone does a great artist find the conclusion of his mission. Even Wagner reached it. Others, like Mozart, live there as if it were their natural home.[11]

La Grande revue (10 June 1913), pp. 612–613

It is almost exactly a year since *Le Sacre du printemps* was announced to readers of *La Grande revue* as a decisive work,[12] in which for the first time music took it upon itself to respond to the feelings not of a man among men, but of a tribe in which the individual loses his sense of self in the collective enthusiasm, on the occasion of a festival celebrating the blind power of nature. Today this music, which we had only been able to approach via the piano version, is revealed in its full symphonic dimensions, and to say that we admire it is an understatement: we are confounded, and long after it is over we are still listening to the mysterious echoes it awakens, this time in the depths of our soul. Those who want to explain everything will maintain that the music is made up of new chords and rhythms, or on the other hand that it uses nothing that is not already known. What does this matter, since it is certain that the music teaches us an emotion of which we have never before been aware? Such discoveries are rare enough that the work which procures them is spared examination, and we must pity those who would find nothing in it to praise but the skill of the performance. It would be more interesting to show why these combinations of notes and sounds, however unexpected they might be, never rouse us to indignation, and even if they do us some violence they blend with it a delight that makes us greedy for this martyrdom; but that is the inviolable secret of art. The historian will notice that this music answers the boldest wishes of our poets, those who dream of *la vie unanime*,[13] also that it seems to have profited by the lessons in primitive dignity that Gauguin and his emulators asked of primitive peoples; and that it is timely and satisfies a need in our spirit. As for the innocent public, it will feel the vertigo of the music as we did, when it can hear it without ludicrous phantoms appearing at every moment to rob it of its gravity.

The scenery and costumes are not in any way to blame, as they are by Monsieur Roerich, and this conscientious artist has been able to reconcile an obligatory primitiveness with the pleasure of our eyes; but the dancing has ruined everything: the eloquence of the body has an irresistible effect on us; music, if given the lie by it, is in the wrong and is obliterated; her most fervent worshippers, if they are not to feel frustrated, have no alternative but to close their eyes.

Monsieur Nijinsky, a most congenial young man, was a very talented performer. An attempt has been made to make a choreographer of him, and his good faith and zeal are both beyond doubt. What he lacks is genius, if we are willing to reduce the word to the obvious meaning of inventive facility. Even more than the ballet *Jeux*, *Le Sacre du printemps* pointed out his impotence, because the subject called for greater development.[14] Monsieur Nijinsky could only bring together, as in an encyclopedia, postures copied from almost anywhere, from central Africa to far Siberian shores, and from these postures he has deduced only mechanical movements. If he had looked at the savages he took as his models, instead of leafing through treatises on ethnography, he would have recognised a sort of grace in their most disorderly dances, and it was this grace that he needed to apply himself to reproducing, not through their means, but through ours. The composer imitating an exotic orchestra does not renounce his national instruments; our country's dance, like its music, has its language, which is appropriate to our customs, our temperaments, our traditions, our ways of thinking and feeling. It is in this language that the artist must convey the impressions that come to him from nature or a foreign art; he will sometimes be led to enrich it with new expressions; but it is useless to pretend to replace it with another language, which no one understands, not even he who speaks it parrot-fashion, articulating signs whose meaning escapes him.

I must praise the skill, memory and dedication of the performers who did not miss a single contortion, tremor, shake or jump, and equally observed immobility in the most cramped postures and synchronism in the most disparate ensembles. I must above all preserve the memory of music that was worthy of a better fate.

La Revue musicale S.I.M. (1 May 1914), pp. 45–46

Paris committed a cruel injustice, but has just made amends for it with a triumph. Last year, we could not hear *Le Sacre du printemps* for the indignant outcry. At Monsieur Monteux' latest concerts, it was listened to in the most respectful silence, and applauded endlessly. The most severe critics have recognised its power. The most envious composers are reduced to imputing an intrigue or a practical joke.

If, after the scandal of *Tannhäuser*, when political passions had subsided, Wagner had been able to appeal to amateur taste, would he too have been rehabilitated? Maybe, because the true public, the one which comes for pleasure, was beginning to replace the court factions and would have supported the work if it had not been withdrawn after three performances. One must never despair of Paris.[15]

But it is certain, equally, that in fifty years people have learned to love and understand music better. The rivalry between five symphonic concert societies, the existence too of a review such as the one in which these lines will appear, are simultaneously the tokens and the instruments of this undeniable progress. Between artists and society, an alliance has been formed; the former are no longer shown off to guests at evening parties like freaks who must not be approached; they are treated as equals; they too receive guests, and the people who attend the last rehearsal for a particular Sunday concert feel deeply flattered by the honour, and, in spite of their plumes or their furs, they are as well behaved as if they were at a lecture by Monsieur Bergson.[16]

Le Sacre du printemps has benefited from these fortunate arrangements. For the work, in its intrepid boldness, had the potential to surprise more than one timorous listener. But today the concert-going public has become a good public. It asks only to be moved, and it is quite right. I myself had, on reading the score, thought I noticed such and such a procedure wrongly used. These are perfectly useless observations. Such music does not yield up its secrets on reading. It comes into existence in the orchestra, not on paper. The sounds, and the movement of the sounds, which is the rhythm, are its substance.

Monsieur Stravinsky is the master of sounds and rhythm. He knows how to choose and place sounds in such a way that all the noises of nature are evoked. There are the terrors of the night-time, the light touch of wings, the cries, the murmurs, the wailings of outer space, there are the roars of monsters, implacable gallopings, animals crawling, leaps of surprise, starts of agony, fights, anguish, delirium, prostrations, bloody triumphs, and there is the indissoluble union of life and death. Nature appears to us here in her terrible blindness, with neither the attenuation nor the interpretation which our cowardice so long inflicted on it. This is her rough language, which is only completed, reinforced and clarified at times when all she can do is to stammer confused syllables. These are the organs of the earth, but a composer is a keyboard.

Much could be said about rhythm which is not, as simple minds imagine, a matter of hygienic arithmetic, but a subtle contest between duration, intensity, pitch and timbre. Rhythm is only judged by the effect it makes, and here the effect is prodigious. It is like a hurricane, the soul with its personal scruples, modesty and resistances is dispelled, and we let ourselves be borne along like a stone or a leaf. It is drunkenness, ecstasy, annihilation, and when the music stops, the audience is beside itself, prey to an enthusiasm which could only better be described as panic.

'I have,' said Monsieur Stravinsky, 'completed a work of faith.'[17] He has communicated this faith to us. With him we have celebrated the mysteries of the eternal Mother; without horror, we have contemplated human sacrifice and we have shared out the slaughtered flesh.

In 1920, seven years after the first performance, *Le Sacre du printemps* was staged again by the Ballets Russes. With new choreography by Leonid Massine, it was much better received than at the first performances.

Comœdia (16 December 1920), p. 1

At last we have had the privilege of hearing and seeing *Le Sacre du printemps*. Freed from objections, apologies, commentaries and gossip, the work showed forth in its pure power, and the audience response was so enthusiastic that after the last chord, amid the din of the applause which brought to the stage, beside Madame Sokolova, still trembling from her dance of despair, the conductor Monsieur Golschmann, smiling broadly, Monsieur Massine, emotional and serious, Monsieur Stravinsky, adjusting his tortoiseshell spectacles which had been dislodged by his plunging bows, each person remembered another tumult and wondered how a composition in such a sustained style could have been taken as a defiance of common sense or a bad joke.

That is what happened, however, in the same theatre, and in front of the same, or very nearly the same audience. The moment the curtain rose, the murmuring began, soon increasing to jeering and interrupted by furious altercations. As if the untamed ardour evinced by the dancers had passed from the stage to the hall, we saw fists raised, and threatening glances seeking each other out from the orchestra seats to the upper galleries. A few cool-headed members of the audience, however, made efforts to listen to the music. They grasped enough of it to know that it was remarkable, and to conjecture that the choreography rather than the music was inciting the public to revolution.

In the event they were to be proved right. The following year, the work reappeared in a concert performance, under the direction of Monsieur Monteux, and it imposed itself through a clarity, simplicity and strength of which we had not previously had such a striking example. It was music which was to an extent stripped bare, with all its veins standing out, all its muscles in travail, all its motions marked by blows, kicks, exposed palpitations. Melodic music above all, the chords not intervening so as to envelop, nor yet to sustain, but to brighten the melodic line with a more trenchant dissonance, or to whip up its whirling dizziness with muted pulsations.[18] With no refusal, resistance, or discussion, we were seized by the throat, carried off as if into a sorcerors' round dance, and Monsieur Nijinsky's error was no doubt not to have complied docilely enough with the injunctions of the music, and – drawing his inspiration rather from the subject matter – to have interrupted the continuity with successive entrances, as also to have exaggerated, more than the music required, the contortion or dislocation of the attitudes. This error was particularly appreciable in the final dance where Madame Karsavina, with her feet constantly turned inwards in a voluntary violation of the rules of dance, seemed to be asking for mercy.

Monsieur Massine listened only to the music. That is why there is nothing episodic about his choreography, and why it does not resort to any props. Where does the action take place? It matters little. On the stage we will see neither tents nor huts, nor a sacred enclosure, nor a sacrificial stone. The ground, and the sky: that is the decor. Men and women wear almost uniform robes, white or red, and the latter are savages only in the narrow black plaits hanging about their heads. Only the young girl designated as the victim will have blond hair, not for reasons of ethnography, but to make her more virginal. And there will not be a ritual murder, but only an exasperated dance in which the body, leaping about, striking the earth, flinging up its arms, nodding its head, as if incited by intolerable pain, seems to be trying to deliver itself from itself, until one last falling leap brings an end to its agony. Here Madame Sokolova, whom we already admired, almost a year ago, in *Le Chant du rossignol* where she danced the role of Death, showed a precision, a suppleness, and a poignant grace in the grip of terror, which brought the performance to a close with a long ovation. But in the previous scenes, we had already been amazed by the symphony of gestures, evoking images of work or combat, but without direct representation, just as the composer transposes the noises of nature into notes and chords, instead of reproducing them: sitting on the ground, the women oscillate their arms as if they were endlessly weaving an imaginary cloth, the men bring down their fists like axes, or else provoke each other to fight and take turns to feint blows to one another's chin, like boxers, while the women, hands cupped over their eyes, convey anxious curiosity. There are also ternary groups trying to break apart, but not succeeding, there are inert captives whom the conqueror takes on his back, there are hands held up in fervent supplication, and the intertwined march at the beginning of the second tableau which holds the dazed girl prisoner in its loops. I do not think that even in *Le Chant du rossignol* Monsieur Massine showed such free or harmonious inventiveness. For the young ballet master that is a new success, and for the art of choreography it is a precious model.

Since a certain evening when I had the privilege of attending a ballet danced by the artists of His Majesty King Sisowath of Cambodia, I believe I know the principle of the art of choreography. For it was on that evening that I saw, for the first time, fairies and demons fighting without weapons, through a mutual exorcism of gestures, and a legendary prince declaring his love without placing his hand on his heart.[19] But we must strive to attain a no less ideal beauty for the steps and figures of European dance. Monsieur Massine draws closer to it with each of his creations, and to my mind, that is the most magnificent praise I can bestow on him.

Notes

1 'Musique surhumaine, révélation des puissances élémentaires, dédales, tourbillons, rumeurs, voix lointaines, souffles vivants, frissons de l'espace, troubles, extases, effroi, initiations cruelles et célébrations mystérieuses: le culte de la nature trouve sa liturgie.'

2 In fact the date was 9 June 1912, and Laloy's recollection later in this paragraph that the first performance took place 'a few days later' must be incorrect. On 1 June 1912 Laloy had written to Stravinsky: 'I remind you of our hope that you will come on Sunday, to 17 bis, rue des Capucines, Bellevue. We will be *en famille*. It will be a great honour for my home. You can come by taxi, train or even boat. Monsieur and Madame Debussy will also be there.' V. Stravinsky and Craft (1978), p. 87. On 25 June 1912 he wrote the advance review translated on pp. 271–272. A letter from Debussy to Stravinsky dated 8 November 1912 says: 'Our reading of *Le Sacre du printemps*, at Laloy's house, is always present in my mind. It haunts me like a beautiful nightmare and I try, in vain, to reinvoke the terrific impression. That is why I wait for the stage version like a greedy child impatient for promised sweets.' This letter appears in Stravinsky and Craft (1962), pp. 63–64, and Stravinsky adds a footnote: 'Which Louis Laloy, the critic, incorrectly attributes to the spring of 1913. What most impressed me at the time and what is still most memorable from the occasion of the sight-reading of *Le Sacre* was Debussy's brilliant piano playing.' Interestingly, Ravel also played the duet version of *Le Sacre* with Stravinsky, in 1913 at Clarens in Switzerland, while the two composers were working on a performing version of Mussorgsky's opera *Khovanchina*.

3 According to V. Stravinsky and Craft (1978), pp. 87 and 613, at this stage the piano-duet arrangement was only complete as far as Part I.

4 In fact, this article has not been located in *Comœdia*, and no clues to its whereabouts have been found.

5 A brief description of some of Laloy's colleagues at *Comœdia* has been omitted.

6 The Chinese philosopher Chang Tzu produced a work of some 100,000 words or more in the 4th century BC. The work is usually called 'the Chang Tzu'. The title of the second chapter is 'Discussion on making all things equal'.

7 The *Oxford English dictionary* defines *elytron* (French *élytre*) as the outer hard wing-case of a coleopterous insect (such as a beetle or weevil).

8 Futurism, which produced dynamic, subversive works of art inspired by the machine age, began in 1909 with a manifesto by the Italian writer F.T. Marinetti. Primarily a movement in literature and the graphic arts, it also had some musical manifestations, most notably in the instruments which Luigi Russolo invented to produce various sorts of noise, and Laloy is referring to two of them. Russolo (1885–1947) set out his ideas in *L'Arte dei rumori* (*The art of noises*, 1913).

9 'Ce sont les terreurs de la nuit, les frôlements d'ailes, les cris soudains, les murmures, les plaintes de l'espace, ce sont les mugissements des monstres, les galops implacables, les approches rampantes, les bonds de surprise, les sursauts d'agonie, les combats vertigineux, les angoisses, les délires, les prostrations, les triomphes sanglants, et c'est l'union indissoluble de la vie et de la mort. La nature nous apparaît ici dans son aveuglement terrible, sans les atténuations et les corrections que si longtemps notre lâcheté lui infligea. C'est son rude langage, complété seulement, renforcé et éclairci, alors qu'elle ne sait qu'en balbutier les syllabes confuses. Ce sont les orgues de la terre, mais un musicien est un clavier.'

10 In an article published on the day of the first performance, Stravinsky described *Le Sacre du printemps* as 'une œuvre de foi' ('a work of faith'). The article, in *Montjoie* (29 May 1913), was based on an interview which Stravinsky had given to Ricciotto Canudo; Stravinsky later disowned it. It is reproduced in Lesure (1980), pp. 13–15.

11 Laloy continues in *La Musique retrouvée*: 'The wish I expressed at the end of this article was fulfilled, the following year, by Stravinsky's *Le Rossignol*, given in June 1914, with scenery by Alexandre Benois, on the stage of the Opéra where the Ballets Russes season was held that year. I was happy to acknowledge this in another article in the same journal.' An article on *Le Rossignol* then follows: it is translated on pp. 284–288.

12 See p. 271.

13 Literally 'unanimous life'. The reference is to the doctrine of 'unanimism', conceived by the French writer Jules Romains (1885–1972). Romains gave a definition: 'By unanimism . . . understand simply the expression of unanimous, collective life. We experience a sense of the life which surrounds and exceeds us.' His poem, *La Vie unanime* (1908), explores the concept:

> Et le mélange de nos âmes identiques
> Forme un fleuve divin où se mire la nuit.
> Je suis un peu d'unanime qui s'attendrit.
> Je ne sens rien, sinon que la rue est réelle,
> Et que je suis très sûr d'être pensé par elle.

[14] Laloy was also highly critical of the choreography Nijinsky devised for Debussy's *Jeux*, which was first performed on 15 May 1913, a fortnight before *Le Sacre du printemps*. He considered the movements Nijinsky devised 'puerile inventions of an uncultured mind':

> This fluid, sustained music, which weaves its imponderable yet strong lines in space, required movements which like it were prolonged, rounded and smoothly joined. Monsieur Nijinsky punctuates it in small units, as happy as a schoolboy to be able to place on each note a movement of the head, arms or legs, and so attentive about counting off the stems of the quavers and crotchets that he takes no notice of the melody, or the rhythm, or even those slurs that run along the top of our scores showing ignoramuses and deaf people the construction of the phrases.
>
> *La Grande revue* (25 May 1913), pp. 403–405

These remarks are consistent with Stravinsky's later complaints about Nijinsky, and with what Debussy wrote to Robert Godet about the choreography: 'It's ugly, even Dalcrozian. It appears it's called stylization of gesture.' Laloy also criticised 'the aggressive ugliness of Monsieur Bakst's design' and went on to say, 'It is a matter of profound regret that Monsieur Debussy's music should have been subject to [Nijinsky's] experiments.' (p. 405)

[15] Wagner's *Tannhäuser* was performed at the Paris Opéra in 1861. Wagner had refused to add a ballet in accordance with Parisian taste, and as a result the first three performances were disrupted with shouting and whistling. The work was then withdrawn.

[16] The philosopher Henri Bergson, who had a high public profile. For a brief discussion of his ideas, see p. 5, and also L. Laloy, 'M. Henri Bergson et la musique', *Comœdia* (9 February 1914), p. 3.

[17] See above, note 10.

[18] 'Musique en quelque sorte dénudée, toutes les veines en saillies, tous les muscles en travail, tous les mouvements marqués par des frappements, des battements, des palpitations à découvert. Musique mélodique avant tout, les accords n'intervenant pas pour envelopper, [ni] encore pour soutenir, mais pour aviver le chant d'une dissonance plus tranchante, ou en fouetter de sourdes pulsations le tournoyant vertige.'

[19] In 1906 Laloy attended a private performance given by the visiting Cambodian ballet in Paris. He wrote up his observations in an article, 'Musique et danses cambodgiennes', *Le Mercure musical* (15 August 1906), pp. 98–112; an extract is quoted in *La Musique retrouvée*, pp. 152–158. Laloy returned to the subject in 'Les Principes de la danse cambodgienne', *La Revue musicale*, vol. 3, no. 9 (1 July 1922), pp. 1–7.

Le Rossignol

Le Rossignol was Laloy's favourite Stravinsky work. Unlike Laloy, most critics were very disappointed with it: one wrote of the 'unbearable cacophony' of Act II. This article first appeared in *Comœdia* in June 1914, after the first performance, and it is reproduced in *La Musique retrouvée*.[1]

Notes for this section begin on p. 288.

La Musique retrouvée, pp. 219–223 and *Comœdia* (4 June 1914), p. 3

A masterpiece, as has been declared here right from the first. A pure masterpiece. Superhuman music, not, as with a certain fanatic of pride,[2] through renunciation, negation and defiance, but through the exaltation of gentleness, calm and love. Supernatural music, but without anything sham; a magic mirror in which matter becomes transparent, space luminous, and in which every perceptible appearance, while not vanishing, lets itself be penetrated right to the point where it joins the invisible, the ineffable, the non-existent.[3]

The revelation of *Le Rossignol* takes possession of our soul and renews it; only the revelations of *Parsifal*, *Boris Godunov*, *Pelléas et Mélisande* and *Saint Sébastien* are comparable. What a fortunate time we live in, with so many unexplored perspectives being discovered one after the other! It does seem that music, according to one of Wagner's prophecies, is the art of the twentieth century. Art in the full sense of the word: not the art which merely entertains, or is limited to the pleasure of the senses, or the satisfaction of reason, but the one which, as the interpreter of the highest mysteries, communicates directly to the heart of man what religion, using words, cannot faithfully represent.[4]

People who do me the honour of glancing through these weekly divagations will perhaps remember that recently I attempted to transcribe an already pious admiration for Monsieur Stravinsky's previous composition, *Le Sacre du printemps*. Borrowing a magnificent metaphor from one of the great minds of China, I showed that Stravinsky had in that work become the master of the organs of the earth and was able to command their immense wind-power at will. I ended with the wish also to hear, in the future, organs which are even more powerful in their eternal harmony, those of heaven.[5] I did not know this wish was so close to being fulfilled, nor so completely. For the music of heaven is certainly bringing down its enchantment on us; but, like the immortals in Taoist legends who are carried off to the clouds along with their domestic pets and the flowers from their gardens, it has taken away all the resonances of matter and now gives them back to us just as rich, as strong and diverse, but transfigured by peace, majesty and bliss.

To superficial minds this music will seem difficult, because sharps, flats and naturals occur frequently. For this encumbrance we must blame only our notation which persists in using a diatonic scale in which the successive semitones occur only by accident, whereas our composers manage to divide the octave into twelve equal semitones. This system is not new; it was instituted in China in the era of the legendary emperors, then prudently held in reserve until the day when artists became proficient enough to use it. The late, but rapid, civilization of the West rightfully reclaims this share, among several others, of the ancient wealth.

The music of *Le Rossignol* is entirely chromatic in its principle, which however does not mean that it is devoid of definite modes, or that it goes perpetually round and round in a maze of semitones. All its notes always have reference to a common origin and though, when the music imitates the song of the nightingale, the music happens to bring the intervals closer together to the point where it is as whimsical as the winged singer, elsewhere on the other hand it denies itself the semitone, blending only minor thirds with the whole tones, according to the almost indifferent equilibrium which the Chinese have assigned to all liturgy. Here people will speak of local colour, and quite wrongly. I said once that the days of exoticism were over. This score gives me definitive proof. Indeed the Chinese elements which we find in it are not added, out of complaisance with the subject, to a foreign way of thinking: they flow from that way of thinking. The reason why the Emperor's retinue advances to the strains of a march which is free of semitones is not that he reigns over the land bordered by the Great Wall; it is because such sounds carried within them the stamp of a solemn, implacable opulence which the author had in his mind. No detail ever juts out or demands attention; the work unfolds in such a constant flow that nothing surprises us in a world in which nothing is familiar.

When *Le Sacre du printemps* appeared, the more timorous among us tried to excuse the author's harsh language in consideration of the savages he wished to portray. He protested vigorously that the language was his own, not that of his characters, and would serve him in any circumstances. In fact, the same combinations of supposedly incompatible notes are found in *Le Rossignol*; but the feeling is altered. I showed, a propos of *Le Sacre*, how our own art, after a long detour, was going to follow the route whose starting point only had been marked out by the Far East. *Le Rossignol* goes further along this route. There is no doubt that the next work, whatever its subject, setting and means may be, will continue in the same direction. And, moreover, there is no element of premeditation: it is our music's necessary progression; genius guesses it by intuition and uses it at will.

It is the same language, but with no harshness, no frenzy, no obsessiveness, no terror, no violence. *Le Sacre du printemps* brought melodies into collision in furious dissonances. Here the same encounters of notes form unexpected consonances, with multiple vibrations, with rainbow-coloured reflections. What spell has been used? Only academic pedants will speak of dissonances, because they will not find any of the chords catalogued in treatises. But those who are content to listen to the music and give themselves up to their impressions will be delighted to let their ears be filled with these sonorities which are inspired by bells, drums, gongs, suspended stones, as also by waves shuddering, droplets of water falling or stars twinkling, but which surpass them in beauty. Music which admits only simple chords – those which are directly deduced from the given scale – is all on the surface. But this music, in which notes chosen by design intersect, brush past each other and give each other colour, half opens translucent depths which obliterate rays of light. It has the supple strength of jade: the blended lustre, the variable grain and the sense of inner movement.

Compact and folded in on itself, it does not spread out. An inflection suffices, with no repetition, no transposition, no development. Each episode appears and vanishes in a moment. But that moment has sufficed to show everything.[6] This rapidity of suggestion is a new quality in Monsieur Stravinsky, one which he shares only with the greatest masters of the art, a Mozart, a Mussorgsky, a Debussy. But he espouses it without renouncing any of the decisiveness that was always part of his thinking. Shorter, his melodies have such clear-cut outlines and are set in such bold relief that they immediately etch themselves in the memory. Sometimes they are borne along by moving harmony, and sometimes, like the song of the nightingale, they spring forth in the empty space where their echo vibrates vaguely. Always recognisable, the melodies provide the work with its correspondences and frameworks: thus the Emperor's march, triumphal in the second tableau, becomes funereal in the third: thus the fisherman's song concludes each of the three tableaux,[7] resembling itself, mysterious because of its freshness, differently nuanced.

Delicacy and power are united. There is nothing abrupt, and nothing ugly. Even the lively agitation of the courtiers under the lanterns in the dark garden is unconflicted. Even the mechanical nightingale, a present from the Japanese Embassy, makes a noise of clicking springs which further adds to the charm. It is because, in this work, reality leaves its envelope and dissolves into dream. There is nothing as comfortable or as sweet as a dream. There is also nothing more moving.

Emotion reigns, and is poignant. In the first tableau, there is the servant's naive reaction to the stupidity of the courtiers who take the heifer's lowing and the frogs' croaking for the song of the nightingale. In the second, there is the formidable splendour of the procession, then the bird's lament which provokes tears and at the same time gives comfort for them. In the third, there is the haunting call of the ghosts; then, conjured up by the nightingale, the voices of those who are no more, and their song is uncertain, timid, and so saddened with futile affection that, as death does, we would like to go to them; finally there is the austere sorrow of a life extinguished, and the peaceful happiness of a resurrection which is like an apotheosis. The highest virtues of the spirit and heart are celebrated in this music: penetration, clarity, meditation, authority, goodness. He who is able to pay such worthy homage to them is not only a great artist, but a great sage, and his composition leaves behind it a memory perfumed with regret and hope.[8]

May he therefore permit me to recall these words which a Chinese man we know has just dedicated to him with a cursive brush at the base of a portrait: *Kan-en-t'ien-yueh.* (*Thank you for the heavenly music.*)[9]

Since then I have continued to follow Stravinsky in all the developments of his thinking, and as with Debussy I have admitted that he was right each time he left the path he himself had traced out and went boldly in search of unknown truths. It is because I love Stravinsky that I loved in succession *Les Noces*, *Histoire du soldat*, *Mavra*, the Concerto, *Œdipus*. However, for *Le Rossignol* I have a predilection whose causes must perhaps be sought in the Far East. Stravinsky well knows this, and as he likes to make jokes, he says to me, '*Le Rossignol* is a present I've given you. It's a flask of marc-brandy[10] I've slipped into your pocket.'[11,12]

Notes

1 The text translated here is a conflation of the two sources. Another review by Laloy, in *La Grande revue* (10 June 1914), pp. 526–528, substantially duplicates the review in *Comœdia*; however, two passages from it have been added here as notes.

2 i.e. Wagner

3 'Musique surnaturelle, mais sans rien de fictif; miroir magique où la matière devient transparente, l'espace lumineux, et où toute apparence sensible, sans s'évanouir, se laisse pénétrer jusqu'aux attaches de l'invisible, de l'ineffable, de l'inexistant.'

4 In the review in *La Grande revue* (10 June 1914), p. 527, Laloy writes:

> For the first time modern art has created the visionary theatre called for by our wishes, which only Shakespeare was able to give to his time. And here as in Shakespeare, the fable is strengthened by the deepest and most true feelings of the human soul, and it isolates and magnifies them. This time, the Far East restores to Europe a freedom of invention which Europe has never accepted. Andersen's nightingale charmed the Emperor of China with its songs and saved him from death. The authors of the drama understood, much better than the story-teller, how this event could be turned to advantage. One of them, Monsieur Benois, conceived scenery similar to those Chinese paintings from the Sung and Yüan dynasties in which glowing rubies, sapphires and emeralds sparkle amid subtle mists. The other, Monsieur Stravinsky, wrote music which with European notes and instruments evokes the resonances of bells, drums and suspended stones, as also the song of the nightingale, the rustling foliage and the quivering waters. For in this work the whole of nature takes on life spontaneously, without man's intervention, according to the custom of a mentality which is more abstract than that of Europe and which could be called pantheistic, if the word did not also imply a distinction between appearances and ideas.

5 See pp. 273 and 275.

6 'Ramassée et repliée sur elle-même, elle ne s'étend pas. Une inflexion lui suffit, sans répétition, sans transposition, sans développement. Chaque épisode, en un instant s'y projette, puis s'efface. Mais cet instant a suffi pour tout montrer.'

7 Stravinsky uses 'act' rather than 'tableau' in *Le Rossignol*.

8 In his review of *Le Rossignol* in *La Grande revue* (10 June 1914), p. 528, Laloy writes:

> A masterpiece of sweetness, of meditation, of goodness and also of penetration, power and courage. A nobility of mind finding its most apt, discreet and fervent expression. These are beauties which one does not only admire: one worships them. Art becomes religion and, better than through words, shows us the eternal way.

That review concludes:

> We must thank Monsieur Stravinsky for a sublime lesson, and he himself, in the generosity of his heart, would insist that beside his own name we should also mention those of Monsieur Benois, who supported him with such poetic tableaux, and Monsieur de Diaghilev, without whom *Le Rossignol*, not to mention *Le Sacre du printemps*, or even *Petrouchka*, would never have seen the light of day.

9 It has not been possible to find this portrait.

10 Marc-brandy is particularly strong type of brandy, made in Bourgogne, which is close to Laloy's native region.

11 'Stravinski le sait bien, et comme il plaisante volontiers, il lui arrive de me dire: «Le *Rossignol*, c'est un cadeau que je vous ai fait. C'est un flacon de marc que j'ai glissé dans votre poche».'

12 This concluding paragraph appears only in *La Musique retrouvée*, not in the *Comœdia* article.

Le Chant du rossignol

Stravinsky made a ballet out of the music for *Le Rossignol*, though with substantial cuts: all of the music from Act I and large sections of Acts II and III were omitted. *Le Chant du rossignol* was first performed in Geneva in December 1919.

Comœdia (4 February 1920), p. 1

After *Le Tricorne*, a hyper-Spanish ballet,[1] comes *Le Chant du rossignol*, the essence of Asia.

The point of departure is the tale by Andersen which had already lent its subject to the very moving drama performed in 1914 under its exact title, *Le Rossignol*. The Emperor of China learns that a nightingale is enchanting the fishermen by the sea with its songs, and directs that the marvellous bird be brought to him. Great preparations are made to receive it at the palace: 'The walls and the porcelain tiles shone in the glow of a hundred thousand golden lamps; the most gorgeous flowers, along with the loveliest little bells, lined the corridors. All the coming and going created a twofold draught which set all the bells ringing and meant that people could not hear each other speak.'[2]

But the Emperor of Japan sends the Emperor of China a mechanical nightingale which naturally is much more successful than the living bird. The latter, indignant, flies away, and the Emperor falls ill with longing.

The Emperor is dying. Lying in his bed, completely abandoned, he divines about him the motionless shadow of Death, and hears the murmur of dark voices: they are his life's actions, good and bad, which have come back to take his soul. Frozen with horror, he tries in vain to repel the spectres; his body is paralysed, his lips cannot speak, his eyes cannot see. And then a delightful song is heard in the distance, draws nearer. Filled with pity, the nightingale has returned. Death himself is seduced and listens to the bird. So that it will sing again, he gives it the Emperor's crown which he had already taken. 'The nightingale sang and sang; it told of the peaceful cemetery where the white roses grow, where the lime-tree spreads its perfumes, where the fresh green grass is watered by the tears of those who are still living. And Death suddenly felt an urge to return to his garden, and vanished through the window like a cold, white mist. The Emperor comes back to life, and, when the funeral procession of courtiers comes to bury him, he stands up and simply says, "Good-day!"'

The score of *Le Rossignol* has three acts, magnificently illustrated by Monsieur Alexandre Benois.

It was a marvellous performance with an intensity of emotion which verged on the inexpressible. We are revisiting it today, but now it is summarised, condensed, concentrated and, with the vocal line and the words omitted, uniquely conveyed by the movements, groupings and gestures of the characters. The two nightingales are no longer singing nightingales, but dancing nightingales. One episode follows another without transition or explanation. The music has taken on the solidity of a symphony. The search for the nightingale, which previously comprised the first act, with its ironic dialogues, has been omitted. The fisherman's song has been shifted to the orchestra where it is stated by the trumpet by way of a prelude. The preparations for the feast and the imperial march have been fused. The nightingale's song, reduced to its main motifs, with no repetitions or variations, comprises, once the bird has made its entrance, both the melody which enchanted the courtiers and that which was to ward off Death. Madame Karsavina, draped in translucent white, embroiders this melody with restrained leaps and tremulous flutterings which scrupulously follow its inflections. Monsieur Idzikovsky is the mechanical nightingale; imprisoned in his varnished carapace, this witty dancer entertains us with the stupid way he half opens his beak in time with the music, jumps clumsily and lifts up his short wings in accordance with signs from his watching showman.[3]

Such is this new ballet, the last of the three this Russian season was to introduce.[4] The ingenuity is as remarkable as the performance, and I do not want to end without thanking Monsieur Ansermet, who was designated by Monsieur Stravinsky to conduct the reduced orchestra in this finely-wrought score, and who gave the subtlest nuances their true value.

Notes

1 *El sombrero de tres picos* (*The three-cornered hat*) by Manuel de Falla. Laloy writes about this work, and raves about the performances given by Karsavina and Massine, in *La Musique retrouvée*, pp. 264–265.

[2] This is a quotation from Hans Christian Andersen's tale, *Le Rossignol*. So many editions exist that it is impossible to say which one Laloy used.

[3] Comments about other performers have been omitted.

[4] Diaghilev's previous two ballets were *La Boutique fantasque*, to music by Rossini arranged by Respighi, and Falla's *Le Tricorne*. Both had their first performance in London in 1919.

From *Pulcinella* to *Œdipus rex*

La Musique retrouvée, pp. 265–269

Famous after *Petrouchka, Le Sacre du printemps* and *Le Rossignol*, as if he dreaded the prisons of glory, this powerful composer fled from his own example and from 1914 onwards undertook researches which since have made each of these works an audacious experiment. *Pulcinella*, like *Le Chant du rossignol*, which appeared during the same period and reduced the sung *Rossignol* to a ballet, made a trial of a linear orchestra, written entirely, as the technical expression goes, in real parts, in other words made up only of melodies which are superimposed, with no interpolated notes, and what is more, so as to keep their outline clear, articulated by a single instrument. Of the two works, *Pulcinella* seemed to me the more successful, for the reason, I think, that Pergolesi's tunes, conceived for solo voice, lend themselves to a solo instrumental rendition better than motifs initially destined to be elements in more complex combinations.[1]

The score of *Les Noces* was finished, for piano, as early as 1914. It was only staged in 1923. The author needed a long period of study to find an acceptable solution to the instrumentation problem he had set himself, which consisted – with variety of colour suppressed this time – in accompanying the voices with the notes from four pianos and the rhythm of the percussion instruments. It had no other subject than the celebration of a village wedding according to the most ancient customs of Russia. Nor any more costumes, the male and female dancers having their work uniforms, black skirts and leather belts. As decor, a backdrop representing the wooden house, the bedroom with the bed and its pile of eiderdown quilts. Strictly reduced to melody and movement, austere as a church chant and as fervent, the work provoked an enthusiastic reception in which, despite my best efforts and to my great regret, I have never been able to join wholeheartedly. Never, in the theatre, has *Les Noces* given me the impression I have had from reading the score. The execution of the vocal parts, which was always defective, certainly had a great deal to do with my disappointment. But what repulses me also, I confess to my shame, is the austere set purpose. In vain people tell me, and in vain I repeat to myself that a reaction against charm was necessary, that the fewer instruments an artist has at his disposition, the better he shows his muscular strength, that he is curious to test out his idea, as one tests a steel bar, by cutting it away to the critical point where it will break, and that it is quite right that the composer, in order to take a bigger leap, should rein himself in. These are reasons, and therefore poor reasons, if I keep them in my mind when I should simply be all eyes and ears. It is the case with *Les Noces*: I cannot forget, when I listen to it and watch it in the theatre, the precepts of the sthetic it serves to verify, I have thoughts of hygiene, and I see the reins.[2]

Histoire du soldat, given for the first time in Geneva in 1919 by the Pitoëff company, *Renard* and *Mavra*, presented by the Ballets Russes in 1923, the Concerto performed at the Opéra, under the direction of Koussevitsky, in 1924, and *Œdipus rex*, which appeared last year, do not give rise, as far as the music is concerned, to the same objections. I mean that Stravinsky's intention to deprive himself is much less noticeable, form and thought more in accord. *Histoire du soldat* is a suite for solo instruments, more profound and pure in sentiment; the Concerto treats a Classical subject in the modern style; *Mavra* is an opéra-comique without recitatives, whose arias are charming. Why must *Histoire du soldat* be interrupted by the recitation of an interminable text, why must the plot of *Mavra* be unintelligible to the spectator who does not know the tales of Pushkin, and why must it be impossible to grasp a word of *Renard* on account of prosody which is incompatible with the music, as with *Œdipus rex*, whose words are Latin, pronounced in Russian, accentuated without rhyme or reason?

I know the answer to this question. There is an answer to everything. The music is given greater importance by depriving it of everything which could put people on the wrong track. Without the support of a specified subject, or an explicit sentiment, it will certainly only be admired for itself, like a coquettish woman who puts her suitors to the test by renouncing all finery. It is a system like any other, but I prefer an art without systems. A composition has another aim than to show how one makes a composition. The interest comes from outside, and beauty is given to it as a bonus. All this, fortunately, does not prevent Stravinsky from writing truly successful music on whatever pretext, for the sap flows, throws off stakes, resists pruning, and in the narrow beds of a garden by Le Nôtre[3] pushes up its wild foliage and fantastical flowers. Stravinsky can allow himself all the debauches of theory: he will always be a master musician.[4]

Notes

[1] No substantial review of *Pulcinella* has come to light. In a short review of the work in *Comœdia* (17 May 1920), p. 1, Laloy briefly describes the staging and choreography, and Stravinsky's use of melodies by Pergolesi, asking: 'Did he have the right to make such use of them? Without a doubt, since his composition is charming. In art, the only politics is that of results, and a masterpiece achieved at the cost of sacrilege would be no less admirable for that.'

[2] 'Mais ce qui me rebute aussi, je l'avoue à ma honte, c'est cette austérité de parti pris. On a beau me dire, et j'ai beau me répéter à moi-même qu'une réaction était nécessaire contre le charme, que moins l'artiste a d'instruments à sa disposition, mieux il montre sa force musculaire, qu'il est curieux d'éprouver sa pensée, comme on éprouve une barre d'acier, par un évidement poussé jusqu'au point critique où la rupture se produira, et qu'il est bon que le musicien, pour prendre plus d'élan, se mette la ceinture. Ce sont là des raisons, donc de mauvaises raisons, si je les garde dans l'esprit quand je devrais simplement être tout yeux et tout oreilles. C'est le cas pour les *Noces*: je ne puis oublier, quand je les écoute et les regarde au théâtre, les préceptes de l'esthétique dont elles apportent la vérification, j'ai des pensées d'hygiène, et je vois la ceinture.'

[3] André Le Nôtre (1613–1700) was the Director of Louis XIV's gardens. He is famous for having designed gardens in the Classical style for the Tuileries and Versailles.

[4] 'Tout cela n'empêche pas Stravinski, par bonheur, d'écrire sous n'importe quel prétexte une musique vraiment à toute épreuve, car la sève y afflue, renverse les tuteurs, résiste à la taille, et dans les étroites plates-bandes d'un jardin de Le Nôtre épanouit ses frondaisons sauvages et ses fleurs fantastiques. Stravinski peut se permettre toutes les débauches de théorie: il restera toujours un maître musicien.'

Mavra

The opera buffa *Mavra*, which lasts about twenty-five minutes, was first performed by the Ballets Russes at the Opéra on 3 June 1922.

Comœdia (5 June 1922), p. 1

It is a little domestic drama. The old lady, on the advice of her daughter, and after pouring out her troubles to a neighbour, hires a chambermaid. But it was treacherous advice. The chamber-maid is only a hussar in disguise, who sings a duet with the girl, and the old woman comes back unexpectedly and catches him shaving.

Monsieur Kokhno has staged this ironic novelette by Pushkin very skilfully.[1] Its ironic effect is heightened by Monsieur Survage's decor, with its split-level design that contrasts with the crinolined costumes, and especially by Monsieur Stravinsky's music which superimposes a cavatina-style vocal line on a reversed orchestra, in which the wood-wind and brass are increased at the expense of the violin and viola, which are both reduced to one solo instrument, and of the cellos and double basses which have sole responsibility for the basso continuo. An extraordinary orchestra that chirps, chirrs, gurgles, screeches, grunts, hoots, sobs, guffaws, a fiery orchestra that bounds and prances, yet is always contained and directed by a strong hand, which turns it to its own liking, calms it, strokes it and makes it set out anew, only to stop it again, shuddering, with a barely perceptible pressure.[2] Never had the composer shown such mastery. No doubt *Le Sacre du printemps* uses richer, more massive sonorities; but here the *tour de force* is achieved with a balance that is never [stable . . . heard] several times, and will be.[3]

Notes

1 *Mavra* is based on Pushkin's *The little house in Kolomna*: Pushkin called it a dramatic poem. In a pamphlet, *Pushkin: poetry and music* (1940), Stravinsky wrote: '[. . .] the depth of Pushkin's dramatic poem, in a high

degree lyrical, or rather its spiritual nucleus, as well as his method of transmitting this depth, i.e. Pushkin's poetic structure of rhymes, had interested me much more than the abstract ideas which one could draw from the story itself.' The pamphlet is reproduced in White (1979), p. 589.

2 'Extraordinaire orchestre, qui gazouille, stridule, gargouille, glapit, grogne, ulule, sanglote, s'esclaffe, fougueux orchestre qui bondit et se cabre, toujours contenu cependant et dirigé par une main puissante, qui le tourne à son gré, l'apaise, le flatte et le fait repartir, pour l'arrêter de nouveau, tout frémissant, d'une pression à peine sensible.'

3 A missing line evidently says Laloy thinks the work deserves – or perhaps needs – to be heard.

Les Noces

Here Laloy writes an advance notice of the first performance of *Les Noces*. The work was to be given by the Ballets Russes, to which the first sentence refers.

Comœdia (4 June 1923), p. 1

On 13 June they return to us for a short, but well-filled season. It will take place at the Théâtre de la Gaîté-Lyrique where, two years ago, the first performance of *Le Bouffon* (*Chout*) by Prokofiev was given, and it will include eight performances up to 21 June. From the first evening, a new work will be presented.

It was ever thus. Monsieur Serge de Diaghilev, founder and director of this famous company, is too great an artist to be content with established successes. How many directors would live comfortably with a repertoire which includes *Petrouchka, Les Danses du Prince Igor, Shéhérazade, Le Sacre du printemps, Le Rossignol, Les Contes russes, Le Tricorne, La Boutique fantasque, Le Spectre de la rose, Pulcinella*?

But it is not a matter of living comfortably. It is not a matter of making investments. One must forge ahead. A work has been successful? So much the better. But from then on it belongs to the past, and only the future interests a creative genius. Debussy was asked to give us another *Pelléas*. 'What's the use?', he said to me. And he composed *Le Martyre de saint Sébastien*. Similarly, in each of his seasons, Monsieur de Diaghilev guides his collaborators in a different direction, composers, painters, choreographers, and carries his investigations into uncharted regions. Every season, too, it is to the Parisian public that he first wants to show the fruits of his researches and that is why, every year, his return is so impatiently awaited: we know that he will not come empty-handed and that he will bring a 'surprise'.

Les Noces will be this year's present. I can confirm that it is beautiful, for I already know the music and I know how the stage version will be modelled on it. Last summer Stravinsky played the newly finished score to me, and I immediately recognised a work equal in power to *Le Sacre du printemps*, but in a form which is quite different and without precedent up to now.

I wrote formerly in this same publication, taking up a famous comparison made by a Chinese philosopher, that *Le Sacre du printemps* gave us the music of the earth.[1] Here, we have the music of Man. A nuptial ceremony reduced to its essential rites: presentation of the fiancé and fiancée, procession, offering. A chorus, [. . .] from which four soloists [. . .][2] will at times emerge, will celebrate this festival which, in all times and for all peoples, is the festival of humanity; its necessary, joyful festival. No specific determination, no liturgy affirming a dogma, no local colour. The orchestral mixtures will not be applied forcefully to melodies which will appear in the pure state, in the natural state, enveloped only by the quivering sound of four pianos and sustained by the alternating pulsations of six percussion instruments. Monsieur Georges Auric and Mademoiselle Marcelle Meyer will be two of the pianists: the participation of such performers is a significant tribute.[3]

The staging and choreography will have the same quality of simplification. For the decor, coloured backdrops. Only two costumes, one for all the men, the other for all the women. Madame Goncharova, whose marvellous inventive abilities have been appreciated since *Le Coq d'or*,[4] conceived this decor and these costumes. Madame Nijinska, the great artist of choreography, thus had at her disposal not distinct characters with roles, but elements which were identical and so to speak interchangeable. She took advantage of them to produce moving constructions, the most vigorous and best-defined we have ever seen on the stage.[5]

Les Danses du Prince Igor, *Les Contes russes*, *Petrouchka*, *Le Sacre du printemps*, *Chout*, *Parade*, *Pulcinella* together with *Les Noces* will make up this season's program. Was I not right to say that it would be well filled?

Notes

1 See p. 273.

2 Names of performers have been omitted.

3 The French pianist Marcelle Meyer (1897–1976) was a specialist in the contemporary music of her generation. A friend of *Les Six*, she also worked with Ravel, and recorded his piano music complete. The other pianists in this performance of *Les Noces* were Francis Poulenc and Hélène Ralli.

4 Rimsky-Korsakov's opera *Le Coq d'or* (*The golden cockerel*), first

performed in Moscow in 1909, was performed in Paris by the Ballets Russes in 1914. The dancers mimed the action, and the singers stood on rises on each side of the stage.

5 Again, names of performers have been omitted.

Various works from the 1920s

This short review covers the two Suites for small orchestra (1921 and 1925), the Concerto for piano and wind orchestra (1924), *Le Baiser de la fée* (1928), and the *Capriccio* for piano and orchestra (1929).

La Revue des deux mondes, vol. 104, no. 24 (1 December 1934), p. 698

The Orchestre Symphonique de Paris, under the author's direction and with the cooperation of one of his sons who is an excellent pianist,[1] offered us some recent works by Monsieur Stravinsky. We had already heard *Le Baiser de la fée* in the theatre, thanks to Madame Ida Rubinstein, a benefactress of music and dance. In concert, it is a charming, poetic symphony, on themes by Tchaikovsky. This composer who was the delight of Russia in the last century possesses a delicate grace, but also a slightly anaemic langour, of which Stravinsky has cured him, ridding the ideas of everything that makes them insipid so as to retain only their musical substance, and immersing them in a restorative orchestra which gives them back fresh colours. The Concerto for piano and orchestra [sic], through a contrasting turn of mind, imposes Classical discipline on the inborn passion of the author's mind; cast into this prepared mould, his ardent music immediately hardens and takes on extraordinary relief. Two little suites, transcribed from piano for orchestra,[2] evoke memories of Naples, Spain, the Russian people, in brief visions which take shape suddenly and vanish almost immediately, or perhaps it is dances of yesteryear, waltz, polka, galop; nothing could be more intense or more subtle. The *Capriccio* for piano and orchestra is a sparkling work, whose brilliance however is at one with the music and not an adornment to it; for the orchestra with its vibrant lines stands out and receives the impulsion of the percussive piano like a harmonious drum. Through this feeling for sonority and rhythmic accompaniment, the Russian composer draws near to the Far East, but with our instruments and according to the laws of our musical logic.

Notes

[1] Soulima Stravinsky (1910–1994) gave extensive concert tours in Europe and America, and became an American citizen.

[2] The two Suites for small orchestra were arranged from pieces for piano duet: *Three easy pieces* (1915) and *Five easy pieces* (1917).

Œdipus rex, *Jeu de cartes* and the suite from *L'Oiseau de feu*

Laloy is reviewing a concert which was to be broadcast, and he says that it was played to a full house. The conductor was Stravinsky.

***La Revue des deux mondes*, vol. 108, no. 43 (1 January 1938), pp. 227–229**

[The 'opera-oratorio', *Œdipus rex*,] dates from the period when Stravinsky, in an unheard-of effort, and not without risk to his good name, renounced the attractions of rhythm and the delights of colour, in quest of a less sensuous, more pure art. They were difficult years, when at times one might have thought that, in reaction against himself, he was taking scruple too far and becoming abstract. Several of his friends quarrelled with him about it. He listened to them without a word and continued on his steep, obscure road, sure of reaching his goal eventually. And he was right. *Œdipus rex* is one of the finest proofs.

However, it must be admitted that the demonstration left us still with a few doubts, when it was given on the stage of a large theatre, a few years ago, through the good offices of Diaghilev.[1] We must not blame the performance, which was admirably discreet and dignified, but rather the vast proportions of the hall and its luxurious appearance which called for a different type of magnificence. As its double appellation indicates, the work can pass unharmed from the theatre to the concert hall, and that is where I had the privilege of hearing it, in the self-communion it requires.

It is not a drama, but a series of meditations in music, based on the events of a tragic story. The Greek language invited local colour; our own, the element of the pathetic. That is why Jean Cocteau chose Latin, which is more remote from us, yet sufficiently intelligible, and above all consecrated by the usage of the Roman Catholic liturgy. Indeed in this work the music finds its deepest source in the religious sentiment which pervades human emotion, and imposes a rigid form which is not a constraint, but which by confining it reinforces it and allows it to soar. This music is hewn from living matter, in vigorous lines and with powerful harmony, a sanctuary of faith, solidly founded in nature on earth, but rising up towards the protecting sky, in ardent prayer.

Jeu de cartes, the music of which we were hearing for the first time, uses an analogous constraint to a different end and benefits equally from it. It is a ballet, completed in November 1936 and given in New York in April 1937, which stages a poker game. But there is no need at all to know the rules of this game in order to follow the changes of fortune; for the music admits no rules other than those of Classical ballet. The composer who so willingly surrendered to the fury of rhythm in his early works, here constantly submits to the metre and symmetry which are the only basis of the steps and figures of a light, purified dance where grace always prevails over instinct. This necessity was so well understood by him, and he was able so judiciously to draw in the lines between points which were marked out in advance, that there is nothing more evocative. On stage, no doubt, appropriate costumes would allow us to identify the king, the queen, the jack, and not to confuse spades with hearts. In a concert rendition, these obligatory disguises matter little to us: now it is only a matter of *pas de deux* or *pas de quatre*, solo variations, or simulated fights, in which only the music enters into dance, and nothing more is needed for this imaginary performance in which a rhythmical tempo carries along the supple, finely-wrought melodies that are adorned only by their unfailing limpidity.

The suite from *L'Oiseau de feu*, which finished the concert, dates from 1911.[2] It is a youthful, and already a masterly, work. All the resources of harmony and orchestration, skilfully employed, beautify the feast, with the simultaneously naive and sumptuous taste in which the Ballets Russes of that period gloried. Still sensitive to the sweet ambiguities of chromatic alteration, the iridescent effects of blends of sounds and the nostalgia of folk-songs, the music is embroidered over a fairy tale and highlights its charm and freshness. We always take great pleasure in hearing it, but also see quite well that the author had to move on.[3]

Notes

[1] *Œdipus rex* was first performed as an oratorio by the Ballets Russes at the Théâtre Sarah-Bernhardt on 30 May 1927, with Stravinsky conducting. Its first performance as an opera was given in Vienna the following year.

[2] Laloy writes 1909, but that is the date of the ballet.

[3] Except for this paragraph on the suite from *L'Oiseau de feu*, no Laloy reviews of the early Stravinsky ballets have come to light. However, he writes briefly about them in *La Musique retrouvée* (see p. 31), and in an article on the Ballets Russes he draws a contrast between Rimsky-Korsakov and the Stravinsky of *Petrouchka*:

> Rimsky-Korsakov always remained a spectator: he found joy in colours, in contours, in actions, and smiled placidly at the external world. Stravinsky is not able thus to defend his soul against the temptations of sounds: he lets it and them move lightly among human beings and breathe in their life. Through this capacity for sympathy, he transfigures the crowd's jostling into furious enjoyment, and is able to take unforgettable snapshots of the emotions that move like flashes of lightning across the mechanism of the puppets [. . .]
>
> 'Les Ballets russes', *La Grande revue* (25 June 1912), pp. 849–850

Perséphone

In this review of the first performance of the melodrama *Perséphone*, Laloy summarizes Stravinsky's artistic development over the previous twenty-five years, demonstrating a perceptiveness not often encountered in other critics of the period. He then discusses the composer's aims in the new work.

La Revue des deux mondes, vol. 104, no. 21 (1 June 1934), pp. 693–696

Madame Ida Rubinstein's ballet company, in giving us *Perséphone*, has renewed, on the stage of the Opéra, the mysteries of Eleusis, in the spirit and form necessary to produce a profound emotional response.[1]

Monsieur Stravinsky attains in this work a simplicity which can be called Classical although it does not recall – or rather because it does not in any way recall – the procedures consecrated before his time by the practice of the masters to achieve that effect. He has been striving towards it for a long time, restraining at all costs the dazzling ardour which so seduced us in *L'Oiseau de feu*, *Petrouchka* and *Le Sacre du printemps*. We were able to admire unreservedly certain works in this second manner, like *Le Rossignol* and *Histoire du soldat*, in which the reform had not yet been carried to its furthest point and so left him his freedom of movement, and his richness of colour. But other works betrayed a voluntary abstention and from time to time donned borrowed forms. He continued, however, deaf to our cries of alarm, digging in stony ground, plunging into the night, and he was certainly right, for he is now coming out of the tunnel into the light, into another land where his wishes are fulfilled.[2]

This music is all in one block, and everything is set firm; there are no external details.[3] The orchestration has its usual instruments, and even a piano, and thus obtains varied colours which are never added together, and were conceived in the same moment as the design to which they point; but the design imprints its own emphasis on the harps – by turns assiduous or intermittent – on the compact bassoon chord which marks time on the spot, or on the sinister underworld flute. There is no development: that would be rhetoric. The accompaniment motifs are repeated as in the meanders of Greek art, surrounding the central melody with their geometric regularity and yet also in agreement with this melody which unfolds in the resulting space but never yields to the temptation of making a detour. It is direct and inflexible. No oscillation betrays a stirring of the heart: that would be Romanticism. The thought which inspires the melody is detached from the person, who is absorbed in contemplation. He prays, not for himself, but for all who are present at this service: there are no original words in a liturgy.

Remaining always faithful to itself, the melody avoids the trap of the human voice and does not allow itself to be distracted from its course either by the particular meaning or shape of the phrase, nor even by the expressive or tonic accent[4] of the text. What counts, for me, said the author in a preliminary manifesto, is not the word but the syllable.[5] The result is that we have difficulty in grasping the words, but it is true that only the syllable, by the sonority it contributes, is in direct relationship with the music. The rest is the concern of the poet and not the composer who, if the poem is effective, cannot double back without redundancy and pleonasm: to each his craft. In the mysteries of Greece, as in those of Egypt, what was important was the correct articulation of the syllables and especially the right timbre of the vowels they contained. Those who suffered from faulty utterance could not become adepts, and the priests of Eleusis were chosen from among the Eumolpides, that is from the family of harmonious voices. Vocal melody takes on its supreme power when it ceases to adhere closely to the discourse, because then it translates the ineffable: Mozart's arias, Gregorian chant, the ancient music of China reach this emancipation by different routes. These are the mysteries of music.

But Stravinsky's music is following yet another road. The choruses have the naive quality of a simple song. The recitor[6] psalmodises on an even pitch or, on the other hand, at long intervals carves out an energetic litany. These are only superficial analogies: the atmosphere is not the same. This simplicity is not immediate, but results from a meditative quality with which it remains impregnated. Sentiment, no longer evaporating in fleeting vapours, takes on a concentrated ardour, and a soul is manifested all the more strongly for being gathered in on itself and giving away no secrets. It is the soul of a believer, a Christian of our time, and even, if my information is correct, very piously orthodox,[7] but from that pagan cult the permanent ideas of sacrifice and devotion. Very modern in sound and scales, the music of *Perséphone* yet comes to us from the depths of the ages: crafted not in the round, but in square relief like the ancient sculptures of Greece, it imprints in the memory of those who are able to hear it the seal of its superb, hieratic power.[8]

Notes

[1] Two paragraphs telling the story of *Perséphone*, and praising the text by the French writer André Gide (1869–1951), have been omitted.

[2] 'Il continuait pourtant, sourd à nos cris d'alarme, fouillant un sol ingrat, s'enfonçant dans la nuit, et certes il faisait bien, car voilà qu'il sort du tunnel et reparaît au jour, dans une autre contrée où ses vœux s'accomplissent.'

[3] 'C'est une musique d'un seul tenant, où tout fait prise, sans détails extérieurs.'

[4] Tonic accent: an accent placed on a syllable by pronouncing it more strongly than the surrounding syllables.

[5] Stravinsky's article in *Excelsior* (29 April and 1 May 1934) includes discussion of the syllable:

> I must, as I have been asked to write about the music of *Perséphone* and I scarcely have time to do so, draw the public's attention to a word which contains an entire program: *syllable* and also the verb *syllabize*. [The latter word is a neologism: in French Stravinsky writes *syllaber*, rather than the usual *syllabiser*.]
>
> Therein lies my main preoccupation.
>
> In music, which is time and regulated tone, by contrast to the confused sound found in nature, there is always the syllable. Between it and the entirely general meaning – the mood which bathes the work – there is the word which canalizes scattered thoughts and focuses discursive meaning. For *Perséphone* I wanted only syllables, fine, strong syllables, and then a plot. In this desire, I congratulate myself on having met Gide, whose text, highly poetic but free of jerkiness, was to provide me with an excellent syllabic structure.

White (1979), p. 580. The translation is by the present writer.

[6] The role of Persephone, performed by an actress/dancer, is spoken throughout. Laloy slips up here and writes the masculine form 'le récitant' rather than the feminine 'la récitante'.

[7] Laloy's information was correct: Stravinsky had rejoined the Russian Orthodox Church in 1926.

[8] 'Toute moderne par le son et la gamme, la musique de *Perséphone* vient cependant à nous depuis la profondeur des âges ; taillée sans ronde[-]bosse, en relief carré comme les anciennes sculptures de la Grèce, elle imprime dans la mémoire de qui sait l'entendre le sceau de son pouvoir hiératique et superbe.'

Appendix 1

Personalia

Apaches (literally 'hooligans'). An group of young men who between 1900 and 1914 enthusiastically followed the arts in Paris, and gave support to Ravel, who was one of them. Included André Caplet, Manuel de Falla, Léon-Paul Fargue, Tristan Klingsor, D.-E. Inghelbrecht, Florent Schmitt, Déodat de Séverac, Ricardo Viñes, Emile Vuillermoz, and (briefly) Stravinsky.

Auric, Georges. (1899–1983) French composer, one of *Les Six*. Ardent supporter of Satie. Wrote ballet *Les Enchantements d'Alcine* with Laloy (1928). President of Société des Amis de Louis Laloy.

Bakst, Leon. (1866–1924) Russian painter and stage designer, associated with Ballets Russes. His use of very rich colour revolutionized stage design and also fashion. Designed Debussy's *L'Après-midi d'un faune* and Ravel's *Daphnis et Chloé*.

Bathori, Jane (pseudonym of Jeanne-Marie Berthier). (1877–1970) French singer who specialised in contemporary French music. Her book *Sur l'interprétation des mélodies de Claude Debussy* (Paris, 1953) gives insight into performance practice.

Baudelaire, Charles. (1821–1867) French Symbolist poet, famous for his translations of Edgar Allan Poe and for his collection of poems, *Les Fleurs du mal* (1857), of which Debussy set five.

Bédier, Joseph. (1864–1938) French medievalist. Wrote an adaptation of the Tristan and Isolde romance, *Le Roman de Tristan* (1900). Taught Laloy French at the Ecole Normale Supérieure.

Bellaigue, Camille. (1858–1930) Influential French music critic. Studied piano at Conservatoire. Principal critic of *La Revue des deux mondes* from 1885 onwards; succeeded by Laloy. Highly conservative and a vehement critic of Debussy.

Bergson, Henri. (1859–1941) French philosopher. Influential tracts included *Le Rire* (1900) and *L'Evolution créatrice* (1907). Won Nobel

Prize for literature in 1927. Taught Laloy French at Lycée Henri IV, Paris.

Blanche, Jacques-Emile. (1861-1942) French painter. Friend of Debussy; painted two portraits of him. Closely associated with Diaghilev and the Ballets Russes.

Bordes, Charles. (1863-1909) French conductor, teacher and composer. Co-founded the Schola Cantorum with Alexandre Guilmant and Vincent d'Indy (1894). Established the Chanteurs de Saint-Gervais, dedicated to resurrecting Renaissance choral repertoire.

Calvocoressi, Michel-Dimitri. (1877-1944) Writer, translator and music critic of Greek parentage, educated in France. Friend and supporter of Ravel; one of the *Apaches*. Settled in England after 1914.

Caplet, André. (1878-1925) French composer and conductor. Won Prix de Rome 1901. Friend of Debussy. Collaborated with him on orchestration of *Le Martyre de saint Sébastien*; also orchestrated *Children's corner* and *La Boîte à joujoux*.

Casella, Alfredo. (1883-1947) Italian composer, pianist and conductor. Studied composition with Fauré. Friend of Debussy. Founded a number of music societies in Rome after 1917.

Chevillard, Camille. (1859-1923) French composer and conductor. Son-in-law of Charles Lamoureux; became conductor of the Concerts Lamoureux after his death. Active exponent of Russian composers in France.

Claudel, Paul. (1868-1955) French poet, playwright and diplomat. His writing used mystical and Roman Catholic themes. Plays included *L'Annonce faite à Marie* (1912) and *Jeanne d'Arc au bûcher* (1939).

Cocteau, Jean. (1889-1963) French writer, poet, playwright and film-maker. Collaborated with Picasso and Satie on ballet *Parade* (1917). Promoted younger generation of French composers including *Les Six*.

Colette (Sidonie-Gabrielle Colette). (1873-1954) French writer. Married for some years to Henri Gauthier-Villars (Willy), with whom she collaborated on the famous *Claudine* series. Her book *En pays connu* contains recollections of Debussy.

Colonne, Edouard. (1838-1910) French violinist and conductor. Founder and principal conductor of Concerts Colonne, succeeded by Gabriel Pierné. Popularized works of Berlioz.

Combarieu, Jules. (1859–1916) French musicologist and music critic. One of the first doctoral candidates in music at the Sorbonne. Founded early *Revue musicale* in 1901, with Laloy as unofficial editor-in-chief.

Diaghilev, Serge de. (1872–1929) Russian impresario, founder of the Ballets Russes. Commissioned Debussy's *Jeux* and Ravel's *Daphnis et Chloé*, and works from Stravinsky, Falla, Prokofiev, Poulenc, Auric and Sauguet.

Dukas, Paul. (1865–1935) French composer and music critic. Famous for opera *Ariane et Barbe-bleu* (1906) as well as the very popular *L'Apprenti sorcier* (1897).

Duncan, Isadora. (1878–1927) American dancer who, without formal training, pioneered modern dance. Took inspiration from Ancient Greek art. Worked in Europe and America. She lived a tragic life, and died strangled by her own scarf.

Durand, Jacques. (1865–1928) Director of the French music publishing house Durand, founded by his father Auguste in 1891. Close friend of Debussy.

Falla, Manuel de. (1876–1946) Spanish composer. Drew on Spanish folk tradition , but was also influenced by Debussy and Ravel. Works included zarzuelas, operas, ballets and songs.

Fauré, Gabriel. (1845–1924) French composer. Taught Ravel 1898–1903. Director of Conservatoire 1905–1920. Wrote incidental music, chamber music, piano pieces and songs, including the song cycle *La Bonne chanson* (1894).

Franck, César. (1822–1890) French composer and organist of Belgian birth. Wrote many sacred works, including oratorio *Les Béatitudes* (1879). Taught Charles Bordes, d'Indy, Duparc, Chausson.

Franc-Nohain (pseudonym of Maurice-Etienne Legrand). (1873–1934) French poet, playwright and journalist. His play *L'Heure espagnole*, which Ravel set to music, dates from 1904.

Garden, Mary. (1877–1967) American soprano, born in Scotland. Sang the role of Mélisande at the first performances of *Pelléas et Mélisande* (1902). Also performed in London and the U.S.A. Greatly appreciated by Debussy for her 'delicately fragile, crystal voice'.

Gauthier-Villars, Henri ('Willy'). (1859–1931) French writer and music critic, married for some years to Colette. Wrote for many periodicals including *L'Echo de Paris*, *Gil blas* and *La Revue blanche*. Employed ghost writers including Emile Vuillermoz.

Honegger, Arthur. (1892–1955) Swiss composer. One of *Les Six*. Works included orchestral piece *Pacific 231* (1923) and dramatic psalm *Le Roi David* (1921). Prolific in all genres.

d'Indy, Vincent. (1851–1931) French composer and teacher. Studied with Franck. One of the founders of the Société Nationale de Musique (1871) and Schola Cantorum (1894). Operas included *Fervaal* (1897) and *L'Etranger* (1901). Wrote books on Franck, Beethoven and Wagner.

Inghelbrecht, Désiré-Emile. (1880–1965) French conductor and composer. One of the *Apaches*. Championed the music of Debussy and Ravel. Founded Orchestre National de la Radiodiffusion Française (1934).

Jean-Aubry, Georges. (1882–1949) French music critic and musicologist. Travelled in England and Europe to advance the cause of contemporary French music. Friend of Debussy. Edited the English periodical *The Chesterian* 1919–1940.

Klingsor, Tristan (pseudonym of Léon Leclère). (1874–1966) French poet, painter and composer. One of the *Apaches*. Wrote a poem praising the 'tender, ironic heart' of Maurice Ravel. Compositions included *Chansons de ma mère l'Oie* (*Mother Goose songs*, 1905).

Koechlin, Charles. (1867–1951) French composer and music critic. Studied with Fauré. Wrote books on Debussy and Fauré and reviews for *La Gazette des beaux-arts*, *La Chronique des arts et de la curiosité*, *Le Ménestrel* and *La Revue musicale*.

Lalo, Pierre. (1866–1943) French music critic. Son of the composer Edouard Lalo. Principal music critic of newspaper *Le Temps* from 1898. His conservative views were very influential.

Lamoureux, Charles. (1834–1899) French violinist and conductor. Founded Concerts Lamoureux (1881). Popularized Wagner's music dramas in France.

Liebich, Franz. (1860–1922) British pianist. Studied with Hans von Bülow. Played much contemporary music. Friend of Debussy. His wife, Louise Liebich, wrote one of the first biographies of Debussy.[1]

Louÿs, Pierre. (1870–1925) French poet and novelist. Close friend of Debussy until 1902. Poems used themes of voluptuousness and mysticism. Debussy set his *Chansons de Bilitis* (1894) to music.

Maeterlinck, Maurice. (1862–1949) Belgian Symbolist playwright and poet. Plays included *Pelléas et Mélisande* (1892), *Alladine et Palomides* (1894), *La Mort de Tintagiles* (1894) and *L'Oiseau bleu* (1908).

Mallarmé, Stéphane. (1842–1898) French Symbolist poet and literary critic. Famous for his Tuesday literary gatherings. Poetry included *L'Après-midi d'un faune* (1876) and *Divagations* (1896). Translated poems of Edgar Allan Poe into French.

Maritain, Jacques. (1882–1973) French philosopher. Supported Catholic orthodoxy and opposed the philosophy of Bergson. Writings include *La Philosophie bergsonienne* (1913) and *Science et sagesse* (1935).

Marnold, Jean. (1859–1935) French music critic, co-founder with Laloy of *Le Mercure musical* (1905). Exceptionally convoluted prose style, almost unintelligible when it came to Ravel, whose works he championed.

Massine, Leonid. (1894–1979) Russian dancer and choreographer with Ballets Russes 1913–*c.*1920. Choreographed Cocteau and Satie's *Parade* and Stravinsky's *Le Sacre du printemps* and *Le Chant du rossignol*.

Mendès, Catulle. (1841–1909) French writer. Spokesman for Wagner's music in France. Wrote libretto of Chabrier's opera *Gwendoline* (1885) and Massenet's *Bacchus* (1909).

Messager, André. (1853–1929) French composer and conductor. Wrote many operettas. As Director of Music at Opéra-Comique in Paris, conducted first performances of Debussy's *Pelléas et Mélisande* (1902).

Migot, Georges. (1891–1976) French composer, music critic, writer and painter. Pupil of Widor. Prolific in most genres. Wrote a 'lyric and choreographic symphony', *Hagoromo*, with Laloy (1921).

Milhaud, Darius. (1892–1974) French composer, one of *Les Six*. Ballets included *Le Bœuf sur le toit* (1919) and *La Création du monde* (1923). Wrote several theatrical works with Paul Claudel.

Nijinska, Bronislava. (1891–1972) Russian dancer and choreographer, sister of Vaclav. Danced with Ballets Russes 1909–1913. Choreographed Stravinsky's *Les Noces* and *Le Baiser de la fée* and Ravel's *Boléro* and *La Valse*.

Nijinsky, Vaclav. (1890–1950) Russian dancer. Came to Paris with Diaghilev in 1909 and made a brilliant career. Less successful as a choreographer, of *L'Après-midi d'un faune*, *Le Sacre du printemps* and *Jeux*. Career terminated *c*.1917 by mental illness.

Périer, Jean. (1869–1954) French baritone. Created the roles of Pelléas in Debussy's *Pelléas et Mélisande* and Ramiro in Ravel's *L'Heure espagnole*. Also a gifted actor, appearing in plays and films.

Pierné, Gabriel. (1863–1937) French conductor and composer. Contemporary of Debussy at Conservatoire. Won Prix de Rome 1882. Principal conductor of Concerts Colonne 1910–1932.

Poulenc, Francis. (1899–1963) French composer and pianist. One of *Les Six*. Best known for his songs and chamber music. Also two ballets, *Les Biches* (1923) and *Aubade* (1929).

Prunières, Henri. (1886–1942) French musicologist. Student of Romain Rolland. Founded *La Revue musicale* (1920). Wrote books on Monteverdi and Lully and produced a complete edition of Lully's works.

Redon, Odilon. (1840–1916) French painter and lithographer. His paintings, in the Symbolist tradition, were primarily of flowers, landscapes and literary or mythological subjects.

Régnier, Henri de. (1864–1936) French Symbolist poet. One of the founders of *Le Mercure de France* (1890). Quotations from his works appear in Ravel's *Jeux d'eau* and *Valses nobles et sentimentales*.

Roger-Ducasse, Jean. (1873–1954) French composer. Studied with Fauré. Taught at Conservatoire. Works included *Au jardin de Marguerite* for choir and orchestra (1905) and the successful opera *Cantegril* (1931).

Roland-Manuel (pseudonym of Roland-Manuel Lévy). (1891–1966) French musicologist and composer. Pupil and close friend of Ravel. Interested in Orientalism. Taught at Conservatoire and Schola Cantorum.

Rolland, Romain. (1866–1944) French novelist, playwright, critic and musicologist. Wrote numerous books on music including a seven-volume work on Beethoven. Also a multi-volume novel about the life of a composer, *Jean-Christophe* (1905–1912).

Rouché, Jacques. (1862–1957) Highly respected and influential Director of Théâtre des Arts and later of Paris Opéra, where he was assisted by Laloy as Secretary-General. Adopted new practices in stage design and lighting from Germany and England.

Roussel, Albert. (1869–1937) French composer. Claimed he was born too close to the Mediterranean ever to want to imitate Wagner. Taught at Schola Cantorum. Wrote opera-ballet, *Padmâvatî*, with Laloy (1923).

Rubinstein, Ida. (1880–1960) Russian dancer and impresario. Began with the Ballets Russes but later formed her own dance company, which staged Debussy's *Le Martyre de saint Sébastien* (1911).

Saint-Saëns, Camille. (1835–1921) French composer, pianist, organist and explorer. One of the founders of the Société Nationale (1871). Highly conservative. Disapproved of much of Debussy's and Ravel's music.

Satie, Erik. (1866–1925) French composer. Highly individualistic, with little formal training. Mentor of *Les Six*. Collaborated on ballet *Parade* with Cocteau and Picasso (1917). His loathing for Laloy was reciprocated.

Schmitt, Florent. (1870–1958) French composer and music critic. Won Prix de Rome 1900. One of the *Apaches*. Outspoken on musical issues of the day. Wrote orchestral and choral works, piano pieces and songs.

Séverac, Déodat de. (1873–1921) French composer. Studied with d'Indy. Lived in southern France; his music was inspired by the local countryside. Wrote piano pieces, songs, and operas including *Le Cœur du moulin* (1908).

Les Six. Group of French composers formed after World War I: Auric, Louis Durey, Honegger, Milhaud, Poulenc and Germaine Tailleferre. Linked with Satie and Cocteau. Name came from an article by Henri Collet, 'Les Cinq russes, les six français et M. Satie' in *Comœdia* (16 January 1920).

Toulet, Paul-Jean. (1867–1920) French poet and writer. Travelled in Spain and the Orient; interested in Chinese culture. Friend of Debussy.

Verlaine, Paul. (1844–1896) French Symbolist poet. Debussy, Ravel and Stravinsky set his poetry to music. His volumes of poems included

Fêtes galantes (1869), *La Bonne chanson* (1870) and *Les Poètes maudits* (1884).

Viñes, Ricardo. (1875–1943) Spanish pianist. Deeply interested in literature and painting. One of the *Apaches*. Gave first performances of many works by Debussy and Ravel.

Vuillermoz, Emile. (1878–1960) Influential French music critic and composer. One of the *Apaches*. Wrote for *Comœdia*, *Excelsior*, *Le Temps*. Books included *Musiques d'aujourd'hui* (Paris, 1923) and *Histoire de la musique* (Paris, 1949).

Whistler, James Abbott McNeill. (1834–1903) American painter and etcher. Lived in Paris then London. Influenced by Japanese painting. His most revolutionary paintings were the *Nocturnes* (1877).

Willy. See **Gauthier-Villars, Henri.**

Notes

1 Very little information is available about Franz Liebich. Most of the details given here are taken from an entry in W. Lyle, *A dictionary of pianists* (London, 1985), p. 169, under the name Frank Liebich. On balance, it seems likely that the entry refers to Franz Liebich, particularly as the author notes that 'with his wife's collaboration, he developed a lecture-recital on Chopin in which she delivered the lecture and he delivered the illustrations at the keyboard'. No other information about Louise Liebich has come to light.

Appendix 2

Chronological list of principal compositions by Debussy, Ravel and Stravinsky

The dates listed are the dates of composition and of any revisions.

Debussy

L'Enfant prodigue	1884; rev. 1908
Printemps	1887
La Damoiselle élue	1888
Ariettes oubliées	1888
Cinq poèmes de Baudelaire	1890
Fantasy for piano and orchestra	1890
Suite bergamasque	1890; rev. 1905
Deux arabesques	1891
Fêtes galantes I	1891
Proses lyriques	1893
String quartet	1893
Prélude à l'Après-midi d'un faune	1894
Chansons de Bilitis	1898
Nocturnes	1899
Suite *Pour le piano*	1901
Pelléas et Mélisande	1902
Estampes	1903
Fêtes galantes II	1904
L'Isle joyeuse	1904
Trois chansons de France	1904
Images I (for piano)	1905
La Mer	1905
Images II (for piano)	1907
Children's corner	1908
Trois chansons de Charles d'Orléans	1908

Ibéria	1908
Rondes de printemps	1909
Préludes I	1910
Trois ballades de François Villon	1910
Le Martyre de saint Sébastien	1911
Rhapsody for clarinet and orchestra	1911
Gigues	1912
Khamma	1912
La Boîte à joujoux	1913
Jeux	1913
Préludes II	1913
Syrinx	1913
Trois poèmes de Stéphane Mallarmé	1913
Berceuse héroïque	1914
En blanc et noir	1915
Etudes	1915
Noël des enfants qui n'ont plus de maison	1915
Sonata for cello and piano	1915
Sonata for flute, viola and harp	1915
Sonata for violin and piano	1917

Ravel

Shéhérazade (overture)	1898
Pavane pour une Infante défunte	1899
Jeux d'eau	1901
String quartet	1903
Shéhérazade (song cycle)	1903
Noël des jouets	1905, rev. 1913
Sonatine	1905
Introduction et allegro	1905
Miroirs	1905
Cinq mélodies populaires grecques	1906
Histoires naturelles	1906
Rapsodie espagnole	1908
Gaspard de la nuit	1908
L'Heure espagnole	1909
Chants populaires	1910
Ma mère l'Oye (piano duet)	1910
Ma mère l'Oye (ballet)	1911
Valses nobles et sentimentales	1911
Adélaïde, ou le Langage des fleurs	1912
Daphnis et Chloé	1912
Trois poèmes de Stéphane Mallarmé	1913
Piano trio	1914
Le Tombeau de Couperin	1917
La Valse	1920
Le Tombeau de Claude Debussy	1920
Sonata for violin and cello	1922
Tzigane	1924
L'Enfant et les sortilèges	1925
Chansons madécasses	1926
Sonata for violin and piano	1927
Boléro	1928
Piano concerto for the left hand	1930
Piano concerto in G	1931
Don Quichotte à Dulcinée	1933

Stravinsky

This list covers only the period relevant to the present volume, not Stravinsky's later career.

L'Oiseau de feu	1910
Petrouchka	1911
Le Sacre du printemps	1913
Three Japanese lyrics	1913
Le Rossignol	1914
Berceuses du chat	1916
Renard	1916
Le Chant du rossignol	1917
Histoire du soldat	1918
Rag-time	1918
Piano-rag-music	1919
Pulcinella	1920
Symphonies of wind instruments	1920
Suite no. 2 for small orchestra	1921
Mavra	1922
Les Noces	1923
Octet	1923
Concerto for piano and wind orchestra	1924
Sonata for piano	1924
Suite no. 1 for small orchestra	1925
Œdipus rex	1927
Apollon musagète	1928
Le Baiser de la fée	1928
Capriccio for piano and orchestra	1929
Symphony of Psalms	1930
Violin concerto	1931
Duo concertante	1932
Perséphone	1934
Concerto for two solo pianos	1935
Jeu de cartes	1936

Bibliography

L'Avant-scène, vol. 9 (March–April 1977), special issue devoted to *Pelléas et Mélisande*.

Hommage à Eliette Schenneberg, Dôle (1991).

'Hommage à Louis Laloy', *L'Information musicale*, vol. 4, no. 151 (31 March 1944), pp. 245–247.

'Liste chronologique des principales créations et reprises montées [à l'Opéra] sous la direction de Jacques Rouché', *Revue d'histoire du théâtre*, vol. 10, no. 3 (1958), pp. 286–290.

Ansermet, E. (1980), 'Debussy', *La Revue musicale de Suisse Romande*, vol. 33, no. 2 (May), pp. 65–69.

Audel, S. (1963), *Francis Poulenc: mes amis et moi*, Geneva.

Augé, P. (ed.) (1928–1933), *Larousse du XXe siècle*, 6 vols, Paris.

Auric, G. (1979), *Quand j'étais là*, Paris.

Barbey, V. (1937), 'Naissance de *Padmâvatî*', *La Revue musicale*, special issue (November), p. 344.

Barraqué, J. (1962), *Debussy*, Paris.

Bartoli, J.-P. et al. (1992), 'Claude Debussy, *Pelléas et Mélisande*. Bibliographie commentée', *Analyses musicales*, vol. 19, no. 4, pp. 31–106.

Bathori, J. (1938), 'Souvenir', *La Revue musicale*, special issue (December), pp. 179(371)–181(373).

Bathori, J. (1953), *Sur l'interprétation des mélodies de Claude Debussy*, Paris.

Bellaigue, C. (1921), *Souvenirs de musique et de musiciens*, Paris.

Bernard, R. (1948), *Albert Roussel, sa vie – son œuvre*, Paris.

Bertrand, P. (1947), *Le Monde de la musique: souvenirs d'un éditeur*, Geneva.

Blanchart, P. (1958), 'Agenda et chroniques du Théâtre des Arts', *Revue d'histoire du théâtre*, vol. 10, no. 3, pp. 222–265.

Blanchart, P. (1958), 'Jacques Rouché au Théâtre des Arts. Saisons 1910–11 à 1912–13', *Revue d'histoire du théâtre* vol. 10, no. 3, pp. 211–221.

Blume, F. (ed.) (1949–1979), *Die Musik in Geschichte und Gegenwart*, 16 vols, Kassel.

Boschot, A. (1931), *La Musique et la vie*, Paris.

Boucourechliev, A. et al. (1972), *Debussy*, Paris.

Boulanger, N. (1926), 'Lectures on modern music. Debussy: the *Préludes*', *The Rice Institute pamphlet*, vol. 13 (April), pp. 153–177.

Bredel, M. (1982), *Erik Satie*, Paris.

Brenet, M. (1905), [Review of L. Laloy, *Aristoxène et la musique de l'antiquité* (1904)], *Le Mercure musical* (15 October), pp. 450–451.

Briscoe, J. R. (1990), *Claude Debussy. A guide to research*, London.

Brody, E. (1977), 'Viñes in Paris: new light on twentieth-century performance practice', in E. H. Clinkscale and C. Brook, eds, *A musical offering: essays in honour of Martin Bernstein*, New York, pp. 45–62.

Bruneau, A. (1901), *La Musique française*, Paris.

Buckle, R. (1979), *Diaghilev*, London.

Buckle, R. (1980), *Nijinsky*, rev. ed., London.

Bullard, T. (1971), *The first performance of Igor Stravinsky's 'Sacre du printemps'*, Ph.D. thesis, University of Rochester, Eastman School of Music, 3 vols, Ann Arbor, Michigan.

Byrnside, R. L. (1980), 'Musical impressionism: the early history of the term', *The musical quarterly*, vol. 66, no. 4 (October), pp. 522–537.

Caillard, C.-F. and J. de Bérys. (1909), *Le Cas Debussy*, Paris.

Calvocoressi, M.-D. (1913), 'Maurice Ravel', *The musical times*, vol. 54 (1 December), pp. 785–787.

Casella, A. (1933), 'Claude Debussy', *The monthly musical record*, vol. 63 (January), pp. 1–3.

Casella, A. (1955), *Music in my time: the memoirs of Alfredo Casella*, trans. S. Norton, Norman, Oklahoma.

Chalupt, R. (1956), *Ravel au miroir de ses lettres*, Paris.

Chantavoine, J. (1912), *Musiciens et poètes*, Paris.

Charette, J. M. (ed.) (1990), *Claude Debussy through his letters*, New York.

Chennevière, D. (1913), *Claude Debussy et son œuvre*, Paris.

Chimènes, M. (1991), 'Un portrait de Debussy. Lettre de Léon-Paul Fargue à Auguste Martin'. *Cahiers Debussy*, nouvelle série no. 15, pp. 59–61.

Coeuroy, A. (1922), *La Musique française moderne*, Paris.

Coeuroy, A. (1923), *Musique et littérature*, Paris.

Coeuroy, A. (1928), *Panorama de la musique contemporaine*, Paris.

Colette. (1936), *Mes apprentissages*, Paris.

Collaer, P. (1955), *La Musique moderne 1905-1955*, 2nd ed., Brussels.

Cooper, M. (1961), *French music from the death of Berlioz to the death of Fauré*, London.

Cortot, A. (1931), *La Musique française de piano*, vol. 1, Paris.

Craft, R. (ed.) (1982–1985), *Stravinsky. Selected correspondence*, 3 vols, New York.

Deane, B. (1961), *Albert Roussel*, London.

Debussy, C. (1927), *Lettres de Claude Debussy à son éditeur*, Paris.

Debussy, C. (1970), *Prelude to 'The afternoon of a faun'*, ed. W. W. Austin, New York.

Debussy, C. (1987), *Monsieur Croche et autres écrits*, ed. F. Lesure, rev. ed., Paris.

Didier, B. (ed.) (1994), *Dictionnaire universel des littératures*, 3 vols, Paris.

Dietschy, M. (1962), *La Passion de Claude Debussy*, Neuchâtel.

Dietschy, M. (1977), 'Louis Laloy', *Bulletin de la Société des Amis de Meudon* vol. 41, no. 142 (spring–summer), pp. 2276–2286.

Dietschy, M. (1980), 'Debussy interprète de ses propres œuvres', *Schweizerische Musikzeitung*, vol. 120, no. 1 (January–February), pp. 12–14.

Dietschy, M. (1990), *A portrait of Claude Debussy*, trans W. Ashbrook and M. G. Cobb, Oxford.
Dufourcq, N. (ed.) (1957), *Larousse de la musique*, 2 vols, Paris.
Dukas, P. (1948), *Les Ecrits de Paul Dukas sur la musique*, Paris.
Dumesnil, R. (1924), *Le Monde des musiciens*, Paris.
Dumesnil, R. (1938), 'Debussy's principles in pianoforte playing', *The Etude*, vol. 56 (March), pp. 153-154
Dumesnil, R. (1946), *La Musique en France entre les deux guerres*, Paris.
Durand, J. (1924-1925), *Quelques souvenirs d'un éditeur de musique*, 2 vols, Paris.
Emmanuel, M. ([1926]), *'Pelléas et Mélisande' de Claude Debussy: étude historique et analyse musicale*, Paris.
Falla, M. de. (1939), 'Notes sur Ravel', *La Revue musicale*, vol. 20, no. 189 (March), pp. 81-86.
Farwell, A. and L. Laloy. (1907), 'La Musique américaine', *Le Mercure musical*, (15 October), pp. 1039-1045.
Février, J. (1939), 'Les Exigences de Ravel', *La Revue internationale de musique*, vol. 1, nos. 5-6 (April), pp. 893-894.
Flattot-Mouffard, A. (1986), 'Louis Laloy, musicologue Franc-Comtois et Claude Debussy', *Mémoires de la Société d'émulation du Doubs*, vol. 28, pp. 67-77.
Flattot-Mouffard, A. (1987), 'Louis Laloy et Albert Roussel. A propos d'un anniversaire', *A.R.D.I.A.M.* vol. 19 (December), pp. 2-5.
Fokine, M. (1961), *Fokine: memoirs of a ballet master*, London.
Follet, R. (1988), *Albert Roussel: a bio-bibliography*, New York.
Garden, M. (1952), *A l'envers du décor: souvenirs d'une grande cantatrice*, Paris.
Gatti, G. M. (1921), 'The piano works of Claude Debussy', *The musical quarterly*, vol. 7, pp. 418-460.
Gauthier, A. (1962), *Debussy. Documents iconographiques*, Geneva.
Gauthier-Villars, H. (1907), 'Pierre Lalo contre Ravel, Louis Laloy pro Ravel', *Le Mercure de France*, (1 April), pp. 528-532.
Gillmor, A. M. (1988), *Erik Satie*, Boston.
Gilman, L. (1915), *Nature in music and other studies of the tone-poetry of today*, London.
Gilman, L. (1951), *Orchestral music: an armchair guide*, New York.
Goubault, C. (1984), *La Critique musicale dans la presse française de 1870 à 1914*, Geneva.
Goubault, C. (1986), *Claude Debussy*, Paris.
Grammont, M. (1976), *Petit traité de versification française*, Paris.
Griffiths, P. (1992), *Stravinsky*, London.
Grigoriev, S. L. (1953), *The Diaghilev ballet 1909-1929*, London.
Gubisch, N. (1980), 'La Vie musicale à Paris entre 1887 et 1914 à travers le journal de R. Viñes', *La Revue internationale de musique française*, vol. 1, no. 2 (June), pp. 154-248.
Harding, J. (1975), *Erik Satie*, New York.
Haskell, A. (1968), *Ballet russe*, London.

Hell, H. (1959), *Francis Poulenc*, London.
Hébert, M. (1904), 'Notes prises à une conférence faite par M. Laloy', *Le Guide musical* (3 April), pp. 309–311.
Hill, E. B. (1924), *Modern French music*, London.
Hirsbrunner, T. (1982), *Igor Strawinsky in Paris*, Berne.
Honegger, A. (1938), 'Ravel et le Debussysme', *La Revue musicale*, special issue (December), pp. 66(258)–67(259).
Howat, R. (1988–1989), 'Debussy et les musiques de l'Inde', *Cahiers Debussy* vols. 12–13, pp. 141–152.
Howat, R. (1994), 'Debussy and the Orient' in A. Gerstle and A. Milner, eds, *Recovering the Orient: artists, scholars, appropriations*, pp. 45–81, London.
Inghelbrecht, D.-E. (1947), *Mouvement contraire. Souvenirs d'un musicien*, Paris.
Inghelbrecht, G. and D.-E. (1953), *Claude Debussy*, Paris.
Jardillier, R. (1922), *Claude Debussy*, Dijon.
Jardillier, R. (1927), *Pelléas*, Paris.
Jarocinski, S. (1976), *Debussy: Impressionism and Symbolism*, London.
Jean-Aubry, G. (c. 1917), *An introduction to French music*, London.
Jean-Aubry, G. (1918), 'Some recollections of Debussy', *The musical times*, vol. 59, no. 903 (1 May), pp. 203–209.
Joly-Ségalen, A. and A. Schaeffner. (1962), *Ségalen et Debussy*, Monaco.
Jou-Kia, H. and L. Laloy. (1912), 'Histoire de la révolution chinoise', *La Grande revue* (25 May), pp. 225–243.
Jourdan-Morhange, H. (1945), *Ravel et nous. L'homme, l'ami, le musicien*, Geneva.
Keck, G. R. (1990), *Francis Poulenc: a bio-bibliography*, New York.
Keller, G. (ed.) (1982), *The piano in concert*, 2 vols, Metuchen, New Jersey.
Koechlin, C. (1927), *Debussy*, Paris.
Koechlin, C. (1935), 'Sur l'évolution de la musique française avant et après Debussy', *La Revue musicale*, vol. 16, no. 155 (April), pp. 264–280.
Koechlin, C. (1952), 'Claude Debussy et le Debussysme dans l'époque', *La Revue musicale*, vol. 210 (January), pp. 55–64.
Laloy, L. (n.d.), 'Jean-Jacques Rousseau musicien' in P. Lalo et al., *Histoire du théâtre lyrique en France depuis les origines jusqu'à nos jours*, vol. 1, pp. 141–150, Paris.
Laloy, L. (1901), 'Le Genre enharmonique des Grecs', *La Revue musicale* (February and March), pp. 33–45, 90–94.
Laloy, L. (1901), 'Promenades et visites musicales. III: Une nouvelle école de musique: Le cours de M. Vincent d'Indy', *La Revue musicale* (November), pp. 393–398.
Laloy, L. (1902), 'Palestrina et Victor Hugo', *La Revue musicale* (July), pp. 326–328.
Laloy, L. (1903), 'Phonographes et gramophone', *La Revue musicale* (31 May–1 June), pp. 223–225.
Laloy, L. (1903), 'Vincent d'Indy', *La Revue musicale* (15 December), pp. 693–699.

Laloy, L. (1904) *Aristoxène de Tarente et la musique de l'antiquité*, Paris, repr. Geneva, 1973.

Laloy, L. (1904) 'Au jardin des chansons', *La Revue musicale* (15 December), pp. 586–593.

Laloy, L. (1904), 'Isadora Duncan et la danse nouvelle', *La Revue musicale* (15 May), pp. 249–253.

Laloy, L. (1904), *Lexique d'Aristoxène*, Paris.

Laloy, L. (1905), 'Déodat de Séverac', *Le Mercure musical* (15 June), pp. 134–135.

Laloy, L. (1905), 'Le Drame musical moderne.' I: 'La Légende héroïque: *Fervaal*'. II: 'Les Véristes: Zola-Bruneau'. III: 'Les Véristes français: Gustave Charpentier'. IV: 'Claude Debussy'. *Le Mercure musical* (15 May, 1 June, 1 July and 1 August), pp. 8–16, 75–84, 169–176, 233–250.

Laloy, L. (1905), 'Un dernier mot sur Alfred Bruneau', *Le Mercure musical* (15 August), pp. 288–292.

Laloy, L. (1906), 'Musique et danses cambodgiennes', *Le Mercure musical* (15 August), pp. 98–112.

Laloy, L. (1907), 'Le Chant grégorien et la musique française', *Le Mercure musical* (15 January), pp. 75–80.

Laloy, L. (1907), 'Les Ecoliers', *Le Mercure musical* (15 April), pp. 367– 372.

Laloy, L. (1907), 'Les Idées de Jean-Philippe Rameau sur la musique', *Le Mercure musical* (15 November), pp. 1144–1159.

Laloy, L. (1907), 'Musique nouvelle [on Dukas' *Ariane et Barbe-bleue* and R. Strauss' *Salome*]', *Le Mercure musical* (15 June), pp. 645–651.

Laloy, L. (1907), 'Musique russe', *Le Mercure musical* (15 May and 15 June), pp. 500–501, 652–656.

Laloy, L. (1907), 'Musiques étrangères', *La Revue de Paris* (15 June), pp. 755–782.

Laloy, L. (1907), 'La Notation musicale', *Le Mercure musical* (15 December), pp. 1299–1301.

Laloy, L. (1907), 'Les Partis musicaux en France', *La Grande revue* (25 December), pp. 790–799.

Laloy, L. (1908), 'Le Budget de la musique en 1908', *S.I.M.* (15 January), pp. 1–3.

Laloy, L. (1908), 'La Musique de l'avenir', *Le Mercure de France* (1 December), pp. 419–434.

Laloy, L. (1908), *Rameau*, Paris.

Laloy, L. (1908), 'Rimski-Korsakov', *S.I.M.* (15 July), pp. 739–741.

Laloy, L. (1909), 'Chanson des royaumes', *La Nouvelle revue française* (August, September and October), pp. 5–14, 130–136, 195–204.

Laloy, L. (1909), *Claude Debussy*, rev. 1944, Paris.

Laloy, L. (1909), 'Le Quintette de Florent Schmitt', *La Nouvelle revue française* (August), p. 79.

Laloy, L. (1909), 'Wagner et les musiciens d'aujourd'hui', *La Grande revue* (10 April and 10 May), pp. 558–566, 160–164.

Laloy, L. ([1910]), *The future of music; coming changes outlined in regard to composer, conductor and orchestra*, trans. L. Liebich, London.

Laloy, L. (1911), 'Maurice Ravel, Claude Debussy, Ricardo Viñes', *La Grande revue* (25 April), pp. 846–848.
Laloy, L. (1911), 'Opium, fumée d'opium et morphine', *La Grande revue* (25 June and 10 July), pp. 786–800, 116–128.
Laloy, L. (1912), 'Les Ballets russes', *La Grande revue*, (25 June), pp. 844–850.
Laloy, L. (1912), 'La Convention d'opium', *La Grande revue* (25 July), pp. 385–388.
Laloy, L. (1912), 'Danses d'Asie', *Revue musicale S.I.M.* (15 February). pp. 39–40.
Laloy, L. (1912), 'L'Histoire de la musique à la Faculté des Lettres', *La Grande revue* (25 October), pp. 748–753.
Laloy, L. (1912), *La Musique chinoise*, repr. 1979, Paris.
Laloy, L. (1913), [Review of the ballet *Dolly*], *La Grande revue* (25 January), pp. 401.
Laloy, L. (1913), 'Le Bal de l'Opéra', *Revue musicale S.I.M.* (1 April), pp. 49–50.
Laloy, L. (1913), 'Cabarets et music-halls', *Revue musicale S.I.M.* (15 February, 15 March, 15 April, 15 May, 15 June, July–August), pp. 53–56, 53–57, 52–55, 67–68, 57–58, 51–53.
Laloy, L. (1913), 'Le Gala de Claude Debussy', *Revue musicale S.I.M.* (15 June), p. 68.
Laloy, L. (1913), *Le Livre de la fumée*, Paris.
Laloy, L. (1913), 'L'Origine de la musique', *Revue musicale S.I.M.* (September–October), pp. 14–25.
Laloy, L. (1913), 'Le Tango', *Revue musicale S.I.M.* (1 February), pp. 47–49.
Laloy, L. (1913-1914), 'Music-halls et chansonneries', *Revue musicale S.I.M.* (1 December, 1 January, 1 March, July–August), pp. 48–50, 47–48, 53–56, 45–46.
Laloy, L. (1914), 'M. Henri Bergson et la musique', *Comœdia* (9 February), p. 3.
Laloy, L. (1914), 'Le Musicien dans la société moderne', *Comœdia* (25 June), p. 2.
Laloy, L. (1914), 'René Lenormand. *Etude sur l'harmonie moderne*', *Comœdia* (29 January), p. 3.
Laloy, L. (1919), 'Gabriele d'Annunzio [sic]', *Excelsior* (3 February), p. 4.
Laloy, L. (1919), 'M. Camille Chevillard', *Excelsior* (11 August), p. 4.
Laloy, L. (1919), 'Musiques militaires', *Excelsior* (7 September), p. 4.
Laloy, L. (1919), 'Paderewski', *Excelsior* (7 April), p. 4.
Laloy, L. (1920), 'Reprise de *Parade*', *Comœdia* (23 December), p. 1.
Laloy, L. (1921), 'Art lyrique et budget', *Le Courrier musical*, vol. 23, no. 6 (15 March), p. 89–90.
Laloy, L. (1921), 'Le Danseur fou', *Excelsior* (24 January), p. 4.
Laloy, L. (1921), 'Déodat de Séverac', *Excelsior* (23 March), p. 4.
Laloy, L. (1921), 'Les Emigrés', *Excelsior* (9 May), p. 4.
Laloy, L. (1921), '"On connaît le mot de Rossini . . ." [on the death of Saint-Saëns]', *Excelsior* (26 December), p. 4.

Laloy, L. (1921), 'Un sculpteur [Rodin]', *Excelsior* (16 May), p. 4.
Laloy, L. (1922), *Le Chagrin dans le palais de Han*, Paris.
Laloy, L. (1922), 'Les Etudes classiques au Conservatoire', *Le Courrier musical*, vol. 24, no. 13 (July), p. 219.
Laloy, L. (1922), *Légendes des immortels; d'après les auteurs chinois*, Paris.
Laloy, L. (1922), 'Les Principes de la danse cambodgienne', *La Revue musicale*, vol. 3, no. 9 (1 July), pp. 1-7.
Laloy, L. (1922), '"Tout le monde" [on Mussorgsky's *Boris Godunov*]', *Excelsior* (6 March), p. 4.
Laloy, L. (1923), 'A Dôle', *Excelsior* (28 May), p. 2.
Laloy, L. (1923), 'Physique et musique', *Le Courrier musical*, vol. 25, no. 1 (1 January), p. 2.
Laloy, L. (1923), 'Un musicien [tribute to Albert Roussel]', *Excelsior* (7 June), p. 2.
Laloy, L. (1924), 'A Monte-Carlo. Festivals français', *Le Courrier musical*, vol. 26, no. 3 (1 February), p. 76.
Laloy, L. (1924), 'Ronsard musicien', *La Revue musicale*, special issue (1 May), pp. 11-20.
Laloy, L. (c.1925), *Contes magiques, d'après l'ancien texte chinois de P'ou Soung-lin*, Paris.
Laloy, L. (1925), 'Marie Jaëll', *La Revue musicale*, vol. 6, no. 7 (May), pp. 139-143.
Laloy, L. (1925), 'La Musique et les philosophes chinois', *La Revue musicale*, vol. 6, no. 4 (1 February), pp. 132-139.
Laloy, L. (1925), 'L'Opéra' in L. Rohozinski (ed.), *Cinquante ans de musique française de 1874 à 1925*, vol. 1, ch. 1, pp. 1-117, Paris.
Laloy, L. (1926), 'Ce que je pense d'Erik Satie', *Le Courrier musical*, vol. 28, no. 11 (1 June), p. 301.
Laloy, L. (1927), *La Danse à l'Opéra*, Paris.
Laloy, L. (1928), *La Musique retrouvée, 1902-1927*, repr. 1974, Paris.
Laloy, L. (1930), 'Le "Groupe des six"', *Le Courrier musical*, vol. 32, no. 1 (1 January), p. 5.
Laloy, L. (1930), 'Hommage à Diaghilew [sic]', *La Revue musicale*, special issue (1 December), pp. 57(441)-61(445).
Laloy, L. (1930), 'Le Meurtre de Rameau et sa résurrection', *La Joie musicale*, vol. 8 (5 November), pp. 3-4.
Laloy, L. (1930), '*Tristan* et *Pelléas*', *La Joie musicale*, vol. 6 (16 May-15 June), p. 6.
Laloy, L. (1930), *Une heure de musique avec Beethoven*, Paris.
Laloy, L. (1931), 'M. Vincent d'Indy', *La Revue des deux mondes*, vol. 101, no. 1 (1 January), pp. 221-225.
Laloy, L. (1933), *Miroir de la Chine: présages, images, mirages*, Paris.
Laloy, L. (1935), *Le Rêve du millet jaune: drame taoiste du XIIIe siècle*, Paris.
Laloy, L. (1942), *Comment écouter la musique*, Paris.
Laloy, L. (1943), 'Souvenirs sur le maître', *Comœdia* (27 March), pp. 1, 3.
Laloy, L. (1943), *Trois drames de l'Asie*, Paris.
Laloy, L. et al. (n.d.), *Musica-album. Claude Debussy*, Paris.

Laloy, L. et al. (1924), *Ronsard et la musique*, Paris.
Landormy, P. (1910), 'M. Claude Debussy et l'avenir de la musique française', *Le Courrier musical*, vol. 13, no. 3 (1 February), pp. 98–101.
Landormy, P. (1946), *La Musique française*, Paris.
Laurencie, L. de la. (1904), 'Notes sur l'art de Claude Debussy', *Le Courrier musical* (1 and 15 March), pp. 141–149, 181–185.
Laurencie, L. de la. (1905), *Le Goût musical en France*, Paris.
Lejeune, D. (1991), *La France de la Belle Epoque. 1896–1914*, Paris.
Lenormand, R. (1913), *Etude sur l'harmonie moderne*, Paris.
Lépine, J. (1930), *La Vie de Claude Debussy*, Paris.
Lesure, F. (1963), '"L'Affaire" Debussy-Ravel', in *Festschrift Friedrich Blume zum 70. Geburtstag*, pp. 231–234, Kassel.
Lesure, F. (1986), 'Crime d'amour ou fêtes galantes. Un projet verlainien de Debussy 1912–1915', *Cahiers Debussy*, nouvelle série no. 10, pp. 17–23.
Lesure, F. (1990–1992), 'Ravel et Debussy', *Cahiers Maurice Ravel*, vol. 5, pp. 27–33.
Lesure, F. (1994), *Claude Debussy: biographie critique*, Paris.
Lesure, F. (ed.) (1962), 'Correspondance de Claude Debussy et de Louis Laloy (1902–1914)', *La Revue de musicologie*, vol. 48, no. 125, pp. 3–40.
Lesure, F. (ed.) (1977), *Esquisses de 'Pelléas et Mélisande' (1893–1895)*, Geneva.
Lesure, F. (ed.) (1980), *Debussy. Iconographie musicale*, Geneva.
Lesure, F. (ed.) (1980), *Igor Stravinsky: 'Le Sacre du printemps': dossier de presse*, Geneva.
Lesure, F. (ed.) (1993), *Claude Debussy. Correspondance 1884–1918*, Paris.
Lesure, F. and R. Langham Smith. (eds) (1977), *Debussy on music*, London.
Lesure, F. and J.-M. Nectoux. (eds) (1975), *Maurice Ravel*, Paris.
Lesure, F. and R. Nichols. (eds) (1987), *Debussy letters*, London.
Liebich, L. (1908), *Claude-Achille Debussy*, repr. 1925, London.
Lifar, S. (1954), *Serge Diaghilev: sa vie, son œuvre, sa légende*, Monaco.
Lockspeiser, E. (1962–1965), *Debussy: his life and mind*; London, rev. 1978, Cambridge.
Long, M. (1938), 'Souvenir de Maurice Ravel', *La Revue musicale*, special issue (December), pp. 172(364)–174(366).
Long, M. (1960), *Au piano avec Debussy*, Paris.
Long, M. (1971), *Au piano avec Ravel*, Paris.
Long, M. (1972), *At the piano with Debussy*, trans. O. Senior-Ellis, London.
Mansell Jones, P. (ed.) (1973), *The Oxford book of French verse*, 2nd ed., London.
Marnat, M. (1972), 'Jouer Debussy: ombres ou lumière', *La Musique de tous les temps*, vol. 8 (June), pp. 14–16.
Marnat, M. (1995), *Ravel: souvenirs de Manuel Rosenthal*, Paris.
Marnold, J. (1911), *Musique d'autrefois et d'aujourd'hui*, Paris.
Mason, D. G. (1938), *Music in my time and other reminiscences*, New York.
Mauclair, C. (1914), *Histoire de la musique européenne, 1850–1914*, Paris.
McDonald, W. J. (ed.) (1967), *New Catholic Encyclopedia*, 17 vols, repr. 1981, Washington D.C.

McMillan, J. F. (1992), *Twentieth-century France: politics and society 1898–1991*, London.

Messager, A. (1964), 'Les Premières représentations de *Pelléas*', *La Revue musicale*, vol. 259, pp. 57–60.

Michel, F. (ed.) (1958–1961), *Encyclopédie de la musique*, 3 vols, Paris.

Millington, B. (1992), *The Wagner compendium. A guide to Wagner's life and music*, London.

Miomandre, F. de. (1944), 'Souvenirs sur Louis Laloy', *Le Journal* (11 May), vol. 3.

Myers, R. H. (1960), *Ravel: life and works*, New York.

Myers, R. H. (1971), *Modern French music: its evolution and cultural background from 1900 to the present day*, Oxford.

Newman, E. (1918), 'The development of Claude Debussy', *The musical times*, vol. 59, no. 903 (1 May), pp. 199–202.

Nichols, R. (1987), *Ravel remembered*, London.

Nichols, R. (1992), *Debussy remembered*, Portland, Oregon.

Orenstein, A. (1975), *Ravel, man and musician*, New York.

Orenstein, A. (1990), *A Ravel reader: correspondence, articles, interviews*, New York.

Orledge, R. and R. Nichols (1995), *Satie remembered*, London.

Pâris, A. (1995), *Dictionnaire des interprètes et de l'interprétation musicale au XXe siècle*, Paris.

Pasler, J. (ed.) (1986), *Confronting Stravinsky: man, musician and modernist*, Berkeley.

Pasler, J. (1987), '*Pelléas* and power: forces behind the reception of Debussy's opera', *Nineteenth-century music*, vol. 10, no. 3 (spring), pp. 243–264.

Perlemuter, V. and H. Jourdan-Morhange (1988), *Ravel according to Ravel*, London.

Perloff, N. L. (1991), *Art and the everyday: popular entertainment and the circle of Erik Satie*, Oxford.

Peter, R. (1931), *Claude Debussy*, 6th ed., Paris.

Petit, J. (ed.) (1973), *Jacques Maritain, Emmanuel Mounier. Correspondance*, Paris.

Pincherle, M. (1957), *Albert Roussel*, Geneva.

Poueigh, J. (1921), *Musiciens français d'aujourd'hui*, Paris.

Randle, D. (ed.) (1986), *The New Harvard dictionary of music*, Cambridge, Mass.

Ravel, M. (1913), 'A propos des *Images* de Claude Debussy', *Cahiers d'aujourd'hui* (February), pp. 135–138.

Ravel, M. (1938), 'Esquisse autobiographique', *La Revue musicale*, special issue (December), pp. 16(208)–23(215).

Rey, A. (1974), *Erik Satie*, Paris.

Ricou, G. (n.d.), 'La Générale de *Pelléas et Mélisande*' in P. Lalo et al., *Histoire du théâtre lyrique en France depuis les origines jusqu'à nos jours*, vol. 3, pp. 69–81, Paris.

Rivière, J. (1910), '*Claude Debussy* par Louis Laloy', *La Nouvelle revue française* (January), p. 131.

Robert, P. (ed.) (1964), *Dictionnaire alphabétique et analogique de la langue française*, 6 vols + supplement, Paris.
Rohozinski, L. (ed.) (1925), *Cinquante ans de musique française de 1874 à 1925*, 2 vols, Paris.
Roland-Manuel. (1928), *Maurice Ravel et son œuvre dramatique*, Paris.
Roland-Manuel. (1947), *Maurice Ravel*, trans. C. Jolly, London.
Rolland, R. (1914), *Musiciens d'aujourd'hui*, 6th ed., Paris.
Rolland, R. (1978), *Jean-Christophe à Paris*, vol. 1, *La Foire sur la place*, 74th ed., Paris.
Rouché, J. (1958), 'Portraits', *Revue d'histoire du théâtre*, vol. 10, no. 3, pp. 291-312.
Sachs, M. (c.1939), *Au temps du Bœuf sur le toit*, Paris.
Sadie, S. (ed.) (1980), *The New Grove dictionary of music and musicians*, 20 vols, London.
Samazeuilh, G. (1947), *Musiciens de mon temps*, Paris.
Satie, E. (1977), *Ecrits*, Paris.
Sauguet, H. (1958), 'Jacques Rouché et la musique', *Revue d'histoire du théâtre*, vol. 10, no. 3, pp. 266-269.
Sauguet, H. (1990), *La Musique ma vie*, Paris.
Schaeffner, A. (1930), 'Du *Capriccio* à la *Symphonie de psaumes*', *Feuilles musicales*, vol. 3, no. 10 (December), pp. 327-329.
Schloezer, B. de. (1926), 'Festival Strawinsky [sic]', *La Revue musicale*, vol. 7, no. 5 (1 March), pp. 268-269.
Schmitz, E. R. (1950), *The piano works of Claude Debussy*, New York, repr. 1970, Westport, Connecticut.
Seldin, T. (ed.) (1977), *France, 1848-1948*, vols 1 and 2 of *The Oxford History of Modern Europe*, Oxford.
Séré, O. (1911), *Les Musiciens français d'aujourd'hui*, Paris.
Shattuck, R. (1984), *The banquet years: the origins of the avant-garde in France, 1885 to World War I*, rev. ed. Salem, New Haven.
Shera, F. H. (1925), *Debussy and Ravel*, London.
Souris, A. (1962), 'Debussy et Stravinsky', *La Revue belge de musicologie*, vol. 16, pp. 45-56.
Stravinsky, I. (1936), *An autobiography*, New York.
Stravinsky, I. (1959), *Poetics of music*, Cambridge, Mass.
Stravinsky, I. and R. Craft. (1959), *Memories and commentaries*, London.
Stravinsky, I. and R. Craft. (1962), *Expositions and developments*, London.
Stravinsky, I. and R. Craft. (1962), *Stravinsky in conversation with Robert Craft*, Harmondsworth, Middlesex.
Stravinsky, I. and R. Craft. (1967), *Themes and episodes*, 2nd ed., New York.
Stravinsky, I. and R. Craft. (1969), *Retrospectives and conclusions*, New York.
Stravinsky, I. and W. Nouvel. (1936), *Chronicle of my life*, London.
Stravinsky, V. and R. Craft. (1978), *Stravinsky in pictures and documents*, New York.
Stuckenschmidt, H. H. (1968), *Ravel: variations on his life and work*, trans. S. Rosenbaum, Philadelphia.

Suarès, A. (1938), 'Ravel: esquisse', *La Revue musicale*, special issue (December), pp. 48(240)-52(244).

Talvart, J., J. Place and G. Place. (eds) (1928-1976), *Bibliographie des auteurs modernes de langue française*, 22 vols, Paris.

Teyte, M. (1958), *Star on the door*, London.

Teyte, M. (1962), 'Maggie Teyte talks to Frank Granville Barker. Memories of Debussy', *Music and Musicians*, vol. 26, no. 12 (August), pp. 16-17.

Thompson, O. (1937), *Debussy: man and artist*, repr. 1967, New York.

Thoraval, J. et al. (1972), *Les Grandes étapes de la civilisation française*, Paris.

Thoumin, J.-A. (1957), *Bibliographie retrospective des périodiques français de la littérature musicale 1870-1954*, Paris.

Tiénot, Y. and Y. d'Estrade-Guerra. (1962), 'Debussy et Erik Satie', *Feuilles musicales*, vol. 15, nos. 4-5 (June-July), p. 86.

Tiersot, J. (1918), 'Claude Debussy', *Le Courrier musical*, vol. 20 (15 April), pp. 171-174.

Tiersot, J. (1924), *Un demi-siècle de musique française (1870-1919)*, 2nd ed., Paris.

Timbrell, C. (1992), 'Claude Debussy and Walter Rummel: chronicle of a friendship, with new correspondence', *Music and letters*, vol. 73, no. 3, pp. 399-406.

Tinan, Mme G. de (Dolly Bardac). (1973), 'Memories of Debussy and his circle', *Recorded sound*, vols 50-51 (April-July), pp. 158-163.

Tollefson, R. (1970), 'Debussy's pedalling', *Clavier*, vol. 9, pp. 22-33.

Toorn, P. C. van den. (1987), *Stravinsky and 'The rite of spring'. The beginnings of a musical language*, Berkeley.

Tosi, G. (ed.) (1929), *Correspondance de Claude Debussy et P.-J. Toulet*, Paris.

Tresize, S. (1994), *Debussy, 'La Mer'*, Cambridge.

Trillig, J. (1982), *Untersuchung zur Rezeption Claude Debussys in der zeitgenössischen Musikkritik*, Tutzing.

Vallas, L. (1933), *Claude Debussy: his life and works*, trans. M. and G. O'Brien, London.

Vallas, L. (1946-1950), *Vincent d'Indy*, 2 vols, Paris.

Vallas, L. (1958), *Claude Debussy et son temps*, rev. ed., Paris.

Vallery-Radot, P. (1938), 'Claude Debussy: souvenirs', *La Revue des deux mondes*, vol. 108, no. 45 (1 May), pp. 390-418.

Vallery-Radot, P. (1958), *Tel était Claude Debussy*, Paris.

Vallery-Radot, P. (1964), 'Allocution', *La Revue musicale*, vol. 259, pp. 21-24.

Vallery-Radot, P. (1964), 'Allocution', *La Revue musicale*, vol. 259, pp. 147-151.

Vallery-Radot, P. (1964), 'Claude Debussy et le culte de l'amitié', *La Revue musicale*, vol. 259, pp. 107-109.

Viñes, R. (1935), 'Trois aristocrates du son', *Le Monde musical*, vol. 12 (31 December), pp. 356-358.

Vuillermoz, E. (1910), 'En l'an 2010', *S.I.M. Revue musicale* (August-September), pp. 520-529.

Vuillermoz, E. (1920), 'Claude Debussy', *Le Ménéstrel*, vol. 82, nos. 24 and 25 (11 and 18 June), pp. 241–243, 249–251.
Vuillermoz, E. (1923), *Musiques d'aujourd'hui*, Paris.
Vuillermoz, E. (1944), 'Louis Laloy', *L'Echo de la France* (18 March), p. 3.
Vuillermoz, E. (1957), *Claude Debussy*, Geneva.
Watelin, L. C. (1924), 'La Genèse d'un monument: le monument à Claude Debussy', *L'Art et les artistes*, vol. 18, pp. 197–199.
Watson, B. (ed.) (1968), *The complete works of Chuang Tzu*, New York.
Wéber, E. (ed.) (1962), *Debussy et l'évolution de la musique au XXe siècle*, Paris.
White, E. W. (1962), 'Stravinsky and Debussy', *Tempo*, vols. 61–62, pp. 2–5.
White, E. W. (1979), *Stravinsky: the composer and his works*, 2nd ed., London.
Widor, C.-M. (1927), *Fondations: portraits de Massenet à Paladilhe*, Paris.
Wolff, S. (1953), *Un demi-siècle de l'Opéra-Comique (1900–1950)*, Paris.
Wolff, S. (1962), *L'Opéra au Palais Garnier (1875–1962)*, Paris.
Wood, H. (1938), *My life of music*, London.

Index